MIDDLE ENGLISH MOUTHS

The mouth, responsible for both physical and spiritual functions –
eating, drinking, breathing, praying and confessing – was of immediate importance to medieval thinking about the nature of the human
being. Where scholars have traditionally focused on the mouth's
grotesque excesses, Katie L. Walter argues for the recuperation of
its material 'everyday' aspect. Walter's original study draws on two
rich archives: one comprising Middle English theology (Langland,
Julian of Norwich, Lydgate, Chaucer) and pastoral writings; the
other broadly medical and surgical, including learned encyclopaedias
and vernacular translations and treatises. Challenging several critical
orthodoxies about the centrality of sight, the hierarchy of the senses
and the separation of religious from medical discourses, the book
reveals the centrality of the mouth, taste and touch to human modes
of knowing and to Christian identity.

DR KATIE L. WALTER is Senior Lecturer in Medieval English
Literature at the University of Sussex. She is the editor of *Reading Skin
in Medieval Literature and Culture* (2013), *The Culture of Inquisition
in Medieval England* (with Mary Flannery, 2013) and a special issue
of *Textual Practice* on 'Prosthesis in Medieval and Early Modern
Culture' (with Chloe Porter and Margaret Healy, 2016). Dr Walter
has published essays on the body, skin, flesh and the senses, as well as
on medieval literary theories and reading practices.

CAMBRIDGE STUDIES IN MEDIEVAL LITERATURE

General Editor
Alastair Minnis, *Yale University*

Editorial Board
Zygmunt G. Barański, *University of Cambridge*
Christopher C. Baswell, *Barnard College and Columbia University*
Mary Carruthers, *New York University*
Rita Copeland, *University of Pennsylvania*
Roberta Frank, *Yale University*
Jocelyn Wogan-Browne, *Fordham University*

This series of critical books seeks to cover the whole area of literature written in the major medieval languages – the main European vernaculars, and medieval Latin and Greek – during the period c.1100–1500. Its chief aim is to publish and stimulate fresh scholarship and criticism on medieval literature, special emphasis being placed on understanding major works of poetry, prose and drama in relation to the contemporary culture and learning which fostered them.

A complete list of titles in the series can be found at the end of the volume.

MIDDLE ENGLISH MOUTHS

Late Medieval Medical, Religious and Literary Traditions

KATIE L. WALTER

University of Sussex

CAMBRIDGE UNIVERSITY PRESS

CAMBRIDGE
UNIVERSITY PRESS

University Printing House, Cambridge CB2 8BS, United Kingdom

One Liberty Plaza, 20th Floor, New York, NY 10006, USA

477 Williamstown Road, Port Melbourne, VIC 3207, Australia

314–321, 3rd Floor, Plot 3, Splendor Forum, Jasola District Centre, New Delhi – 110025, India

79 Anson Road, #06-04/06, Singapore 079906

Cambridge University Press is part of the University of Cambridge.

It furthers the University's mission by disseminating knowledge in the pursuit of education, learning, and research at the highest international levels of excellence.

www.cambridge.org
Information on this title: www.cambridge.org/9781108426619
DOI: 10.1017/9781108551106

First published 2018

Printed in the United Kingdom by Clays, St Ives plc

A catalogue record for this publication is available from the British Library.

ISBN 978-1-108-42661-9 Hardback

For my family

Contents

Acknowledgements

This book's story has journeyed with me for longer, and to more places, than I had ever expected – from its first beginnings in a conversation with Felicity Riddy at York, through a PhD at King's College, Cambridge, then off over the Channel to be rethought in the industrial heartland of Germany, before finding its final form – in between steadying stints in Cambridge libraries and (less steadying ones) in an Alaskan brewery – comfortably nestled in the Sussex Downs. I am grateful to many whose paths I have crossed and who have cheered and helped and goaded along the way.

My thanks to Cambridge University Press and the two anonymous readers whose comments were valuable in helping me re-envision the scope of this project. Thanks are also due to Jacqueline Tasioulas (my doctoral supervisor) and Nicolette Zeeman. Conversations with Nicky about Langland, nature and the body have shaped the thinking in this book in ways more profound than can be footnoted. I owe much to her generosity, support and encouragement.

Others have given benevolently of their time and expertise, including Christopher Cannon, Helen Cooper, Edwin Craun, Isabel Davis, Luuk Houwen, Peter Murray Jones, Robert Mills, Richard Newhauser, Jean-Pascal Pouzet, Susan Powell, Elizabeth Robertson and Barry Windeatt, as well as Tom Healy and Margaret Healy and my colleagues in the Centre for Early Modern and Medieval Studies at Sussex. There have been many who have brightened library tearooms with conversation, enlivened conferences or offered hospitality, including Daisy Hay, Virginia Langum, Ruth Ahnert and Sebastian Ahnert. Daniel DiCenso and Eva and Christian von Contzen have provided invaluable Latin expertise, from which my translations have greatly benefited, as well as friendship. Mary Flannery, who has been an excellent friend and collaborator, has read and reread substantial portions of this book: thank you.

Long before this book's beginnings, my parents, David and Christine Walter, were my greatest and longest-suffering supporters. They remain so, and the ways they have helped and encouraged me are countless. Without them the journey would have been longer and harder. I am grateful to Natalie and Luke Cathie for a place to stay, to Melodie Walter for continental jaunts and to all three of them for laughter and distractions.

James Wade has been a patient and expert reader, a wise and incisive interlocuter and an uncomplaining maker of coffee and bringer of treats. More than this, he is the very best of travelling companions. Edith Constance, who slept in my arms as I finished this book, will undoubtedly make our next journey both sweeter and noisier. I dedicate this book to my family, with love.

Abbreviations

EETS	Early English Text Society
MED	*Middle English Dictionary*
NML	*New Medieval Literatures*
N&Q	*Notes & Queries*
PL	Patrologiae cursus completus. Series Latina, [gen. ed.] J.-P. Migne (Paris, 1844–64)
YLS	*Yearbook of Langland Studies*

Introduction: Everyday Mouths

> Nothing seems more ineffable, more incommunicable, more inimitable, and, therefore, more precious, than the values given body, *made* body by the transubstantiation achieved by the hidden persuasion of an implicit pedagogy, capable of instilling a whole cosmology, an ethic, a metaphysic, a political philosophy, through injunctions as insignificant as 'stand up straight' or 'don't hold your knife in your left hand'.[1]
>
> – Pierre Bourdieu

The human mouth is, for the most part, strikingly absent from the indices of scholarly works on the medieval period. Where it does appear it is usually in its capacity as the organ of speech, where it tends to be dissolved into language or relegated to the realm of metaphor; or when it is caught *in extremis* – that is, when it is grotesque or monstrous, when its borders are transgressed, or when it opens or eats to excess.[2] Mundane, literal references to the material mouth, however, are commonplace enough in medieval texts themselves; perhaps it is their commonplaceness, the very mundanity of mouths, that makes them seem so unremarkable. The premise of this book is, therefore, somewhat counterintuitive: it proposes that the human mouth – and especially its everyday, physical aspect – is centrally implicated in discourses of physical, ethical and spiritual good. Responsible for both physical and spiritual functions, such as eating and breathing, but also prayer and confession, the mouth is deeply enmeshed in medieval thinking about what it means to be human, and about sin and salvation. It is, in fact, as this book contends, the principal point where human and Christian identity is bestowed, maintained and ultimately dismantled. In this regard, a study of medieval mouths contributes towards a history both of the human body and of medieval Christianity.

This claim is grounded in readings of the mouth in two Middle English literary traditions: religious and (in very broad terms) medical or

I

biological – what might be referred to as vernacular theology and vernacular medicine respectively. It is in the later medieval period (in particular from the mid fourteenth century on) that theology and science undergo a process of vernacularisation from Latin into Anglo-Norman and into Middle English, both in the form of translations and original productions.[3] The understanding of the mouth that emerges in the intersections of these two traditions discloses a discourse of the care of the self that has powerful reverberations for our reading of medieval texts and our understanding of late medieval devotional practices. Latin traditions, particularly those stemming from the twelfth century, from which vernacular discourses of the care of the self in part derive, similarly disclose a close relationship between medicine and religion; vernacularisation, however, marks a widening access to these learned traditions and facilitates reading between medical and religious ideas. This book traces the discourses (representations, beliefs, practices) of the human mouth that emerge in the intersections of learned, Latinate culture and popular, Middle English learning. These discourses are part of the spectrum of 'kynde' – or 'the natural' – explored by many late medieval, and specifically Middle English, writers;[4] by extension, so too are they part of late medieval debates about epistemology which question the relationship of knowledge to the subject of ethics, to 'doing well' and to getting saved.

'Kynde' has rich connotations in the fourteenth century, often positioned in some ways against what is often referred to in Middle English as 'clergie' (or 'learning'). However, 'kynde' designates, variously, knowledge which inheres naturally in the human (that is, to take William Langland's phrase in *Piers Plowman*, 'kynde knowyng'), as well as knowledge which is about nature (observed as well as taught).[5] 'Kynde' is therefore situated in the Pauline–Augustinian tradition of *via positiva*, profoundly influenced in the later medieval period by the rise of Aristotelianism, where the visible natural world and the human body provide a commentary on the invisible and divine.[6] Descriptions of the physiology, anatomy and pathology of the mouth accordingly provide a gloss for spiritual processes, such as confession and self-knowledge, and disclose themselves to be not only figures of spiritual processes but the literal bases of them. 'Kynde' is also situated in the tradition of *experientia*, which might be understood as learning through living in the world. Importantly, *experientia* values being-in-the-world and sensate experiences, including those of sin and suffering: it therefore creates the possibility that even fallen human experience can bring spiritual benefit.[7] This book contends that the mouth – and especially the senses of taste and touch, which are defined in Middle English natural philosophy as the 'boistous', that is, 'earthy' senses – peculiarly directs us to a medieval discourse of lived experience. This discourse derives its value not from the transcendence of the body but from being-in-the-body – for example, from the sometimes sinful, sometimes painful experiences not only of eating and speaking, but also defecating and vomiting. On the surface at least, 'kynde' knowledge about the mouth is, however, particularly mundane, and is conveyed in injunctions as seemingly insignificant as 'chew your food properly' and 'scrape clean your teeth', and in instructions for, and the practice of, caring for children and the self (the appropriate age to wean a child, how to teach a child to speak, when and how to eat, how to cure toothache or bad breath). This everyday kind of knowledge is deceptively ordinary; it forms, in fact, what we might understand to be a kind of body *hexis* that, in Pierre Bourdieu's words, is capable of 'instilling a whole cosmology, an ethic, a metaphysic'. It is thus the values 'given body, *made* body' that this book explores; the ways in which the experience and pedagogy of the mouth develops 'a "moral organism" akin to and embodied in the physical organism'.[8]

* * *

Middle English Mouths takes its point of departure from several influential approaches to the body with a long history in medieval scholarship. Mikhail Bakhtin's theory of grotesque realism, formulated by 1940 but first translated into English in 1968, makes the mouth the leading feature of the grotesque body: 'The distinctive character of this body', he writes, 'is its open unfinished nature, its interaction with the world. These traits are most fully and concretely revealed in the act of eating; the body transgresses here its own limits: it swallows, devours, rends the world apart, is enriched and grows at the world's expense.'[9] Suggestively characterising the movement and oppositions between carnival and lent, official and non-official culture, seriousness and communal laughter, Bakhtin's formulations have been very influential on interpretations of medieval bodies.[10] His description of the openness of the grotesque body's 'open unfinished nature', and its capacity to traverse and travesty hierarchies and spheres, remains a powerfully generative idea for thinking about the relationship of the body to the world, and to political and cultural structures. But its broader theoretical framework has limitations: its concentration on the body in excess ('all that is bodily becomes grandiose, exaggerated, immeasurable'); its antagonism to religious seriousness; and its strict boundaries between official ('classical' body) and non-official ('grotesque' body) cultures.[11] David Williams pinpoints the problem inherent in the term grotesque, since 'the terms "monster," "grotesque," and "fantastic" are generally used more or less interchangeably'.[12] If eating and drinking, for Bakhtin, are manifestations of the grotesque, they are also, as medieval commentaries on the body and the quotidian disclose, manifestations of the body at its most human. It is therefore necessary to articulate and appropriate more carefully the concept of the grotesque in thinking about the mouth; in turn, it also seems necessary to recuperate some of the operations of the mouth that are otherwise (and sometimes uncritically) associated with the grotesque. In his critique of the use of Bakhtinian theory in early modern scholarship, Michael C. Schoenfeldt has usefully suggested that we should see carnival in the context of the 'calendrical process of self and communal regulation'.[13] In this way, the grotesque, excessive aspects of human experience are not fixed or totalising but part of a spectrum: understanding bodily experiences to be temporal allows us to view traditionally 'grotesque' aspects of human behaviour (eating, chewing, spitting, vomiting, defecating) without *necessarily* invoking laughter, subversion and monstrosity (although, importantly, it does not preclude any of these aspects emerging). Schoenfeldt suggests that mundane bodily functions such as eating and defecating might better be understood in terms of the 'care of the self', a notion he borrows from Michel Foucault, who identifies discourses of the care of the self in the medical regimen of the Classical period: 'medicine', Foucault asserts, 'was not conceived simply as a technique of intervention ... It was also supposed to define, in the form of a corpus of knowledge and rules, a way of living, a reflective mode of relation to oneself.'[14] Here Foucault articulates an understanding of medicine that is bound up with the concerns of both everyday care and individual identity, concerns which are similarly intertwined in the late medieval writings discussed in this book.

A second influential approach to the medieval body takes its lead from the turn to embodiment and the 'new materialism'. In this vein, Caroline Walker Bynum's early work was seminal in raising the profile of the body as a site of religious experience.[15] Here, the mouth appears often obliquely – in relation to the Eucharist, or the ascetic eating practices at the centre of the lifestyles of those who achieve the status of saints or mystics. In many ways, Bynum's approach and the studies which it inspired value flesh and fleshliness, exploring the manipulation and modification of the body and considering in particular how this might be used to subvert hegemony and patriarchy in medieval society or for postmodern readers. At the same time, it tends to stress the *corps morcelé*, dismemberment, torture, bodies in pain, the violent, the bizarre, the wondrous and the supernatural.[16] These tropes of the body abound in medieval texts and have particular resonance with religious discourses that emerge within them (Franciscanism, affective piety, *imitatio Christi*, hagiography and martyrdom, fast and feast, the Eucharist and the suffering humanity of Christ).[17] But this focus tends to elide the discourses of those who, in pursuit of the mixed life, go about eating, drinking, having toothache, experiencing the feel of words in the mouth, defecating, falling unwell, feeling healthy, learning about the world, about the self and about God, forgetting again and dying.

More recently, however, the interest in embodiment and materiality has developed in ways that make these everyday experiences an increasingly important focus, including the turns to 'affect', to material culture and (everyday) objects.[18] Bynum's 2015 work, *Christian Materiality: An Essay in Religion in Late Medieval Europe*, is a case in point. Going beyond the category of the body to 'the study of matter itself', it highlights the tangibility of late medieval devotional objects, and situates questions about the human body and corporeality in broader medieval theories of matter and its changeability.[19] As Bynum's stress on the tangible suggests, so too has medieval scholarship seen a related emphasis on the senses. Recent cultural and anthropological histories, attune to the category of 'experience', thus rethink the senses in terms of 'multisensoriality' – their interrelation and collaboration – rather than treating them as isolated or fixed.[20] It is in the context of the shift to multisensorality that this book intervenes by making a case for the centrality of taste and touch in discourses of worldly and spiritual experience, in which their value is predicated in not only their collaboration with, but their very difference from, the other senses.

The attention to affect, objects and the senses has done much to broaden the horizons of scholarship on the human body. At the same time, however, animal studies and disability studies have both offered important critiques of the kinds of narratives and histories that have emerged in the past several decades. Medieval natural philosophical descriptions of the human body tend to have in mind a male, idealised form, and often derive value from man's comparison with, as well as his difference from, animals. As Karl Steel summarises, 'critical animal theory stresses that the categories "human" and "animal", as well as the assumption of any absolute limit between human and animals, must be radically rethought'.[21] Disability studies has similarly problematised accounts of the body that either overlook or are (implicitly) forged against impaired or disabled experiences of the body.[22] Medical discourse, in delineating sickness and impairment, can provide an important counterpart to the 'ideal' bodies of natural philosophy. But so too can attentiveness to natural philosophical descriptions of lifecycle stages and bodily functions, as well as to medical regimen for the daily care of the self, go some way to countering static understandings of 'the body', pointing to inherent flux and change (in aptitude, health and so on), as well as exposing what the human has in common with animals, plants and material objects. This also affords some recognition of human vulnerability, and of the ways in which impairment, sickness and suffering change and recalibrate the experience of the body.

Sharing a commitment to embodiment and materiality, scholarly thinking on the everyday derives energy from an anthropological emphasis on 'the domain of the lived experience and the effect of the social realm on the human body'.[23] The notion of the everyday body is kindred with that of the care of the self, taking in, in Schoenfeldt's terms, the body's calendrical flux and change, as well as sensate experience lived in the world. The work of Felicity Riddy does much to articulate further the perspective afforded by the category of the everyday, which, as she describes it, makes possible compassionate, matter of fact and valorising responses to bodily experiences and behaviours.[24] Writing on a fourteenth-century Middle English romance, *Le Bone Florence of Rome*, Riddy identifies a spectrum of bodies in the poem:

> Sick, deformed and wounded; needing to be fed, clothed, kept warm and given rest; eroticised, tormented and vulnerable; the corpse – all these varieties of the body in time are accommodated by the poem, and not as animal but as human … In all this there is, it seems, no abjection: the body is not shrunk from and does not defile. It is multivalent: sometimes funny; at others appalling; at others no more than matter-of-factly there to be contended with: fed, rested, clothed. It is what the poem understands humans to be: what I call the everyday body.[25]

For Riddy, the everyday perspective does not find the conditions of the body (sickness, deformity, woundedness, sex, hunger, the onset of death) at odds with morality or with living well: 'the everyday body is vulnerable and needy, but it is not despised as worthless flesh; its processes may be dirty and smelly but they are not morally filthy'.[26] This begins to raise the possibility that the everyday body may provide (religious) opportunity to those for whom living in the world (rather than withdrawing from it) is very much a necessity. In taking up the everyday body and its care, this book is limited in its capacity to speak to the particularised experiences – especially of disability, but also of gender – of those who are differently embodied from the male, and often normative, bodies of philosophy and medicine.[27] Approaching the body through the category of the everyday cannot, for example, fully account for the experience of disability, where neither sickness nor impairment might be temporal, but rather lived with permanently, and where the experience of vulnerability too is differently inflected.[28] It does, however, offer a corrective to fixed and static accounts of the body, and works with a sense of the importance of finding more fluid understandings of what it means to be human.

Reading Habits

In the medieval period, everyday care of the self does not just extend to the body but, as Foucault suggests, to the body and soul as a related whole, and so encompasses medical, ethical and religious concerns. The influx of Classical and Arabic learning into the West around the twelfth century quite fundamentally provides a new corpus of natural philosophical, medical and surgical works to be taken up by and integrated with existing *theological* as well as medical traditions; the body and its passions are increasingly the subject of books, both Latinate and Middle English. Indeed, the second half of the fourteenth century sees the beginning of an explosion in the vernacular translation and production of medical, surgical and scientific treatises.[29] In the same period, too, the production and vernacularisation of pastoral and devotional works proliferates significantly. Scholarship on vernacular theology, seen to stem from the 'educational drive' of the Fourth Lateran Council in 1215, is considerable but perhaps has not given due consideration to its relationship with the parallel developments in vernacular science. The increased concern with the health of the body, however, might represent the other side of the coin to the concern with providing 'guides to spiritual health'.[30]

The notion that natural philosophy, medical and pastoral works are counterparts in the care of selves requires that we understand the readership of scientific and medical texts to be wider than an exclusively academic or professional one, but also that we conceive of a late medieval practice of reading between medical and religious traditions. The different genres of medical texts have been seen to correlate directly with a hierarchy of users – for example, the guild-trained surgeons and barbers would be the target audience for surgical books.[31] However, the medium of Middle English opens up medical knowledge to the perusal not just of university and professional readers, but arguably 'anyone literate'.[32] The boundaries of readership of vernacular science are, therefore, necessarily fluid. Laymen and women, as well as clergial writers, might read and appropriate such 'natural' or medical material for themselves and for their own ends. It is also clear that some translators of medical treatises 'imagined an audience beyond that of scholars and medical practitioners. They seem to have seen the vernacular medical translation as a kind of medical sermon, with a pastoral, indeed charitable, function in mind.'[33] This places some medical translating activity in the same vein as vernacular theology, where works such as John Mirk's sermon cycle, the *Festial*, and a whole host of other vernacular penitential and confessional manuals are written in order to instruct lewed parish priests and their unlearned parishioners. We should, of course, be careful about what we understand the 'good' of this material to have been. As Julie Orlemanski reminds us, in the form of vernacular medicine 'medieval men and women confronted a set of therapeutic models and explanatory terms that often failed – failed, that is, to be understandable to readers and to provide the physical relief sought'.[34]

While questions thus might be raised both about the comprehensibility of vernacular biology and medicine, and about the efficacy of such knowledge for either physical or spiritual healing, the medieval habit of reading across genres nonetheless posits the complementarity of natural knowledge and medicine, on the one hand, and devotional poetry and prose, on the other.[35] Indeed, as Judson Boyce Allen in *The Ethical Poetic* observes, textual and generic distinctions of this kind are largely modern rather than medieval ones.[36] The vernacular habit of reading in the cross-flow of genre is exemplified in the character of manuscript miscellany: Lincoln Cathedral, Dean and Chapter Library MS 91, a fifteenth-century miscellany copied by Robert Thornton, for example, further to its romances and devotional texts, includes three charms for toothache, a prescription for 'scyatica' and a prose medical text, *Liber de diversis medicinis*.[37] But it is also central to the reading practice of Chaucer's *Canterbury Tales*, where, as R. A. Shoaf has suggested, the boundaries between the medical and the penitential are blurred. Foregrounding the Nun's Priest's tale's debt to medical regimen, Shoaf argues that it 'has an idea of the body humanely dieted'; the collection's final tale, that of the Parson, in turn, is a 'tale on the care of the self'. In other words, the one tale about the effects of food on the body complements another tale about the process of penance and receiving forgiveness.[38] Such reading and compositional practices are calibrated by the conviction that ethics and spiritual processes are founded in the body and its physiology; that knowledge *about* the body is therefore valuable, even necessary, for salvation.[39]

This medieval habit of reading between medicine and theology, or between the body and soul, fosters in turn the incorporation of medical knowledge into Middle English *pastoralia* and devotional works. The extent to which vernacular theology draws upon medicalised knowledge suggests that in teaching priests how to care for the souls of their parishioners, or in teaching the laity to care for their own, these texts also necessarily teach how to care for the body.[40] William Langland's concern in *Piers Plowman* with the psychosomatic whole, epitomised by Holy Church's caution that 'it is nought al good to the goost [soul] that the gut asketh, / Ne liflode [necessary] to the likame [body] that leef [pleasing] is to the soule', is telling of a more general medieval belief in the interdependency of body and soul and of the importance of being able to treat and indeed to read about both.[41] Thus, for writers and readers of vernacular theology, an understanding of the causes of sin, for example, might encompass more technical medicalised knowledge of the science of conception and the regimen for pregnant women, as it does in the early fifteenth-century *Dives and Pauper*:

> Also meen [men] been enclynyd to synne, oon more þan anothir be excees, of mete and drynk, be myskepyngge of his fyue wy3ttys [senses]. And for þese same causys oon is enclynyd to bodyly sekenesse more þan anothir. For synne oftyntyme is cause of bodyly sekenesse. Also þe mysdyetyngge of þe moder qhyl [while] she is wyt childe or be mysdysposicioun of þe fader / or of þe modyr or of bothyn qhanne [when] þe chyld is begetyn.[42]

The *Dives* author makes clear that, for some, eating and drinking too much, and for others, unregulated sensory perception (the 'fyue wy3ttys'), inclines them to sinful behaviour; inextricably, this failure in the care of the self leads both to sin and to bodily sickness. The 'mysdyetyngge of þe moder qhyl she is wyt childe' has consequences, not only for the health of mother and child, but also for the child's own future inclination to sin. At the heart of Middle English *pastoralia* and devotional poetry, then, is a fundamental concern with the care of the self (the proper control of diet, the regulation of the sense perceptions and of sexual intercourse) that either moderates or fires man's predisposition both to sin and sickness – that is, his habits.

As *Dives and Pauper*'s anxiety over the consequences of the bad habits arising from the 'mysdeyetyngge of þe moder' or the 'mysdysposicioun of þe fader' discloses, Middle English pastoral instructions also make clear that virtue acquisition is necessarily founded in everyday practices such as those prescribed in regimen and diets.[43] *Habitus*, as Aristotle conceives it in the *Nichomachean Ethics* and the medieval period likewise understands it, is not inherent but acquired through repeated acts.[44] These repeated acts become, in turn, a permanent disposition (i.e. for moral or immoral actions).[45] *Habitus* differs from but is founded upon *natura*, being learned from experience, but also through education.[46] The taught aspect of *habitus* is derived not exclusively from formal educational institutions (monastery, school, church) but also from the domestic sphere. In other words, the learning that forms *habitus* is practised, lived in and lived out, and – as this book shows – partly accrued through the mouth (in the sensory experiences involving taste and touch) and derived from mundane knowledge about its care, such as that about how food is to be chewed and teeth to be cleaned.

The questions which haunt the production and readership of both medical and religious texts in the vernacular consequently concern the relationship of knowledge to salvation: if questions of how much food is consumed, the fitting time for sexual intercourse and the proper regimen of pregnant women are so closely bound up with sin and with human ability to live ethically, what knowledge, scientific and medical as well as catechetical, is necessary? What knowledge is natural, inhering in the self, and what knowledge needs to be taught? What are the value and limits of the various kinds of knowledge? What are the consequences of the lack or abuse of learning by the clergy for lay salvation? What are the implications of lay interpretation and appropriation of that knowledge? As the following chapters explore, this book contends that, despite the complexity of the late medieval epistemological debate with which vernacular theology is implicated, the pastoral tradition makes clear that knowledge about the body, and specifically about the mouth – encompassing physiology, psychology, anatomy, pathology, medicinal remedy, surgery and regimen – is written into the knowledge necessary for salvation.

Everyday Sense

The bodily basis of epistemology in the medieval period is widely acknowledged; the specific role of the mouth in acquiring (both 'kynde' and 'clergial') knowledge and in performing the repeated acts which form dispositions, however, needs to be given greater consideration. Following Aristotle, not only sensate existence but also cognition and the operation of reason is widely, if sometimes controversially, understood to be dependent upon sense perception; thus Thomas Aquinas in the thirteenth century asserts, 'all our knowledge takes its rise from sensation'.[47] While recent scholarship on the senses has begun to reappraise the 'lower' senses, it is still the case that sight has commanded the most scholarly attention in medieval contexts and is accordingly privileged in discussions of the acquisition of knowledge in general and spiritual knowledge in particular.[48] The scholarly preoccupation with vision is corroborated by a similar primacy of vision in medieval science. The Middle Ages inherit a hierarchy of the senses from natural philosophical traditions as well as early patristic ones, which is correlated with the topographical arrangement of the face.[49] In this scheme, the eyes, located at the top of the head, are the most noble of the sense organs. Taste (located in the mouth at the bottom of the face) and touch (located in all the limbs of the body, but also in the mouth and tongue) are the least noble. Sight, since it acts on light, is especially connected with knowledge as illumination or revelation. In the later medieval period, the rise of the science of optics (transmitted from Arabic science) furthers the prestige of vision – Roger Bacon making the claim that vision 'is the noblest of our senses. It is the sense upon which all human science depends.'[50] Indeed, or so it has been claimed, ' "All early natural philosophers acknowledged that vision is man's most noble and dependable sense". The same is true of theologians – Aquinas remarks that "the sense of sight has a special dignity; it is more spiritual and subtle than any other sense".'[51] These kinds of designations in the realms of natural philosophy and medieval science have led some critics to a kind of visual essentialism, in which sight is central not only to the acquisition of knowledge but to the construction of the sense of self. Thus, Carolyn Collette asserts:

> We think of sight as central to our lives because it is central to our physical existence. Seeing means being able to navigate in the world ... Throughout the Middle Ages the sense of sight was similarly regarded as central.[52]

Dallas Denery also claims in his work on optics and theology in the later medieval period:

> In many respects, people had come to think about themselves primarily in visual terms, in terms of a somewhat amorphous distinction between what appears and what exists.[53]

Such visual essentialism has not gone uncriticised.[54] Indeed, the recent scholarly move to analyse the senses in terms of interaction and collaboration goes some way to rethinking the 'lower' senses more positively.[55] The greater recognition of the ways in which sight, for example, is understood to be founded on touch in medieval theories makes clear that in order to understand vision we also need to understand touch.[56]

However, while medieval discourses are not monologic they very often erect stark distinctions between the senses to think about their differing epistemological contributions. A re-examination of medieval sources and traditions suggests that taste and touch have a particular value, not always afforded to sight and the other senses, in directing us to lived experience. Taste and touch are, this book contends, rather more important to human and Christian identity – particularly in the context of the fallen human condition, and to the acquisition of both mundane and spiritual knowledge – than is normally assumed. This capacity of taste and touch derives precisely from the binary distinctions that scholarship on the senses has been at pains to dismantle.

Medieval accounts of sense perception, whilst insisting on the bodily basis of all the senses, associate sight with distance, disembodiment and atemporality, and taste and touch with embodied experience.[57] It is this difference that grounds the physical, ethical and spiritual good of the mouth. In standard medieval accounts, such as that in John Trevisa's translation of *De proprietatibus rerum*, the senses are outlined as follows:

> [Kynde] setteþ þe yȝen in þe ferþer and ouerpartie of þe heed … for þe witte of sight is more sotile and more nobil þan oþir wittes. Kynde settiþ þe instrumentis and lymes of herynge in þe middel of þe roundnes of þe heed … Kynde setteþ þe wit of smellinge aftir þe eiȝen as myddel and mene bitwene þe siȝt and taast, for þe witte of smellynge is more boistous þan þe siȝt and more sotile þan þe taast. Þerfore þe tonge is sette last, þat is þe instrument and lyme of taast and touche; þe worchinge þerof is aboute greet and boistous substaunce.[58]

Sight is 'sotil', that is, rarefied, refined, in some way partaking in less of the substance, the very stuff, of the body and of the earth.[59] The 'sotilnes' of sight, iterated elsewhere in *On the Properties of Things* ('siȝt is more sotile and more lifliche [keen] þan þe oþir wittis', I, III), accounts for the ability of the human to 'knowiþ sodeinliche þinges þat ben fulle fer' (I, 108). Elaine Scarry suggests in *The Body in Pain*: 'vision and hearing are, under ordinary conditions, so exclusively bound up with their object rather than with their bodily location' that 'through them, one seems to become disembodied'.[60] Resonating with Scarry's description of vision and hearing, Middle English 'sotil' therefore implies a heightened, transcendent, immaterial knowing at a distance, one in which temporality is prone to collapse.

In contrast, taste and touch are 'boistous', that is, reified, coarse, dominated by the element earth and by the body.[61] (Smell, though often classed along with taste and touch as a lower sense, more properly here, since it is neither truly subtle nor truly 'boistous', occupies a medial place and state – it is 'myddel and mene' between sight and taste – in the Aristotelian model.)[62] The natural philosophers' assertion that the tongue ('þe instrument and lyme of taast and touche') acts upon 'greet and boistous substaunce' underscores the quality that marks the difference between the eyes and the mouth: to taste and touch requires direct contact with the objects sensed, they cannot keep at a distance, but necessarily work at close quarters and act in and on bodies. The knowledge accrued by mouth is therefore everyday, experienced, about the body and about the world. These 'boistous' qualities have been made the basis for claims for the inferiority and ignobility of taste and touch and the knowledge they acquire, but I suggest that, in the context of medieval discourses of the natural which make possible the recuperation of fallen human conditions and experiences, they are also the grounds for their valorisation and their affective, cognitive and spiritual power.[63]

A focus on the mouth roots knowledge and learning in the lived experience of the body (*experientia*) and points, not to a division between body and soul, but to the conditions that make us human. In turn, for readers and critics of medieval bodies, reintegrating and recuperating taste and touch into the spectrum of ethical and spiritual modes of learning provides a way of reformulating contemporary and medieval theories of the body and capturing something of medieval being-in-the-world that a focus on eyes and sight or on 'body as metaphor' tends to eschew. The following chapters therefore offer explorations of the value and power of the example of the mouth as it emerges in reading between biology and medicine, on the one hand, and vernacular theology on the other.

The Archive

The archive of vernacular biology and medicine drawn on in this book comprises translations of medical and surgical works, such as those of Lanfranchi of Milan (c.1295) and Guy de Chauliac, as well as natural philosophical works, such as Trevisa's translation of *De proprietatibus rerum*. The Middle English treatise known as *Lanfrank's 'Science of Chirurgie'* makes available c.1380 a surgical work in English perhaps for the very first time.[64] More influential than Lanfrank's surgery is Guy's. Originally composed in Latin as the *Inventarium seu collectorium in parte cyrurgicali medicine* (written in Avignon, 1363, also known as *Chirurgia magna*), Guy's text was quickly translated into French and other vernacular languages.[65] If translations of medical texts such as these proliferated in this period, wholescale translation of encyclopaedias into Middle English was a more unusual endeavour. Trevisa's translation of Bartholomaeus's thirteenth-century work (completed at Berkeley, Gloucestershire in 1398/9 and surviving in eight manuscripts) evidences something of the ambition the late medieval vernacular project reaches. More important than its availability in English, however, is the evidence for its use in its Latin forms, along with other encyclopaedias and works of natural philosophy, by theologians, pastoral writers and devotional poets alike.[66] Indeed, Michael Twomey observes that: 'For English preachers, it would seem that Bartholomaeus' encyclopaedia is a source for *exempla* ... For literary authors, both religious and secular, Bartholomaeus' encyclopaedia is far and away the encyclopaedia of choice.'[67] Along with Vincent of Beauvais's compendious thirteenth-century *Speculum maius* and the writings of the scholastics Thomas Aquinas and Albertus Magnus, *De proprietatibus rerum* is therefore taken as a principal witness of the learned ideas about the body and soul that would be known and understood by many late medieval writers.[68]

This book's counterpart archive of vernacular theology comprises both *pastoralia* and the devotional poetry and prose of William Langland, Julian of Norwich and John Lydgate, among others. The following chapters draw on Englishings of Lorens of Orléans's *Somme le roi* and William Peraldus's *Summa de vitiis et virtutibus* (available, in fact, in eight different Middle English translations, including *Speculum vitae*, *The Book of Vices and Virtues* and *Book for a Simple and Devout Woman*), sermon collections such as John Mirk's *Festial* (c.1380) and catechetical instruction such as *Dives and Pauper* (1405–10).[69] These works – in their adherence to their sources and their deviations from it – bear out a late medieval valuation of the natural and the exemplary, grapple with the relationship of knowledge to salvation and posit a contiguity of the physical and spiritual, the physiological and the ethical. Pastoral works such as these, along with natural philosophy and medicine (in both English and Latin), together form the resources drawn on by writers such as William Langland. Extant in around fifty copies ('perhaps a small proportion' of the total made), *Piers Plowman* (B-text, c.1379) is positioned precisely in the interface between learned Latinate traditions and popular Middle English learning, a position that Fiona Somerset has called 'extraclergial': 'outside of the clergy', '"lewed" or lay in status or alliance, but possessed of "clergie" or learning nonetheless'.[70] As a result, *Piers Plowman* appeals to a mixed audience, one that is both learned and 'lewed', clerical and lay.[71] From within this extraclergial position, Langland provides a searing critique of what he perceives as the contemporary crisis of virtue and bad habits.[72] He also provides one of the most sustained Middle English considerations of 'kynde', and of the ways in which 'human beings have the capacity to "read" or see spiritual lessons "reflected" in nature'.[73] Thus Nicolette Zeeman argues:

> Langland makes rich and cogent claims about the powers of the natural ... Langland's notion of *kynde* is moral, communitarian, familial, 'kindly',

loving, experiential, bodily; it is associated with the proper use and sharing of material goods and a positive view of the life and functioning of the body.[74]

This valuation of the natural, which A. V. C. Schmidt has also identified in the poem's pervasive use of 'elementary images', characterises it as a peculiarly powerful example of the spiritual value of the everyday and what might be termed the 'boistous' body.[75] Furthermore, both Rosanne Gasse and Louise Bishop have claimed the importance of medicine to the poem, observing 'the subject of medicine in *Piers Plowman* goes substantially beyond the realms of metaphor and allegory', and that 'medicine is the vehicle for epistemological, lexical, and pious analysis in *Piers Plowman*'.[76] Langland's poem is therefore an important witness to the centrality of the mouth to religious discourses and forms the core of this book's argument, each chapter of *Middle English Mouths* turning to examples from it. I put Langland's poem into conversation with other works of vernacular theology and Middle English poetry, such as Julian of Norwich's late fourteenth-century *Showings*, the second recension of Guillaume de Deguileville's *Le Pèlerinage de la vie humaine* (1355) – a poem with a strong influence on Langland in particular and medieval English literature in general – in its English version by John Lydgate (1426), and Geoffrey Chaucer's works.[77] Not typically understood as a vernacular theologian, Chaucer's thinking is nonetheless generated, as Langland's, Julian's and Lydgate's, from a profound engagement with both vernacular medicine and biology and Middle English *pastoralia*.

The Chapters

Drawing on these Latin and vernacular archives, the chapters of this book build accretively around a core set of the mouth's properties: the first chapter outlines the mouth's implication in the tripartite system of the soul; the second moves to think about the mouth's place in the body, in particular in its topographical and hierarchical arrangements. The next three chapters are more tightly focused on the properties of the mouth itself, treating first the ways in which taste, touch – and teeth – found all human knowledge and provide the model for ethical epistemological modes in which eating figures knowing, and food stands in for sapiential knowledge. Chapter 4 stays with the sensory physiology of the mouth – the ways in which taste and touch penetrate more deeply into the body interior, are more 'felt' and bring about material change – as properties that underlie medieval beliefs about the power of kissing. The final chapter turns to surgical interventions in the mouth, especially to the teeth and tongue, to explore the corrective work of pastoral care, the paradigmatic *habitus* of grammar and the discipline of confession.

Middle English Mouths starts out in Chapter 1, 'Natural Knowledge', by thinking about the different constellations of 'kynde', and the way in which this tradition understands that the natural provides a form of commentary or gloss on the unseen and divine. What is it that the mouth teaches 'kyndely'? Drawing on Latinate and vernacular mediations of natural philosophy and medicine, this chapter delineates medieval understandings of the mouth's physiology. Belief that the soul is the entelechy of the body establishes that bodily form and functioning have consequences for the soul. Moreover, belief in a *tripartite* soul, in which the lower parts (the vegetable and the sensible) are fully embodied, establishes the mouth's implication with three interrelated ensouled systems: those of the viscera, the heart and the brain. As the entranceway into the body, the mouth's role in judging what – and how much – enters into it is crucial to physiological health, as well as to ethical status. Moreover, in the system of the viscera the mouth is a key agent in a processual model – moving from mouth to stomach, to the anus and back out to the earth – that is not only one of the medieval period's most powerful means of thinking about a spiritual economy of interchange between high and low, inside and outside, but which defines human experience as one of flux and change, of daily cycles and life stages. The mouth, however, is not just anatomically connected to the lower body through passageways such as the gullet and oesophagus; it is also connected through sinews that are the means of communication between the soul and the body's parts. A physiological model posits multiple origins of speech, which is above all material, sent to the mouth to be voiced. In the systems of the brain and heart, the mouth mediates knowledge accrued through the senses of touch and taste. Natural philosophical discourses disclose multiple ways of valuing and ordering the senses, in which the distinct qualities of taste and touch – their reliance on direct contact, their greater sensitivity to pleasure and pain, as well as to material change – provide the grounds, in particular circumstances, for their superiority. This 'kynde' knowledge of the mouth forms the book's frame for rereading vernacular theology. These rereadings seek to exemplify the value of understanding Middle English bodies within less fixed, binary categories, as this first chapter begins to do through its closing discussion of the material aspect the tripartite understanding of the soul gives to medieval interior spirituality. In addition to recuperating the category of the everyday and the flux and change of lifecycle stages, I suggest that, following the tripartite model of the soul, we should look to the varied lessons learned from the body surface and the body interior, as well as from introspection of the reasonable soul.

Taking up one of the most common surface readings of the body, Chapter 2, 'The Reading Lesson', focuses on the meanings given to the upright body of man and the place of the mouth within it. Influentially formulated in Ovid's *Metamorphoses*, man's upright posture, according to a surface reading, reflects the heavens and liberates the eyes from a preoccupation with earth to seek God. The perspective of the tripartite soul offered in Chapter 1, however, cautions against surface readings of the body that are detached from biology. Middle English descriptions of anatomy and physiology offer variant readings of the lessons that can be derived from the upright body of man, which disclose instead the power of the mouth and the lower body to shape and direct human ethics. Works of vernacular theology draw on the powerful model of cyclical exchange provided by the mouth and the soul system of the viscera in reading the human body. This reframes man's upright bearing as one of a spectrum of postures, directed by the temporal rhythms of the body interior. Reading the place of the mouth within the body's topography in the interstices of physiological knowledge and vernacular theology challenges our recourse to fixed and totalising categorisations of the medieval body. Moreover, the positive lessons about the mouth that vernacular authors derive from nature direct us to a more attentive reading of the moral and spiritual consequences of having a body bent towards the earth. The codification of the body in which those who have acquired virtue might always maintain an upright posture is an ideal untenable (and indeed undesirable) in the conditions that characterise being human: body posture might be reversed as much through willed reason or natural need as through accident or becoming animal. Chapter 2 thus also turns to natural philosophical descriptions of the lifecycle stages of infancy and old age. An upright body, in these accounts, is a learned posture, achieved only with difficulty, and subject to daily reversal as well as perennial decline. What is perhaps the most radical lesson this natural example teaches is that in falling or kneeling, just as in other perversions of the upright posture, the power and extension of the senses are recalibrated: sight is diminished and taste and touch are intensified.

Exposing the vulnerable human condition, Middle English discourses make the care of the self – attending to temperate eating, drinking and sleeping and to maintaining an upright body – central to cultivating habits that will achieve salvation. This vulnerability, especially to taste and touch, characterises the physiology and sensibility of the newly born child and the lifecycle stage of childhood. Chapter 3, 'Tasting, Eating and Knowing', sets out natural philosophical descriptions of childhood and the medical regimen appropriate for children. In these contexts, the child's susceptibility to taste and touch is understood to correlate directly with moral disposition and cognitive capacity; the growth of teeth is associated, with the capacity not only to eat, but also to speak, to learn, to make moral judgements and to act rationally. The special care required of the mouth in childhood continues, however, not only into the pastoral concern with adult eating habits, but also into valorised modes of learning modelled on the mouth and its properties. This chapter focuses on three epistemological modes that derive their moral and spiritual efficacy from the mouth: *sapientia*; the related practices of *meditatio* and *ruminatio*; and the monastic habit of reading texts while eating. These traditions are founded in the mouth's sensory epistemology, on the one hand, and in the connection between food and knowledge, on the other. Mediated in *pastoralia* and poetry to vernacular and lay audiences, these clerical instruments of *habitus* are taken up to delineate how everyday practices of reading texts, consuming knowledge and eating food become sites of learning how to do well in the world. Discussions of the relationship between real and spiritual taste, and real and spiritual food, are also opportunities for vernacular authors to explore the relationship between the natural and the spiritual, and between the body's physiology and ethical and cognitive work, as well as the value of different epistemological modes. The coincidence of food and knowledge in works of vernacular theology reveals something about authors' and readers' understanding of the mouth's place in the question of what it means to be human: the governance of the mouth is at the very heart of ethical life, but so too is it at the heart of both original sin and its remedy. The mouth's natural properties – what and how we learn through it, the appetite to taste and to know mediated by it – provides a natural commentary not only on what it means to be human, but the mechanisms of harmatiology and soteriology.

Chapter 4, 'The Epistemology of Kissing', argues for an understanding of the kiss that situates it primarily within the category of the natural. As a discussion of the patristic commentaries on the kiss shows, there is a long tradition expounding the kiss's significance through analogy to natural functions of the mouth, such as breathing and speaking. This tendency is given impetus from the twelfth century on by the renewed engagement with the relationship of the tripartite soul and body, fostered by the encyclopaedism of the thirteenth century, and made available more widely through the vernacularisation of the fourteenth century. Drawing on natural philosophy and medicine, this chapter outlines the ways in which the transformative powers of kissing are rooted in a sciential knowledge of the physiology of the senses and modulated by the natural properties of the mouth – as an organ of nourishment and respiration, as well as a threshold in the body. Taste and touch are understood to mediate a deeper experience of pleasure and pain; so too are they understood to effect a greater extent of material change. This establishes a paradigm in which sensory encounters through kissing penetrate into the body interior, make deeper impressions than the other senses, and continue to act at distance, after contact has ceased. Secondly, the natural transformations that take place in the mouth – in saliva and on air drawn into the body for breath – sensitise the mouth as a threshold space, where alterations are made both in bodily and extra-bodily material. In the commentary tradition, breath is understood to convey something of the core of an individual within it, and so raises what is potentially at stake in a mouth-to-mouth kiss: the mingling and joining of two souls or minds. From a 'kynde' perspective, the kiss is therefore understood to arise out of practices of the care of the self – as the surplus of food and drink, or the expression of spiritually valorised affection and like-mindedness. Alongside this 'kynde' tradition, however, is a pastoral concern with the transformative, supernatural possibilities of the kiss, of which Judas's kiss of betrayal is made the example *par excellence*. This chapter thus also establishes the supernatural potency of the kiss as it emerges in vernacular pastoral works: the kiss has the power not only to penetrate into the body interior but also to traverse spiritual realms. The kiss in medieval traditions is thus multidirectional: it drives into the body, stretches into the world and crosses into hell.

The extension of the material into the spiritual, exemplified by the kiss, gives urgency to the care of the self in medieval guides to spiritual health. Chapter 5, 'Surgical Habits', looks to both the experience of medieval medical care, and textual descriptions of the mouth's passions and their treatments, in order to show the ways in which surgical interventions in the mouth are also understood to have spiritual effects. In so doing, this chapter provides a particularised discussion of the interaction between everyday bodily practices and the cultivation of *habitus*, which forms a thread running throughout the book's chapters. It starts out by foregrounding the cultural agency of the barber-surgeon, here used as a loose catch-all term for the 'medical' figure involved in a range of crafts from hair-cutting and shaving to the more technical crafts of bloodletting and forms of surgery. Reading between vernacular medicine and works of vernacular theology demonstrates the literal and imaginative affiliation of the barber-surgeon and the confessor. As the barber-surgeon works to shave the body and pare back its superfluities, so too does the confessor trim the superfluities of sin in the soul. Moreover, since bodily form is understood to have a real effect on the soul, the work of the barber-surgeon in some ways facilitates the work of confession. More specifically, this chapter contends that oral surgical interventions in the mouth provide a peculiarly powerful analogy for thinking about the material and spiritual effects of speech. The medical tradition establishes an oral surgical lexis of filing, scraping, shaving and rubbing that is taken up in both learned Latinate traditions of grammar and in vernacular discourses of confession. The 'kynde' understanding of the surgical effects of speaking, made available in vernacular encyclopaedias and pastoral texts alike, finds more specific analogy in the sacrament of penance, where the lexis of filing, shaving, scraping and shaving recurs in the threefold reformation process of contrition, confession and satisfaction. This chapter demonstrates vernacular understandings of the surgical effects of speaking, and of the tongue itself as a literal and figurative instrument of ethical action and correction. The efficacy of both surgery and speech, however, is called into question, especially in bodies habituated to sin, which might be resistant to these natural ethical strategies. The book thus concludes with the question, itself posed by vernacular theology, about the extent to which the physical care of the mouth has the power to shape virtue or reform the soul.

CHAPTER I

Natural Knowledge

❡ To kepe sobrenesse techeþ vs kynde and holi writ and alle creatures. ❡ Kynde, for amonges alle bestes þe man haþ lest mouþ after þe gretnesse of his body. ❡ And also a man haþ of oþere membres double, as two eien, two eeren, but he ne haþ but on mouþ. In þat techeþ kynde þat men schul ete litel and litel drynke, for kynde is of litle sustenaunce, and bi to moche mete kynde is ofte ouer-þrowe.[1]

— *The Book of Vices and Virtues*

'Kynde' – that is, nature, but also natural experience – teaches man through the example provided by the body and its parts. Relative to the size of his body, man's mouth is small, and while the other organs of sense are doubled, man has just one mouth.[2] The lesson this teaches us is of 'sobrenesse', or measure:[3] we do not need great quantities of food and drink (if we did, we would have two mouths), and, indeed, it is 'bi to moche mete' that our 'kynde' is overthrown.[4] In this passage from *The Book of Vices and Virtues*, 'kynde' is both Nature, our teacher, and human 'nature' itself, as well as natural need. That which we learn 'kyndely' through the body works in conjunction with that which we learn through 'holi writ' (the Scriptures and Christian authorities), as well as through observing the natural world ('alle creatures').[5] 'Kynde knowledge', here, is not antithetical to taught, clergial knowledge, but part of a spectrum encompassing the experiential, the exemplary, the taught and the revealed. Together, these interlacing forms of knowledge teach that a life styled by soberness is necessary, not only for bodily health, but because it puts all 'þouȝtes and þe willes and alle meuynges of þe herte and alle þe wittes of þe body vnder þe lordschip of riȝt and resoun'. Measured eating is thus central to the daily care of the self, making possible the rule of reason over the body's sensory perceptions ('wittes'), inclinations or feelings ('meuynges'), desires ('willes') and thoughts. So too does it make possible – literally and by analogy – the rule of God over the individual: 'herto bryngeþ sobre loue to God, þat put þe herte in þe wille of God'.[6] The anatomy of man's mouth both glosses and provides the literal basis for spiritual temperance, ethical action and 'sober' love for God.

The pastoral tradition from which *The Book of Vices and Virtues* stems articulates a prevalent strain of medieval thought (outlined in this book's Introduction) in which knowledge learned naturally, through nature, but also knowledge *about* nature forms part of the knowledge necessary for salvation. As Edwin Craun has observed in an important article on 'comparative physiology' and the tongue, this valuing of the physiology of the mouth for ethical learning in fourteenth-century *pastoralia* is generated by the rise of Aristotelianism in general and works such as John of Wales's (d.1295) *De lingua* in particular. Thus Craun notes that *De lingua*:

> develops the ethical potential of Aristotelian descriptions of the human tongue as a body part in and of itself and in comparison with the tongues of other animals … John initiates in Britain a sustained attention to physiological description of form and function as a basis for knowing what is vicious and virtuous in the use of the tongue, then for discovering how to shun the former and embrace the latter.[7]

As with the tongue, so with the other parts and functions of the human body. It is this mode that is taken up in *Piers Plowman*, a poem notable, in Nicolette Zeeman's terms, for its 'rich and cogent claims about the powers of the natural'.[8] Thus in this poem the dreamer meets with 'Kynde' (indistinguishable in this formulation from God, suggesting that nature is part of a divine whole) who bids him 'thorugh the wondres of this world wit [understanding] for to take', and leads him 'thorugh ech a creature, Kynde my creatour to lovye' (B.XI.322–5): the natural here both teaches and arouses love. Similarly, at a basic level, a pastoral work such as John Mirk's *Festial* glosses the visible world with spiritual meaning, and devotional poems, such as that translated by John Lydgate in *The Pilgrimage of the Life of Man*, seek to demonstrate how natural knowledge must operate under the frame of taught knowledge.[9] As these examples show, the late medieval valuation of the natural – rooted in the Pauline–Augustinian tradition of the *via positiva*, fostered by the so-called 'twelfth-century renaissance', and disseminated in part through the encyclopaedism of the thirteenth century – assumes that nature and the natural can provide a gloss on the unseen, the immaterial and the divine.[10] Thus Bartholomaeus Anglicus justifies his encyclopaedic work (quoting directly from St Paul, Romans 1:19–20) on the grounds that 'vnseye þinges of God beth iknowe and vndirstonde by þinges þat beth iseye' (1, 41). If the tradition of the *via positiva* provides a justification for the writing of books about nature in both Latin and the vernacular, so too, particularly in the context of the rise of Aristotelianism and its emphasis on learning through the senses, does the human body achieve a textual status: natural bodily experience and physiology provide a form of commentary on the self, Scripture and the divine.[11] But this kind of natural knowledge, as *Piers Plowman* articulates and *The Book of Vices and Virtues* demonstrates, should also lead to love for God – that is, it should comprise not *scientia ut scientia* but *scientia ut sapientia*. This mode of learning, then, is not just descriptive but emotive: it stirs, variously, contrition for sin and praise of the Creator.

In outlining late medieval knowledge about the mouth – its anatomy and physiology – this chapter provides the groundwork for the book's investigations into the ways in which the mouth forms a commentary on processes such as sinning, speaking, prayer and confession; on being saved; or on knowing the self and loving God. But human physiology is more than just gloss: as this chapter will show, the proper functioning of the body's physiology (our 'kynde') forms the literal basis for acting ethically, loving God and doing intellectual work, as well as for the spiritual processes we sometimes think of as transcending or abstracting the body. In order to establish what 'kynde' teaches about the mouth, this chapter draws upon encyclopaedic works – principally John Trevisa's translation of Bartholomaeus Anglicus's *De proprietatibus rerum*, as well as Latin texts, such as Albertus Magnus's *De animalibus* and Vincent of Beauvais's *Speculum maius*. It also looks to vernacular translations of medical texts, such as those of Lanfrank's and Guy de Chauliac's surgeries. As these texts demonstrate, we must begin by establishing the place of the mouth in the body–soul composite that makes up the human. Medieval belief in a tripartite soul situates the mouth in multiple interacting systems: further to the ways in which the mouth serves the reasonable part of the soul (through speech, for example), the mouth also serves the vegetable and sensible parts. The mouth thus interchanges with three main body–soul systems: those of the viscera, the heart and the brain. In disclosing the dependency of sensory and intellective functions on nutritive ones, these systems show that the mouth is implicated in the acquisition of ethical and spiritual knowledge. In the system of the viscera, governed by the vegetable part of the soul, the mouth participates in a processual movement, whereby things are brought into the body, driven down into the bowels, and from thence either sent to be made into body (including the *spiritus* that carry out the soul's offices) or back out of it into the earth. The mouth is shown to be intimately associated with, and in some ways analogous to, both stomach and anus. Even words are disclosed by the system of the viscera to be made in the very same sinews as those that serve appetite in the stomach. Understanding how a tripartite soul works in the body and its parts therefore reframes how we understand medieval theories of speech: the system of the viscera makes clear that there are multiple, and sometimes competing, sources of speech, which it is the mouth's task to articulate.

The sensible functions of the soul operate in both the heart and the brain. In this system, the mouth accrues knowledge principally through taste and touch. Importantly, the structure of the *via positiva* – that we move from knowledge about nature to a knowledge of God – itself mirrors the fundamental structure of learning through the senses. While all sensory perception is felt in the heart and processed in the brain in similar ways, sensory knowledge accrued by the mouth is distinctive in terms of how necessary it is for existence, the elemental qualities of the objects it acts upon and the effect it has on the body. These differences are at times the grounds for the denigration of the mouth and of the senses of taste and touch, but they are also the basis for their value and, for some authors, their superiority over the other senses: acting directly, inwardly, on earthy mundane objects, taste and touch are deeply felt and make changes in the body. If consideration of the vegetable operations of the mouth reinforces an understanding of the temporal, cyclical nature of the human body, its sensible operations direct us to the lived experience of the body in which the senses collaborate in making ethical living possible.

Natural knowledge – in all its iterations – about the tripartite soul and the place of the mouth within it offers compelling grounds, as I explore in the final section of this chapter, for allowing a material aspect to late medieval practices of self-knowledge and interiority. Middle English pastoral texts share with natural philosophical and medical texts an understanding of the interpenetration of the material with the spiritual. A knowledge (however rudimentary) of the processes of digestion and assimilation and of the operation of the five senses, for example, is essential to understanding how to use the mouth to cultivate virtue rather than vice, to do well while living in the world. As a result, interior spirituality – typically understood in scholarship to characterise late medieval devotional practice and to be rooted in the introspection of an *immaterial* soul – needs to be expanded to accommodate a sense of the body interior, with its nerves, veins, *spiritus* and words running between its organs and limbs. The mouth as the main entrance into this body interior itself becomes a site for rethinking the binaries of body–soul, inner–outer, as well as the opposition of sight and hearing to taste and touch.

The Tripartite Soul

The influx of natural philosophical works into the West in the twelfth century facilitated a fundamental reappraisal of the relationship between body and soul, in particular one that accommodated the soul's biological operations.[12] Aristotle's belief that the soul is the entelechy (or form) of the body and Galen's anatomical model (influenced by Platonic notions of three distinct souls), developed by Avicenna and harmonised by scholastic theologians, became the medieval standard (though a standard that was not without contradiction and debate).[13] Perhaps most significantly, this adherence to the soul as the body's entelechy *necessitates* a body in medieval thinking; human identity requires the unity of body and soul and is therefore fully corporeal. John Trevisa's translation of *De proprietatibus rerum* asserts (citing Aristotle): 'a soule is *endelochia* [entelechy], þat is, þe firste acte and perfeccioun of a kindeliche body þat haþ lymes and myȝt to haue lif' (I, 92). Indeed, he elaborates, the soul 'coueitiþ' and 'desireþ kyndeliche þe onynge wiþ þe body' (I, 102) – that is, the soul of its very nature yearns after union with the body. The soul's natural desire for and dependency on the body is underscored by the understanding that two potencies of the soul, the *vegetabilis* and *sensibilis*, have bodily locations. Following Aristotle's division of the soul's virtues, *On the Properties of Things* records the standard medieval view that the soul has three powers: the *vegetabilis* which gives life (common to plants, animals and man); the *sensibilis* which gives feeling and movement (common to animals and man); and the *racionalis* which bestows reason (unique to man).[14] The reasonable soul, either not localised or posited as residing in the heart (or, in some accounts, the brain), is thought to be separable from the body.[15] In contrast, the *sensibilis* and *vegetabilis* – located in and ruled over by the liver, heart and brain – are fully integrated with and dependent on the body, and are held to die with it. The reasonable part of the soul, moreover, depends on the proper operation of the sensible and vegetable parts in order to act in and through the body.[16]

This tripartite understanding of the soul gives to medieval epistemological theories a material, embodied basis (as works such as *The Book of Vices and Virtues* testify); it also gives a materialist aspect to late medieval interiority, whereby the individual sought to come to self-knowledge and, thus, to knowledge of God.[17] Medieval beliefs about the virtues of the two lower parts of the soul, and how the mouth operates in relation to them, disclose the dependency of sensory and intellectual functions on nutritive ones. It also shows that while taste and touch are valued differently from the other senses, they are not straightforwardly 'brutish', as critical orthodoxy still tends to hold. Matthew Milner's study of the senses, while pointing to more varied assessments, recounts the standard summary: 'touch was ranked the lowest because of its ubiquity throughout the body and lack of intellective use', and further, that, 'because of its explicit connection to "nutryment"', taste 'was even more removed from intellective processes'.[18] Traditionally, the eyes and ears are held to be the noble organs, and sight and hearing the noble senses, valuable for cognition and reason, engaged in learning and understanding; smell, while in some functions associated with taste, occupies a middle ground; the mouth and nerve-filled flesh, taste and touch, on the other hand, are held to be base – necessary for existence and life in the world, but of limited value for cognition and reason and without relevance for taught or spiritual knowledge. The tripartite model of the soul, however, demonstrates a rather more complex, fluid relationship between principles of the soul and parts of the body: perhaps against our expectations, in all three soul systems, the mouth is implicated, not merely in preserving life, but in knowledge acquisition and cognitive processes. Furthermore, the tripartite model of the soul also figures the mouth as the means of expressing not only reason, but also the wants and passions of the body and its parts, even if these wants and passions are at times contradictory.

Food for Thought: Being, Eating and Speaking

The lowest potency of the soul, the vegetable, works in the viscera. *On the Properties of Things* elaborates that this level of the soul, since it is responsible for reproduction, nourishment and growth, gives life or 'desireþ to be' whereas the sensible part of the soul 'desireþ to be wel' and the reasonable 'to be best' (i, 102). In this regard, the mouth is fundamental to the vegetable part of the soul: it is the vehicle for ingesting food and drink, without which life cannot persist, as well as the means of discriminating, through the senses of taste and touch, between what is harmful and what is beneficial to bring into the body. If the vegetable part of the soul *desires* 'to be', taste and touch (centred in the mouth) are necessary for the human 'to be' at all: medieval authorities follow Aristotle, who writes in *De anima* that 'these senses are indispensable to the animal, and it is clear that without touch' – and this includes taste, since taste is a kind of touch – 'it is impossible for an animal to be' (other senses are held rather to be necessary *ad esse bene*, 'in order to be well').[19] Without taste and touch – without the mouth – and a sensitive body, man could not move through the world nor find (beneficial) nutriment within it. The soul's (vegetable) desire 'to be' (or to eat) is therefore bound up with the mouth's (sensible) desire to taste and touch – a connection borne out in received medieval medical traditions which understand parturition as being brought about when the foetus can no longer find enough nutriment in the uterus.[20] After birth, the child's experience continues to be centred on the mouth, as tasting and touching condition not only its means of survival but also its first means of encountering the world. The vegetable part of the soul, however, does not merely serve the mundane, if vital, acts of eating and drinking; it also serves the assimilation of food and drink into the body, and the transformation of digested matter into bodily spirits. It thus fundamentally both shapes human form and facilitates the sensible and cognitive faculties of the second part of the soul, the *sensibilis*.

One of the consequences of the new availability of Classical and Arabic learning, and the 'naturalist optimism' it fosters,[21] is that explanations of processes such as generation and growth in the human body (as Philip Reynolds has described) are naturalised or desacralised.[22] Following the understanding that it is the *vegetabilis* that serves appetite, but also, crucially, digestion, assimilation (i.e. turning food into the material of the body), retention and excretion, theologians come to accept that it is food that is turned into the flesh and materials of the body. This raises questions and creates anxiety about bodily wholeness and the effect of food on the identity of the consumer.[23] It is here that the mouth's senses and judgements are shown to be necessary for the human in order 'to be' in morally urgent ways – not just in preserving life, but also (in ways that sight, hearing and smell are not) in shaping the form that life, physical and moral, will take. If the mouth's judgements over *what* enters the body have profound implications for human form and identity, so too do its judgements over *how much*. Measured eating and drinking is vital not only to maintaining bodily form, but also, as works such as *The Book of Vices and Virtues* make clear, in facilitating the rule of the reasonable part of the soul through the 'spirits' (*spiritus*) that perform its offices.

Essentially, the role of the *vegetabilis* is to restore that which is lost by the body (of man, beast or plant): however, as the body grows older this part of the soul begins to fail and ultimately dies with the body.[24] In the medieval medical tradition, the human body is understood to be in a constant state of decay; it is naturally leaky and loses matter through sweat, spit and other bodily excretions, as well as being vulnerable to accidental spillage through injury or sickness. Humours, which are made from food, are therefore needed to restore that which is lost by the body.[25] The mouth is a vital agent in this process, as *On the Properties of Things* describes:

> For þe mouþ first fongiþ [receives] mete, and chiewith it, and sesouneþ it and makeþ it abel to digestioun, and sendiþ it to þe stomak, and þerfore kynde makeþ þe mouþ moist withinne to tempre and chaunge þe esiloker [the more easily] þe drynes of þe mete by moisture of þe mouþ. (1, 201)

The mouth not only brings food into the body, breaking it down through chewing so it can be swallowed, it also 'seasons it' ('sesouneþ it'), that is 'bring[s] (food) to a desired state or consistency' (*MED*, s.v.), which the stomach is able to digest.[26] Once received and digested by the stomach, the most subtle parts of food are drawn by the veins to the liver where they are transformed by the presence of heat into the four humours. These humours are then distributed to the members of the body and assimilated as flesh and the 'species' of the limbs and organs. Thus, for example, the liver and stomach 'lediþ [transport] and chaungiþ þe mete into þe kinde of membris' (1, 164), and the *vegetabilis* 'oneþ [joins] hit [the food] to þe þing þat is ifedde' (1, 97): food is literally 'made one' with the eater, transformed into human flesh.[27] At each stage of digestion, that which cannot be assimilated by the body is separated out and excreted. As the entranceway into the body and the first stage in the digestion process, the mouth is deeply implicated with a body–soul system that creates a passageway through from the higher to the lower bodily stratum, conveying, ingesting, assimilating and excreting food and drink. Indeed, the linea between mouth and anus creates an interior space that is continuous with the outside of the body. Unlike the eyes, ears and nose, the mouth's movement is directed deep down into the body, as the earthy things taken into it not required to maintain bodily form and physiological function pass through the stomach, intestines and anus and back out into the earth.

Chaucer deploys these kinds of natural lessons about the mouth's anatomy and physiology in and through the figure of the Prioress in *The Canterbury Tales*. The Prioress, we are told, has a small mouth (it is 'ful smal'); accordingly, she exercises fastidious control over what enters into her mouth and demonstrates (seemingly) exemplary table manners: 'At mete [the table] wel ytaught was she with alle', Chaucer the Pilgrim observes, 'She leet no morsel from hir lippes falle'; and 'Wel koude she carie [carry] a morsel [e.g. to her mouth] and wel kepe / That no drope ne fille upon hire brest'.[28] The Prioress herself makes the mouth the central subject of her Prologue and her Tale, where she further pursues an alimentary logic: the anatomical linea between mouth and anus here surfaces in the description of the tale's setting – on a street that 'was free and open at eyther ende' – and the mouth's downward thrust manifests in the fate of the tale's 'litel clergeon' (a seven-year-old Christian boy).²⁹ Provoking the neighbouring Jews to seek his death, the boy's daily, public sung devotion (the *alma redemptoris*) to the Virgin Mary ends (or finds one sort of end) in the place Jews purge their 'entraille [bowels, intestines]' – a 'wardrobe' or privy.³⁰ Thus, while the Prioress takes up what the mouth teaches 'kyndely' in her lifestyle as in her tale, she troubles the idea of the good to which it can lead: her concern with her mouth betrays an obsessive anxiety over food and eating;³¹ her anti-Semitic tale displaces the natural digestive and excretory systems, to which the mouth is central, on to (murderous, thus unnatural) Jewish bodies and so short-circuits its health-bringing, renewing cycle.³² Chaucer's Prioress therefore invokes but holds off the possibility of the natural and spiritual benefit that the mouth's interaction with the lower body can bring.

The digestion process, further to purging waste and restoring bodily matter, restores and renews the spirits that provide the medium between body and soul and through which the potencies of the soul are performed.³³ These spirits, as *On the Properties of Things* explains, 'haþ many names':

> by worchinge of þe lyuour he hatte *spiritus naturalis*, in þe herte *vitalis*, and in þe heed *animalis*. We schal nouȝt trowe [believe] þat þis spirit is manys resonable soule but more soþely þe chare þerof and cariage and propre instrument. For be suche a spirit þe soule is ioyned to þe body, and wiþoute þe seruice of suche a spirit þe soule visþ no parfit worchinge in þe body. (1, 123)

The *spiritus* is the 'chare' (seat) and 'cariage' (vehicle) of the soul – or, in the words of the Middle English translation of Lanfrank's *Science of Cirurgie*, 'bitwixe a mannys bodi & his soule a louely byndynge'.³⁴ As Bartholomaeus's definition of *spiritus* indicates, in the first stage of digestion the liver purifies humours, making the spirit *naturalis* (which is rarefied blood). This is then moved by way of the veins and sent to the heart, where it is purified further and made into *vitalis*, which is the pulse of life (that is, breath). The same spirit is sent by way of arteries into the den of the brain where it is made into *animalis*, which is a more subtle form of spirit. (In a fourth stage, the spirit is sent to the testicles or to the uterus where it is refined even further to provide the male and female spermatic material necessary for conception and generation of a child.) From the brain, an intricate network in the body allows the *spiritus* to move through a series of sinews to 'wosen' (arteries), to veins and to 'smale weyes', enabling sensation and movement (1, 99).[35] However, if this spirit is damaged through overeating or undereating, causing blockages in the sinews, the accord and unity of the body and soul is dissolved and the reasonable spirit is hindered from working in the body.[36]

Fundamental to medical theory, such beliefs about the body–soul relationship also lie at the heart of medieval theories of governance, daily regimen and the care of the self. As Giles of Rome's *De regimine principum* (1277–80) explains, in John Trevisa's translation: although reason and understanding 'be not a bodilich vertu, nerþelees it vseth in his doyng bodilich membris and lemys [limbs]. Wherfore 3if þe body is distempred [out of balance], resoun may not frelich [freely] vse his owne doynge.'[37] Thus the humoural imbalance resulting from bad digestion can cause, as Vincent of Beauvais's *Speculum doctrinale* details, 'loss of reason, stupefaction, extreme lethargy, epilepsy, and madness'.[38] Similarly, Lanfrank's surgical treatise records that through digestive disorders, such as constipation or 'flix [flux] of þe wombe' (diarrhoea), 'boþe her heerynge & oþere comoun wittis ben troublid', that is, the outer wits or senses, as well as the 'priuy vertues þat ben troublid as ymaginatif', that is, the inner wits or cerebral faculties.[39] And *On the Properties of Things* relates how overeating prevents proper digestion, producing fumes or 'smoke' that rise to the brain. This smoke disturbs the 'substaunce and þe vse of resoun, and ryueþ [damages] and apeireþ [impairs] þe tongue þat telliþ what resoun meneþ, and makeþ þe tonge stamere and faille, as it is iseye in dronken men' (1, 146). The effects of food on reason are thus manifested as a diminished control over bodily organs and as a rupture between what reason 'means' and what the tongue 'tells'.

Some examples in medieval medical texts draw the line between mouth and stomach even more tightly, establishing them as analogous organs and as intimately connected with each other. Thus certain bodily disorders produce dysfunction in the mouth mirrored in the symptoms experienced in the digestive system. Guy de Chauliac describes in his *Cyrurgie* how humoural imbalance that causes 'wlaffynge' (stuttering or stammering) also causes diarrhoea: because of excessive moisture in the sinews and 'brawnes' (muscles) under the tongue, 'wlaffynge or rattelynge [stuttering] men ben most taken wiþ a longe dyarie (i. fluxe)'.[40] Verbal and faecal diarrhoea are expressions of the same pathological condition: a loss of control over speech is mirrored and mimicked by a loss of control over defecation. In other words, the lower body has an inextricable connection with the upper body and is analogous to it. The connection between control over the mouth and control over the anal sphincter frequently spills over from a physical into a moral one in medieval thinking. Thus, in *Piers Plowman*, Envy has a 'flux' of foul mouth (B.v.177); the couple that marry for money do not produce children but an offspring of 'foule' words that issue out as excrement (B.ix.162–9). *An Alphabet of Tales* records the fate of the blasphemous man whose mouth was 'turnyd into his ars, & efter euer whils he liffid [lived], all þe filthe and þe degestion of his bodie come out at his mouthe, & noght at his nache [anus]'.[41]

If the analogy of mouth and stomach furnishes the medieval imagination with powerful images, it is the sinews (repeatedly in the medical examples cited above) that provide the literal connection of mouth and stomach. What is understood to move through these sinews is not mere matter, however, but rather ensouled matter, with sensory and cognitive content. Vincent thus records the effect that obstacles in the sinews can have on the mouth's sensing and speaking faculties: dyscrasia in 'the nerve through which taste is "felt"' leads to a privation of taste; that in 'nerves through which words are formed', to a privation of words.[42] This has implications for the role of the mouth as the organ (and bodily agent) that makes exterior what is interior and for its function more generally in the body as a sign. Albertus Magnus similarly describes how the stomach and lower lip have a 'common boundary', because of 'a binding nerve [*nervus ligans*]'. This means that 'a movement of the lower lip is a sign that vomiting is imminent, for the latitudinal fibers of the stomach are already moving to eject the food'.[43] This suggests a literal form of body language, establishing communication between the mouth and stomach in the form of a physical sign, that is drawn deeper still by the sinew that the *Cyrurgie* terms variously the 'reuersif synowe' or the 'double synowes'.[44] This sinew, which conveys the sensory signals for appetite (or hunger) from the stomach, also conveys 'voice': 'considre double synowes, descendynge to þe stomak and to þe bowels, croked aȝeyne for þe felynge and turnynge aȝen to wiþynne aboue next þe þroote, for þe voyce'.[45] Indeed, both Guy and Lanfrank warn against the danger of cutting this sinew, 'for by þe kyttynge of it þe voyce is lost' and 'of þe whiche kuttynge or prickynge euermore is maad hosnesse [hoarseness]'.[46] By means of this 'reuersif synowe', which descends to the stomach and ascends again to the throat, the stomach is directly connected with the sinews that work to create speech.[47] What this also underscores is the materiality of speech in medieval understandings, which emerges from a mingling of matter (making up words themselves) in the sinews and in the veins.[48]

The biological interchange between stomach, heart, brain and mouth sets up the potential for competing discourses of the body, facilitated physiologically by common boundaries between the stomach and mouth and by sinews that run to the stomach and turn again 'for voice'. *On the Properties of Things* bears out this notion of the body's multivocality. It records (following Isidore of Seville) that the mouth 'is þe messanger of þe soule, for we tellen out by þe mouþe what we conseyuen raþer in soule and in þou3t' (1, 200). In other words, the mouth is understood to act on behalf of the higher part of the soul, as a mediator of reason, which is the godlike part of man. Indeed, the tongue should (as we have seen above), in a properly regulated body, tell 'what resoun *meneþ*' (1, 146, my emphasis), that is, express what reason intends to convey. This seems to ascribe to the mouth the activity of translating or construing.[49] The pastoral text *Dives and Pauper* similarly records, citing Aristotle's *De interpretatione*, 'þat speche is tokene of þou3tis in þe herte, for it is ordeynyd þat man be his speche schulde schewyn þing to ben or nout to ben as he felyt & þinkyth in his herte'.[50] But, as *On the Properties of Things* continues, so too do the mouth and its parts 'schape þe voys of literal speche', and work 'to tokene in propir interpretacioun *disposiciouns of lymes* and *passiouns of þe soule*, as wreþþe and frendeschip, sorewe and woo' (1, 199, my emphasis): that is, the mouth externalises bodily wants – the morbid dispositions, but also the inclinations or concerns of the limbs – as well as the 'passiouns' (the sufferings, feelings) of the soul.[51] The 'reuersif synowe' therefore provides a physiological reminder of the ways in which, in medieval thinking, speaking is dependent on eating, but also that speaking is not, in some ways, so very different from eating. More than simply maintaining human life, the mouth–stomach system makes possible, through creating and restoring *spiritus*, the very materials required for feeling, thinking, speaking and the operation of reason. As the body–soul systems of the brain and heart also make clear, the mouth's role is not merely material (i.e. to produce the matter to be acted upon by the soul) but active: desiring and experiencing; shaping and interpreting affect, thought and reason; and speaking for all three parts of the soul and for the body. However, the insistence that the mouth should express a proper 'token' (or sign) of the limbs' 'disposiciouns' is at once destabilised by the accompanying process of 'interpretacioun', which inevitably makes the 'token' susceptible to multiple readings.

This creates the potential, not only for a disjunction between the thoughts of the heart and the words of the mouth, or for the social failure of the body as a sign, but also for the mouth's misguided pursuit of food and drink, as pastoral writers make clear. Thus, the ability of uncontrolled appetite and eating to overthrow reason is commonly attributed to the body's own competing discourses and instability as a sign. In Passus I of the B-text of *Piers Plowman*, the dreamer encounters the figure of Holy Church who instructs him on the ways in which God has provided man with 'liflode at nede [the necessities of life] / In mesurable manere' (18–19). Warning against gluttony and 'delitable drynke' (34), she teaches that:

> 'Mesure is medicine, though thow muchel yerne.
> It is nought al good to the goost that the gut asketh,
> Ne liflode to the likame [body] that leef is to the soule.
> Leve nought thi likame, for a liere hym techeth –
> That is the wrecched world, wolde thee bitraye.
> For the fend and thi flessh folwen togidere,
> And that seeth thi soule and seith it in thin herte.' (B.1.35–41)

Not everything the gut asks for is good for the soul, nor is what is pleasing and beneficial to the soul always nourishing to the body. Holy Church's view of man (like the medical tradition's) is multivocal: the 'gut asketh', the soul 'seeth' (sees) and 'seith' (says) it in the heart.[52] Thus, Holy Church establishes two important notions, shared with the medical tradition, which have a bearing on ethics: (1) the potential contradiction or variance (multivocality) between the speech acts of the 'gut' and those of the 'soule', and (2) the need to discern the origin of bodily signs and speech ('Leve not thi likame') – for, as Jill Mann suggests in her essay on Chaucer's 'Miller's Tale', 'like language, the body is polysemous'.[53] If we bring a physiological understanding of the mouth to Langland's image of the gut – here representing the stomach, but also more generally the viscera, the anus and so a lower bodily stratum – we can infer that the gut speaks, just as the soul does, through the mouth.[54] The discourse of the gut might therefore take up the subjects of lack, hunger, appetite and love, but also itself might be the source of low, base speech, bawdy tales and sin. Similarly, medieval *pastoralia* vividly depicts the body's multivocality in discussions of the vice of gluttony – when God bids the glutton to fast his stomach bids him rather to ' "ete þy mete in al ese" '.[55] *Pastoralia* also imagines the discord *between* body parts: the stomach cries ' "A, dame þrote [throat], þou sleest me! I am so ful þat I breste [burst]!" ' But the glutton's tongue answers: ' "Þeiȝ þou breste, þis good mossel [mouthful] schal be ete" '.[56] The possibility of competing bodily discourses so vividly dramatised in the pastoral tradition is thus one rooted in medieval beliefs about physiology and anatomy, the test, and 'medicine', for which is the all-important principle of 'measure'.

To summarise, then: in the system of the viscera the mouth interchanges with the stomach and the anus. It is involved in a processual movement down through the body and out again that points to its cyclic nature. Paying attention to the ways in which the lowest, vegetable part of the soul works through the mouth and its parts reminds us that even mundane processes, such as eating and excreting, are ensouled, and further, that they are not separate from but intimately connected with cognitive processes and with the rule of reason in the body. It also reminds us that processes we often think of as immaterial or spiritual are, in medieval thinking, rooted in the material: words are matter (made from food) and speaking is physical, sharing in and arising from the same systems responsible for hunger, appetite and digestion. This calls into question assessments, for example, that a body part's connection with 'nutriment' necessarily correlates with a distance from 'intellective processes'. Measured eating, it turns out, is the literal basis for learning, but also provides a powerful model for understanding different, and sometimes competing, kinds of knowledge and knowledge acquisition. Thus attention, in turn, to the second part of the soul, the *sensibilis*, reminds us that the mouth, through taste and touch, also accrues a specific kind of knowledge that is valuable for cognition and for reason. In medieval models of epistemology, all knowledge is dependent upon the operation of the sense perceptions, which gather knowledge about the world and self.[57] As Thomas Aquinas contends, 'we are of the kind to reach the world of intelligence through the world of sense, since all our knowledge takes its rise from sensation'. In this context, Aquinas influentially outlines a model of the *via positiva*: Scripture 'puts forward spiritual things under bodily likenesses; at all events the uneducated may then lay hold of them.'[58] If we take this seriously, what *kind* of knowledge does the mouth, through taste and touch, accrue?[59]

Rereading the Senses: Sensing, Feeling, Knowing

The *sensibilis*, or the sensible part of the soul, operates in the brain (or in the heart and brain, depending on the authority followed).[60] *On the Properties of Things* records that the *sensibilis* is located in the 'most subtle' chambers of the brain from where it gives feeling and movement to the limbs (1, 98) via the sinews. The sensible part of the soul 'knows' through the outer wits (the sense organs) and 'apprehends' through the inner wits. Adhering to the medical model of cerebral processing, Bartholomaeus records that the inner wits (*sensu interiori*) are located in three regions of the brain: in the first is *ymaginatiua*, where the outer wits are carried, ordered and collated; in the second is *logica* or the *estimatiue* virtue, which discerns good from evil; in the third is *memoritiua* or the 'vertue of mynde' (1, 98) where the judgement of the middle chamber is sent in order to 'bringe it forþ in acte and in dede' (1, 107).[61]

The outer wits (or sense organs) operate physiologically in similar ways, although with some important differences. Taking up the terms of the Aristotelian 'causes' deemed to govern 'all activity and change in the universe', *On the Properties of Things* explains that:[62]

> to make it [taste] parfite þe *casuales* effectiue, material, and informatiue, þat beþ inempned [enumerated] in oþir wittes, ben nedeful. For þe vertue þat hatte *animalis* is cause efficient, doynge and makynge. Þe cause material and instrumental is in þe tonge with what longeþ þerto and makeþ þe vertue of taste parfite. (1, 117)[63]

The efficient cause of taste is the spirit *animalis* – as Lanfrank explains in his *Science of Cirurgie*, veins bring the spirit *vitalis* to the brain where it is digested, becomes *animalis* and 'resseyueþ naturel foorme of vndirstondynge' – which is carried out from the foremost chamber of the brain to the tongue and roof of the mouth by way of the sinews.[64] As adumbrated in Bartholomaeus's account, taste thus operates by six pairs of sinews, originating in the brain, that are 'ipiʒt' (that is, fixed, embedded) in the middle of the tongue, which spread in bows and branches to the outer parts of the tongue (1, 117).[65] The anatomical description of the Middle English translation of Guy's *Cyrurgie* specifies that, further to the 'tastynge and mouynge synowes' of the fourth and sixth pair which come to the tongue, sinews from the third pair come to the lips and to the roots of the teeth.[66]

In order for the sinews to receive the humours of the object tasted, the tongue is hollow and porous – or 'spongie' in the words of London, British Library, MS Sloane 6: 'Tastyng is a vertu goyng out fro þe sensitiue soule. sette in þe spongie flesch of þe tong demyng þe contrariosite [differences] of sauores and þat falleþ of þam' (f.18v). The process of taking the likeness of an object sensed in the mouth, *On the Properties of Things* continues, is facilitated by 'spotel' (spittle), brought to it by 'strenges [frenum]' in the side of the tongue (1, 208). This spittle is:

> [the] mene bytwene þe wit of taast and þe þing þat is itasted, for no þing is itaastid by þe wit of taast but þe sauour þerof be presentid by þe spotil to þe lyme of taast. Þerfore þe spotel is ichaungid aftir þe qualite of þe sauour of þing þat is itastid. (1, 209)

Spittle, which mediates (is the 'mene') between taste and objects of taste, is literally transformed in the process of tasting and touching, taking on the 'qualite' (which here refers to the complexion or humour) of the thing sensed or ingested.[67]

Once acted on by spittle, the spirit *animalis* 'takeþ a liknes of propirtees þerof, and þanne he presentiþ hem to þe doom of þe soule' (1, 117).[68] In concert with the sensing properties of the soul centred in the tongue, the action of the mouth and the mundane matter of spittle provide materials for the soul's judgement, not only about what will and will not be incorporated into the body, but also as a building block for further cognitive and intellectual processes. These processes remain fully embodied and material. By means of the same sinews which run to the organ of sense, the likeness of the object is sent back, either by way of the heart to the brain or directly to the brain, to the *ymaginatiua*, where it is literally, physically impressed on to the cold, moist matter of the brain. From here the likeness moves to the middle ventricle of the brain where the *aestimativa* (intuition or instinct) acts upon it (this is not reason, since this function is common to the cerebral processes of both humans and animals, but discerns whether something is good and desirable, or if it is, instead, to be eschewed). This judgement, in turn, is then sent to the memory to be stored.[69]

While all the outer wits essentially function in a similar way – the spirit *animalis* is brought to them from the brain and brings back a likeness of the sensed object to the brain to be 'digested' – they are in fact not uniform, but differ in terms of how fundamental they are to the human (as we have already seen), the distance at which they act, the particular quality of the perception they mediate and the kind of effect they have on the body. Bartholomaeus's encyclopaedia thus records (following Aristotle):

> Of þe wittes þe siȝt is most sotil for þe kinde þerof is fury [fiery]. Þe heringe haþ meche of þe aier, for soun is of aier ismyte. And þenne moost sotil is þe smellinge, for þe kynde þerof is smoky. And þanne þe taast, for þe kinde þerof is watirry. And þe laste and þe most boistous of alle his þe gropinge, for þe kinde þerof is erþy and is nedeful to fele harde þinges as bones and senewis, rowe [rough] and smethe, colde and hote. (1, 108)[70]

The senses here are placed on a descending scale, at the top of which is the quality of 'sotilnes' and at the bottom that of 'boistousness'. Sight is the most 'sotil' and acts on 'sotil' (or fiery) things, and as such it and its objects are rarefied, partaking in less of the substance of the earth than the other senses. The sense of sight can thus act at a distance; it knows 'sodeinliche [suddenly] þinges þat ben fulle fer' (1, 108).[71] In contrast, taste and touch and their objects are 'boistous', that is, reified and dominated by the element earth. The 'boistousnes' of taste and touch is necessary to discern the tangible qualities that knowing-at-a-distance cannot – rough, smooth, cold and hot, but also the material presence of other bodies, the bones and sinews of which they are composed. While all the senses in some ways touch their objects (even sight is understood as a form of touch – or, perhaps better, is predicated on touch), it is nonetheless the case that taste and touch are associated particularly with direct, unmediated contact.[72] As *De anima* asserts:

> All the other senses, e.g. smell, sight, hearing, apprehend through media; but where there is immediate contact the animal, if it has no sensation, will be unable to avoid some things and take others, and so will find it impossible to survive. That is why taste also is a sort of touch; it is relative to nutriment, which is just tangible body.[73]

Taste, like touch, is unmediated and requires direct contact between the object tasted and the mouth: neither of these senses can keep at a distance, but necessarily work at close quarters and act in and on bodies.

This immediate contact is important for the way in which taste and touch take likenesses from their objects: that is, touch (and taste as a kind of touch) mediates and shapes a particular kind of interaction with and relationship to objects in the world. The property of the objects sensed by sight is 'fury'; that of hearing is 'airy'; that of smell is 'smoky'; that of taste is 'watirry'; and that of touch 'erþy'.[74] More precisely, *On the Properties of Things* describes how the tongue acts upon 'greet [thick] and boistous substaunce' (1, 172). As a result, the degree to which the body is altered or affected by sense perception differs. *On the Properties of Things* thus catalogues: touch or 'gropinge' (and so also taste) is 'more boistous and more material þan oþir wittis. Þerfore he holdiþ þe more strongliche þe impressiouns and prentinges of þingis þat plesiþ oþir greueþ' (1, 120).[75] Further: 'eueriche þing þat is ifelid makeþ a changinge in þe lyme of þat felinge. So seiþ þe philosofir [Aristotle]' (1, 120). The 'boistous' senses, more directly connected with the heart, are more 'felt', more directly mediate pleasure or pain and bring about material change in the body. As a locus of taste and touch, the mouth (more so than, say, the eyes) is subject to (and the medium of) material change through the objects it senses.[76] This constitutes part of the limitations of taste and touch, but also their value.[77] Thus, while in the *Summa theologiae* Aquinas understands taste and touch to be less cognitively complex senses because they entail 'natural immutation' (i.e. the body undergoes a change in the process of sensation), in his *Commentary on the Metaphysics of Aristotle* he ranks touch second only to sight on the basis that this sense, more than the others, discerns the differences *between* bodies and accrues more information about their features.[78]

In *Speculum doctrinale*, Vincent of Beauvais elaborates the particular physiological reason for the intensity in which things are felt in the organs of touch (and so also of taste): the coarseness of the mouth or of the surface of the body makes material alteration difficult; passions likewise do not 'operate in it quickly, because of its thickness which resists and also prohibits. And just as it is pleased more strongly, it is also hurt to a greater extent.'[79] Thus, while taste and touch mediate direct contact with the objects they sense, this does not mean that they take likenesses from their objects more easily than the other senses: rather, their very coarseness makes this a more difficult process, which in turn accounts for the stronger experiences of pleasure and pain they mediate.[80]

While medieval models of taste and touch are not uniform, these examples begin to map out several qualities inhering in taste and touch: the knowledge they convey to the soul about the self, the world and others in it is direct and inward; they make a deeper and longer-lasting impression on the *ymaginatiua* in the brain and on the body; they effect material change; and the degree of pleasure or pain that arises from them is stronger and more 'felt', not just by the body but also by the soul. This Aristotelian account of sensation is repeated in encyclopaedias such as Bartholomaeus's and Vincent's, but it is also followed in treatises on governance and regimen, such as Giles of Rome's *De regimine principum*. Thus Trevisa translates: 'we hauen strengere likynge in tast and in touching þan in siȝte, huryng and smellyng' for two reasons. First, 'we ben more ioned [joined to] and nerere to þe likynge þat we hauen in tast and in touching þan to þe likynge þat we hauen in oþere wittes'. Secondly, 'sencible delectacioun in tast and in touching semeth iordeyned more strayt and inmediate, þat is sone after, to oure kepyng and sauacioun'.[81] The pleasure we derive from taste and touch is predicated not only on our nearness to and our unmediated experience of those objects we taste and touch, but also on their importance for our 'kepyng' and 'sauacioun', that is, the preservation of life itself. *On the Properties of Things* explains that touch, uniquely, is in fact the foundation of all the other senses without which they could not function: 'þe wit of gropinge is þe ground and þe foundement of þe oþir wittis' (I, 120).[82] Thus the 'sauacioun' Giles refers to is the preservation of life and sensation itself, but the contiguity of the physical and the metaphysical, so clearly attested in medieval natural philosophy, opens up the possibility that the ways in which we learn and experience by mouth might also be literally more necessary for spiritual salvation. While, at least in the context of Giles's discussion, these perceptions of taste and touch form the basis of medieval arguments for the particular need to regulate everyday practices in relation to the mouth (and, in fact, since here touching is a euphemism for sexual intercourse, the genitals), so too, for some medieval philosophers, do they become the basis for arguments about the superiority of taste, as they do in the *Summa de saporibus*.[83]

The *Summa de saporibus* begins by asserting that there are two modes of knowing things: experience and reason, both of which are dependent on the senses.[84] The author's interest is therefore in the quality of the knowledge each sense organ accrues and how truly it is able to judge and know the object sensed. In this regard the writer concludes:

> only taste singularly and principally is fitted to search out the nature of things above the rest of the senses. In fact, through it we judge completely and perfectly the nature of things and indeed even of complexions.[85]

Here, emphatically, the only way to know something truly is to taste it; the other senses know but imperfectly (i.e. not substantively) and are therefore often deceived. This claim is based firstly on the propinquity of the mouth to the object tasted and, secondly, on the fact that a likeness of the property of the thing tasted crosses over into the body:

> For by the instrument of taste the whole thing is tasted according to its substance and density [lit. heavy or coarse smokiness] and thus the whole substance of the thing tasted and all its properties become known and are completely combined. Wherefore, [taste] grasps the nature of things better than all the others.[86]

That which is tasted (unlike that which is seen or touched) is brought into the body in order to be known by it. The knowledge accrued by the mouth is therefore deemed to be better than that accrued by the other sense organs. Further evidence of taste's superiority is the fact that unlike the other sense organs which only have two, in this account, six sinews connect the mouth to principles of the soul. Thus *Summa de saporibus* asserts: 'To the tongue come six sinews from the brain, through which a great quantity of animal spirit comes to the instrument of taste', compared, for example, with the nose to which come 'only two sinews, through which comes a small quantity of the animal spirit'.[87] That man has only one mouth but two eyes might teach him a lesson about moderation, but for this author, that the mouth is served by six sinews and the eyes and nose only by two teaches him that it is *more* spiritual.[88] Here, the greater quantity of *spiritus animalis* in the mouth makes taste literally more spiritual than other senses and therefore able to know more fully and completely than the others. Such a position suggests that medieval discourses about the sense perceptions are more varied than we normally assume. If the *Summa de saporibus* author's claims for the superiority of taste are not typical, it nonetheless reveals a logic, operating more widely in medieval contexts, in which the mouth's nearness to, rather than its distance from, objects in the world can be valorised.

In the soul system of the *sensibilis*, the knowledge learned by mouth is gained through direct contact with objects, mediated by saliva through its six sinews, felt deeply in the heart and imprinted in the brain. Such knowledge is both more felt and makes more material change in the body. What is learned by the mouth is not only most necessary for existence, but it grounds all other sensory perception. For some, it is also the most spiritual of the senses since it is able to know most fully and completely. But in acting upon 'boistous' objects – nails, shoes, weapons, fabric, food[89] – the mouth's knowledge is peculiarly mundane and everyday. An understanding of the operation of a tripartite soul thus has far-reaching implications for medieval ethical and cognitive models and the valuation of the mouth within them. A knowledge of the imbrication of the lower vegetable and sensible parts of the soul with the body makes up the spectrum of knowledge about nature that is good for salvation. It also gives a potentially materialist aspect to medieval interiority, since an understanding of the soul includes its physiological situatedness.

To this point in this chapter, I have described the natural knowledge about the mouth as it is delineated in the intersections of learned Latinate traditions and their vernacular counterparts in the later medieval period. If the body achieves textual status in Latinate traditions of *natura*, the foregoing discussion suggests what understandings of the mouth are available to clergial readers and writers for glossing the unseen, immaterial and divine. The movement towards vernacularisation makes available to a wider audience both a sciential knowledge of the mouth and a pastoral tradition motivated by comparative reading between nature, the human body and spiritual truths. This is not to make the claim that readers of vernacular theology in this period understand the mouth's physiology in the precise terms of either Latin or vernacular medical traditions. It is, however, to direct us towards the ways in which – in a culture which habitually reads between guides for bodily and spiritual health – vernacular theology shares in, and derives spiritual benefit from, forms of knowledge about the physiology of the mouth and its place within the body–soul composite. The chapters which follow will take up this natural knowledge of the mouth to frame discussions of the upright posture of man, eating and knowing, kissing, speaking and confessing. I close this chapter by exploring in more detail the ways in which vernacular theology absorbs something of learned understandings of the tripartite soul and the inside of the body in its figuring of the category of interiority. The disciplines of medieval self-knowledge – interior reflection and confession – have been variously understood as essentially antimaterialist (as a movement away from the body into the immaterial soul), and predicated on a process of *visual* introspection. Vernacular notions of the 'inner man', however, accommodate a sense of the embodied nature of the lower parts of the soul, as well as of the structure of the body interior. So too, in some discourses, do the practices of self-knowledge accommodate reflection on the felt experiences of the body and of the mouth, demonstrating a sense of a material interior, in which the mouth is the entranceway and the means by which this material interior is externalised and expressed.

Materialist Interiority

The concept of self-knowledge is a common one in the fourteenth century – Langland, Mirk and Lydgate all, for example, iterate the Neoplatonic injunction to 'know thyself'.[90] This Delphic maxim, engraved on the temple of Apollo, has a long history in Classical and Christian thinking, as Joseph S. Wittig summarises:

> A central facet of Western spirituality since the days of Ambrose and Augustine was the Christianized, Neoplatonic γνωθι σεαυτόν [*nosce teipsum*, know thyself]. Gathering force especially through Augustine's influence and receiving fresh impetus in the later Middle Ages from the writings of the Victorines and of St Bernard, 'Christian Socratism' evolved into a commonplace program of spiritual ascent and fused with other ascetical traditions.[91]

Broadly speaking there are two quite different impulses behind medieval traditions of self-knowledge. In one, drawing upon Aristotle and Cicero, 'the resources of human knowledge are ... essential in the process of knowing oneself'.[92] The other, epitomised by the Pseudo-Bernardine phrase taken up in *Piers Plowman*, 'multi multa sciunt et seipsos nesciunt' (B.XI.3), rejects 'intellectual curiosity about the natural world'.[93] Traditions of self-knowledge therefore are positioned both within and against traditions of *natura* and *scientia*. In their medieval iterations, however, they have been understood to be essentially antimaterialist. Thus Wittig, outlining the tradition of spiritual ascent through self-knowledge, writes of 'the necessity for the whole inward journey of the soul, to withdraw from the influence of the body'.[94] Caroline Walker Bynum in turn has suggested that 'what they thought they were discovering when they turned within was what they called "the soul" (*anima*), or "self" (*seipsum*), or the "inner man" (*homo interior*)', that is to say an immaterial 'image' of God in the self.[95] Accounts of these 'technologies of the self' characteristically emphasise, on the one hand, their antimaterialism, and, on the other, their reliance on vision and visual processes. Thus Dallas Denery's study of confession – a medieval practice posited as central in discovering the interior self – is concerned with 'seeing and being seen', and Jennifer Bryan, in her analysis of medieval notions of the self, suggests both that scholars' interest in the body has led to a neglect of the category of 'inwardness', and that, where the body might have a role to play, devotional writers tend 'to emphasize vision, and to downplay other modes of knowing and sensing'.[96] The complex relationship of the tripartite soul to the body, along with the nuanced discussion of taste and touch adumbrated in natural philosophy, however, suggests that a focus neither on the body nor on the 'inferior' senses should necessarily direct us away from the category of inwardness.

Isidore of Seville, in the seventh-century *Etymologiae*, observes that: 'Human beings have two aspects: the interior and the exterior. The interior human is the soul [and] the exterior is the body.'[97] This dualistic conceit, however, resists precise interpretation: if the soul is the interior man, how do we separate out the inside of the body both from the soul and from the outside of the body (i.e. is the inside of the body in fact 'exterior')? *On the Properties of Things* cites Isidore's division of man ('Isider spekeþ of double maner man, of þe inner man and vtter man', I, 91) in the first entry of Book III on the soul. Bartholomaeus asserts that he will first 'trete of þe inner man' (I, 91) and proceeds to catalogue the rational soul, the tripartite soul, as well as sense perception, its cerebral processing and the *spiritus* which perform the soul's work.[98] Since the medieval soul is tripartite, one might therefore more usefully discuss the body surface (flesh, skin, orifices, sense organs), the body interior (encompassing the internal body structure, principal members, the cerebral processes enacted through sense perception and the 'lower' vegetable and sensible functions of the soul) and, finally, that more strictly separate category of the reasonable soul, the *intellectus* or mind (which might be located in either the heart or the brain or might act metaphysically through the whole body, but which is always separable from it).[99] Such a tripartite perspective, in moving us away from any strict adherence to body–soul dualism, is more properly reflective of the late fourteenth-century position. In *Piers Plowman*, the personification of the soul, Anima, explains the different meanings of her many names, including: 'whan I feele that folk telleth, my firste name is *Sensus* – / And that is wit and wisdom, the welle of alle craftes' (B.xv.29–30). The senses – the source ('welle') of all human knowledge ('craftes') – are enmeshed in and inextricable from the material body and from being in the world.[100] Langland's very definition of the soul therefore includes not only the body interior but, by implication, the surface organs of sense.

Vernacular encyclopaedic and poetic descriptions of the soul bear out a slippery sense of what 'inner' might connote. The increase in both written and visual representations of the body interior, made available through vernacular medicine, further suggests that a consideration of the 'inner man' might also include the interior bodily organs. Julian of Norwich's *Showings* evokes precisely the internal layers exposed and unfurled by anatomical illustration: 'as þe body is cladd in the cloth, and the flessch in the skynne, and the bonys in the flessch, and the harte in the bowke'.[101] This bodily knowledge launches reflection on the mystery of the spiritual enclosure of the human soul within God. Henry of Lancaster's devotional treatise *Le livre de seyntz medicines* (1354) likewise provides a striking example of the ways in which notions of interiority might include a medicalised sense of the interrogation of the body interior. Henry prays that he might be opened before God, as a body is opened up before surgeons at Montpellier, in order 'to see and to know how the veins, nerves and other parts are situated inside', so that he might be able to expose the sin in his own body interior.[102] Here, self-reflexive scrutiny is played out on the body's surface and within its material interior as much as within an immaterial soul.

To many medieval people, before the advent of widespread autopsy and dissection practice, natural philosophical descriptions of the 'inner man' evoked a hidden, unknowable world which, simultaneously, was the goal and medium of getting to 'know thyself'.[103] Indeed, rendering into English Bartholomaeus's stated reason for presenting the science of the soul, Trevisa reveals something about the project of medieval encyclopaedic knowledge itself: the properties of the tripartite soul are described in order that 'bestissche men and simple' know more openly what they are made and 'componed' of (1, 90). The *MED* defines the meaning of 'bestissche' as 'unspiritual', 'man in the natural state not guided by divine revelation'. Although autopsy (surgical rather than merely external examination) and dissection practice (both of which might be viewed as part of the process of desacralising nature) were established as part of normal legal procedure and university instruction in Italy in the late thirteenth century, neither was common in northern Europe until later: as Katharine Park observes, 'with the exception of the University of Montpellier in southern France, there are few known references to autopsies and only one to a dissection in Germany, England or France before the late fifteenth century, including the relatively important medical faculty at Paris'.[104] However, it is this kind of 'inner man' that anatomies and surgeries increasingly, through vernacular translations and lay circulation, make available in the late fourteenth century. Works such as Guy de Chauliac's *Cyrurgie* describe dissection techniques even if its practice remained untypical for another century.[105] The medical illustrations known as the Fünfbilderserie comprise a series of five anatomical illustrations of the body interior, which sometimes represent the *spiritus* (here, either the soul or breath) as a black grain located in the heart.[106] These illustrations plot the unseen *spiritus* on to the map of the interior body, providing a physical anatomy of an invisible soul. The *dessins anatomiques* illustrating the *Chirurgie* of Henri de Mondeville (1306) too are representative of the kinds of anatomical drawings that might serve to further the shifting perceptions of the inner man (the inside of man is suddenly made 'exterior', for example), and resonate with hagiographical illustrations of flayed saints (such as St Bartholomew) holding their skin.[107] Notably, Danielle Jacquart and Claude Thomasset suggest that Mondeville's anatomical drawings were likely to have been used in training 'non-Latinist surgeons and barbers' in France, implying an expanding access to body knowledge of this kind.[108] These anatomical descriptions and illustrations provide the medieval reader with a literal gloss on the *homo interior*.

While Julian and Henry disclose an expansive understanding of the category of interiority, one that includes the body interior, both, in these instances, retain a sense of the *visual* nature of introspection. An exemplum in Mirk's *Festial* suggests the potential instead for a focus on the mouth and on the 'inferior' senses to launch confessional scrutiny and obtain self-knowledge. The narrative style of the *Festial*, a mixture of exegesis, hagiography and illustrative homilies, makes particular use of the body 'as a public teaching device'.[109] Accordingly, as Judy Ann Ford has claimed, the *Festial* privileges *experientia* and what might be termed natural (or 'boistous') knowledge over scriptural authority: the *Festial* 'prefers the avenues of acquiring knowledge open to the illiterate, namely visual images, oral tradition, and direct revelatory experience'.[110] A *narracio* for the sermon for Palm Sunday renders a version of the widely known 'triumph exemplum' based on the Roman custom (recorded in the *Gesta*

Romanorum) of bestowing 'triple honour' as well as 'triple annoyance' upon a victorious soldier on returning through the city.[111] The exemplum is explicitly positioned in traditions of self-knowledge, since a slave (as part of the 'annoyance') is to enjoin the conqueror 'to know himself'.[112] Mirk's condensed version of the exemplum is interesting in two respects. Firstly, Mirk uses it as a model for confession, and secondly he makes a striking departure from the source material by introducing mouth-beating:[113]

> whan he [the conqueror] come thorowg [through] any cite, þere schulde a man standen by hym in þe chare [chariot], and beton hym in þe mowthe with a braunch of olyf, sayng þus: '*Anothe delytes*', þat is to sayne: know þiself! know þiself! As þo3 [though] he sayde to hym þus: 'Þo3 þou haue þe victori now, hit may happon þat þou schalt anoþur tyme haue þe werre [worse], and so turne þe into also mykul [much] vilanye os now is done þe worchep. Wherefore be nowte proude of þineself!'
>
> Þus, gode men and wommen, þus 3e schal beton 3oure seluen in þe mowþe of 3oure sowle wythinneforþe wyth þe braunche of olyf, þat is, wyth þe vertu of mekenes, and so holde 3ow meke in herte.[114]

The 'real', historical example of the Roman custom should suggest to Mirk's parishioners that the experience of pain felt in the mouth is a literal mode of remembering what it means to be human, recalling man's fallen, sinful origins and the fickleness of Fortune. Secondly, the motif of mouth-beating becomes a model for the process of introspection: 'gode men and wommen, þus 3e schal beton 3oure seluen in þe mowþe of 3oure sowle wythinneforþe wyth þe braunche of olyf'. Self-knowledge, humility and meekness begin with a painful experience in the mouth – literally for the Roman conqueror, and imaginatively for Mirk's parishioners. But so too does the victory over mortality and sin that is won through oral confession ('clene schryuing of mowþe'). This exemplum roots introspection in bodiliness and stages it in the mouth. In turn, the (real and imagined) action of beating the mouth itself is shown to have corrective value. Self-knowledge, here, is not just produced through speech, or through a reflection on the immaterial soul, but also in the (recollected) felt experiences and materiality of the mouth.

The natural knowledge about the body–soul relationship, forged in the intersections of Latinate and vernacular encyclopaedias and medical texts, fundamentally reframes our understanding of the ethical and spiritual potential of the mouth. Imitating the medieval habit of reading between sciential knowledge of the body and ethical knowledge of the soul, the chapters which follow bring 'kynde' knowledge about the mouth to bear upon readings of Middle English pastoral literature and devotional poetry. These works of vernacular theology do not necessarily demonstrate either a precise knowledge of the mouth's physiology or familiarity with learned medical treatises. However, reading the mouth in the interstices of vernacular biology and medicine, on the one hand, and vernacular theology on the other, discloses its profound place in medieval discourses of physical, ethical and spiritual good. The tripartite soul implicates the mouth in two embodied soul systems, the *vegetabilis* and the *sensibilis*, which generate powerful commentaries on the processes of sin and salvation. In the first, the *vegetabilis*, the mouth interchanges with the stomach and anus; it establishes (in a properly regulated body) a healthful flow into, down and out of the body in digestion and excretion; eating, in turn, provides the materials for feeling, speaking and thinking. This processual, cyclical model necessitates the care of the self: overeating can lead to both sickness and sin; but so too, as *The Book of Vices and Virtues* outlines, can a diet of measure lead to the governance of reason and love of God. In the second, that of the *sensibilis*, the senses of taste and touch accrue a kind of knowledge that derives its value from nearness to, rather than transcendence of, the earth. These senses are not only necessary for existence, but are the foundation for all sensory perception. The qualities of the perception these senses accrue form the basis of an epistemological mode – experienced and felt, bringing about material change in the self – that has a profound reach in vernacular theology. Recuperating the everyday, lived experience of the body, this epistemological mode makes the mouth a site for fundamental spiritual lessons. Within this context, the mouth disrupts the traditional binaries of body and soul, inner and outer, material and spiritual. It is therefore a peculiarly liminal site in the body, effecting interchange between inside and outside, material and spiritual, but also, at times, collapsing the distinction between them. Recognising the material aspect of medieval interiority directs us to the ways in which the human body – man's single mouth; his six sinews – provides a gloss on spiritual processes, at the same time as it is the literal basis of them. It also cautions us against surface readings of the mouth detached from the body interior and its physiological milieu.

CHAPTER 2

The Reading Lesson

One of the most common lessons derived from medieval readings of nature is that man's upright body mirrors the natural ordering and hierarchy of creation. Exemplifying the way in which values are 'given body, *made body*', standing upright is equated with man's divine quality and intellective capacity;[1] the directions 'above', 'high', 'upwards' correspond with heaven and so with the morally good. It is also upon this upright posture that man's difference from beasts is predicated; it is a trace of the *imago dei*, witnessing man's nobility and rationality. This has been made the basis of rigid interpretations of medieval space and the body; thus, according to Mikhail Bakhtin, 'in the medieval picture of the world, the top and bottom, the higher and lower, have an absolute meaning both in the sense of space and of values'.[2] In this schema the head and the eyes are aligned with the heavens, God and the good, the lower body and its functions with the earth, the bestial and the bad. From this perspective, reversing or deforming an upright posture is therefore a denigration of the human, threatening to make him look (and behave) no different from beasts. The mouth itself, since it is at once both high and low, is a disruptive element in the body's hierarchy: as the instrument of speech it shares in the nobility of man, but in its connection with the stomach and anus, and in its position last in the face, it also slips into the ostensibly offensive lower body. Yet, since the body is not fixed or static but processual and subject to daily flux and change, movement from high to low, and from upright to bent, is a necessary part of being human. This chapter argues that late medieval discourses in fact display a nuanced reading of the lessons learned from nature in which the lower body is not always offensive and the nearness of the mouth to the earth is not always denigrating but a natural experience, needful for health, with cognitive and spiritual potential.

This chapter begins by re-examining the idealising trope of the upright body of man and its counterpart, that of the bent body, as they are outlined and moralised in natural philosophy and *pastoralia* alike. From a medicalised perspective, an upright posture is necessarily temporal; from a theological perspective, moreover, the condition of being 'fallen' means that the Christian must relearn, but also reread, 'natural' bodily postures in the world. Ovid's poetic meditation in the *Metamorphoses* on the upright posture of man, as it is quoted and reworked in medieval encyclopaedias and Middle English devotional literature, forms the focus of the first part of the chapter. A variant of this trope in John Lydgate's *Pilgrimage of the Life of Man* establishes the normative version of body topography in which the ideal of the upright posture, facilitating noble vision to contemplate the heavens, is perverted by the mouth's orientation towards, and preoccupation with, the earth. The mouth's downward drive here is indicative of a failure of 'natural' knowledge – that is, a misreading of man's relation to the earth and the heavens. This is, however, a surface reading of body topography. The perspective of the body interior – again, delineated in encyclopaedias and also in medical texts – establishes that an upright posture is, in fact, needful for good digestion and to cultivate an ethical relationship, not of the eyes and vision to heaven, but of the mouth to the stomach, anus and the earth. In other words, an upright posture is necessary for continence: it has everything to do with the operations of the vegetable part of the soul in eating, digesting, purging and defecating, but it does so, as works of vernacular theology such as Julian of Norwich's *Showings* make clear, in order to create time and place for devotion, for cognitive work and contemplation. In this second version, the body's anatomical arrangement comes to be predominantly about the mouth and its interorientation between serving the material needs of the body and the acquisition of ethical and spiritual knowledge. Returning, in the final part of this section, to surface readings of man's upright body, I demonstrate that, alongside normative readings, which associate an upright posture with the epistemology of vision, is a variant reading in which the purpose (or *telos*) of an upright posture facilitates instead an ethical epistemology of taste. The Ovidian trope as it occurs in John Trevisa's Middle Englishing of *On the Properties of Things* thus discloses that man's upright body gives to man a 'high' mouth, with which he is able to taste heaven.

However, as medieval texts also understand, an upright posture is a learned one – not 'natural' to the lifecycle stage of infancy, and reversible in old age and the experiences of sickness or bodily impairment. It is, moreover, reconfigured in the daily care of the self – in forms of work as well as in rest and leisure – in ways that are salutary, as well as that lead, through unregulated, intemperate lifestyles, to sickness. Medieval discourses are thus also engaged with the question of how to reorient and retrain the body to cultivate an 'upright' disposition in a world where both vicious and virtuous behaviour require a spectrum of bodily postures. The second part of this chapter examines the traditions in which meditation on, as well as experience of, the 'bent' body becomes the source of ethical good, in order to show in turn the value derived from the mouth's association with the lower body and its closeness to (rather than distance from) the earth. The posture of kneeling as it is configured in natural philosophy and pastoral works, such as the *South English Legendary*, is cognate with the prepartum, less distinctly 'human', topography of the foetus. To kneel is thus a performative lesson in man's origins, the difficulty with which uprightness is achieved, and the value of temporarily obscuring vision and of feeling what it means to be in a body.

With this lesson in mind, I turn to those works of vernacular theology that reveal an understanding of the essentially cyclical experience of the body, which 'naturally' moves between prostrate, bent and upright postures. Two particular experiences are taken up as examples *par excellence* – falling and vomiting – of the ways in which low, 'base', bodily experiences have a healing or reforming potential. The natural experience of the everyday rhythms of rising and falling, and the influence of the mouth within it, profoundly informs medieval theologies of sin: from the particular perspectives of the traditions of the *felix culpa* and the valuation of the natural, authors such as William Langland and Julian of Norwich show that sinning, which is experienced as a fall, naturally precedes and itself precipitates rising, and therefore can, in fact, bring its own spiritual benefit. Being low (bad or bestial) can ultimately lead to being high (good or god-like), but so too are these low/high experiences more ambiguously valued than some scholarly formulations of medieval space and the hierarchy of the body would suggest (i.e. low can itself be good).[3] Furthermore, everyday experiences, as well as lifecycle stages such as infancy and old age, alter the functioning of the senses and recalibrate their value. As Langland's Ymaginatif and Julian's parable of the lord and servant show, falling as a figure for the effects of sinning radically diminishes the capacity of vision and intensifies the senses of taste and touch, which becomes the grounds for reorientation towards God. Vomiting, as both the symptom of sin as well as a figure for confession in medieval pastoral discourses, works its physical and spiritual benefit through a similar process of temporary sensory impairment. Thus, in *Piers Plowman*, as Gloton falls and vomits he loses both his upright posture and his capacity to see at a distance in ways that parody the reforming process of confession. As the literal embodiment of his sin, however, Gloton's example places pressure on the analogy of both sin and its remedy to bodily processes. Through Gloton, I suggest, Langland explores the limits of the capacious category of the natural and its value for ethics and soteriology.

Finally, this chapter closes with the reading lessons taught the dreamer in *Piers Plowman* by Ymaginatif in Passus XII and by Dame Studie in Passus X, which restage and reframe medieval glossatory traditions on the topographical arrangement of the body and the place of the mouth within it. In the first lesson, the question asked by the unlearned about why Adam and Eve covered their genitals when it was their mouths that sinned teaches the dreamer the limits of natural knowledge – or, rather, the problem of surface readings of body topography and the instability of the body as a sign. This recalls an earlier lesson taught by Dame Studie, in which those guilty of the intellectual sin of curiosity – a desire for knowledge beyond natural need – have as both punishment and remedy the toppling of vision and the (ethical) privileging of the mouth. Medieval ethics, therefore, *does* correlate upright posture and seeing with upright living, but it also grapples with how to 'do well' when an upright posture cannot be maintained and when seeing is no longer possible. It is in this fallen state that the mouth, taste and touch, as well as the bodily need for both nourishment and purgation, become primary.

Seeing Heaven, Eating Earth

The difference between the upright posture of man and the bent bodies of animals has long been made the basis for asserting both man's nobility and his place in the hierarchy of creation below the angels but above the created world. Aristotle asserts in the *Historia animalium* that 'in man, above all other animals, the upper and lower parts are arranged in accordance with their natural positions; for in him, upper and lower are the same as in the case of the universe as a whole'.[4] This model of man as a microcosm – widely influential in the domains of medicine and astrology and in theories of government – is commonly repeated in, and indeed very often provides an ordering principle for, the catalogues of medieval encyclopaedias and works of natural philosophy.[5] The correspondence of the head with the heavens also corresponds with the ability to accrue knowledge through vision – an ability predicated on man's upright body posture. Variations of Ovid's verse – 'Whereas other animals hang their heads and look at the ground, he [the Creator] made man stand erect, bidding him look up to heaven, and lift his head to the stars' – find widespread iteration in medieval contexts, and in texts with quite different relationships to traditions of 'kynde'.[6] Chaucer's translation of Boethius's *Consolation of Philosophy*, with its Aristotelian influence, records that 'only the lynage of man [the human race] heveth [raises] heyest his heie heved [high head], and stondith light with his upryght body, and byholdeth the erthes undir hym'.[7] But so too, the author of *The Cloud of Unknowing* – expounding a Neoplatonic, negative form of theology – writes, after having discussed the bodily ascension of Christ into heaven, that:

> for þis seemlines it is þat a man, þe whiche is þe seemliest creature in body
> þat euer God maad, is not maad crokid to þe erþewardes, as ben alle oþer
> beestes, bot upriȝte to heuenwardes; for whi þat it schulde figure in licnes
> bodely þe werke of þe soule goostly.[8]

Distinguishing him from beasts, man's upright body materialises – figures 'in licnes bodely' – the nobility of the reasonable soul, allowing him to bear his head high in order to see and to know. While the *Cloud*-author emphasises the figurative meaning of man's upright body, it is at once intertwined with physiology and cognition, since body posture not only figures but also literally enables vision and knowledge.

It is therefore often the redirection of the body and the mouth down into the earth that pastoral discourses equate with sin and a loss of human nobility: the propensity of the mouth for the 'boistous' – that is, the mundane, the coarse, the element earth – threatens the ability of the body to figure and, in turn, to obtain God and the good. This is the upshot of Guillaume de Deguileville's pastorally minded treatment of the trope in *The Pilgrimage of the Life of Man*, which also highlights the problem of the 'boistousness' of taste and the mouth, since being human can begin to look too much like being animal.[9] As Kellie Robertson has argued, Deguileville's poem is concerned with the 'danger of Aristotelian naturalism', and this episode performs a rejection of reading nature as a guide to understanding God.[10] In Lydgate's translation, in response to Nature's rage at the unnatural 'mutacion' of 'bred in-to flesshe, wyn in-to blood' (3,280–1) in the sacrament of the altar, Grace Dieu rebukes Nature for failing to look up at the heavens and understand the limits and bounds of her earthly authority:

> 'Ye Resemble (who lokë wel,)
> Vn-to the wyldë swyn savage,
> Wych that renneth in hys rage
> In the woodys large & grene,
> And ne kan no ferther sene
> But to the frut that he hath founde,
> And the Acornys on the grounde,

ffor to fille hys hongry mawe.
ffor he, in his swynys lawe,
Off hys rudnesse bestyal,
Ne kan no ferther se at al
Toward the hevene, nor the tre
Wher he receyveth hys plente,
That bar the frut for hys repast [nourishment],
Al that ys from hys myndë past;
ffor to the acorn al only,
And to hys ffoodë fynally
Ys set hys herte & al hys thouht;
ffor he in soth ne recchet nouht
Off alle the surplus neueradel.'

(3,710–29)

By taking up the trope of the upright human body in a discussion of the transgression of Nature, Deguileville locates the garnering of knowledge with the senses and when driven by bodily appetite within the broader debate in the poem (and in the later medieval period) about revealed knowledge (or *sapientia*) and knowledge learned through nature (or, in this particular context, *scientia*).[11] Nature's re-education by Grace Dieu, here, draws on the knowledge that can be gained through comparative observation of nature (of men and pigs), at the same time as it points out its limits in explaining divine mysteries. Grace Dieu thus reveals the need for taught, revealed knowledge *about* nature to guide spiritual understanding of the natural. Grace Dieu accuses Nature of having the restricted vision that comes from being busy about one's 'bely joye'. The wrong *telos* – his heart is set on food 'fynally' – obfuscates the potential nobility of the mouth. This state is clearly precipitated by (or has caused) the loss of reason: Nature resembles the 'wyldë', 'savage' swine which runs in his 'rage'. Grace Dieu equates this excessive, unthinking quest for food with an unlearned state: the swine behaves as he does because of his 'rudnesse bestial'. Being 'rude', a synonym for 'boistous', is associated with a limited capacity for vision and a peculiar awareness of the mouth and taste and touch. The swine, with his bent body and his head stooped over the earth, 'kan no ferther sene' than the fruit and acorns he devours from the ground, unable to look up and read the heavens or even to see the trees – that is, the 'surplus', the rest or the 'beyond' – to recognise the source of the fruit he eats. Nature's failure, like the swine's, like the man busy about his 'bely joye', is precisely the failure to move beyond the natural, material world to what it figures or where it comes from. Thus, iterating the need for pastoral instruction, the 'rude', *lewed* man, without *clergie* and without the practice of measure (or medicine), will pervert his body topography and become bestial. When driven by appetite, placing his 'boistous' mouth close to the earth, man risks losing his reason and thereby becoming unable to read God in the material world or find him in the heavens.[12]

Taking up a similar image, *Book for a Simple and Devout Woman* likens those who fall into the sin of 'backbiting' to the swine which 'kepeþ no more his mouþe from filþe þan he doþ his fete'.[13] Like the swine, instead of savouring flowers and herbs, if the backbiter sees any villainy or sin that stinks foul 'he draweþ and henteþ [seizes] hit in his mouþe to telle þat filþe abrode oueralle þer he comeþ'.[14] Here, man in the state of sin – bent towards the earth – inverts topography and causes his mouth to occupy the same position as his feet. What is more, this fallen topography also corresponds with a corruption of the sense of taste and an inversion of the function of the mouth: drawn, not to savour flowers, but to eat filth, the mouth of the backbiter spreads words-as-excrement. Likewise, *The Book of Vices and Virtues* figures those in whom reason is dead as living like beasts: because 'here wittes ben mysturned [misdirected] and roted [corrupted]', like a sick man or pregnant woman, they 'fyndeþ betere sauour in a sour appel þan in any bred of whete [wheat], or as a child fyndeþ sauour in a cole more þan in any good mete'.[15] *The Book of Margery Kempe* (c.1436) records a tale 'be the maner of exampyl' in which a priest, wandering ('wil') in a wood for the benefit of his soul and taking rest in an arbor, has a vision of a 'gret and boistows' bear devouring the blossoms of a beautiful pear tree. 'Turnyng his tayl ende', the bear then 'voydyd hem [the blossoms] owt ageyn at the hymyr party [hinder part]'.[16] Unable to read beyond the surface, the priest of the tale requires the aid of a palmer to recognise that he is like the flower-excreting bear when he performs the 'sacrament of the awter [altar]' in a state of sin. This is barely allegory: spiritual food (the Eucharist) is made subject to the same process as natural food as a result of the priest's sinful disposition. Margery's exemplum pursues a logic natural to the human body, but displaces it on to the prone, bent body of the bear. In so doing, the exemplum teaches that priestly service requires the proper subordination, indeed negation, of the lower body and its functions. If the mouth's closeness to earth, in these accounts, brings the human into the register of the animal and the debased, converting sacramental blossoms into excrement, so too does closeness to earth denigrate the senses – diminishing vision and giving man an unhealthy taste for sour apples and filth. This, however, allows for the possibility that ethical knowledge (taught and experienced) is implicated not only in regulating appetite and alimentation, but also in training the senses – more specifically, in re-educating the powers of the sense of taste which, when no longer corrupted by sin, can be redirected towards its proper (divine) ends.[17]

The surface reading of the topographical arrangement of the body, which emphasises the epistemology of the senses, is rewritten from the perspective of the body interior as an ethics of eating, digestion and purgation. More than mere figure for the 'werke of þe soule goostly', the upright body physically and physiologically allows man to see both the heavens and 'the erthes undir him'. It also places a distance between the mouth and the earth, and between the mouth and the stomach and anus. The otherwise natural affinity of mouth and stomach/anus is elsewhere suggested in Aristotle's assertion that the oesophagus is 'in fact not required of necessity for nutritive purposes; for it has no action whatsoever on the food. Indeed there is nothing to prevent the stomach from being placed directly after the mouth.'[18] The oesophagus is therefore understood in some ways to be a necessary consequence of man's upright posture, helping to establish a seemly distance between the mouth and the earth. Henry Daniel's *Liber uricrisiarum* (c.1376–9), an early witness to the project of translating medicine in England and extant in over twenty manuscripts, underscores this natural resemblance of mouth and anus, terming them the upper ('ouere') and lower ('neþer') holes. In describing the stages of digestion, Daniel notes: 'The first digestiown hath purgacioun to his superfluites the ouere and the neþer hole, [*scilicet*] þe mowthe and the tayle-ende.'[19] It continues, the mouth purges by 'golpyng', 'rosping [belching]' and 'brakyng [vomiting]'; the anus by 'egestiown [elimination]' – '[*id est,*] shityng, crakkyng, and wlisping benethin [farting "beneath"]'.[20] As Hanna's edition notes, '*benethin* indicates the transferred use of the terms properly referring to oral sounds'.[21] Sin is manifested in the body through the literal collapse of the distinction between the mouth and anus and their functions: medieval exempla tell, for example, of the blasphemous man whose mouth 'turnyd into his ars, & efter euer whils he liffid [lived], all þe filthe and þe degestion of his bodie come out at his mouthe, & noght at his nache [anus]'.[22] However, the anatomy of the interior of the body does not simply support the structure of its external topography and reinforce the moralisation of high as good and low as bad; it is instead shown to be crucial to physiology and the operation of the soul, creating the time and place for eating, digesting and excreting, and so also for thinking and devotion.

This is exemplified by descriptions of the stomach in Middle English natural philosophy and in devotional works alike. *On the Properties of Things* records that:

> þe stomak, and specialliche of a man, is narouȝe and strayte in þe ouer partie and wide and brood in þe neþer partye. And þat is nedeful for a man gooþ more vpriȝt þan oþir beestis, and his mete gooþ dounward alwey, and þerfore þe neþir breede [breadth] and þe widnes of his stomak is profitable to fonge [receive] þerin þe more mete and drynke. And he is synewy to resceyue and haue sotilnes of felinge and vertue and strengþe of appetite. (I, 244)

In other words, the upright body establishes a vertical movement from the mouth, down through the stomach – narrow at the top and wide at the bottom – and out into the earth that is central to the digestion process and to the health of the body. As the tripartite model of the soul makes clear, good digestion is central to the physiology of cognition. Albertus Magnus writes, for example, in *De animalibus* that a well-functioning stomach aids the brain, 'but a bad stomach destroys it'.[23] Middle English devotional works, in turn, show that a properly functioning stomach is central to the work of salvation.

Julian of Norwich in the long text of her *Showings* meditates on the upright body of man to understand the 'meanes' that God has bestowed upon the Christian, specifically prayer, with which she can seek help from God:

> A man goyth vppe ryght, and the soule of his body is sparyde [closed] as a purse fulle feyer. And whan it is tyme of his nescessery, it is openyde and sparyde ayen fulle honestly. And that it is he [God] that doyth this, it is schewed ther wher he seyth he comyth downe to vs to the lowest parte of oure nede. For he hath no dispite of that he made, / ne he hath no disdeyne to serue vs at the sympylest office that to oure body longyth in kynde, for loue of the soule that he made to his awne [own] lycknesse. For as þe body is cladd in the cloth, and the flessch in the skynne, and the bonys in þe flessch, and the harte in the bowke [trunk of the body], so ar we, soule and body, cladde and enclosydde in the goodnes of god.[24]

Echoing the words of Trevisa's translation – man 'gooþ more vpriȝt' – Julian is drawing upon a natural philosophical tradition about the anatomy and physiology of the human body in order to extrapolate spiritual truth. The noun 'soule' punningly refers to both the reasonable soul and – as has been variously suggested – to 'digested food' or to 'sustenaunce'.[25] Julian's description of the 'soule' being 'sparyde as a purse' that 'is openyde and sparyde ayen fulle honestly' further mirrors physiological descriptions of the stomach's operation. Daniel's *Liber uricrisiarum*, for example, explains that once the stomach has drawn what it needs from food and drink the 'remanawt' passes out through the '*porta stomachi, anglice* mawe-ȝate [gate of the stomach]', so-called because 'hit is shet til þat nede of kende deliueryth þe fode oute of the stomac', and after 'hit shettith himselfe ageyn as he was beforne'.[26] Disclosing the material aspect of late medieval interiority, Julian blends the spiritual and the material in this image of food enclosed in the stomach, in turn, wrapped in the anatomical layers of the body (flesh is covered in skin, the bones by flesh and so on), just as spiritual nourishment is contained in the soul and, in turn, enclosed in God.[27] Evoking the downward movement of God's goodness, Julian establishes eating and digesting as an allegory of prayer and confession, but she is also talking about real food. Located in our mouths, prayer obtains – brings into the body – God's goodness which, once swallowed, makes its way through the body, quickening it, making it grow and making it upright, just as food does. But so too is God's goodness shown literally in the provision of food that restores the body and in the process whereby superfluous matter is excreted from it, as the body opens and closes again as is necessary (or, in Daniel's terms, 'nede of kende').[28] Moreover, Julian suggests that God performs the care not just of the soul but literally of the body by the timely nourishment of it and evacuation of the bowels: 'whan it is tyme of his nescessery, it is openyde and sparyde ayen fulle honestly'. (In this way, sin and reparation of sin too are emunctory functions.)[29] Natural, necessary, everyday rhythms of the human body here model the necessary rhythms of daily devotion, as well as the processual patterns of God's reforming work of salvation.

In the *Pilgrimage*, Grace Dieu also explains that the continence and control of the human stomach and of defecation are ordered and performed by the soul, in terms that, like Julian's, suggest that this process is both performed as a kind of service and motivated by compassionate care for the human. This is perhaps somewhat surprising given that the broader context for Grace Dieu's discussion is instruction of the Pilgrim in the three foes – one of whom is his own body. This foe, Grace Dieu explains, accompanies the Pilgrim everywhere, lies in his bed, and

> 'Affter hys [the body's] replecyoun,
> He may nat purge hym on no syde [nowhere]
> But thow [the soul] hym lede, & be hys guyde;
> In chaumbre, goyng to pryvee,
> Hys chaumberleyn thow mustest be:
> Wyth-outë the (yt stondeth so)
> That he sothly may no-thyng do.' (9170–6)

The body here is figured, momentarily, less as a dangerous foe than as a helpless child, who, after eating his full, needs the intimate care of a soul who will help to 'purge' him. Far from transcending or rejecting the body, the soul is implicated, as God is in the *Showings*, in 'the lowest parte of our nede'. In contrast, bodies perverted by vice display no such continence. Avarice in the *Pilgrimage* has a 'sak' on her back and a 'sachel' round her neck: her body is populated with mouths and bellies that characterise her as a consumer.[30] Anything that she takes into her body she does so '[o]ff entent (be wel certyen) / Neuere to taken yt out ageyn'.[31] The entrance to her sak is 'large and pleyne', always open, but the way to convey it out again is 'narow and streyght'.[32] Again recalling the terminology of natural philosophy ('þe stomak, and specialliche of man, is narou3 and strayte in þe ouer partie and wide and brood in þe neþer partye'), Avarice's stomach inverts its natural design to facilitate the passage of food into and out of the stomach again; instead, this stomach works to prevent things taken into it from leaving ('it will nevar ysswe [come] out ageyn').[33] So, too, has Avarice's inside become outside: exposing the physiological and anatomical workings of sin by figuring it with interior bodily organs relocated to the surface of the body, Deguileville demonstrates a markedly material understanding of human interiority.

Both Julian and Deguileville demand that their images be read literally as well as allegorically: there is a real correlation between measured eating, good digestion and timely excretion and the human ability to behave rationally and spiritually. As Albertus Magnus elucidates in *De animalibus*, because the human body retains food and excretes only when necessary, man does not need to be constantly concerned with satiating hunger and so his preoccupation can turn to spiritual things:

> It follows from these facts [i.e. the anatomy of the stomach and the intestines] that food stays for a long time in these passages. And then there are two consequences for a human from this fact. One is that he is not always concerned about food as are the animals which have short and straight intestines from which food emerges quickly, even undigested. The second is that he does not continuously and foully emit dung in bits and pieces as do certain other animals. Rather, it stays and is collected in the lower intestines until it is ejected all at once at an appropriate time and in an appropriate place.[34]

Albertus makes explicit here the logic implied in Bartholomaeus's observations in *On the Properties of Things* as to why it is needful that 'a man gooþ more vpri3t' than animals. Without the oesophagus, stomach and intestines, man would continually eat and excrete; his mouth and anus by turn would be constantly attached to earth. Similarly (and explicitly demonstrating the involvement of the soul in the process) Lanfrank writes in the *Science of Cirurgie* that the nerves (sinews carrying *spiritus*, the agent of the soul) function in the gut so 'þat a man schulde not as soone as he hadde ete, anoon riȝt go to sege [*MED*, s.v. 'to go to stool, void the bowels or bladder'] as doiþ a beest'.[35] If continence distinguishes man from beasts, he must first learn this control over the anal sphincter when a young child. Such control once gained can be lost through injury and in old age. *The Book of Margery Kempe* recounts an episode in which Margery's husband, John, after an accident 'at gret age' turns childish again, and so:

> lakkyd reson that he cowd not don hys owyn esement [relieve the body through excretion] to gon to a sege, er ellys he wolde not, but as a childe voydyd his natural digestyon in hys lynyn clothys ther he sat be the fyre er at the tabil, whethyr it wer, he wolde sparyn no place.[36]

Under pressure from her neighbours, Margery undertakes to care for her (perhaps wilfully) incontinent husband. Margery notes that 'therfor was hir labowr meche the mor in waschyng and wryngyng and hir costage [expenses] in fyryng [maintaining a fire]', which 'lettyd hir ful meche fro hir contemplacyon'. Margery's narrative underscores the ways in which the rhythms and needs of the everyday body – at the centre of the domestic life she has been at pains to escape – put pressure on contemplative life and devotion.

It is both the upright anatomy of man and the proper functioning of the visceral organs – mouth, gullet, stomach, intestines and anal sphincter – that facilitate man's capacity for contemplation and prayer, even at the most practical level, since they create time and place for devotion. This same anatomical and physiological logic underlies Bridget of Sweden's understanding of how the soul operates as a vessel for receiving spiritual things by analogy to the organs – heart, stomach and bowels – which receive things into the body. In the words of a fifteenth-century Middle English translation of her *Liber celestis*, the soul is like the stomach, 'þat is, a wise ordeynyng of a mannes tyme and his werkes, for ryght as þe mete is dified [digested] in þe stomoke, so suld a man ordeyn hys tyme and hys werkes to þe wirshipe of Gode'.[37] The natural example provided by the interior body in these texts thus works as it does in an anonymous treatise, preserved in Oxford, Bodleian Library, Bodley MS 4, discussed by Edwin Craun. Bodley MS 4 records the desire of the wise man, 'in his habits of speech, to be like a swan', because the swan's long neck means its tongue will be 'separated far from its heart'.[38] 'To meditate on comparative physiology', Craun thus observes, 'is to grasp one's moral aspirations and nature's *mores*, to grasp how to use properly the functions of organs (the heart as the center of perception, emotion, and thought; the mouth; the tongue)'.[39] In the case of these discussions of man's upright posture and the arrangement of the body's internal organs, the lesson extends to one about the proper use of the oesophagus, stomach, intestines and anus as well.

As these examples show, a surface reading of man's body suggests that, mirroring the natural ordering and hierarchy of creation, his upright posture facilitates vision in order that man might survey the world at a distance and look up and see heaven. When we remain on the surface, the mouth's place in this topography might be seen to be merely disruptive: it inclines the body to earth and is responsible for the loss of man's nobility. From the perspective of the interior body, however, an upright body posture is shown instead to facilitate measured eating, good digestion and timely excretion, and it is this, in turn, that means man has time and place for contemplation and devotion: relieved of an obligation to continually seek food, the mouth is able to confess sin and offer up prayer and praise to God. Reading from the inside out also shows that, while an upright body establishes an ethical relation between the mouth and the earth (i.e. their distance), the mouth's drive down into the lower body is vital to maintaining physical and moral uprightness. This opens the possibility, in turn, that one of the lessons derived from reading the human body might be this: that an upright posture facilitates not noble, 'sotil' vision, but rather the 'boistous' work of the mouth itself. It is this very possibility that Trevisa's translation of Bartholomaeus's citation of the Ovidian verse in *De proprietatibus rerum* holds out.

Book III of *On the Properties of Things*, which treats the 'inner man', begins by compiling authorities on the question of what a 'man' is composed. The very first given is a citation from Isidore, in which he takes up Ovid's comparison of the downward bent of beasts with the upright bearing of man in the *Metamorphoses* to bear out his etymology of 'man' in both Latin and Greek:

> as Isider seiþ by a mysvse, *homo* 'a man' haþ þe name of *humo* 'þe erþe' seþ þat he is nouȝt imaad onliche of body but componed of body and sowle. Þerfore a man hatte *antropos* in grewe [Greek]. *Antropos* is to menen 'arered vp' for þe spirit is arered vp by gouernaunce to þe contemplacioun of God his makere. Þerfore þe poete seiþ:

> *Pronaque cum spectent animalia cetera terram*
> *Os homini sublime dedit celumque videre*
> *Iussit et erectos ad sidera tollere vultus.*

> Þe menynge is þis: oþir bestis lokeþ donward to þe erþe, and God ʒaf [gave] to man an hiʒe mouþ and hete [bid] hym loke vp and se heuen, and he ʒaf to men visagis arerid toward þe sterres. Also a man schal seche [seek] heuen and nouʒt putte his þouʒt in þerþe and be obedient to þe wombe as a best.⁴⁰
> (1, 90–1)

While Latin 'homo' points to the human connection to earth (according to Isidore, from the Latin for 'þe erþe', or soil [*humus*]), the etymology of 'antropos' contains within it the physiological basis that makes an upright posture possible: 'þe spirit is *arered vp* by gouernaunce to þe contemplacioun of God his makere' (my emphasis).⁴¹ 'Areren' means both to raise upright and, more specifically, 'physiol. of "humours" and "heat": to ascend or make ascend' (*MED*, s.v.). In other words, the *spiritus* (made from humours under the action of heat in the digestion process) means the body can be raised upwards. The bodies of animals in contrast are heavier, have less *spiritus* and less natural heat, making an upright body physiologically impossible. In turn, the 'gouernaunce' of the 'spirit' is inextricable from the proper regulation of eating, drinking and digestion. This is exemplified by a citation from Ovid's poetic meditation in the *Metamorphoses* on 'Os homini sublime dedit'. In Trevisa's translation Ovid's 'os' is rendered 'mouth': this lexical choice is significant, since 'face' or 'head' are also possible, and indeed are always preferred in Modern English translations.⁴² So too is the translation of 'os' as 'face' preferred in John Lydgate's *Reson and Sensuallyte*, where the Ovidian verse is rendered thus:

> Man was set in the hyest place
> Towarde heven erecte hys face,
> Cleymyng [claiming] hys diwe [rightful] heritage
> Be the syght of his visage,
> To make a demonstracion.⁴³

In Lydgate's interpretation, the upright direction of man's face facilitates vision and, in turn, knowing at a distance or speculative *scientia*. 'Demonstracion' refers to the 'process of demonstrating or proving; a logical proof; scientific demonstration' (*MED*, s.v.) – thus reading nature (here the upright body of man) provides scientific proofs of man's nobility.

In contrast, Trevisa's translation of 'os' as 'mouth' opens up different epistemological possibilities. While ascribing a 'high' mouth – not 'face' – to man is part of a discourse, unfolding in natural philosophy and scholastic theology, in which the distance of the human mouth from earth liberates the sense perceptions to seek and learn about God, it also begins to suggest that it is from the placement of the mouth itself that man derives his capacity for reason and intellectual activity; more, that man learns – tastes – of the heavens with his mouth.[44] Vincent of Beauvais's treatment of the trope in *Speculum naturale* points to a similar possibility. Here he records: 'Man is not created like beasts, without reason, which we see leaning forward to the ground, but the upright form of the body puts us in mind of heaven, to *taste* [*sapere*] what is on high' (my emphasis).[45] John of Wales's thirteenth-century *De lingua* is even more explicit. Reflecting on Isidore's etymology, he observes: 'nature teaches that, with his mouth, he [humankind] ought to seek and taste those things that are upward, and not what is earthly'.[46] In his perceptive reading of this passage of *De lingua*, Craun suggests that:

> while such language is metaphorical, the immaterial Creator of nature being savored and delighted in by mind and reason and will, not by the bodily tongue, such a sensory metaphor achieves its power and clarity from the continuum of a spirit-based experience that embraces the bodily and the mental.[47]

The interdependency of body and soul in medieval beliefs – 'the continuum of a spirit-based experience that embraces the bodily and the mental', in Craun's terms – gives energy to this metaphor; I would go further and suggest that it also allows the possibility of a literal, material aspect. In contrast with Lydgate's 'demonstracion', these natural philosophical texts emphasise that the upright body of man specifically facilitates a sapiential, tasty kind of knowledge. Connecting man's capacity for spiritualised thought with the location of the mouth in the body, Trevisa's Middle English translation thereby raises the possibility that 'boistous' taste, like 'sotil' sight, can seek heaven and garner knowledge not just about food and the earth but of the self and of God. The mouth thus has vertical 'pull' in both directions – down into the body, but also, as here, up into the heavens.

From this perspective, the normative reading of the surface of the body that correlates the category of 'uprightness' with the spatial position of the head, the eyes and the heavens, and so with seeing, begins to look less like a cultural hegemony and more like a temporally conditioned lesson. Reading in the cross-flow of genre, vernacular medicine offers a second reading through the body interior that recuperates the everyday, 'lower' bodily processes of eating, digesting and excreting as part of the 'good' of the human, both facilitating and exemplifying cognitive and spiritual effort. The gloss of the upright posture that instead correlates 'uprightness' with the mouth and with the sense of taste likewise offers a more fluid way of thinking about topography, one which retains rather than abstracts the mouth's connection with food and eating, and which points to an ethical epistemology of taste.

These variant readings – from Lydgate's transgressive Nature, to Julian's meditation on 'a man goyth vppe ryght' and to Trevisa's 'high mouth' – of body topography show that the mouth, in medieval commentaries on the 'natural', is an unstable element. Without the support of taught, revealed knowledge, without a properly educated sense of taste, we might pervert this upright topography. The slippage of the mouth from the head to the lower body – its tendency not only to drive down into but also to conflate with the stomach, anus and the earth, in a way that neither the eyes nor the other sense organs can – gives the lie, however, to claims for a stable human ontology, or indeed spirituality, which divorces the human body from the earth. Both an upright posture and distance from earth are, in fact, learned dispositions and acquired through governance – infants do not possess it – which old age will reverse. Once learned, body posture is not fixed or static but processual and so is subject to daily flux and change. The slippage of the mouth is therefore shown to be part of a cyclic (physical and spiritual) physiology in which things taken into the body both renew it and are excreted from it. In this context, natural experience is more powerful than taught knowledge, showing the spiritual benefits of feeling over seeing. It is also here that the value of the 'high' mouth of man is derived more literally, not from its association with the upper spectrum and with a spiritual sense of taste, but from its implication, indeed, imbrication with the lower body and with what the mouth knows through its closeness to, not its detachment from, earth.

Learning to be Upright

As Aristotle remarks in *De partibus animalium*, the upright stature of man (like his continence) is achieved only with maturity. It is not an attribute of the newly born child; rather it is learned, facilitated by the process of growth and is therefore parallel with, and arguably the outward sign of, the development of an intellectual and rational capacity which regulates appetite and subordinates material need to the rule of reason. Indeed, after birth but before maturity (and so before willed or natural falling back to earth), children crawl or creep on the ground like animals and cannot raise their bodies or their heads: their eyes as well as their mouths are near to earth and not kept separate from it.[48] Thus *On the Properties of Things* explains:

> þe ouer partye of a childe is heuyere [heavier] þan þe neþir partyes, and
> þerfore in þe bigynnynge of his walkinge a childe crepiþ on feet and hondes

and þan aftirward he rereþ his body a litil, for þe ouer partye wanieþ [grows smaller] and worþith [becomes] more liȝt and þe neþir parties wexen and encresen and worþen more heuy. (1, 300)

Accordingly, children are also understood to be deficient in intelligence and do not know good from evil.[49] The nearness of infants' mouths to earth correlates with their preoccupation with food: birth is a quest for food and life is characterised by the pursuit of the satiation of appetite. As the 'De puero' passage of *On the Properties of Things* relates:

> [Children] thinkiþ onlich in wombe ioye, and knowiþ nouȝt þe mesure of here owne wombe. Thei coueiten and desiren to ete and drinke alwey. Vnnethe [reluctantly] þey risen out of here bed and axen [ask for] mete anon. (1, 301)

In the lifecycle stage of childhood, the mouth is overwhelmingly connected with the stomach, with the lower body and the earth, but also, in ethical terms – if such a propensity in the child is unchecked – with sin. As Thomas Hoccleve reflects in 'La Male Regle de T. Hoccleve' (1405/6), while Reson advised him 'to ete and drynke in tyme attemprely [moderately]', 'wilful youthe' would not obey. For twenty years he has thus consumed both food and drink 'outrageously':

> The custume of my repleet abstinence,
> My greedy mowth, receite of swich outrage,
> And hondes two, as woot my negligence,
> Thus han me gyded and broght in seruage
> Of hir þat werreieth euery age,
> Seeknesse ...[50]

In 'La Male Regle' it is both a badly governed mouth and the habit of only stopping eating when stuffed that simultaneously retard Thomas (such youthful misrule should have lasted 'two yeer or three' but instead persists for twenty) and age him prematurely through sickness (he now has no desire to 'daunce' or 'skippe').[51] This childish, unruly appetite for food and desire to taste should – though might not – be superseded by measure and temperance as the body is educated, makes itself upright and the human becomes mature and rational.

Willed, temporary reversion to this infantile – indeed, prepartum – posture is a peculiarly powerful reminder of the difficulty with which uprightness is achieved, as medieval moralisations of embryology elucidate.

On the Properties of Things, for example, records that, far from upright, the embryo is first curled and bent in the uterus:

> For whanne a childe is igendred, he is so ischape þat þe kneen ben vpward, and by iust ioynynge of þe kneen þe yȝen bene ischape and made holouȝ oþir rounde; *secundum verbum philosophi, genua comprimit arta gena*, þat is here to menynge men wepen þe rather ȝif þey knele, for kynde wole þat þe yȝen and þe kneen hauen mynde where þey were ifere [companions] in þe modir wombe in derknes ar he come into þe liȝt. *Huc usque Isidorus*. (1, 267)

Following Aristotle (*'secundum verbum philosophi'*) and explicitly drawing upon Isidore's gloss (which Isidore develops from what he posits as the shared etymology of *genu* (knee) and *gena* (cheeks)), Bartholomaeus asserts that the eye sockets are formed in the embryo by the knees, which are drawn upwards.[52] If birth and growing up result in the capacity to stand upright, and so put a distance between the eyes and the knees, kneeling reverts the body to prepartum topography. Those uterine companions, the eyes and the knees (which were 'ifere in þe modir wombe'), are thereby reconnected, with the effect, firstly, of obscuring vision ('men wepen'), and secondly of reminding what it was like to be in the dark or, in other words, to be unsaved. Notably, the eyes are shown here, contrary to models which only assign the eyes a place in the upper bodily spectrum, to have an intimate connection with the lower body. That Bartholomaeus posits that the knees and eyes have in mind ('hauen mynde') their prepartum experience points to how deeply cognitive structures, and indeed soteriological ones, are embedded in medieval physiological and anatomical descriptions. Kneeling in the world is thus a form of natural knowledge, precipitating contrition by recalling man's sightless, sinful origins and need for salvation.[53]

'The Legend of St Michael' in the thirteenth-century *South English Legendary* provides another wonderfully evocative Middle English version of this uterine body topography, which similarly emphasises the cognitive and reforming potential which inheres in bodily movements. Also following Isidore, the legend records that before the child is born he lies in the womb and is 'ibud [bent, curled] as an hare' lying in a burrow; his legs are bowed and the heels are drawn up to the 'bottocs', the knees to either eye and the head is 'ibuyd' downwards, with the arms pulled up to the elbows and the fists to the chin. The back is all 'ibud' so that he is almost round in shape. It concludes,

Al ibud him is þe rug [back] · so þat nei rount it is
Man ware of [from where] comþ al þi prute [pride] · for þer nis non iwis

Þou makest þe so hei [high] her · and to man nelt abowe
Loke hou croked þou were þere · & to wan þou mi3t þe powe
Þou nemi3test no3t [might not] holde up þin heued · ne enes [once] vndo
  þin ei3e
Wannene com it [how does it happen] suþþe [after] to bere · þin heued so
  heie.[54]

Given these beginnings, on what grounds does man hold now his 'heued
so heie', the poem asks? The man 'nelt abowe' provides a figure – further,
a reminder – not of God and the heavens, but rather of a prepartum
experience, and of our lowly, sinful origins, but also our original
vulnerability. The 'bowed' or 'crooked' uterine topography, along with its
attendant sightlessness (the foetus can 'ne enes vndo þin ei3e'), is in marked
contrast with its counterpart: the upright man who surveys at a distance. If
kneeling brings us back down to earth, doing so is neither 'unethical' nor a
diminishment of reason, but rather a means of realigning our relationship
with and dependency on a saving God. Such a sentiment is shared by the
author of *Dives and Pauper*, who explains that by kneeling we 'knowlechyn
þat we moun nought stondyn in vertue ne in goodnesse ne in wele but
only by hym [God]. Qhanne [when] we fallyn al doun to grounde to God
we knowlechyn þat but he helde vs and kepte vs we shuldyn fallyn to
nought.'[55] Beginning to disturb the fit of high and low to 'good' and 'bad',
this conveys the suggestion that closeness to earth (being 'boistous') might
actually bring bodily and spiritual benefit. It is this possibility, holding
out the hope of salvation, which is essential in a world where, as medieval
writers are acutely aware, 'the body must of necessity incline towards the
ground'.[56]

The semi-detachment from earth effected by the upright body is
ultimately reversed in the ageing process: so Bartholomaeus (again,
following Isidore) recalls in *On the Properties of Things* that in old age,
'þe body bendiþ and crokeþ, fourme and schap is ilost', until finally
'asschen [ashes] tofalle and turne in asschen, and poudre into poudre' (1,
293).[57] This process is commonly depicted in illustrations of the medieval
lifecycle. A single manuscript leaf dating to the mid fourteenth century
has five roundels illustrating the ages of man. The first roundel, 'infantia',
shows a child with its knees drawn up and its back bowed, crawling on
the ground, accompanied by a text which relates that 'in infancy man goes
about on hands and feet, in adolescence he walks erect and, finally, in old
age he is bent once again toward the earth, since taken from the earth to
the earth he returns'.[58] Within the human lifecycle, uprightness is therefore
first achieved with great difficulty and finally striven for futilely.

Moreover, after birth and in maturity, since the mouth and the body are innately heavy, the upright bearing of humans is maintained only by considerable physical and moral effort, and is constantly reversed, 'of necessity', as well as rationally – for example, in willed, temporary kneeling – but also through accident and deliberate sin.[59] The codification of the body – in which those disposed to virtue, unlike those disposed to vice, always remain upright – represents an ideal untenable under the conditions which characterise being human: sinning, falling, lying down, kneeling and tasting of the earth are all inevitable but also in some ways necessary. In exposing the vulnerable human condition, these Middle English discourses make the care of the self – attending to temperate eating, drinking, sleeping and to maintaining a capacity for 'uprightness' – central to cultivating habits that will achieve salvation. Indeed, concern with the material needs of the body can bring its own physical, affective, cognitive and spiritual benefits. If the example of kneeling in *The South English Legendary* establishes a more general pattern, its particular benefit is in part predicated on obscuring vision and effecting the closeness of the mouth to the earth. The daily risings and fallings that the body is subject to likewise have wide-reaching implications for the relative capacities of the sense perceptions: falling over (willed or accidental) leads to a diminished ability to see, but it also leads to an intensification of the senses of taste and touch. This holds out the possibility that while the mouth can lead to a fall, it is also the mouth, through the senses of taste and touch, which teaches man about himself and ultimately reorients him to God. Julian's *Showings* and Langland's *Piers Plowman* provide two particularly powerful examples of this natural, processual body logic and its attendant experiential sensory modification to develop theologies in which sinful experience can be made the site of lessons on how to do well.

Fortunate Falling

If we examine body movements in *Piers Plowman*, bodies constantly fall – to their knees and flat on their faces.[60] Lucifer, through his desire to be like the Most High, falls from heaven (B.i.iii–15); Gloton, through his appetite for drink, falls to earth and vomits (B.v.351–5); Sleuth (notably, a by-product of excessive consumption) cannot keep upright and, through his lust for sleep, swoons (B.v.442). It would seem, therefore, that mouths and bodies in *Piers Plowman* cannot help but seek out the earth, drawn by the heaviness of the flesh and by giving sway to the demands of the stomach. The pastoral tradition describes the spiritual and physical inertia of the sinner as 'heaviness', which is defined as: 'whan a man is so heuy þat he loueþ not but to lyn and reste & slepe'; or, elsewhere, 'when man is heuy þat nouȝt elles he doþ bot eteþ and drynkeþ and slepuþ, and leuer haþ [rather] to lese foure masses [fail to attend four masses] þan a mornyng swote'.[61] A 'swote' is 'medicinal or purgative sweating; a fit of sweating induced for therapeutic purposes' (*MED*, s.v.). An undisciplined, intemperate body, in need of therapeutic sweats, interrupts and wastes liturgical time and devotion ('foure masses'). Here, natural human needs – food, drink, sleep, rest – become the conditions conducive to sin. The mouth–stomach's desire has become preternatural and excessive; it has made knowledge, food and sleep 'ends' rather than means.

However, falling in *Piers Plowman* (giving in to the earth's pull) is also an act of contrition; Pernelle falls 'platte' to the earth and cries for mercy (B.v.62–70) and Haukyn swoons with shame as he recognises his sin (B.xiv.326). Falling therefore also signifies desire for God.[62] The pastoral tradition likewise widely understands that if falling – as a figure for sinning – is an inevitable, quotidian experience, getting up again is its remedy: 'if þu eueriche day falle, eueriche day arise and turn to þy Lorde … Forþi if þu ofte falle, ofte þu rise.'[63] In *Piers Plowman*, this daily rising is motivated by natural bodily need, even as the body is the root cause of falling in the first place. Thus, Sleuth gets up because he needs to eat and defecate: 'Were I brought abedde, but if my tailende it made, / Sholde no ryngynge do me ryse er I were ripe to dyne' (B.v.389–90). The bell-ringing calling Sleuth to church is less effective in reorienting him than bodily need. Likewise, when a man falls in a ditch the natural experience of shame, as Ymaginatif explains to the dreamer, is more effective than the counsel or rebuke of Clergie:

> 'For lat a dronken daffe in a dyk [ditch] falle,
> Lat hym ligge, loke noght on hym til hym liste to ryse.
> For though Reson rebuked hym thanne, reccheth he nevere;
> Of Clergie ne of his counseil he counteth noght a risshe [rush].
> To blame or for to bete hym thanne, it were but pure synne.
> Ac whan nede nymeth [picks] hym up, for noye lest he sterve,
> And shame shrapeth hise clothes and hise shynes wassheth,
> Thanne woot the dronken daffe wherfore he is to blame.' (B.xi.425–32)

Once fallen into a ditch, it is natural need – to eat, lest he starve – that will cause him to regain his upright posture and his pursuit of God.[64] For the man in a ditch, taught knowledge will have little effect and punishment would be 'pure synne'. It is rather natural experience, felt in the body, that will make him cognisant of how he has erred. Similarly, *The Book of Vices and Virtues* understands a natural process whereby sin acts at first to deaden the senses; but then, after sleep, to bring the sinner to painful, felt awareness of his or her folly. 'Þe synful man or womman þat slepeþ in dedly synne fareþ as a dronke harlote þat haþ al y-dronke at þe tauerne'; though he is 'so naked and so pore þat he haþ nouȝt', he neither feels it nor complains about it. But when he has slept, when the effects of alcohol have worn off and he has come to his 'senses' again, 'þan feleþ he his harm and knoweþ his owne folye, and þan he waileþ [bewails] his harm'.[65] The experiences of falling and rising gesture towards the ways in which body topography is conceived of as an indicator of spiritual orientation, but also suggest that man's spatial relation to the world is in flux; suffering, falling and nearness to earth are part of the processes which characterise the everyday body. In this context, care of the self in the forms of sleep and rest, responding to the need to eat or to defecate, work their own natural benefit, precipitating rising and re-establishing 'uprightness'.

The experience of sin as sickness or as a form of suffering outlined in Passus XI of *Piers Plowman* and in the pastoral tradition directs us to the particular logic of how the experience of sin might in some ways be beneficial. As Elaine Scarry remarks in *The Body in Pain*:

> As the body breaks down, it becomes increasingly the object of attention, usurping the place of all other objects, so that finally, in very very old and sick people, the world may exist only in a circle two feet out from themselves; the exclusive content of perception and speech may become what was eaten, the problems of excreting, the progress of pains … This constantly diminishing world ground is almost a given in representations of old age.[66]

This sense of a diminishing perception of and extension into the world – the contraction into the *space of the body* – is not just effected in old age (as we see with Margery's aged husband, who has turned childish again, and can no longer use a privy), but in the processes of being born, being unwell, suffering, falling and dying. In these experiences, the primary physical wants of the body (eating, excreting, feeling) become the whole content of thought and speech. If sin, in medieval discourses, is experienced as a form of suffering, then sinning/suffering brings experience back into the space of the body and its needs, restricts vision and privileges the mouth's wants and offices and necessitates as much the body's care as its renunciation.

Julian of Norwich's *Showings* provides a very literal example of this in the vision of a lord and his servant, where the Genesis narrative of original sin is rewritten as a fall, like that of Langland's drunken 'daffe', into a ditch. Julian's version of the Fall draws on the traditions both of the *felix culpa* and of the late medieval valuation of the natural.[67] Thus Julian writes in the *Showings* with a compassionate recognition of the conditions of being human: 'Man is channgeabyll in this lyfe, and by sympylnesse' – or, as a manuscript variant has it, 'frelte' – 'and vncunnyng fallyth in to synne'.[68] Man unwittingly falls into sin through his natural frailty. Original sin in Julian's vision is revealed to be precipitated by the servant's (well-intentioned) running to satiate *the lord's* appetite. (The appetite that drives Adam and Eve to taste forbidden fruit is thus here displaced and revalorised as God's own good desire to eat.) While natural experience in the *Showings* is thus dark and painful, at the same time, the natural is also deeply positive. Sin, as Julian famously asserts, is 'behovable' – that is, not only inevitable but in some ways necessary, and necessary for salvation. This principle is figured most powerfully as a process of falling and rising: thus Julian writes that as 'we falle, hastely he [God] reysyth vs by his louely beclepyng [calling] and his gracyous touchyng'.[69] And elsewhere: 'it nedyth vs to falle, and it nedyth vs to see it', because by the 'assey [or trial] of this fallyng we shalle haue an hygh and a mervelous knowyng of loue in god without ende'.[70]

Adam's Fall, paralleled by Christ's fall to earth in the Incarnation, is the example *par excellence* of this truth, as Julian explicates in the parable of the lord and servant. In this parable, the servant (Adam, but also Christ) is standing waiting to do his lord's (God's) will:

> nott onely he goyth, but sodenly he stertyth and rynnyth in grett hast for loue to do his lordes wylle. And anon he fallyth in a slade [ditch], and takyth ful grett sorow; and than he gronyth and monyth and wallowyth [rolls] and wryeth [writhes], but he may nott ryse nor helpe hym selfe by no manner of weye.[71]

First and foremost, the literal level of the parable establishes what it is like to live in a fallen world and what it is like to fall over. Julian notes that as a consequence of falling the servant 'culde nott turne his face to loke vppe on his lovyng lorde, whych was to hym full nere'; she then continues to outline seven great pains that the servant suffers while lying in the 'slade': (1) the 'soore brosyng [bruising] that he toke in his fallyng'; (2) 'þe hevynesse of his body'; (3) the 'fybylnesse that folowyth of theyse two'; (4) 'he was blyndyd in his reson and stonyd [stupefied] in his mynde'; (5) 'he myght nott ryse'; (6) 'he leye aloone'; and (7) 'the place whych he ley in was alang, harde and grevous' one.[72] Falling over is therefore characterised by three bodily conditions: firstly, the deprivation of both vision and reason. Secondly, the upright body of man (upon which the efficacy of vision depends) is lost, leaving instead an awareness of the body's heaviness (i.e. the difficulty of keeping upright in the first place). Finally, falling is characterised by an intensification of the sense of touch: the experience of bodily pain and suffering. It is, however, precisely this natural experience – the loss of vision, the toppling of the body, the intensification of the sense of touch, the preoccupation with the suffering of the body – that enables the restoration of the servant: the fall leads the lord, not to punish the servant, but to give him gifts.

Imagining both original sin and everyday sin as a fall, Julian's parable of the lord and servant and Ymaginatif's example of the drunken 'daffe' in *Piers Plowman* offer a further challenge to surface readings of the upright body of man. Making sense of the inevitability of sin through the paradigm of natural bodily experience reveals the limitations of the knowledge learned through vision: for the woman or man whose body is bent towards the earth – through sin, but also through everyday need or lifelong impairment – the lessons gained through looking up will go unheeded, as will the admonishments of 'clergie'. Instead, the natural knowledge of *experientia* – knowledge that is felt as bodily need and shame, or as temporal blindness and a bruised, uncomfortable body, and which prompts care of the body or the compassionate care of others – becomes the most powerful remedy for sin.

Piers Plowman returns time and again both to this cyclic, processual understanding of sin, to and the value of natural knowledge – in all its iterations – to it. The theology of sin articulated by Ymaginatif recalls and restages, in particular, an earlier version in the poem, that of the confession of Gloton in Passus V. Here, Gloton's sin is not only experienced as a fall but also as vomition. Like falling, the experience of vomiting is a natural consequence of sin (overeating) and at the same time its remedy. In the medieval medical traditions, vomiting, far from 'grotesque', is rather remedial and beneficial to health. Medieval pastoral discourses draw on this medicalised understanding of vomition in extending their understanding, not only of the processual, inevitable nature of sin, but also of the purgative effects of confession. Vomiting, like the mundane processes of eating, digesting and defecating, is therefore the scene for serious spiritual learning. In the case of Gloton, however, Langland places pressure on a faultline in theologies of sin generated from the natural example of the body: the cyclical nature of sin and its remedy calls into question whether – if this is itself a habit – reformation through it is, in fact, possible.

'Goode spuynge'?

Passus v details what happens when Gloton is waylaid en route to church by the temptations of the tavern.[73] Gloton's tavern-going brings about the reversal of his upright posture and the diminishment of his sensory and sensible faculties, as medieval *pastoralia* commonly warns it will: the glutton, *The Book of Vices and Virtues* observes, 'goþ riȝt ynow [goes in upright enough], and whan he comeþ out he ne haþ no fot þat may bere hym'; and although 'whan he goþ þidre [into the tavern] he hereþ and seeþ and spekeþ and vnderstondeþ', when he leaves, 'alles ben y-lost, as he þat haþ no witt ne resoun ne vnderstondynge'.[74] Having sat until evensong in the tavern and 'yglubbed [gulped down] a galon and a gille [a quarter pint]' (B.v.340), Gloton, belly-grumbling and farting, eventually and predictably tumbles at the tavern's threshold:

> And whan he drough to the dore, thanne dymmed hise eighen;
> He thrumbled [stumbled] on the thresshfold and threw [fell] to the erthe.
> Clement the Cobelere kaughte hym by the myddel
> For to liften hym olofte, and leyde hym on his knowes.
> Ac Gloton was a gret cherl and a grym in the liftyng,
> And koughed up a cawdel [mess] in Clementes lappe.
> Is noon so hungry hound in Hertfordshire
> Dorste lape of that levynge [mess], so unlovely is smaughte [smelled]!
>
> (B.v.350–7)[75]

As Gloton falls, so too does his vision fail – 'thanne dymmed hise eighen'; as L. O. Aranye Fradenburg remarks, 'a failure of vision is at stake in falling'.[76] In stumbling to earth, his power of extension into the world too is diminished. Sin and its attendant suffering thereby limit Gloton's experience of the world to the space of his body, bringing him close to earth and centring his sensing and feeling faculties in his mouth – the taste of bile rising, the purging of vomit, the unpleasant smell which is overwhelming.[77]

The wider context for Gloton's fall, of course, is Reson's call to repentance. In Passus v, each deadly sin makes confession; in so doing, if the efficacy of confession in the case of sin personified is called into question, its capacity to reveal each sin's interior state and essential nature is not. This sacramental frame is crucial to understanding the significance of Gloton's fall. Tempted by Beton the Brewestere's ale and 'hote spices' (304), Gloton is distracted on the way to confession: as such the tavern comes to take the place of the church as the space of bodily and spiritual formation – that is, for the cultivation of habits. By implication, confession temporarily (but repetitively) reverses man's upright bearing and dims his sight. Falling over and vomiting, thus, in various ways figure and parody the reforming power of confession. As Clement helps Gloton to his knees, Gloton's posture recalls the bowed, uterine topography, reminds him of what it is like to be in the dark and intensifies taste and touch: falling works (or, at least, should work) to remind Gloton of his origins and so also of his need for salvation.

If Gloton's tavern visit substitutes for confession in church, it is followed by Gloton's real confession – ' "I, Gloton," quod the gome, "gilty me yelde" ' (B.v.368) – in which he characterises the sin of gluttony as a cycle of eating, drinking and vomiting: having 'overseyen [forgotten]' himself at supper, he would have 'girte [vomited] it up' before he had gone a mile. His confession complete, Gloton weeps and vows to take up abstinence. It is the experience of the consequences of overeating and overdrinking – centred on the mouth, the stomach and the senses of taste and touch – that motivates his stated desire to reform himself.

Meditating on the experience of vomiting is therefore one way of understanding the process of spiritual reformation. This is made clear in the penitential writings of the Frenchman William of Auvergne (c.1180–1249), *Tractatus novus de penitentia* and *De sacramentis* (which are aimed, notably, at the literate laity rather than at a clerical audience). William's writings disclose something in common with the theology of sin taken up by Langland and Julian: as Lesley Smith summarises, William believes that sin is inevitable but also that creation is inherently good; 'his thoughts are always based in the temporal world, and it leads him constantly to make the link between our physical and spiritual lives'.[78] Valuing the natural and reading the created world to learn about God, William quite strikingly ruminates on the physical process of vomiting to expound on confession and its benefits. Outlining vomition (as William remarks, 'literally speaking, [it] is the emptying of the belly … by the agency of the mouth'), William explains:

> just as someone with an upset stomach [*indignatio ventris*], straining to expel what is harmful or unsuitable to it, distends his belly and opens his mouth wide to get rid of it, so too someone with an upset to a noble and holy conscience strains and searches the belly of his heart to throw out and expel detestable and filthy vices and sins, opening his mouth wide for them to leave via the words of confession. Therefore, since the noxious humour of vices and detestable sins is pushed towards the mouth, because of this upset and disturbance of the spiritual belly or conscience, and leaves via confession, this confession is rightly called spiritual vomit, because of the similitude with bodily vomit.[79]

The straining of internal muscles, the distended stomach, the open mouth: the physical movements and posture of confessing (painful, self-revelatory speaking, from within the deep space of the inner man) are the same as those of vomiting. Notably, Bartholomaeus's description of vomiting in *On the Properties of Things* could likewise just as easily describe the process of contrition and the postures of confession as it does vomiting. As Trevisa translates, vomiting is preceded by:

> meuynge and quakinge of lippis, and forsinge [straining] and angwisse [pain] of þe spiritual membres, wlatsomnes [nausea] and abhominacioun, openynge of þe mouþ, strecchinge of tonge, slakynge of veynes, of pipis, of senewis, teres in yȝen, rennynge out of swote, changinge of þe þrote, and bittirnesse and infeccioun of tonge, of palate, and of þe mowþe. (1, 396–7)

This body, on the verge of vomiting (but this could be mistaken for being on the verge of speaking), demonstrates all the evidence of genuine contrition – the mouth opens, the tongue stretches, the eyes weep – necessary for true confession to be made. It is, moreover, felt as a bitter taste on the tongue and on the palate. It is a body in anguish, exposing what lies within it.

The parodic overtones of Christian ritual are clear in the Passus v episode in which Gloton falls and vomits, but it is perhaps more than just parody: it is a literal example of how confession is enacted physiologically and teaches experientially (we all know how it feels to vomit). As medical texts testify, the only remedy for overeating is to purge the body, either through vomiting or through defecating: the remedial action for the sin of gluttony is both a literal and a figural one. As *On the Properties of Things* recalls: deliberate purgation, 'wilfullyche imaad' – which elsewhere Trevisa terms 'goode spuynge' – 'profitiþ' and 'helpiþ'.[80] However undesirable being sick is, like the undesirability of sin, it can be beneficial for the body and even for the soul. As the embodiment of engrained habitual sin, however, Gloton's example tests the logic of the analogy of sin to the body's natural daily cycles. If the body's needs cannot be transcended, is it inevitably the case that life will be experienced not only as always sinful but as a form of suffering? If so, what hope is there of achieving the virtuous *habitus* the pastoral tradition suggests is possible? The poem does not offer easy answers to these questions. However inefficacious it proves to be in Gloton's case, Langland's commitment here nonetheless is to exploring the ways in which the loss of the upright body, the diminishment of sight and the inordinate awareness of taste and touch might usher in salvation.

Where the example of the drunken man's fall into a ditch in Passus XI demonstrates, like the fall of the servant in Julian's parable, the natural value of 'being low', Gloton demonstrates that what happens to upright posture through overeating and overdrinking is unexpectedly close to what happens in confession. These are not the only lessons about the body that the dreamer receives in *Piers Plowman*, however – far from it. In conclusion to this chapter, I turn to Langland's own restaging of the exegetical potential of the topographical arrangement of the body in a set of 'lewed' theological questions about Adam and Eve in Passus X and XII. The first, related by Kynde: why did Adam and Eve cover their 'pryvé membres' once they were aware of their sin? The second, drawing Dame Studie's anger: why did God allow Satan to enter into Paradise? Both questions exemplify forms of intellectual meddling, seeking knowledge beyond natural need, just as Adam and Eve's own original sin does. The oblique answers to these questions direct the dreamer to the mouth's insistent connection to the lower body. Most telling, however, is Dame Studie's suggested remedy for the desire for knowledge beyond need, which proposes to topple sight from its privileged place at the top of the body's hierarchy.

The Dreamer's Reading Lessons

Langland's treatment of the Adam and Eve narrative in Passus X and XII of *Piers Plowman* explicates the kinds of natural lessons that can be learned from reading the human body, while at the same time directing us to the difficulties inherent in doing so.[81] In this case, the lesson is one primarily concerned with the interchange of the mouth with the lower body, and, like the Passus V episode, with the ways in which taste and touch have affective, cognitive and spiritual value. In Passus XII, Ymaginatif – rebuking the dreamer because he 'sekest after the whyes' (B.XII.216) – delineates the difference between taught knowledge and 'kynde' knowledge. Nicolette Zeeman – positing taught knowledge as revelation and 'kynde' knowledge as natural understanding – argues that 'the valuation of the natural [in *Piers Plowman*] presupposes that many moral and spiritual things can be realised in created matter and active, outward life'.[82] Thus Ymaginatif teaches the dreamer to read moral lessons in creation, without desiring knowledge 'beyond need' (i.e. an understanding of the 'whys'):

> 'And Kynde kenned [taught] Adam to knowe his pryvé membres,
> And taughte hym and Eve to helien hem with leves.
>   Lewed men many tymes maistres thei apposen,
> Whi Adam ne hiled noght first his mouth that eet the appul,

Rather than his likame alogh? – lewed asken thus clerkes.
Kynde knoweth whi he dide so, ac no clerk ellis!' (B.XII.229–34)[83]

The primary meaning of 'helien' (*MED*, s.v.) is 'to cover over', 'to conceal', but it also implies 'to cure' or 'to heal', as Adam and Eve, in covering over their naked bodies, attempt figuratively to cover over and remedy their transgression.[84] And yet, as the 'lewed men' invoked by Ymaginatif point out, they cover over the wrong part. Reading for the literal sense of the body, those who are unlearned ask why Adam and Eve cover their 'likame alogh' (lower body), when it is their mouth, located high in their body, which has transgressed? Notably, 'alogh' (*MED*, s.v. 'Of position or direction; low or lower down, below, downward') invokes the terms of body topography: nature relocates the sign of Adam and Eve's oral sin to their lower bodily stratum. While Ymaginatif ostensibly resists providing an answer as to 'why' disobedience should require the genitalia to be covered (it is Kynde's secret knowledge), medieval theology offers several interpretations. To wit, the Genesis Fall both placed sexual feelings outside of the rule of reason (Paradise is no longer at Adam's 'wille') and began the transmission of original sin through reproduction.[85] Most revealing, however, is the gloss the poem itself can be used to create.

Firstly, by drawing deliberate attention to the misdirection of Adam and Eve's covering, Langland makes this all too familiar narrative unfamiliar. At once, we recognise the failure of the body as a sign. Secondly, like the innate heaviness of the body, this displacement of shame to the genitals is a downward movement, characteristic of the tendencies of bodies in the text, but also of the downward thrust evinced by the mouth, through tasting and swallowing, into the bowels and lower body. It also suggests that the mouths of Adam and Eve have in fact interpreted the 'speech' of the gut, signifying its appetite both by tasting and by seeking after food and knowledge – a taste – that will make them as gods.[86] By redirecting the sign of transgression back to its source (i.e. the lower bodily stratum) the covering over of the body's nakedness seems suddenly far more appropriate. Sin – as the debasement and degradation of the *imago dei* that leaves a trace in body topography – pursues a downward logic that reaffirms this displacement of bodily shame from mouth to genitals.

The displacement from mouth to lower bodily stratum in this Adam and Eve narrative, however, recalls an earlier one that occurs in Passus x of *Piers Plowman*. Like Passus v, this passage points out the epistemological and soteriological value of the mouth and of the sightlessness brought about not by a physical fall but by an intellectual one. It also suggests a radical reformulation of the properties of the senses since it ultimately proposes to redefine 'sotil' sight as 'boistous'. Dame Studie this time is beating the bounds of intellectual inquiry, having overheard men (notably sitting and eating at the table) asking why God suffered Satan to enter Paradise and cause Adam to sin. Citing Augustine's caution, '*Non plus sapere quam oportet . . .* ' (B.x.118), Dame Studie says: 'For alle that wilneth to wite the whyes of God almyghty, / I wolde his eighe were in his ers and his fynger after' (B.x.124–5).[87] Associating preternatural knowledge beyond need and its implicit criticism of the wisdom of God with speculative knowing at a distance, the dreamer is shown the value of natural knowledge, which is gained first-hand, inwardly, in the body and by the mouth. Those who misuse learning should firstly be hindered by the confusion and displacement of the bodily senses, and should secondly cover their eyes. Punning on the possible interpretation of 'ers' as ears, 'ers' in this context might also refer to the 'ars'.[88] The first possibility, that of banishing the eyes to the ears, reminds of an image in Deguileville's second recension of the *Pilgrimage* (a text with which Langland would be familiar) of Grace Dieu placing the Pilgrim's eyes in his ears.[89] In the second interpretation, the grotesque image of the eyes being banished to the anus gives them a limited, downward vision of the earth, one which will inevitably become obscured by the filth of excrement. This redirection into the earth is a strange reversal of body topography and physiology. The 'ers' itself is to be covered, stopped up by a finger – an act which would further obscure noble, 'sotil' vision but also prevent the 'behouely' exit of filth from the body.[90] Here, sin as suffering once again redirects human experience back into the body: no longer able to see or hear (the referents of taught knowledge or 'clergie'), the human becomes reliant on the 'boistous' senses of taste and touch (the referents of 'kynde' knowledge or *experientia*). When negotiating the world in the dark, taste and touch become the primary senses that remind man of his human condition, the bounds of his human intellect and his need for God and salvation. In banishing the eyes to the anus, Langland's image effectively topples sight from its privileged position and realigns it with the 'boistous' senses and with the lower body.

The natural lessons learned from observing, and experiencing, an upright body posture are therefore multiform. The commentary provided through a surface reading of the body correlates an upright posture with a hierarchy of the head and the eyes at the top, and the mouth and the lower body at the bottom. The mouth's position in the face, however, as Trevisa's translation of the Ovidian verse shows, also offers a variant reading in which an upright body instead gives to the mouth a noble *telos*. In both variants, however, the emphasis is on an epistemology of the senses, whether of the sense of sight or of the sense of taste (or perhaps both in collaboration). If a surface reading of the body suggests man's nobility derives from his abstraction from the daily concerns of eating and digesting, reading the body inside out reveals instead the cyclic process of decline and regeneration that is central to human experience and to the work of salvation. In this context, the upright body teaches man about the internal arrangement of the organs, and about digestion and excretion. This version of the trope thus correlates bodily form and sphincteral continence with the human ability for rational activities and for the performance of devotion. The cyclical logic, both of bodily posture (in lifecycles and quotidianly) and of the vegetable operations of the soul, is taken up to gloss the human disposition to sin and the process of spiritual reformation: falling and vomiting, in temporally toppling the upright body, dimming vision and centring on the felt experiences of taste and touch, precipitate rising and effect a beneficial purging of the body, needful for health but also for salvation. As Langland's reconfiguration of both the sin of gluttony and the Fall of Adam and Eve epitomises, however, running through these variant readings of the natural body are questions about literal, surface readings: the limits of knowledge gained naturally, through experience, or through observing the created world; and the potential failure of the body as a sign. So too does each variant stage a different proposition about the implication of the mouth, and of the sense of taste in particular, in the acquisition of knowledge. 'Non plus sapere quam oportet,' warns Dame Studie, to those sat talking about God at the dinner table. 'Don't be more wise than you need to be.' Or perhaps: 'Don't taste more than you need to.' While the lessons learned from the mouth are varied, sometimes contradictory or at the limits of the possible, taken together, these medical, pastoral and devotional examples suggest the valuation of taste (and taste as a touch – felt, experienced) as well as or even over sight as characterising the vulnerable (as opposed to the godlike) human condition and so as essential to medieval soteriology. Unlike sight, which (aided by the upright body) facilitates a certain transcendence of the body and of the world – one which cannot be sustained since it also transcends or negates humanness – tasting and touching locate experience in the body and reinforce being-in-the-world. In this way, the mouth can be as much a powerful agent of spiritual reform as the ears or the eyes. The next chapter describes in more detail the mouth's implication in the acquisition of a 'boistous', sapiential kind of knowledge.

CHAPTER 3

Tasting, Eating and Knowing

Medieval natural philosophy establishes that the mouth has a peculiar connection with the earth: preoccupied with seeking food and eating it, its very complexion – its humoural proportions – naturally inclines it downwards. In some ways earthbound, the mouth has thus been deemed unable to participate in the contemplation of the heavens and to be at odds with the acquisition of rational or spiritual knowledge. The traditional exclusion of taste and touch from spiritual knowledge is further predicated on natural philosophical claims for their obverse relation to sight. Sight is defined as 'sotil' (refined) and acts on 'sotil' (rarefied) objects, and so is itself in some ways 'spiritual'. Moreover, since sight acts on light it has a particular association with spiritual illumination and revelation. Taste and touch, in contrast, are 'boistous' (coarse) and act on 'boistous' (reified) objects. They are decidedly concerned with the earth and with fulfilling the mundane needs of living in it. If the eyes accrue knowledge at a distance, the mouth can only do so directly and inwardly. This in turn accords with the binary of knowing things whole (with the eyes) versus knowing things in pieces (with the mouth). The way in which the eyes and mind can know something both at a distance and completely is exemplified in the cerebral mode of dream vision: at the opening of *The Pilgrimage of the Life of Man* the Pilgrim thinks he sees the heavenly city of Jerusalem 'with-Inne a merour [mirror] large & bryht' (318); later he will hear Sapience teach Aristotle that, although the eye is small, 'yet the gretnesse off thy face / A-bydeth there ... / Swych as yt ys, hool & entere' (5986–8). The capacity of vision for seeing whole, for seeing the bigger picture, is seemingly foreign to the mouth: the mouth knows piecemeal, by bringing into the body, breaking with the teeth and by ingestion. Yet, as Chapter 2 demonstrates, medieval glosses of man's upright posture raise the possibility that taste, like sight, can also seek heaven and garner knowledge: 'erecta in cælum corporis ammonet forma, eum quae sursum sunt sapere' ('The upright form of the body puts us in mind of heaven, to *taste* [*sapere*] what is on high').[1] The metaphorical force of 'sapere' here is clear, but so too is the potential for recuperating physical taste as good for obtaining spiritual knowledge, as the variant readings of the body's bent posture bear out. If taste and touch have cognitive and intellectual value, how do their properties shape the qualities of the knowledge learned? This chapter gives sustained attention to the epistemological models which derive their spiritual and moral efficacy from thinking through the particular properties of the mouth and the sense of taste.

Alongside this sensory epistemology, the Middle Ages inherits a tradition in which food is a powerful metaphor for a kind of knowledge, and eating the figure for its acquisition. Contrary to the elemental logic that would make 'boistous' food particularly inapposite as a figure for a valorised, spiritual knowledge, food in this tradition stands in for Scripture and other texts, as well as for theologically difficult knowledge, which requires being broken into pieces if it is to be known at all. Paradoxically, then, the mouth's distinctly unspiritual properties are recuperated here as the most appropriate in accessing knowledge-as-food. Ethical eating is marked by measured, timely consumption, the discernment of flavour and careful chewing. Such eating results in assimilation – that is, the transformation of food into flesh and bones, and into work and action. In the same way, knowledge-as-food requires measure, discernment and careful mastication in order that it be transformed into self and lived out actively. Within this tradition, the knowledge learned through the mouth designates a more material, affective and transformative kind of knowledge than that garnered by the other sense organs.

This valorised epistemology of the mouth finds powerful expression in the tradition of *sapientia*, and the monastic practices of *lectio divina* and of reading Scripture while eating a meal – instruments of clerical *habitus*. The first of these, from Latin *sapere* meaning both 'to taste' and 'to know', draws its character from the properties of physical taste. The tradition of *sapientia* therefore denotes, in Nicolette Zeeman's words, 'affective understanding described as something "felt", made inward and "experienced" by spiritual "taste"'.[2] This affective, felt principle similarly underpins the goals of the related reading and memory practices of the second, *lectio divina*.[3] Within this, *meditatio* and *ruminatio* are particularly associated with eating: that is, with chewing and masticating texts-as-food, which work to bring out the sweetness of knowledge of God.[4] As Mary Carruthers has shown, these epistemological modes have literal, material bases: reinforced through the repeated muscle movement of the mouth speaking words, what is learned is also understood to become embodied as it is processed in the brain, embedded into memory, felt in the heart and performed in deed.[5] The mouth therefore provides a form of commentary on a peculiarly ethical mode of knowledge acquisition.

In the vernacular theology of later medieval England, these epistemological models, drawn from the mouth's physiology and sensory capacities, are powerful instruments: in teaching how to read texts or consume knowledge in order to instil virtuous habits; in probing the relationship between the natural and the spiritual, and between the body's physiology and ethical and cognitive work; and in offering a model in which the everyday body and the daily experiences of tasting and eating are occasions for doing well while living in the world.[6] However, these same properties hold the potential for what should be an ethical mode to become pathological, even destructive. The mouth's sense of taste and its physical power to break, fragment and to bring into the body are therefore also taken up to characterise a counter-model of preternatural, sinful knowledge, marked instead by epistemophilia, by indigestion and by wastefulness. As such, as this chapter explores, the mouth also becomes the stage in works of vernacular theology for thinking through the difficulties or dangers that lay access to clergial knowledge might provoke, and of the limitations of different kinds of knowledge – natural, exemplary, experienced, taught, revealed – for working out one's salvation.

This chapter begins with a discussion of medieval descriptions of the lifecycle stage of infancy – in encyclopaedias, treatises on governance and in regimen for infants and children. It does so in order to show that the mouth's senses and offices are understood to be the primary means of shaping humanness right from the very start of life. In these contexts, the mouth is the newly born child's primary means of experiencing and coming to know itself and the world. The child's body, understood to be in need of a process of hardening, is not only physically, but also morally impressionable. In this phase of life, shaping bodily form is understood simultaneously to foster *mores* and habits. The stimulation of taste and touch, most strikingly, encourages both the growth of teeth and the development of speech. Since taste and touch, as well as the growth of teeth, are understood to have implications for affective, moral and cognitive development, care of the mouth forms the particular focus of regimen for children. The presence of teeth, facilitating the acquisition of speech and the capacity to eat food (as opposed to drinking milk), also heralds, more unexpectedly, the ability to discern good from evil, to enter formal pedagogic structures, as well as to think and to reason.

This kind of knowledge, I suggest, forms an important backdrop for understanding references to the mouth – taste, touch, but especially teeth – in vernacular theology, which I turn to in the second part of this chapter. It suggests, for example, a continuum between the muscular and sensory stimulation, thought to be necessary to the development of teeth and speech in the child, and the potential for everyday acts of eating to shape the content of thought and speech in adulthood. It also shows that taste and touch and the mouth's experiences are the foundation for all subsequent learning. The argument of the second part of the chapter is rooted in close readings of two poems – the pastoral *Speculum vitae*, and Langland's *Piers Plowman*. Both poems in varying ways explore the multiform connections of food and knowledge, and both utilise techniques appropriated from the tradition of *sapientia* and from monastic reading habits.

Speculum vitae's exposition of two petitions of the *Pater noster* prayer gives sustained consideration to the epistemological model provided by the mouth. The first petition ('his name be halwed') offers an opportunity to probe the connections of tasting and knowing established in the tradition of *sapientia*. As a gift, *sapientia* positions an anti-intellectual experiential knowledge alongside and against bookish *scientia*: it tests the limits of what can be learned by taste and what can be learned by sight. Even as it privileges an anti-intellectual form of knowledge, the poem teaches its readers what *sapientia* is through the sciential knowledge of the physical senses. Most strikingly, the gift of *sapientia* is revealed to have bodily effects. Each of the seven spiritual gifts drives out one of the seven deadly sins, grafting virtuous habits in the stead of vicious ones. Specifically, *sapientia* drives out gluttony and inserts measure. *Sapientia*, it turns out, is all about the governance of the mouth. *Speculum vitae*'s account of *sapientia* begins to erode the analogical status of the body (the gloss physical taste provides for spiritual taste) revealing instead the cyclic logic of the interrelation of the bodily and the spiritual (spiritual taste governs physical taste, which in turn cultivates the virtuous *habitus* of *sapientia*; but unregulated physical taste develops the immoderate habits that sour and corrupt spiritual taste).

The fourth petition of the *Pater noster* provides a second opportunity, this time through exegesis of the material and spiritual meanings of bread. Drawing explicitly on the monastic practice of *ruminatio*, the poem's exegesis of the petition 'our ilk day brede today gif vs' brings to the fore questions about the difference, not between taste and sight, but between knowing in pieces and swallowing whole, on the one hand, and between good and bad chewing on the other. In so doing it also betrays anxiety about the access of lay mouths to 'bread' or clergial forms of knowledge. The metaphorical force of eating in this model derives from the way in which teeth break down food into particles in the mouth. The first model, then, draws on the 'kynde' imperative for ordered, regulated eating, in which food is taken into the body in a measured, timely way and thoroughly chewed in order to be digested and transformed into work or actions. The second – counter – model draws instead on the eaterly habits of the greedy man, who swallows his food whole. Paradoxically, this second is both warned against and advocated in pastoral literature, since breaking food into particles might undesirably equate with asking questions about the revealed truths taught by Holy Church. In this context, the body of Christ is the primary test case for exploring the limits and bounds of a vernacular access to knowledge and of the glossatory powers of 'kynde' mouths.

A further counter-model is delineated in *Piers Plowman*, in which mouths are similarly figured chewing and breaking down food, but in a destructive, wasteful way. The monastic habit of reading Scripture while eating provides Langland with a frame for appraising the relationship of reading to eating, and of talking to eating, in a broadened social context, including within lay, vernacular halls. In this poem, the setting of everyday eating is made the grounds for the dreamer to learn – in sometimes competing and contradictory terms – about the ethical status of different epistemological modes, including not only the dangers of 'lewed' access to knowledge, but clergial abuse of it. Langland founds his discussion in, but ultimately goes beyond, the pastoral objective outlined in *Speculum vitae*. Contained within *Speculum vitae*'s exposition of *sapientia* is a corresponding exposition of the categories of the sins of the tongue and the sin of gluttony. Thus, in a cyclical process that moves through the material and the spiritual, *sapientia*, once obtained, will cultivate good eating habits that, in turn, will also influence the content of thought and speech. In particular, *Speculum vitae* invokes the monastic model of reading at the dinner table to show how actual eating forms a commentary on spiritual food, but also, how spiritual thought should be employed to gloss everyday acts of eating with spiritual meaning. It is this pastoral tradition of teaching about the vice of gluttony that Langland takes up and reworks in two dinner-table scenes to offer a sustained exploration of the ethics of knowledge, and of the relationship of knowledge to salvation. One scene is that evoked by Dame Studie in the course of her critique of the economy of the hall; the other is Conscience's feast, attended by the dreamer. In so doing, *Piers Plowman* tests to their limits the actual and metaphorical connections of tasting, eating and knowing at the heart of the epistemological models derived from the mouth.

The chapter's closing discussion returns to Kynde's instruction of the dreamer in how to read lessons in the created world in *Piers Plowman*. While Kynde outlines the ethical knowledge that can be learned through sight, what the dreamer in fact learns about is the human mouths and genitals – that is, about measured eating and drinking, and temperance in sex. The catenation of this natural teaching moment, in which the dreamer undergoes an intellectual fall, with the Fall of Adam and Eve discloses that the imbrication of food and knowledge found at the foundations of becoming human and the very origins of sin is also the archetype, paradoxically, for the means of human redemption. If the mouth structures Langland's retelling of original sin (as it does Julian's), so too does it structure Christ's redemptive act: in the Incarnation, Christ becomes mouth.

Growing Teeth and Beginning to Know

Following Aristotle, Giles of Rome writes in his treatise on governance, *De regimine principum*, that when we are first born (in the words of John Trevisa's translation) our 'knowyng bygynneþ of þe wit of felyng, and þynges þat ben iknowe by felyng ben most iknowe to us'.[7] All knowledge may arise from sensation, but the very first sense through which we learn is the sense of touch. Furthermore, what we learn through touch is 'most iknowe': it is this knowledge that we learn best, and which we come to know most fully. Reminding ourselves of this medieval commonplace underscores the importance of thinking about the senses through the lenses of daily cycles and life stages. In the lifecycle stage of infancy, sight turns out to be rather less important than touch. This understanding of the haptic condition of the newly born child finds a central place in Giles's day-to-day instructions for how children should be looked after and governed; so too does it in Middle English pastoral traditions: 'childryn in ʒougthe welyn asayʒyn [test, experience] and handelyn nyghy alle thyngge,' observes Pauper in *Dives and Pauper*. This accounts for children's particular 'inclynaciouns' (that is, their tendency towards certain sins), but also their especial vulnerability to being harmed through the senses of taste and touch:[8] if children assay the material world through touch, their innate physical softness means they are also peculiarly susceptible *to* touch.

It is not, however, simply that the child is driven by material needs and wants; its very physiology and complexion mean it is most receptive to and affected by these sensory experiences. This is because, as *On the Properties of Things* records, the child's flesh is not yet hardened but rather is 'tendir, neische [soft], quavy' [*MED*, s.v. 'flabby, ?full of moisture'), and 'vnsad' [*MED*, s.v. 'of flesh: not hard, not tough'] (1, 298). As such the child's body is susceptible to being reshaped, or misshaped: 'for tendirnes þe lymes of þe childe mai esiliche and sone bowe and bende and take diuers schappis' (1, 299). The softness of the child's body is a result of its innate heat and abundance of blood, but also, as *De animalibus* records, 'because of its nearness to the sperm' – that is, because it is still like to the quality of the digested food in the uterus from which it is first formed.[9] It is this softness that in part accounts for the child's inability to lift its body upright, but also for its lack of teeth. The malleable softness of the child's body is directly correlated with a moral, ethical impressionability, making it as much a pressing concern for those caring for the soul as for the body. *De regimine principum* therefore observes that

> children ben nesche [soft] and sone ouercome, ȝif þei folwen lecherie and *likyng wiþoute refraynyng*, anoun vicious habites and disposiciouns ben iprented in hem as þe liknes of a seel is sone iprented in þe nesche wex þat is wel itempred [softened].[10] (my emphasis)

Wax-like, children's soft bodies soon shape the inclinations of their morals and so the state of their souls. The 'vicious habites and disposiciouns' that Giles hopes parental governance will prevent children developing are, notably, begun in the mouth. 'Likyng' – *MED*, s.v. 'sensual pleasure', 'desire' or 'appetite' – is first expressed, as Giles notes, as a liking to 'souke tetes and breestes'. Even such natural, necessary appetite, 'wiþoute refraynyng', holds the seeds for vice.[11] This physiological softness, which must be tempered as the child matures, underlies the power of touch and taste in the lifecycle stage of infancy: it is the primary means not only of accruing knowledge, but also of forming character – shaping dispositions to feel, think and act morally. As the child's softness and heat is tempered it is thus able not only to stand upright but to moderate the sensibility of taste and touch, and use with greater efficacy the other senses, especially sight and hearing.

If the child's flesh will harden (reaching, finally, the cold, hardened state of old age), thus dulling it somewhat to the impressions of touch, the tongue's efficacy, throughout the human lifecycle, relies instead on its continued softness. As Aristotle describes in *De partibus animalium*:

> man is the most sensitive of animals, and a soft tongue is most adapted to sensation, being most impressionable by touch, of which sense taste is but a variety, and its softness again, together with its breadth, adapts it for the articulation of letters and for speech.[12]

Essential both for sensation and speech, the softness of the tongue, however, also accounts for its slipperiness. The wall-like hardness of teeth, along with the barrier of the lips, therefore provide necessary checks and measures on the soft tongue, while acting as reminder of the need for moral vigilance over it. *Book for a Simple and Devout Woman* recalls: 'For þat in slippynge þe tonge is sette, þe lyʒtlocor [more easily] to vuel [evil] hit glideþ ... Forþi kynde abowte þe tonge haþ made a bonen walle, þat he his wordis bynde.'[13] In *The Canterbury Tales*, Chaucer takes up this pastoral trope, putting it in the mouth of the Manciple's mother:

> 'My sone, God of his endelees goodnesse
> Walled a tonge with teeth and lippes eke,
> For man sholde hym avyse what he speeke.'[14]

Here the anatomical arrangement of the human mouth (like its comparatively small size) provides a teachable moment. As Craun summarises: 'this constitutes an "Aristotelian" physiological argument, that the corporeal signifies the Creator's will'.[15] Cautious as the Manciple might be about this kind of vernacular, pastoral teaching (he claims, 'I am noght textueel'), as the tale performs, it is nevertheless what mothers teach their children ('"Thus lerne children whan that they been yonge"'), as well as priests their parishioners.[16] Indeed, learning to restrain the tongue, as the Manciple's mother has taught him, is the 'firste vertu'.[17]

As the primary locus, not only of learning and experience, but also of shaping moral dispositions and virtuous speech, the mouth of the newly born child is therefore the particular object of care. In a section on 'De infantulo' in *On the Properties of Things*, for example, Bartholomaeus instructs that, after washing the newly born child:

> Þanne þe roof of þe mouþ and gomez [gums] schulde be frotid [rubbed] with a fingir iwette in hony, to clense and comforte þe inner partye of þe mouþ, and also to excite and cense þe childes appetite wiþ swetnes and scharpnes of þe hony. (1, 298)

Rubbing the gums and inside of the mouth with honey cleanses them, but it is also thought to 'excite and cense' appetite itself.[18] Gynaecological treatises belonging to the *Trotula* tradition circulating in Middle English in this period issue similar instructions. *The Knowing of Woman's Kind in Childing*, for example, instructs that eight to ten hours after birth the child should be given its carer's finger dipped in honey to suck.[19] The stimulation of taste and touch – those senses defined as necessary 'ad esse' – is in some way bound up with stimulating the desire for life itself, as well as the means for preserving it. In some medieval cultures, oral stimulation is in fact a prerequisite for establishing the precise moment human life begins: as Jacqueline Tasioulas notes of Frisian practice, 'there were various customs which accompanied the abandonment of children, one of which was the rule that the child must be exposed before it had received earthly food'.[20] The status of the newly born child – whether it could be abandoned or should be nurtured – thus might turn on the act of tasting and eating.

The passing of food through the mouth and into the body, and the stimulation of appetite and the senses, mark a rite of passage from foetus to human being. Thereafter, the concerns of medieval regimen turn to encouraging the growth of teeth in order to facilitate weaning and the onset of speech. The association of the absence, emergence and loss of teeth with medieval lifecycle stages is a basic but important one because it correlates physical changes in teeth with changing moral, legal and social status. Teeth act as physical signs, accompanying the ability to eat food rather than drink milk, marking a development or deprivation of verbal skill, and intellectual and spiritual change. Their loss in old age signals a return, of sorts, to a second childhood – toothless, and with diminished powers of reason, but also of (sexual) appetite.[21] Albertus remarks in *De animalibus* that there are four lifecycle stages, the first of which is childhood:

> Childhood is divided into infancy [*infantilis*], which is the age of the newborn, the age of movement [*aetas motiva*], in which the child begins to move, and the age which is prior to strength [*aetas ante fortitudinem*]. This is the one which is called the 'implanting of the perfect teeth' since the teeth are already beginning to change and come back. It is further divided into the age which is prior to the lust of the fully grown and mature seed and lustful age [*aetas luxuriantiva*].[22]

The second stage of childhood, which is that 'prior to strength', is also the stage in which 'perfect' teeth are grown (as milk teeth are lost and replaced).[23] Notably, it is the infant's 'nearness to sperm' – accounting for its physical and moral impressionability – that is also understood to account for its lack of teeth at birth, as well as for the subsequent loss of milk teeth and the presence of the material resources to regrow them. As the *Prose Salernitan Questions* (c.1200) makes clear, teeth are formed from the substance of the brain and from marrow from the eyes or cheekbones, the excess of which runs to the gums where cold air causes it to solidify and form teeth.[24] In contrast, the *Prose Salernitan Questions* explains that adults, due to the diminished heat and moisture attendant on aging, do not regrow teeth which have fallen out, since there is no more soft, excess matter available to reform them: 'In the young, phlegm is sent back [to the teeth] and beaten; in the old, heat, from which teeth come, cannot be made in order to restore [teeth].'[25] It is thus the continued heat and moisture of the child's body that accounts for the fact that children, unlike adults, grow, lose and regrow teeth.

The absence or presence of teeth, however, more than merely marks the physical characteristics of different lifecycle stages: it is understood to correlate with both ethical and rational capacities, predominately because of the role teeth play in creating speech. As Shulamith Shahar notes, 'most authors saw a connection between the emergence of teeth and the commencement of speech, and believed that toothlessness hampered speech'.[26] In his *Etymologiae*, Isidore posits the etymology of *infans* as 'qui fari non potest' ('*in*, "not"; *fari*, present participle *fans*, "speaking"').[27] Isidore's definition is commonplace in the Middle Ages; it is, for example, cited in full by Bartholomaeus in *On the Properties of Things*, and faithfully rendered into Middle English by Trevisa:

> childehood þat brediþ teeþ strecchiþ and durith seuen ʒere. And suche a child hatte *infans* in latyn, þat is to mene "nouʒt spekynge", for he may nouʒt speke noþir sowne [sound] his wordes profitabliche, for here teeþ be nouʒt ʒet parfitliche igrowe and isette in ordere. (1, 291)

Lacking teeth (or lacking perfectly grown and ordered teeth), infants do not have the faculty – central to man's rationality – of articulate speech. Because children, after they have acquired their milk teeth and begun to form words, lose their teeth again, it is only with permanent teeth that speech is seen as being more than mere imitation of adult speech and an expression of independent, rational thought.[28] Hence, the emergence of permanent teeth around the age of seven denotes the appropriate time to begin educating the child.[29]

Since the passage from childhood into adulthood (the 'age of reason'), but also into formal pedagogical structures, in part depends on having teeth, the medieval medical tradition displays a particular interest in stimulating the growth of teeth in the young child. In the same way that the mouth is first to be rubbed with honey to stimulate taste and whet appetite, encyclopaedias and medical texts instruct that the gums, teeth and tongue are to be rubbed in order to encourage the growth of teeth and also (by extension) the onset of speech. Vincent, in an entry on the regimen for the infant after birth in *Speculum doctrinale*, instructs that 'when the time of the birth of teeth approaches, the gums should be rubbed often with butter and fat of a hen, and smeared with barley water', and elsewhere, in an entry on weaning the infant ('De ablactatione infantis'): 'when speaking begins, also the teeth should be rubbed, especially at their roots'.[30] The *Trotula* tradition of gynaecological treatises offers identical instructions to rub the gums with butter and goose grease when teeth first begin to appear. Quite explicitly, these actions are not meant simply to bring comfort to the child during teething. The *Trotula* texts continue: 'so that it [the child] might talk all the more quickly, anoint the palate with honey'; as well as, 'after the hour of speech has approached, let the child's nurse anoint its tongue frequently with honey and butter, and this ought to be done especially when speech is delayed'.[31] Guy de Chauliac's *Cyrurgie* (following Arnauld de Villanova) also recommends that the tongue too should be rubbed to encourage speech: 'besynesse of speche and frotyng of þe tonge with sal gemme [rock salt] hasteth þe speche of childerne, as Maister Arnald saith'.[32] The gums, teeth, tongue and palate should therefore all be rubbed, not only when teeth first appear, but also when speech begins, and especially if speech is delayed. Moreover, the physical stimulation of the inside of the mouth with touches and tastes in order to encourage learning to speak is not seen as distinct from the stimulants provided by 'besynesse of speche' – that is, by the child's carer speaking often to it. Similarly, *Trotula* texts suggest singing nursery rhymes and 'talk[ing] in the child's presence frequently'; and *On the Properties of Things* recommends 'semi-sounding' words to the child: since 'he can nouȝt speke þe norse [nurse] whilispiþ [*MED*, s.v. '?articulate slowly or indistinctly'] and semisouneþ [*MED*, s.v. 'semisoun' (n.) 'a slight or soft sound'] þe wordis, to teche þe more esiliche þe child þat can not speke' (1, 304). The encouragement of a child's speech through the nurse's own use of indistinct, half-formed or even nonsense words, which she 'whilispiþ' and 'semiouneþ', suggests that its value is less in its meaning (the word's wholeness or sense is not important), and more in its muscular, voiced movements. Just as in the examples of rubbing the child's mouth, palate, teeth and tongue, these examples similarly show the basis for speech is understood to lie in material, muscular, sensory, indeed tasty, experiences.[33] Talking follows on the heels of tasting and touching.

What the growth of teeth also facilitates is eating meat rather than drinking milk. In the same way that *On the Properties of Things* describes how the nurse should break down words in order to teach the child to speak, so too, before the child has teeth, the nurse 'schoueþ mete in here owne mouþ and makeþ hit redy to þe tooþles childe, þat he may þe eþeloker [more easily] swolewe þat mete' (1, 304). The acquisition of teeth thus heralds both the ability to eat meat and a new cognitive ability (thinking and speaking for oneself follows upon eating for oneself), which gives access to different kinds of knowledge, but also moral consciousness and accountability. *On the Properties of Things* records that

> þe childe is propirliche clepid *puer* when he is iwanied [weaned] from melk and departid from þe brest and þe tete, and knoweþ good and euel. Þerfore he is abil to fonge chastisinge and lore, and þanne he is iput and sette to lore vndir tutours and compelled *to* fonge lore and chastisinge. (1, 300)

The transition from 'infancy' (not speaking) to 'boyhood' is defined by separation from the breast (as a result of the growth of teeth), which heralds both speaking and eating meat;[34] quite strikingly, this lifecycle stage is also marked by a corresponding intellectual and moral development – the acquisition of the knowledge of 'good and euel'. Thus the child can now enter into formal pedagogical structures, since he is able to 'fonge' (receive) 'chastisinge' (discipline) and 'lore' (instruction). Bartholomaeus's description of *puer* creates an equation between the presence of teeth, the ability to eat and to speak, and the capacity for (willed) moral or immoral action, as well as instruction. Such equivalences are founded, of course, not only in natural philosophy, but also in biblical tradition. Thus St Paul influentially correlates eating meat with an ability to discern good from evil in his epistle to the Hebrews (5:12–14):

> For sothe whanne ȝe schulen be maistris for tyme, eftsoone ȝe neden that ȝe be tauȝt, whiche ben the elementis, or lettris, of the bigynnyng of Goddis wordis. And ȝe ben made, tho to whom is need of mylk, and not sad mete. Forsoth ech that is a parcener [partaker] of mylk, is without part of the word of riȝtwysnesse, forsoth he is a litil child. Forsoth of parfit [perfect] men is sad [solid] mete, of hem that for the ilke custom han wittis excersysid, or trauelid, to discrecioun of good and yuel.[35]

Those partaking of milk instead of 'mete' lack literal learning – in short, they do not know their alphabet. Elsewhere, the presence or absence of teeth is a shorthand for this moralised tradition concerning the distinction of milk and meat, innocence and knowledge. St Jerome (d. 420), for example, in a letter to Gaudentius advising him on how to bring up his daughter whom he has dedicated to virginity, describes the stage of girlhood in a similar way: 'She is now a child without teeth and without ideas, but, as soon as she is seven years old, a blushing girl knowing what she ought not to say and hesitating as to what she ought.'[36] Jerome connects, firstly, an absence of teeth with an absence of thought, and secondly, the emergence of teeth with a postlapsarian shame and uncertainty – a knowledge of what is right but a troubled ability to perform it.

It seems, then, that teeth herald an awareness of right and wrong, as well as an ability, through speech, to demonstrate reason, that are prerequisites for full participation in society and for legal majority. Embedded in Isidore's etymology of *infans* – 'qui fari non potest' – are the terms of a legal definition in the Digest of Justinian denying legal majority to an infant (one extending to adults who likewise cannot speak properly, either because they are deaf and dumb or deemed to be mad).[37] Based on Roman law, influential in the West from the twelfth century because of the greater accessibility of the *Corpus iuris civilis*, the Digest prescribes that speechlessness denies legal status.[38] Teeth and the faculty of speech are therefore thought to manifest understanding, reason or intellect; those without teeth and speech are deemed to lack it. This in turn is reflected in a strangely gendered understanding of teeth found in Aristotle, and followed by encyclopaedists such as Isidore and later Albertus and Bartholomaeus. As *On the Properties of Things* records: 'a man passiþ a womman in resoun, in scharpnes of wit and vndirstondinge … Also in eueryche kynde of beestis þe males haueþ more teeþ þan þe females, and nediþ more mete to fede þe body' (1, 307).[39] The implication of this is both a justification and a perpetuation of the belief in the inferior physiology of women and the diminished ability of their bodies to perform rational functions: men have more teeth and eat more food (than women, than children) and are therefore more suited to the acquisition of knowledge, the exercise of reason and the rule of society.

The kind of moral, legal and cognitive status implicated in the presence or absence of teeth is reiterated in Albertus's remarks in *De animalibus* on the sub-stages of childhood (quoted above): the age 'prior to strength' imbricates with the age prior to lust.[40] Teeth are associated not just with appetite, but with an appetite that might spill over into excess, into lust and so into sin. Thus the acquisition of teeth precipitates the onset, when allowed to develop unchecked, of a preternatural appetite (lust) and a (tainted) taste for food and for (sexual, scientific, spiritual) knowledge, in other words, a kind of epistemophilia. Indeed, the *MED* glosses 'toþ' as 'appetite, corporeal desire'. Teeth signify appetite, both natural and inordinate. The devil in *On the Properties of Things* has, for example, a 'toþ of temptacioun' (1, 86). Such connotations reverberate not only in the encyclopaedic and pastoral traditions: Chaucer's Reeve – despite his advancing age – retains the sexual desire of his youth: 'ik have alwey a coltes tooth'.[41] The Wife of Bath keeps her *bele chose* for her husband's 'owene tooth', instead of selling it.[42] Sir Gowther, of human and demonic parentage, is born both with teeth and with a correspondingly voracious appetite through which he slays nine wet nurses and bites off his mother's nipples.[43] In this way, the growth of teeth is both a necessary precursor to becoming a social, rational human being but also a sign of the child's separation from its mother, and a launch into a tasty, tempting, fallen and, when uncontrolled, even monstrous world.

The ontological and epistemological model provided by exploring the mouth in medieval lifecycle stages is one in which knowledge is rooted first in touch and taste. Important not only for cognition, these senses are also central to the moral disposition and cognitive capacity fostered in children. Moreover, stimulating the material insides of the mouth has a literal connection with the development of both speech and moral discernment: tasting leads to talking. Growing teeth and beginning to eat are connected in complicated ways with growing up: that is, with beginning to talk, with transitioning from milk to 'mete', with tempering the sensibility of taste and touch, with making moral judgements and so with exercising, as well as expressing, reason.

If taste, touch and teeth form the foundations for all human learning, the physiology and anatomy of the mouth also provide a model for delimiting the metaphorical association of food and knowledge, eating and knowing. The natural philosophical and medical tradition of lifecycle stages powerfully structures medieval thinking about the correlation between body *hexis* and aptness for knowledge acquisition.[44] The muscular and sensory stimulation of the mouth in the lifecycle stage of childhood provides a continuum with the monastic habit of *ruminatio*. Definitions of childhood and adulthood based on the properties of the mouth shape understandings of the knowledge that is appropriate to the laity and the clergy, as well as frame anxiety about lay access to clerigal knowledge. So too does good governance of the mouth's physiology and anatomy provide the very conditions in which sapiential knowledge can be obtained. These perceptions about the knowledge learned by mouth are tested in the pastoral poem *Speculum vitae*, as the next section explores. In its exposition of the first petition of the *Pater noster* prayer, this poem outlines the relationship between sciential knowledge gained through sight and sapiential knowledge experienced through taste, but it also discloses the slippage between physical and spiritual senses of taste. *Speculum vitae* thus further demonstrates the instability of the figurative gloss provided by the mouth: the material and physical ground the spiritual, which in turn shapes and cultivates the body.

Sapientia

Speculum vitae, a fourteenth-century Middle English translation of *Somme le roi* extant in over forty copies and offering extensive 'septenary catechesis', breaks with its source by structuring its entire contents around the seven petitions of the *Pater noster* prayer.[45] Two of the *Pater noster* petitions provide particular opportunity for its readers to reflect on the connections of the mouth with epistemological modes. The first petition, 'sanctificetur nomen tuum' ('his name be halwed'), obtains the gift of wisdom – *sapientia*.[46] The fourth petition, 'panem nostrum cotidianum da nobis hodie' ('our ilk day brede today gif vs'), contains within it the request for three different kinds of bread – actual, scriptural and that of God's body.[47] Both these petitions and their exegesis make ethical eating absolutely central to them; both, moreover, operate simultaneously on a literal and analogical level.

The first petition, since it obtains wisdom, is also deemed the highest. Wisdom is 'sayde of sauour / Of thinge þat swete es and noght sour. / For when a man es bouxsom / To resayue þe Gift of Wisdome, / He tastes þe sauour what it es / And feles of Godde þe swetnes'.[48] This establishes wisdom as a form of knowledge that is not taught, but is rather received as a gift through prayer: bodily mouth, taste and touch operate here principally as figures. As such, as a mode of knowing, *sapientia* is in some ways anti-intellectual, positioned against *scientia*. However, *Speculum vitae* continues to explain that the receipt of this gift allows man to taste God, '*Als* he þat wil and may tast wele / Þe swetnes of gode licour [wine], and fele / Bi þe mouthe, if he tast right, / Better þan he may bi þe sight' (my emphasis).[49] *Just as* taste can discern the flavour of good wine better than sight, so too does the mouth obtain a fuller experience of God than the eyes. Furthermore, as *Speculum vitae* continues, once God has been tasted, that which was loved in the world will 'bicom fade to þe sight', in the same way that 'Al þat bifore semed clere and bright, / Als water semes fade in shewyng / To hym þat to gode wyne has lyking'.[50] Not only does the taste of wine make that of water taste less in comparison, this taste also recalibrates (just as falling over does) the experience of seeing: a 'lyking' for wine causes water to *look* less clear and bright than it once did, just as the things of earth do after God has been tasted. This sciential knowledge of the operation of the bodily senses, obtained by observing the natural world, is used as an analogy for understanding spiritual taste. However, at the same time, it also teaches us something about bodily taste and its everyday value over and above sight. It thus begins to figure a complex interrelation of knowledge about nature and spiritual understanding, as well as of the implication of the senses (bodily knowledge) in different forms of spiritual knowledge.

The comparative force of taste to sight at this point bifurcates: it operates firstly in relation to the lower, but related, gift obtained by the second petition of the *Pater noster*, understanding. This gift is associated with light and gives clear vision – again, in an anti-intellectual mode – in order to see the state of the inside of one's own heart.[51] Spiritual sight can thus teach a man what he is, but it is spiritual taste that allows him to experience God. The second comparison of taste with sight, however, is of the gift of *sapientia* with speculative *scientia* itself – that is, with knowledge learned through looking at the created world.

Reiterating both that we know God better through taste, just as we know the quality of wine through taste, *Speculum vitae* continues to explain:

> Many philosophers couthe knawe
> Godde thurgh þe creatures þat þai sawe,
> Als it war thurgh a mirour;
> Bot of hym þai had na right sauour.
> Þai sawe þare thurgh Vnderstandyng
> And thurgh Resoun, withouten fayllyng,
> His beaute, his bounte, and his myght,
> Anf his wisdom thurgh þair sight
> Of þe creatures þat Godde wroght …
>   Wharefore þai knewe wele his myght
> Thurgh kyndely way and symple sight
> Or Resoun and Vnderstandynge,
> Thurgh whilk þai hadde anely knawyng.
> Bot of þe luf of Godde ne feled þai noght
> Thurgh taste ne thurgh deuocioun soght.[52]

Through consideration of the created world 'many philosophers couthe knawe / Godde', and yet did not *love* or experience him. The goals of theology run deeper than knowledge for knowledge's sake: for the Christian, *scientia* must be superseded by *sapientia*. The inferiority of a pagan philosopher's knowledge of God is expressed in terms of the kind of knowledge gained through sight as opposed to taste – or rather, of understanding gained only through the physical sense of sight, rather than through physical sight in conjunction with spiritual taste. As such, this example straddles the material and spiritual senses and shows their interconnection. Knowledge of God gleaned from the book of nature with the eyes alone – that is, 'thurgh kyndely way' – is a lesser, 'unsavoury' kind.

Known at a distance – 'als it war thurgh a mirour' – such an indirect mode of knowing does not yield a taste or experience ('right sauour') of God himself. Likewise, if a man overeats and his sense of taste is disordered, he will be hindered from obtaining the gift of wisdom. Thus there are Christians who know God 'by the book', but because their taste is 'englaymed [*MED*, s.v. 'To cover with a sticky or viscous substance, or with filth'] thurgh synne', they may no more taste God than 'Þe seke [sick] man may fele sauour / In gode mete or in gode lycour'.[53] *Sapientia*, instead, building upon (rather than discarding) *scientia*, requires not only sight, but also taste. The senses and their properties are here posited as central to understanding the difference between a sciential and sapiential reading of nature, as well as to understanding the wisdom that comes as a gift from God.

If the discussion of the gift of wisdom in *Speculum vitae* posits the everyday value of the sense of taste at the same time as it takes up taste as a commentary on the spiritual, the slippage between the literal and the analogical is borne out further in the knock-on effects of obtaining wisdom. The gift of wisdom drives out the sin of gluttony and inserts instead the virtues of soberness and measure.[54] In particular, soberness and measure – natural lessons taught to us by observing man's single, small mouth – will deliver a man from thraldom to his belly, order and regulate the activities of eating and speaking, but also set thought, wit and will under the rule of reason, and regulate intellectual inquiry and the quest for understanding.[55] Soberness thus brings 'hele [health]' to both body and soul.[56] The analogical force of the body is here collapsed and the cyclic logic of the interrelation of body and soul is exposed: wisdom will govern a man's mouth, the senses of taste and touch and the activity of eating, but also speaking and thinking.

Speculum vitae's discussion of *sapientia* therefore teaches its lay readers the benefits of physical taste over physical sight (the conditions under which it is better suited than any other sense to obtain knowledge), but it also shows how taste recalibrates sight (we see differently once we have tasted). It further values experiential, spiritual knowledge, figured by taste, over sciential knowledge about nature, accrued by sight, but it does so in ways which show their interrelation. More particularly, it shows the interchange between the material and spiritual in revealing the centrality of good governance of the mouth to acquiring the highest form of spiritual knowledge, wisdom. In its discussion of the fourth petition of the *Pater noster* prayer, the poem sets ruminative chewing against swallowing whole, raising the problematic logic of the analogy of food to knowledge, in which chewing knowledge might lead to the laity challenging clerical interpretation of it. Knowledge learned by mouth, as the practices of *meditatio* and *ruminatio* discussed below show, thus carries the potential to be the most spiritual and the most profound; in lay mouths, however, without education and governance it simultaneously has the potential to be the most transgressive and profane.

Meditatio and Ruminatio

The monastic reading models of *meditatio* and *ruminatio*, in taking up the analogy of eating to knowing, imply active engagement and hard, cognitive work. Eating as a model for learning cannot be made simply to indicate knowledge that is experienced directly and inwardly: it further indicates a kind of knowledge that must be broken if it is to be known at all. Jean Leclercq's study of monastic culture exemplifies the tradition in which eating and learning are forged together in 'active reading', and his description of it, though it has often been cited, is worth repeating here:

> The *meditatio* consists in applying oneself with attention to this exercise in total memorization; it is, therefore, inseparable from the *lectio*. It is what inscribes, so to speak, the sacred text in the body and in the soul.
> This repeated mastication of the divine words is sometimes described by use of the theme of spiritual nutrition. In this case the vocabulary is borrowed from eating, from digestion, and from the particular form of digestion belonging to ruminants ... To meditate is to attach oneself closely to the sentence being recited and weigh all its words in order to sound the depths of their full meaning. It means assimilating the content of a text by means of a kind of mastication which releases its full flavor. It means, as St Augustine, St Gregory, John of Fécamp, and others say in an untranslatable expression, to taste it with the *palatum cordis* or *in ore cordis*. All this activity is, necessarily, a prayer; the *lectio divina* is a prayerful reading.[57]

Knowing inwardly and experientially requires mastication and digestion. Words and texts as food need to be chewed and broken in order to be digested and assimilated, both corporeally and cognitively. St Bernard in his commentary on the Song of Songs, for example, talks of the need to chew psalms with the teeth, 'because if he swallows it in a lump, without proper mastication, the palate will be cheated of the delicious flavour'.[58] Wine and milk can simply be swallowed; but psalms, like food, need to be chewed.

While monastic writing on *meditatio* provides a particular space in which the analogy of mastication is mapped on to modes of learning, it is also common in natural philosophical discourses of cognition. The medieval period inherits a long tradition in which cerebral function is analogous to digestion, as Ynez Violé O'Neill summarises:

> [it was believed that] sensations were apprehended, digested into ideas, and stored as memories in a regular progression through the head from front to back just as nutriments were processed daily through the gastrointestinal tract from top to bottom. The three major stages of the intellectual process were believed to take place in chambers called cells or ventricles (that is, 'little bellys'), which, though located in the head, corresponded in the nutritive process to the 'organs of digestion': the stomach and the large and small intestines.[59]

This digestion (or brain–stomach) analogy is especially persistent as the model for a particular kind of mnemonic and ethical learning.[60] Carruthers, in her work on memory in medieval culture, emphasises the way in which learning needs to be digested in order to become part of – assimilated or incorporated into – the learner: thus *ruminatio* 'familiarizes a text to a medieval scholar, in a way like that by which human beings may be said to "familiarize" their food. It is both physiological and psychological, and it changes both the food and its consumer.'[61] What Carruthers makes clear (and what is implicit in Leclercq's description) is that the link between eating and thinking is not just analogical but physical: we learn (whether from experience or through reading) in conjunction *with* our mouths and our bodies, not just in bodiless mind or soul. The manner of encouraging speech through touches and tastes, outlined in the regimen for the infant, thus forms a continuum with modes of learning appropriate in adulthood, as well as with the reading model in which words are broken down cognitively and experienced simultaneously as the physical movement (tastes and touches) of tongue against teeth, lips and palate.

Speculum vitae's exposition of *sapientia* itself appears within an exposition of the *Pater noster* that is modelled on the prayerful reading of *lectio divina*, as well as on the familiarisation central to medieval memory practices. As the poem tells at its very opening: the *Pater noster* is the first prayer, and the first 'clergie', taught to children.[62] To understand it, we should likewise make ourselves like children. The prayer's prologue – 'Pater noster qui es in celis' – is thus given to us in pieces. Like the nurse who 'shoves' food in her mouth to chew it up first before feeding it to the child, the teacher of the *Pater noster* must first make this prayer palatable in order for it to be learned. The goal of doing so is, firstly, to teach not the 'naked lettre' of the *Pater noster*, but its sense, in order to bring about the accord of heart and mouth and of will and understanding in prayer.[63] Secondly, once committed to memory, the exposition allows the reader to pray the Latin prayer with the mouth while supplying and meditating in the heart upon the full sense of each word and each of the seven petitions it contains. For example, the word 'Pater', among other meanings, 'shewes to our knawing / Þe lengthe of Goddis ay-lastyng. / And thurgh kynde of þe Faderhede, / He askes of vs Luf and Drede', and so on.[64] By the word 'noster' we should understand 'þe largesce of Goddis charyte', which made Christ our brother, but also establishes our kinship with other Christians.[65] 'Qui es' teaches us 'þe depnes of his sothfastnes, / And askes of vs Trouth stedefast'.[66] And by 'in celis' we know something of 'þe heght of Goddes maieste', requiring meekness, strength of will, and 'Pruesce [fortitude]' of heart in response.[67] In other words, for the *Pater noster* to be both understood and efficacious it needs to be broken down, mulled over and assimilated to memory – processes which will in turn mean that the full sweet goodness of it might be tasted.

The value of this mode of knowing – and, indeed, of praying – does not go uncontested in this period. *The Cloud of Unknowing* obsesses precisely with the breakage inherent in speech, but also with this kind of exegetical practice. Thus the author, having instructed that prayer should best be composed of 'bot a litil worde of o silable', advises that if someone 'of his grete clergie' tries to 'expoune þee þat worde & to telle þee þe condicions of þat worde, sey him þat þou wilt *haue it al hole, & not broken ne vndon*' (my emphasis).[68] In contrast to those medieval texts which value knowing in pieces, the negative mysticism of the *Cloud* suggests an anxiety precisely about the mouth – with its teeth, breaking and chewing words – as a model for knowledge. In *Speculum vitae*'s exposition of the *Pater noster*, 'clergie' is taught knowledge made palatable for swallowing – that is, for digestion and memorisation. In the *Cloud*, such clergial sense-making and unbinding of words instead devalues them.

The fourth petition of *Pater noster* – 'panem nostrum cotidianum da nobis hodie' – which obtains the gift of strength by driving out the sin of sloth and inserting fortitude in its stead, provides explicit opportunity in *Speculum vitae* to explain the practice of *ruminatio*.[69] This particular petition of the prayer, moreover, blends eating real food with eating the body of Christ in the Host, and with nourishing the soul with Scripture. In so doing, it underscores the literal as well as the analogical power of *ruminatio*. The petition is explained first as a request for real bread and for things necessary for life: 'In þis we aske strength and myght / For to sustayne our lyf here right.'[70] Such daily bread is, indeed, necessary not just for life, but in order to fulfil 'whyle we lif here al Goddis wille'.[71] The petition is, however, simultaneously a request for spiritual sustenance – 'þat es wytte / To vnderstand Haly Writte' – and for the Eucharist.[72] Actual bread therefore provides the grounds for performing God's will. It is also the figure for the food of Scripture that sustains the soul, as well as for the bread – at once both more 'substantial' and more spiritual – which acts on both the body and soul: the Eucharist.[73]

Somewhat counterintuitively, *Speculum vitae* instructs that the bread of the Eucharist, however, should be eaten whole – hastily, and without chewing: 'Hastyly men suld ay ete it / And gredily, als says Haly Writte – / Als þe gredy man dose gode mete / Þat so gredily wil it ete / Þat þe gode morsels þat er smale / Withouten chewyng swalowes hale.'[74] Such an injunction seems to work against the mouth's natural physiology, and against the grain of most pastoral instruction concerning the regulation of consumption: the right eaterly attitude here is that of the 'greedy' man. Elsewhere, in *Book for a Simple and Devout Woman*, for example, those who 'renne to þe mete as a gredi sowe, and … swoleweþ his mete alle hole' are condemned.[75] Similarly, Mirk's sermon for the first Sunday of Lent in the *Festial* instructs that, in order to remedy the sin of gluttony, 'ȝe moton [must] faston [fast], þat is, note to eton before tyme bot abyde tyl none of þe day. And whanne ȝe ben at ȝoure mete, ete ȝe note to freschelych [vigorously].'[76] The regimen for measured eating in *De regimine principum* – aimed at preventing both bad digestion and the sin of gluttony – underscores the physiological benefits derived from careful chewing: 'kynde ordeyneþ to bestis teeþ, þat mete ichewed wiþ teþ schulde þe better take worchynge [working] of kynde hete and be þe sonnere itorned in to norisching, as wode [wood] ihewe and ihacked smale brenneth þe sonnere and turneth in to fuyre'.[77] Swallowing real food whole is thus not only a symptom of sin, but would seem both to prevent the fullness of its flavour being tasted and to cause indigestion.

Yet *Speculum vitae*'s injunction to swallow the Eucharist whole is in line with conventional pastoral instructions on this sacrament, and indicates a certain anxiety around breaking the sacred body in the mouth and with the teeth. John Mirk's *Instructions to Parish Priests*, for example, cautions that communicants should be careful 'that þey ne chew þat ost to smal, / Leste to smale þey done hyt breke, / And in here teth hyt do steke'.[78] Part of the injunction not to chew might also aim to ward off questions about it. Indeed, the nature of the Eucharist (in Fiona Somerset's words) was 'hotly contested in Latin and English in Oxford and beyond from the early 1380s on'.[79] This debate, intertwined with controversy over the use of the vernacular for Scripture and theology, posed questions (among others) about Christ's presence in the Host, its relation to the form of the bread and wine and so also about the dangers of using Aristotelian natural philosophy to explain supernatural mysteries.[80] John Wyclif asserted that 'the material bread and wine in the Eucharist remained after consecration'; Lollards after him went further in denying that Christ was spiritually present at all in the host.[81] In *Book to a Mother*, a late fourteenth-century work associated with Lollard writings, the figure of eating books becomes a way of spiritually eating Christ's flesh and blood: 'chew' and 'defie [digest]' the life of Christ, the author urges,

> so þat alle þe uertues of þi soule and of þi bodi be turned fro fleshliche liuinge into Cristes liuinge, as bodiliche mete þat is chewed and defied norschiþ [nourishes] alle þe parties of a mannes bodi. And þanne þou etist [eat] gostliche Cristes flesh and his blod whereuere þou be.[82]

A ruminative mode of reading the life of Christ stands in for, and so makes redundant, eating real bread; here, however, unlike in *Speculum vitae*, the author is at pains to delimit the literal and the figurative: the natural example of digestion provides merely an analogy – for a figurative eating of books that points to a figurative body of Christ.

Swallowing whole, for those anxious about lay access to learning, might thus equate with believing without questioning. The alternative translation of the *Somme le roi* offered by *The Book of Vices and Virtues* makes this explicit: by the injunction to swallow the Eucharist whole, the translator explains, it should be understood that the recipient should 'bileue al a-gret þat þat is þe verrey body of Ihesu Crist and his soule and þe Godhed al to-gidere, wiþ-out any sechyng [questioning] or þenkyng how þat may be'.[83] The vehicle for orthodox teaching about the different nature of this divine food is the *defamiliarisation* of the virtuous *habitus* of eating. The example of the Eucharist thus stages the kind of anxiety that the natural example of eating can arouse, whether as an attitude towards the practice of ingesting the body of Christ under the form of bread, or as an attitude towards knowledge – whether taught, natural or revealed, or all three.

In Lydgate's translation of the *Pilgrimage*, instruction on the nature of the Eucharist – 'bread' made by Charity with the help of Sapience – is made an opportunity for reflection on the limits of 'kynde' knowledge and of Aristotelianism.[84] Kellie Robertson further suggests that Lydgate's translation of this episode 'specifically reflect[s] its fifteenth-century moment of production' – namely, concerns over (Wycliffite) heresy in the 1420s.[85] It is Sapience who has given to this bread two particular properties: though this bread is small in appearance, it is plenteous enough to feed the whole world; and, secondly, in 'euery smal party' of this bread, 'Severyd and ybroke asounder, / And departyd her & yonder', lies the same virtue as when it was 'hool and entere'.[86] This provokes the outrage of Nature, who sends her clerk, Aristotle, to reproach Sapience for having broken Nature's laws – namely, that the vessel of bread contains something larger than the vessel itself, and that, in this example, the whole is paradoxically equal to (rather than greater than) its individual parts.[87] Hereby the Pilgrim learns that sapiential knowledge, and God himself, may not be reduced to, or limited by, natural knowledge and natural laws. In the case of the Eucharist, the senses of sight, taste, touch and smell cannot be relied on: only hearing (that is, the teaching of Holy Church) alone will access the truth of its nature.[88] Yet, the *Pilgrimage* also shows the paradox of how something in pieces simultaneously can be whole. It does so by making reference to the properties of the eye and vision: Sapience finally persuades Aristotle of his error by demonstrating to him the capacity for the mind (or heart, as the seat of memory) to hold within it the image of a whole city, and for the eye, or a small piece of mirror, to contain the reflection of the entire face.[89] In this way, so too can a small piece of bread contain within it the body and godhead of God. Preternaturally, in the case of the Eucharist, then, the mouth must consume food whole, without breaking it – that is, without doubting its non-natural nature.

The Eucharist in these examples of vernacular theology becomes a litmus test for what can be learned about the spiritual and unseen through nature, of the capacity of the senses to move from bodily to spiritual knowledge, and of the textual status of the body. *Speculum vitae's* exposition of the fourth petition of the *Pater noster*, however, does not end with the instruction to swallow the Eucharist whole. After Christ's body as bread is swallowed, the process of rumination – chewing over, gleaning knowledge from it – should begin:

> Afterward of þat blissed mete
> Men suld ett als dose þe nete [cow]
> þat eftsons [a second time] chewes þe gresse
> þat he has eten, als his kynde es,
> With lytell and litell, als he shewes,
> And þat es when he þe cude chewes.
> Swa [so] suld a man thurgh deuocioun
> Think when he has swelwed þat mete doun
> And recorde of[t] in his hert and thoght
> Þe gode þat God has for him wroght.[90]

Just as the cow ('nete') regurgitates the grass it has swallowed to chew over again, so too should eating the Eucharist be followed by rumination: recalling in the heart ('re*cor*ding') or thought – or, even, retasting in the mouth – the goodness done by God. *The Book of Vices and Virtues* further elaborates that:

> a man or a womman schal record swetliche and in smale peces be many smale þou3tes al þe godnesses of oure lord and al þat Ihesu Crist suffrid for vs, and þan fynt þe herte ri3t sauour in þis mete and renneþ in-to a gret loue of God and in-to a gret desire to do ynow and suffre for hym al þat he my3t.[91]

As it is figured here, 'recording' is a process requiring sustained attention to 'smale peces', to the fine detail: rather than picturing, for example, an image of Christ on the cross in its entirety, such sapiential knowledge – leading both to love for God and a desire to 'do' afterwards – must be gleaned piecemeal.[92]

Speculum vitae therefore carefully circumscribes the monastic habits of *meditatio* and *ruminatio* to offer pastoral instruction to the laity in palatable form. Breaking up the *Pater noster* prayer into a vernacular form the laity can digest, it also demarcates knowledge that should be swallowed whole in contrast with that which can be eaten. In its vernacular form, *ruminatio* – using the 'kynde' lesson taught by the peculiar digestive system of cows – essentially offers a model for a recollective reading practice focused on drawing out the full sweetness of the nature of Christ's Passion, but not the mystery of transubstantiation. The implication, however, that the laity might in this way access 'mete' rather than milk further troubles the project of vernacularisation.

The association of eating and drinking with different kinds of knowledge is one that is pervasive in biblical and medieval exegetical discourses: St Paul asserts, as we saw above, that infancy accords with a diet of milk; maturity heralds eating solid food.[93] Milk and meat represent kinds of knowledge, often in particular demarcating a form of spiritual food appropriate to childhood or adulthood, the laity or the clergy respectively. Thus Nicholas Love in *The Mirror of the Blessed Life of Jesus Christ* (a text notably circulating under the seal of Archbishop Arundel's approval in the early fifteenth century, in the wake of debates about the vernacular and lay access to knowledge in this form) asserts that 'symple' creatures 'hauen nede to be fedde with mylke of ly3te doctryne & not with sadde mete of grete clargye & of hye contemplacion'.[94] 'Mete' is difficult knowledge. Love claims that the simple, the lay – those who are, in fact, defined by

Love as themselves 'boistous' – need the easier knowledge of milk, suckled from the breasts of Jesus as Mother or Holy Church as Mother.[95] *Speculum vitae* similarly observes that Holy Church feeds us Holy Writ just as a woman, 'thurgh kynde knawen [knowing]', nourishes her child with milk from her breasts.[96] As a mother, who knows 'naturally' how to feed her child, Holy Church nurses the Christian: milk-as-knowledge here is nurturing and nourishing, but also passively ingested. For some Middle English writers, drinking milk and feeding on the divine mother's breast is, however, an unsatisfactory, secondary experience, and so they hunger for something more material, more 'boistous' than milk. Julian of Norwich, for example, demonstrates the superiority of 'mete': 'The moder may geue her chylde sucke hyr mylke, but oure precyous moder Jhesu, he may fede vs wyth hym selfe.'[97] In this eucharistic image, Christ offers his own body as nourishment, but also as a supreme form of knowledge.

Late medieval debates about lay access to clergial (bookish) knowledge, or Scripture itself, thus often pitch 'mete' against milk, knowledge appropriate for 'adults' (clergy) against that appropriate for 'children' (laity). Within this context, swallowing whole might be equated with learning without questioning; eating knowledge, instead, represents learning that must be gained actively and strenuously. Within these discussions teeth are something of an obstacle to be negotiated. Knowledge-as-food must be eaten, chewed with the teeth, swallowed and digested in order to maintain health, but also to produce thought and work. Yet, appetite for food can become preternatural: necessary chewing can become inordinate, leading to indigestion. So too might reckless chewing with the teeth lead to waste and spillage. The model of knowledge-as-food thus causes problems, not only for the laity who might err in interpretation and understanding, but also for the clergy, who might abuse the knowledge that is in their custody. In Middle English pastoral and poetic contexts, the everyday scene of eating in the hall provides more expansive grounds for learning about the interconnections of food and knowledge – the dangers of indigestion and of overeating – but also of the ethical responsibility that comes with possessing knowledge and chewing it with the teeth.

Dinner-Table Ethics

Speculum vitae's exposition of the first petition of the *Pater noster* imbricates the gift of *sapientia* with the mouth's physiology and the offices it performs. In particular, it provides the opportunity to treat the two sins that arise from the mouth: gluttony and 'mala lingua', or the sins of the tongue.⁹⁸ *Sapientia*, when we get down to its nuts and bolts, is all about governance over the mouth. It is thus under the umbrella of *sapientia* that the ten branches of the sins of the tongue and the five branches of gluttony are detailed. The branches of gluttony are: untimely eating, which gives occasion to 'tellynge of trewfles [unedifying tales, but also twaddle] and fables' at the dinner table; overeating, which is attributed to 'foul nurture' (that is, a bad upbringing); eating too quickly, which makes a man eat as a hound does 'caryoun [a carcass]'; eating too fine foods, which wastes goods and money; and curiosity 'to seke gode mete and it to taste', which leads a man to 'recorde' – turn over in his mind, but also boast to others – not the details of the Passion of Christ, but what he has just eaten and how it was served and what 'entremees' (either edible 'delicacies' or the entertainment in between courses) were provided.⁹⁹ Notably, *Speculum vitae* observes when detailing the third branch – eating too quickly – that all food in itself is good. What in fact defines the valence of food is the attitude of the consumer: 'alle maner of mete þat es mans fode / Es gode to þam þat er gode', and particularly, to those who eat with measure and the 'saus' [sauce] of the Dread of God.¹⁰⁰ The remedy prescribed to treat the sin of eating too quickly thus extends even further the literal and metaphorical connections of eating and knowing that the *Speculum vitae* exposition of the *Pater noster* has to this point begun to draw out: this remedy involves thinking about spiritual food while eating – that is, a form of dousing one's real dinner with a metaphorical sauce. The potential efficacy of this remedy is grounded in comparison with the monastic practice of reading at table:

> And by þat mete þat filles right,
> Men suld think, bathe day and nyght,
> Þe swetenes of Godde so gode to fele
> And þe fode þat filles þe hert wele.
> And þarefore men vses of custom
> þis manere thurgh alle Crystendom
> In houses of religyoun
> To rede at þe mete a lessoun.
> Wharefore when þe body þat tyde
> Receyues þe fode on þe ta syde,
> Þe hert on þe tothir syde may fele
> Þe fode þat to it sauours wele.¹⁰¹

Firstly, then, real eating – the movement of the muscles and the mouth's parts, the taste and feel of food – provides a running commentary on, a gloss for, spiritual food: here, not only does real eating work in parallel with knowing, real food also serves to underscore how sweet God's goodness tastes in comparison. Secondly, *Speculum vitae* uses the monastic practice of reading while eating as an example of how to foster good eaterly attitudes: at the same time as the body is fed, so too does the heart receive nourishment, keeping appetite in check. There is evidence from this period that some lay households, such as that of Cicely, Duchess of York (d. 1495), imitated this practice.[102] Margery Kempe (bourgeois rather than noble) makes communal dining the site for 'rehearsing' and expounding – that is, recalling and retelling, but also a meditative form of regurgitation – in *The Book of Margery Kempe*: 'as this creatur sat at mete wyth hir felawshep', we are told for example, 'sche rehersyd a text of a Gospel lych as sche had leryd befortyme wyth other goode wordys'.[103] Another Middle English translation of *Somme le roi*, *Book for a Simple and Devout Woman*, at this juncture in the instruction, provides two salient examples: that of the figure of Toby (or Tobias), the exemplary secular lord of the apocryphal Book of Tobit, and the example of a holy man named Isidore taken from *Vitae Patrum*. Toby, who was widely held up as a model for sharing his food with the poor, sighs with sorrow when he must eat to 'susteyne his kynde'; and Isidore, holding in mind the fact that man was made to eat 'heuenlie fode' in Paradise with God, weeps when he eats earthly food, because it reminds him of the 'seruage' [servitude] in which man lives in this world.[104] The slippage between the literal and the metaphorical, common to medieval discussions of the mouth, is here reconfigured as both the literal and metaphorical are held simultaneously in parallel. In this case, it is the subject matter of thought that should be used to gloss the everyday act of eating and imbue it with spiritual meaning. Eating itself becomes a site of learning, where lessons for doing well, and examples of doing badly, in the world are called to mind.[105]

In Middle English *pastoralia*, then, the everyday practice of dining – a usually communal activity – becomes a particular site for thinking about the interrelation of eating and speaking, eating and reading, and eating and thinking.[106] In *Piers Plowman* the dining table, drawing upon this pastoral tradition, becomes the scene for a sustained exploration of the ethics of knowledge, and in particular, the relationship of knowledge to salvation and to doing well, doing better and doing best. Here the pastoral critique of the 'trewfles', 'fables' and 'entremees' that too often accompany eating in the hall, instead of the reading of Scripture, moral talk or the sharing of food with the hungry, becomes the means for testing to its limits the real and metaphorical connections of eating with knowing.

Scholarship on *Piers Plowman* has thoroughly established the ways in which food and eating are both a means of knowing in a 'kyndely' way and a part of natural bodily need that ultimately prompt the dreamer to 'natural moral effort'.[107] Jill Mann's work emphasises the concrete as well as the metaphorical meanings of food; James Simpson writes of the poem that the divine word *is* man's food and literally sustains the body.[108] Words are reified and food has not just spiritual but also material value. Mann thus explains how Wrath, who makes 'wortes' (herbs or vegetables) out of 'wordes' (B.v.160), introduces 'the idea of eating words' in *Piers Plowman*.[109] Importantly, Mann demonstrates Langland's familiarity with the scholarly technique of *ruminatio* outlined by Leclercq, but she also argues that Langland's use of texts that conflate bread with words is a kind of 'hidden structure' in the poem.[110] As a result, the poem's invocations of food and eating commonly slip from the literal into the figural, the material into the spiritual and back again.

In Passus x, the dreamer meets Dame Studie, the wife of Wit, who had taught him in the previous passus something about the nature of his 'kynde' – about his body and soul, and the consequences of misruling one's wits and making a god of one's belly.[111] Beginning by berating Wit for teaching the dreamer, Dame Studie continues the poem's exploration of knowledge, concerning variously: its misuse; the limits of both 'clergie' and of 'kynde' and of learning through looking; the relation of knowing to doing; and the problematic relation of learning to salvation.[112] In taking up the baton, Dame Studie offers a particular critique of the economy of the hall, where the word of God is little valued and food is not shared but wasted, and also of 'table talk', where the wisdom and privy knowledge of God are meddled with.[113] Thus Dame Studie laments to the dreamer that:

> 'Harlotes for hir harlotrie may have of hir goodes,
> And japeris and jogelours and jangleris of gestes;
> Ac he that hath Holy Writ ay in his mouthe
> And kan telle of Tobye and of the twelve Apostles
> Or prechen of the penaunce that Pilat wroghte
> To Jesu the gentile, that Jewes todrowe –
> Litel is he loved or lete by that swich a lesson sheweth,
> Or daunted [flattered] or drawe forth [advanced] – I do it on God
>   hymselve!
>   But thoo that feynen hem foolis and with faityng [fraud]
>   libbeth [live]
> Ayein the lawe of Oure Lord, and lyen on hemselve,
> Spitten and spuen and speke foule wordes,
> Drynken and drevelen and do men for to gape.' (B.x.30–41)

'Harlotes' (professional entertainers), 'japeris' (jesters), 'jogelours' (minstrels) and 'jangleris' (storytellers) – those in-hall entertainers – receive reward, while those who speak of 'Tobye' and his table ethics, of the apostles or of Christ's Passion, go unvalued.[114] Dame Studie's evocation of the man with Holy Writ 'ay in his mouthe' exemplifies the ethical epistemological model provided by the mouth. In contrast with this, Dame Studie also offers a counter-model of those 'eating badly', who spit, vomit and dribble words-as-food out of the body: such men 'Spitten and spuen and speke foule words, / Drynken and drevelen [slobber, vomit] and do men for to gape' (x.40–1). Not only do they waste food; worse is the effect their unregulated speaking-as-eating has on others: they 'do men for to gape'. That is, they make others talk loudly or jeer (*MED*, s.v.), or perhaps to mirror their own lack of governance by causing the mouths of others to fall wide open in credulous belief. Moreover, while 'atte mete', when the minstrels are quiet, there are both learned and 'lewed' men who 'carpen of [talk, but also to find fault with] Crist':

> 'Thanne telleth thei of the Trinite how two slowe [killed] the thridde.
> And bryngen forth a balled reson [crafty argument], taken Bernard
>   to witnesse,
> And puten forth presumpcion to preve the sothe.
> Thus thei dryvele at hir deys the deitee to knowe,
> And gnawen God with the gorge whanne hir guttes fullen.' (B.x.53–7)

Just as those who speak of 'harlotrie', tell jokes or dirty stories, spill and waste words, those who 'carp' presumptuously and erroneously at the dinner table about the nature of the Trinity gnaw on God 'with the gorge' [*MED*, s.v. 'gullet, esophagus, throat'], having already stuffed full their guts. So too, Dame Studie continues, has she heard noblemen 'etynge at the table / Carpen as thei clerkes were of Crist and of hise myghtes' (B.x.103–4), finding fault with God (as Aristotle does in the *Pilgrimage* on the nature of the Eucharist) and leading other men into wrong belief by questioning why 'Oure Saveour' would 'suffre swich a worm [Satan] in his blisse [Paradise]' (B.x.107). In a far cry from the model proffered by *Speculum vitae*, the dining table in Passus x becomes the scene where ribald tales gloss the eating of food (imbuing it with only profane meanings). The talk is of things that clog up the throat and the stomach, rather than nourish the soul, both interfering in God's knowledge and making a mockery of it, and causing the physical conditions for indigestion.[115]

Passus XIII offers a variation on the theme of this travesty of dining-hall ethics. Here Conscience invites the dreamer to a feast with Clergie, at which a representative of a different (non-allegorical) kind of clergy, a doctor of divinity, is in attendance. The dreamer sits down with Patience at a side table, where they are served the 'sondry metes' (B.XIII.38) of Scripture – the four evangelists, the church fathers – and then the sour loaf of penance, as well as other penitential dishes composed of scriptural quotation. In contrast with the metaphorical food consumed by the dreamer – which, notably, is claimed to nonetheless sustain both soul *and* body – the doctor, seated on the dais, eats real food. Not just any food, however, but those costly, fine sorts implicated in the fourth and fifth branches of the sin of gluttony: thus the doctor eats 'mete of moore cost, mortrews [stews] and potages [soups]' (B.XIII.41). These are accompanied, not with the 'saus of dred', but with the bitter sauce of '*Post mortem*' (B.XIII.43–4). Unbeknownst to him, it would seem, as the doctor consumes real food he also ingests potentially eternal consequences.

All the while, hovering at the edges of these table scenes in Passus x and XIII, are the distressed and the hungry who go without food: God may well be in the nobleman's gorge, Dame Studie observes, but he is not in his works.[116] And as the fine foods consumed by the doctor accumulate, the dreamer grows increasingly angry at his own humble, textual dishes. The dreamer's anger, however, stems not just from the discrepancy in the kind of food they are each given to eat, but from the mismatch between the doctor's words and his works. Despite what the dreamer has heard the doctor preach at St Paul's, 'this Goddes gloton', he observes, 'with his grete chekes, / Hath no pite on us povere' (B.XIII.78–9). The dreamer's critique here continues both to perform the slippage between the literal and the figural, and to hold them in parallel: the doctor's eating habits have a real effect on the poor. But so too does the gloss on the doctor's words provided by his real eating expose a gap: for all his learning and for all his fine words, this doctor has failed to assimilate knowledge-as-food and to 'do' thereafter.

Following the logic provided by the natural example of the body, in which food taken into it must be transformed into the materials of flesh and bone and, in turn, the strength to perform work, knowledge must likewise be assimilated and acted out ethically. Certain modes of acquiring knowledge or attitudes towards it, however, make knowledge indigestible. In Passus xv, it is precisely the potential indigestibility of knowledge that Anima explains to the dreamer through the image of honey: 'The man that muche hony eet, his mawe it engleymeth, / And the moore that a man of good matere hereth, / But he do therafter it dooth hym double scathe' (B.XV.57–9). Honey is sweet, sapiential knowledge.[117] But too much honey makes the 'mawe' (possibly the mouth and throat, but here, finally, the stomach) viscous, and also, in this case, causes constipation, just as the man is paradoxically harmed by good knowledge unless he 'do therafter'. Likewise, those Christians in *Speculum vitae* who know God 'by the book', do not 'fele' him in the heart because their taste is 'englaymed' through sin and so they cannot discern the sapiential sweetness of God. Knowledge beyond need, like the food that is essentially good but is consumed preternaturally, brings sickness and suffering to the body. It is precisely this kind of dinner-table scene – of eating and seeking knowledge beyond need – that drives Dame Studie, citing the Augustinian maxim 'Non plus sapere quam oportet', to wish for the sensory confusion of these overeaters and over-reachers (B.x.117–30): but the consequence of even this kind of indigestible table talk can, within Langland's logic, potentially work its own reform.

The figure of Patience, thus stalling the dreamer's outburst of anger at the doctor with a wink and advising – appropriately – patience, observes: ' "Thou shalt see thus soone, whan he [the doctor] may na moore [i.e. eat no more], / He shal have a penaunce in his paunche and puffe [pant] at ech a worde, / And thane shullen his guttes gothele [rumble], and he shal galpen [gape] after" ' (B.xiii.87–9). Short of breath, mouth gaping wide, the doctor will feel the consequences of his consumption of fine, costly foods in his mouth, and what is left of his capacity to speak will ultimately be relocated to his guts. The doctor will suffer in the ways that echo the description of the glutton's painful condition in *Book for a Simple and Devout Woman*: 'His roppus [guts] schulleþ gurle [rumble] wiþynne, his wombe swelleþ wiþoute as a bladdere, and schal grone wiþ suche sores as he traueiled of a childe.'[118] In the doctor's case we do not find out whether such a 'penaunce in his paunche' will lead to reform, but the physical suffering he experiences as a result of overeating – like Gloton's at the tavern threshold – contains the possibility for it.

The monastic habit of reading while eating is taken up in vernacular theology to delineate an ideal mode of eating, where real eating (the movement of the muscles, the stimulation of taste) provides a commentary on spiritual food (God tastes sweeter). At the same time, the spiritual nourishment of reading keeps appetite in check and, in turn, glosses the mundane act of eating with spiritual value. In *Piers Plowman*, Langland's dinner-table scenes expose instead the fissures between social practice and the monastic ideal. Where literal eating works in parallel with figurative eating in the halls of Toby and Isidore, in *Piers Plowman* it exposes social cracks and hermeneutic fissures. In Passus x, the table is a scene, not for the reading of Scripture, but of 'lewed', transgressive arguments about biblical history and Trinitarian theology. Ribald tales accompany eating, and so gloss real food with profane meanings. Knowledge becomes not only indigestible but a source of social injustice as the poor go hungry. In Passus XIII, the doctor of divinity's eating habits emphasise the poem's central concern with the extension of the material into the spiritual. Preaching one thing with his mouth and doing another, the doctor abuses knowledge. Failing to eat real food with the metaphorical sauce of the fear of God, he eats '*post mortem*' unawares instead. The scene of the dinner table thus reframes the sapiential and ruminative connections of food and knowledge in the poem: more than a model for knowledge acquisition, it is a social relation, about sharing both food and knowledge with the hungry and poor.

Langland's preoccupation with food and knowledge goes beyond, and destabilises, the pastoral project of *Speculum vitae*, in which monastic habits are packaged for vernacular readers. Yet an important principle emerges across pastoral and reformist objectives. A properly governed mouth is central to *sapientia*, as *Speculum vitae* instructs; so too is it at the heart of Langland's social ethics. This chapter finally turns to Langland's meditations on the foundational events of Christian history – the Fall and the Incarnation – and finds that the mouth is at the heart of these too.

Paradise Lost/Regained

Earlier in the poem in Passus XI, prior to attending the feast of Conscience, the dreamer himself falls prey – though through different means – to precisely the kinds of intellectual interfering that those noblemen talking at the dinner table do, who wonder why God would have tolerated Satan's presence in Paradise.[119] At first sight, at this point in the poem, we seem to have moved away from the model of food as knowledge and from a mouth-centric model of epistemology. As the passus unfolds, however, such distinctions collapse. Kynde appears to the dreamer and shows him the wonders of the world, ostensibly modelling the sort of knowledge that can be learned through sight, that is, through observing nature. However, what the dreamer learns is in fact a lesson about the ethics of measure (that virtue which comes as a result of *sapientia*), and of the mouth and the genitals (that lower bodily spectrum with which the mouth is deeply implicated): 'Reson I seigh soothly sewen [follows] alle beestes / In etynge, in drynkynge and in engendrynge of kynde' (B.XI.334–5). This 'sight' provokes the dreamer to question: if reason guides and governs eating, drinking and reproduction in animals, why does it not likewise rule man's mouth and, inextricably, his genitals (B.XIII.368–72)? Reaching thus too high in his quest for knowledge, the dreamer is rebuked by Reson and afterward taught about patient suffering by Ymaginatif.[120] Ymaginatif explains that Reson would have furthered the dreamer's quest for understanding had he but kept his mouth closed:

> 'Ac for thyn entremetynge here artow forsake:
> *Philosophus esses, si tacuisses.*
>   Adam, the whiles he spak noght, hadde paradis at wille;
>   Ac whan he mamelede aboute mete and entremeted to knowe
> The wisedom and the wit of God, he was put fram blisse.' (XI.414–17)

The *MED* glosses 'entremeten' as 'to meddle or interfere (with matters which do not concern one)'. Tellingly, however, this verb is also cognate with those 'entremees' – delicacies or forms of entertainment – provided between courses at feasts. If the dreamer had 'held his peace', as the Latin quotation comments, he would have been a philosopher.

More striking, however, is the parallel Ymaginatif forges between the dreamer's meddlesome question and Adam's *felix culpa*. Whilst Adam did not speak, he possessed Paradise; he lost it at that moment 'whan he mamelede aboute mete and entremeted to knowe / The wisedom and the wit of God'. 'Mamelede' means 'mumble', 'grumble and complain', 'babble' (suggestive of childish, badly formed speech), but the *MED* also suggests tentatively '? to speak with one's mouth full'. Forging a connection between food and knowledge that recurs throughout *Piers Plowman*, Adam's desire for knowledge beyond need, materialised in the act of eating the apple, is figured in terms of *speaking* about 'mete'. Langland thus emphasises that words are both material (speaking words 'eats' the apple) and spiritual (the apple *is* knowledge or contains the desire to know).[121] Thus in this rewriting of the Genesis narrative, eating becomes a (transgressive) speech act: Adam speaks with his mouth full; eating *is* speaking.

Both actions are facilitated by Adam's teeth. Langland thus relates how Wrong 'egged [Adam and Eve] to ille' (B.I.65); Satan likewise recalls how Lucifer 'in semblaunce of a serpent sete on the appultre, / And eggedest hem to ete' (B.XVIII.287–8). 'Eggen' means to urge, incite, but also set one's teeth on edge (*MED*, s.v.). *Cursor mundi* makes this connection between 'eggen', teeth and Adam's sin even more explicit: 'For of þat ilk appel bitt / þair suns tethe ar eggeid yitt': because of the bite of that apple, their sons' teeth are yet set on edge.[122] Adam and Eve are stirred to sin through sharpening the appetite of their teeth. Mann notes that Passus V's specific reference to Adam and Eve eating 'vnrosted apples' makes them 'real apples to us'.[123]

Reified eating, driven by the senses of the mouth (appetite, taste), is the first sin. But clearly, Adam and Eve need to use their teeth to bite and chew these hard, unroasted apples. Indeed, it is because Adam 'freet of [chewed] that fruyt' (B.XVIII.195) that Righteousness (following Isidore's logic in the *Etymologiae*) condemns Adam and Eve to 'chewe as thei chosen ... / For it is botelees bale, the byte that thei eten' (B.XVIII.200–1). Since Adam devoured the apple greedily (*MED*, s.v. 'freten') and gnawed it with his teeth, he and Eve must 'chewe' what they have chosen: the bite of death.[124] Following this logic, if sin comes through a bite, so too does its remedy: if the mouth is the cause of the Fall, so too does it bring about the Incarnation.

God is immaterial. He does not have a mouth, teeth, tongue or lips.[125] The incarnate Christ, however, does have a mouth; indeed he *is* a mouth. The synonymy of mouth with flesh occurs in *Legenda aurea*'s exegesis of the Holy Spirit: the Holy Spirit, so Jacobus de Voragine records, is the breath of our mouth, 'since our mouth is Christ the Lord because he is our mouth and flesh'.[126] In effect, the mouth signifies flesh, matter, embodiment and Christ. In turn, Christ stands simultaneously as a sign of humanity and of the body, but also of the Word. Christ's ability to *be* Word is, from this perspective, entirely dependent on his being bodied and on having a mouth. Likewise, *On the Properties of Things* records among the names for the second person of the Trinity, Christ 'hatte "mowþ" for by hym God spekeþ to þe world' (I, 57). It is the notion of Christ as Mouth that underpins Langland's explanation of what motivates the Incarnation.

In Passus I, in response to the dreamer's question about where he can find Treuthe, Holy Church, calling him a 'doted daffe' (a silly fool), tells him it is a 'kynde knowynge' in his heart, which instructs him in the First Commandment, to love God more than himself and to refrain from sin. Urging the dreamer to live out this commandment, Holy Church shows how Treuthe, who has become identical at this point with love, exemplifies his own compliance with this command through the Incarnation: the works of Christ (who is truth and love) are motivated by love. As Schmidt explains, 'by loving God we obtain direct "natural" knowledge of him, but only because God has revealed himself to man'.[127] Such knowledge is revealed through the material, through Christ's taking on of the element earth. Holy Church's aetiology therefore begins to reframe Christ's motivating love in terms of the natural inclination of the body for food:[128]

> For hevene myghte nat holden it, so was it hevy of hymselve,
> Til it hadde of the erthe eten his fille.
> And whan it hadde of this fold flessh and blood taken,
> Was nevere leef upon lynde lighter therafter. (B.I.153–6)

Made heavy by the weight of flesh, it is Christ's appetite that draws him earthward: he becomes all mouth – a sense that is emphasised by the self-reflexiveness of this image; 'it' was heavy of 'hymselve', and 'it' had eaten 'his' fill.[129] 'Whan it hadde of this folde flesh and blood taken' refers on one level to Christ becoming incarnate, but on another to the nature of Christ's 'food'; he eats (mutable, decaying) flesh, the fruit that Piers strives to protect (Adam is an apple) from the devil. In Passus XVIII, Feith describes Christ's 'joust' after which he will 'walke / And fecche fro the fend Piers fruyt the Plowman, / And legge it ther hym liketh, and Lucifer bynde, / And forbite and adoun brynge bale-deeth for evere' (32–5). 'Forbite' means to 'bite deeply or repeatedly', 'to eat up, devour', 'to utterly destroy' (MED, s.v.). In visual representations and dramatic stagings of Christ's Harrowing of Hell, the entrance to hell itself is often figured as a mouth; readers of *Piers Plowman* would thus perhaps imagine Christ walking through a mouth to fetch Piers's 'fruit' and devour death. Writing on the N-Town 'Harrowing of Hell', Sarah Elliott Novacich observes that Christ's exit through hellmouth on stage along with Adam and Eve itself recalls the transgression of the human mouth in original sin: 'Recapitulated history, carefully ordered and supervised by the redeemer, spills out of the mouth to start once again with its remembered beginning.'[130] The mouth thus frames the history of man's sinful beginnings, his punishment and his rescue. Following the logic of Christ as the second Adam, if death comes through a bite so too must life. In the Incarnation Christ becomes a mouth and works redemption with his teeth – he wounds and breaks (sin, death, flesh, mankind) in his mouth in order to incorporate them into his own body and thereby remake them in his own perfect image.[131]

The coincidence of food and knowledge in *Piers Plowman* thus reveals something about Langland's understanding of the very structure of what it means to be human. The lesson Kynde teaches the dreamer through observing the temperate lives of animals is the difficulty with which man governs his mouth and his genitals. Ymaginatif, in turn, concatenating the dreamer's own 'entermeting' with Adam and Eve's, and with the 'lewed' noblemen at dinner, discloses that the mouth is at the very origin of the human disposition to sin. Ethical life begins with governance of the mouth. In the Incarnation Christ – in becoming 'kynde' – also becomes a mouth. The mouth's natural properties – what and how we learn through it, the appetite to taste and to know mediated by it – provides a natural commentary on what it means to be human, and so also for how it is that Christ was made man.

Within a clerical milieu, the tradition of *sapientia*, the reading practices of *meditatio* and *ruminatio* and the habit of reading while eating all derive their affective, ethical, cognitive and spiritual value from thinking through the particular properties of the mouth and the sense of taste. These epistemological modes suggest that we learn from the natural example of the mouth (the kind of eating that leads to good digestion models an ethical mode of knowing). They also disclose that what we learn through physical taste and touch is the foundation of all learning (there is a literal connection between eating and work, but also we learn in conjunction with the movements and sensory experiences of our bodies and our mouths). What we learn through the mouth is therefore not only useful for everyday knowledge about the food and the earth, but it is also implicated, in multiform ways, in cognition and reason. We learn spiritual truths (the sweetness of God), for example, through the gloss provided by physical tastes. But so too is the ethical and spiritual value of physical eating a product of a cognitive *habitus* (the value of what we eat is shaped by the content of thought or the words in our mouth as we eat it). These pastoral understandings of the ethical and spiritual good (as well as bad) of the mouth are profoundly shaped by 'natural' descriptions of the physiological conditions of different lifecycle stages, and of the relationship of practices of bodily care to moral dispositions and intellectual capacity. In the context of the everyday body, attentive care of the mouth in childhood and the fostering of dinner-table ethics into adulthood are at the core of fashioning bodies that can be saved.

These epistemological modes derived from the mouth are powerful instruments in vernacular theology – in cultivating an ethical relationship between eating and knowledge, and in delineating the interpenetration of the material and the spiritual. The potential for eating knowledge to become transgressive, however, especially in the mouths of the unlearned, means that works such as *Speculum vitae* carefully circumscribe eating as a model, directing the work of mastication towards an affective gleaning of the Passion of Christ rather than chewing over the difficult problems of the nature of the Eucharist. In its vernacular forms, the (ideal) practice of reading at the dinner table recuperates the everyday act of eating as a scene for moral lessons and spiritual learning. Drawing on this pastoral tradition, Langland demonstrates a deep valuation of the mouth's epistemological modes in *Piers Plowman* – they form the very structure of his poem and of his understanding of what it means to be human – at the same time as he understands the mouth to be prototypically ambivalent. *Piers Plowman* continually probes the mouth's faultlines: man's habitual lack of governance over his mouth that is at the root of original sin; the social crisis of both food and knowledge revealed in the gap between what people say and what and how people eat; the limits of textual food in satiating physical hunger. However, even in its excessive aspects, the mouth remains a potential source of good. Knowledge begins in the mouth – for the newly born child, as for Adam – but it is also ultimately completed in it: in the body as it is transformed into labour and action, in the sapiential model that governs eating and glosses it with spiritual meaning, and in the salvific work of Christ who eats in order to incorporate man into himself. Eating as the scene for learning demonstrates the profoundly ethical slippage of the mouth – between inside and outside, the material and the figural, but also between earth and heaven.

CHAPTER 4

The Epistemology of Kissing

Kissing punctuates Christian ritual and worship – from kissing the pax as part of the liturgy of the Mass to touching and kissing devotional objects and books.[1] The kiss is thus a marker of the affective, embodied register of medieval piety, as well as a social gesture or a sign in the social and political body.[2] As a material act, kissing always already extends beyond the body and its boundaries, and thus moves quickly into the realm of the symbolic. More than ritual symbol or expression of worship, however, to kiss a sacred object also often carried the hope of deriving some spiritual benefit from it – the indulgences gained through kissing an image of the wound of Christ, for example, or the healing effected through kissing a shrine or a relic.[3] Devotional practices therefore imbue the kiss, as a form of touch, with transformative possibilities.

To some extent, the potentially supernatural effects of kissing lie outside natural explanation and participate in more popular beliefs about the power of touch, but medieval thinking, as we have seen, does not make the natural and supernatural mutually exclusive categories.[4] Indeed, the potential for change through touch inheres in natural philosophical descriptions of sensory physiology. Touch and taste have a deeper connection with the heart than other sensory perceptions; so too do they have a particular capacity to produce pleasure and pain and to effect material change. The kiss thus takes on something of the natural powers of taste and touch to penetrate and to alter the body. However, part of the power of touch as it is realised in a kiss (as opposed, say, to touching with the hand) also derives from the natural properties of the mouth: its situation at the threshold of the human; its role as an instrument of respiration and as the organ of both eating and speaking. Breath and breathing are not just associated physiologically with the mouth; they are also associated with the nose and so with the sense of smell, a sense that when rightly ordered aids discernment, but when disordered becomes a vehicle of contagion.

Within a materially inflected understanding of words and speech, the kiss is a form of language in the world, expressing interior intention and thought. As an intensely charged stage for multisensory encounters, the kiss as a taste is analogous to eating; the kiss as breath might literally be infectious. Still further, and in distinction from any other bodily sense, organ or act, the kiss performs spiritual exchange in mingling saliva and breath – the material *spiritus* that mediates between and binds together body and soul, and that, in some accounts, carries something of the very core of the individual soul within it.[5] In this way, the kiss in the late medieval period belongs to the categories of the natural and the social, but it extends into the spiritual.

Kissing, then, does things to and between bodies; it is an act in the world that cannot be detached from its internal process and physical effect. This chapter establishes the 'kynde' properties of the kiss as they are forged in the intersections of learned, Latinate traditions and popular Middle English learning. It does so in order to show that a sciential understanding – of the operation of taste and touch, of the mouth's physiological action on air drawn in as breath, and on food and drink through saliva – forms part of the pastoral concern with, and the poetic power of, the kiss. This 'kynde' context of the kiss directs us to the place of the mouth within the physiological and sensory structures of desire: kissing arises from the superfluities of food and drink; it materialises and manifests affective and cognitive states. So too do the mouth's natural properties sensitise the kiss as a locus not just for physical, but also for spiritual, change and interchange – between bodies and also between realms.

This chapter first outlines the patristic tradition of the kiss before turning to twelfth-century discussions such as those of Bernard of Clairvaux and Aelred of Rievaulx. In the commentaries of the early church fathers on biblical examples, two natural analogies are taken up to gloss the spiritual significance of the kiss: firstly, that we kiss with our lips makes it analogous to speech, which is also formed on the lips. Secondly, since the mouth is the point at which breath is drawn in and exhaled, kissing is figured as partaking in respiration. Drawing on these analogies, patristic and monastic considerations of the kiss foreground its spiritual nature – as a sign of unity (the kiss externalises interior affection), of the Holy Spirit (as a form of breath), but also, most strikingly, as a figure for both the desire for Christ (as a touch, direct contact) and Christ himself (as a liminal point of exchange between the material and the spiritual). Twelfth-century discussions take up these patristic understandings, but they also expand further upon the psychophysical aspects of kissing. In *De spirituali amicitia*, for example, Aelred situates the kiss in the context of the natural functions of the body: breathing and eating. In kissing mouth to mouth, Aelred suggests, breath is exchanged, effecting a form of spiritual union between those who kiss. As a gloss for spiritual friendship, the kiss is a symbol of an intellectual union (a form of likemindedness), but its metaphorical energy draws on the literal exchange the kiss performs.

It is this disposition to view the kiss within the context of the mouth's natural functions that the rise of encyclopaedias, which detail the tripartite soul and its imbrication in the body, fosters in the thirteenth century. In this context, the natural properties of the kiss are deeply rooted in the soul system of the heart, which is responsible for spiritual (i.e. respiratory) functions, but also the processing of sensory perceptions. In physiological terms, as this chapter outlines, taste and touch hold the greatest potential to transform the body and thereby the soul. So too do they introduce temporal alterity in the body – felt experiences of pleasure and pain are caught up and delayed – in the material of the body; the likenesses they imprint in the body leave their traces for longer and continue to act at a distance. As the medium between the sense of taste and the thing tasted, saliva itself is altered – continually with every new mouthful – into the quality of that which has been tasted. Breath is implicated in a system whereby air is drawn in from outside the body and altered and purified in the mouth before it is sent to the heart. Saliva and breath therefore both show that the mouth instantiates a pattern of reciprocal exchange – spiritual and physical – between bodies.

Sharing in these natural properties, the kiss is on a continuum with, at the same time that it goes beyond or is in some ways superfluous to, the physiological functions of sensing, eating, drinking and (in the dreamer's words in *Piers Plowman*) 'engendrynge of kynde' (B.XI.335). Techniques of the care of the self, including regimen and diet, in part give rise to it; pastoral care seeks to regulate it. It is these shared pastoral and medicalised understandings of the kiss, to which the second part of the chapter turns, which profoundly shape Langland's figuring of Haukyn in *Piers Plowman*. In an extended close reading, I argue that Haukyn's kiss cannot be divorced from its wider multisensory milieu, operating in a structure – detailed in Middle English *pastoralia* – that begins in sight and ends in touch. Haukyn's confession as it unfolds across Passus XIII–XIV reveals his literalising mode of reading the world, at the heart of which is a sensory pathology. All his sensory faculties are directed towards his body and the earth. The passus therefore sets out to re-educate Haukyn about his senses, about the relationship of body and (tripartite) soul and about the relationship of the material to the spiritual. In this context, Haukyn's kiss is shown to be embedded in the vegetable and sensible faculties of the soul. Situated thus in the spectrum of 'kynde' in the poem, Haukyn's kiss is a 'taste' – arising from the surplus of natural bodily need and a debased mode of experiencing and learning in the world – that exposes the problem of misdirected ends. In other words, Haukyn's kiss teaches us about the very core of what it means to be human; about the structures of human desire; the place of the mouth within it; and the need for knowledge about the body, the body interior and the soul in the care of the self.

In addition to this 'kynde' understanding of the kiss, Middle English *pastoralia* also testifies to osculatory consequences that lie outside natural explanations, but are, instead, a result of divine or diabolic intervention. In these contexts, the kiss functions to give witness to a supernatural encounter, or to materialise the hidden interior. Even here, however, the kiss is not abstracted from interior physiology – from the sensory properties of taste and touch, the inner processes that produce speech and the naturally transformative powers inhering in saliva and breath. The kiss therefore functions as a natural form of gloss on spiritual status or sin. The example *par excellence* is Judas's kiss of betrayal. This chapter finally explores the accounts of Judas's kiss in the *Festial*, *The Gilte Legende*, *Dives and Pauper* and other vernacular pastoral works. Christ's kiss, continuing to act at a distance, alters the very substance of Judas's own mouth through touch. However, the effects of the kiss – Judas's soul is drawn out through his stomach – further expose Judas's dissemblance and internal dysfunction. As the 'lewed' questions voiced in *Dives and Pauper* about why Judas's soul did not leave his body through his mouth show, Judas's disintegrating body is understood to provide a natural form of commentary on his sin. The lessons it teaches are twofold: the power of the kiss as a touch; and the problem of the kiss as a sign. Mirk's *Festial* provides a further example of the power of the kiss to unmake the self in a *narracio* about an adulterous man. Heightened by the understanding of the mouth as a threshold – indeed, of hell itself as a mouth – the pastoral warnings that lecherous kisses lead to hell are literalised in the *Festial narracio*, revealing the kiss to be multidirectional: a kiss can extend into the realm of the spiritual as well as out into the world or back down into the body. In so doing, the kiss exposes and abstracts the mouth's core function in the body: the making and unmaking of both human and Christian identity.

Spiritual Kisses

The early church fathers found particular scriptural resources for thinking about the kiss in the Old Testament Song of Songs, in the New Testament account of Judas's kiss of betrayal and in St Paul's injunctions concerning the kiss of peace. While the church fathers strongly figure the kiss as a sign, the kiss nonetheless remains a physical, embodied action informed by an understanding of the mouth's place in the body: in their discussions, they very often situate the kiss within broader reflections on the mouth and its offices, in particular on the role of the lips and the mouth in materialising the interior thoughts and intentions of the heart and mind. John Chrysostom, for example, explains the human impulse to kiss by analogy with the human capacity to speak: the mouth 'is the organ which most effectively declares the working of the soul', thus we hurry to kiss each other after an absence, and greet one another with a kiss.[6] Ambrose praises the mouth – as an instrument of speech, but more so, as Nicolas Perella notes, 'as the organ for the kiss by which man gives expression to peace and love'.[7] Most influentially for Middle English *pastoralia*, Augustine (for example, when reflecting on the kiss of peace) aligns kissing with speaking in understanding the kiss as one of the mouth's means of making exterior what is interior and of expressing intentions, affections and thoughts.[8] Thus he understands Judas's kiss of betrayal (again in Perella's words) as a 'prototype of a lack of correspondence between the lips and the heart'.[9]

The kiss, then, borders on the interior and the exterior and takes place between the spiritual and the material. It is thus also understood to symbolise the divine mystery of the fusion of God with the human soul, of the spirit with the flesh. In commentaries on the Song of Songs, for example, the trope of Christ as Mouth is transformed into one of Christ as Kiss. The kiss itself is glossed, by early commentators such as Origen of Alexandria and Gregory of Nyssa, as the Word, but also as the desire for Christ's (corporeal) presence.[10] Medieval commentators similarly take up the kiss to figure the transformative effects of the Incarnation, of the joining of flesh with spirit, man with God. Honorius of Autun (1080–1154), glossing Song of Songs 1:2–4 ('Let him kiss with me with the kisses of his mouth'), writes, for example: 'let him who has promised become incarnate now after all this time and kiss me with his presence'. Honorius further characterises the kiss as the Word of the Father (i.e. the Son), since: 'by a kiss flesh is joined to flesh, and spirit companions spirit; and thus Christ is joined to the Church by way of the flesh, and the Church is associated with his divinity through the Spirit'.[11] Bernard of Clairvaux

(1090–1153), in his *Sermones super cantica canticorum*, writes on the same passage: 'Let the mouth that kisses signify the Word who takes on [human nature]. And the mouth that is kissed, the flesh that is taken on.'[12] Bernard thus interprets the kiss variously as the Incarnation (the kiss unites the divine and the human) and as the request of the soul (as the betrothed) for a kiss (the Holy Spirit) from the Word (Christ).[13] In this context, the kiss expresses both a desire to receive the Holy Spirit and a longing for the real, corporeal presence of God. Even when a symbol, the kiss is pointedly material, signifying the Word made flesh and the body.

From the twelfth century on, this spiritual value of the kiss in the Latin West is derived in part from renewed thinking about the natural and about the relationship between body and soul. As Arjo Vanderjagt remarks, as an act that limns the physical and the spiritual, the kiss becomes 'the focal point [in twelfth-century Latinity] of discussions on the relation between body and soul by the actors themselves and also by their modern interpreters'.[14] Similarly, Perella identifies a resurgence of interest in the kiss from the twelfth century as a result of the new availability of 'treatises that seek to explain the complex stirrings and movements of the heart, and the passionate investigation into the psyche of man'.[15] Aelred of Rievaulx's (1109–66) *De spirituali amicitia*, which considers kissing in the context of spiritual friendship, bears the influence of both patristic traditions and the burgeoning interest in nature and natural philosophy facilitated by the transmission of Classical and Arabic learning. Thus Aelred typically deploys the medieval mode of learning through nature or experience: 'let us consider', he writes, 'the propriety of this fleshly kiss, so that we may pass from carnal things to spiritual things, from the human to the divine'.[16] Aelred foregrounds the physiology – or, in Perella's words, the 'scientific realism' – of kissing as a way of thinking about its spiritual effect, and although Aelred makes a distinction between a fleshly kiss (a joining of the lips) and a spiritual one (a joining of minds), this fleshly kiss extends into the spiritual:

> The life of mankind is sustained by two types of nourishment, food and air. Without food a person is able to live for a while, but without air this is not possible for even an hour. So while we live, we take in air through the mouth and exhale it again. What is exhaled and inhaled is called 'breath.' Thus, in one kiss two spirits meet one another, and they are mixed together and so made one. From this mingling of spirits there grows up a kind of mental agreeableness, which elicits and joins together the affection of those who kiss.[17]

Aelred's meditation on kissing digresses to think about the primary acts of the body performed by the mouth that are fundamental and necessary to human life itself. Taking up the discourse of natural philosophy ('the life of mankind is sustained by two types of nourishment'), Aelred places the kiss in the context of gustation and respiration, considering how these functions inform the physiology of kissing. The impossibility of life without breath suggests to Aelred that something quintessentially human – partaking in the nature of the soul – is conveyed in the breath. Aelred believes that kissing mingles breath or spirit, which causes a spiritual change in those who kiss: it stimulates 'mental agreeableness', a kind of likemindedness. Although medieval theologians by and large do not think the reasonable soul *is* breath, but rather believe that breath is a product of the tripartite soul's virtue, the association made by Aelred between the breath and soul commonly resurfaces in religious discourses.[18] What this points to is the recourse by theological thinkers to natural bodily processes, to physiology and to an understanding of the body–soul relationship (as informed by natural philosophy and medicine) in thinking about the effect and meaning of kissing. In other words, kissing, for Aelred, is not merely a sign but a meeting of lips sought out in order for ensouled bodies to act upon each other and bring about a change in the reasonable soul – one which is part of man's spiritual ascent when it is noble, but corrupting when directed towards the wrong ends.[19] While Aelred goes on to describe spiritual and intellectual kisses that do not involve actual contact or joining of lips, it is nonetheless the fleshly kiss that naturally models the kind of exchange – exemplified in the exchange of breath – these figural kisses effect between souls and minds.[20]

The mouth, in the kiss, figuratively becomes the most potent, liminal point of access between selves and between God and man. As a result, in this context, the *spiritual* senses of taste and touch (over and above the spiritual sense of sight) are made the pinnacle of spiritualised contact between bodies. As Perella notes:

> [in this] inversion of the traditional (Platonic) hierarchy of the senses which placed sight above all ... taste and touch are the most exalted. This was a development whose importance was to be second to none in the history of western mysticism. And with the sense of touch the kiss was the supreme expression.[21]

Thus in *The Book of Margery Kempe*, visionary experience provides the stage for the exchange of spiritual kisses between Margery and Christ, marking out her singular intimacy with him: Christ instructs that she '"mayst boldly take me in the armys of thi sowle and kyssen my mowth, myn hed, and my fete"'.[22] But Margery also seeks out material kisses – from those she encounters who remind her of Christ, but most strikingly from the (contagious) lepers she had formerly despised. Warned by her confessor not to seek out kisses from male lepers, Margery goes 'to a place wher seke women dwellyd whech wer ryth ful of the sekenes and fel down on hir kneys beforn hem, preyng hem that sche myth kyssyn her mowth for the lofe of Jhesu'.[23] Proxies through which Margery is able to perform devotion to Christ, these kisses also manifest her sanctity: she is immune to (or untroubled by) the danger kissing lepers poses, since their breath, as the medical tradition outlines, 'stenkiþ and infectiþ oþir'.[24]

In the context of the late medieval valuation of the natural, the kiss's power derives not just from the spiritual senses, or from its capacity to figure and gloss mystical union. As Aelred's consideration of the kiss reminds us: the physical kiss is understood to begin in the body and penetrate to the soul; moreover, it participates in the body's spiritual functions (breath) and its physical sensory processes – as Woolgar points out, kissing was literally understood to be 'a special form of touch'.[25] So too is the kiss a special form of physical taste. The increasing availability of natural knowledge about the mouth in the later medieval period situates the kiss within the spectrum of 'kynde' – a part of the epistemology of the sensing body – but also sensitises it as a threshold site where physical and spiritual transformation takes place. As the next section shows, the understanding of the kiss that is forged in the intersections of learned Latinate traditions and popular Middle English learning draws on the properties of the mouth, and especially its natural capacity – through taste, touch, saliva and breath – to penetrate and to alter the body and the soul.

'Kynde' Kisses

In medieval understandings, as Woolgar observes, 'sensory perception was a much more open process, not just a form of transmission of information about objects, but one which enabled tangible qualities and, indeed, spiritual or intangible qualities to be passed from one party or object to another'.[26] Like all the senses in an Aristotelian model, taste and touch mediate, through their organs, a likeness of the object sensed to the faculty of imagination, where it is impressed on the material of the brain and leaves a physical trace. In contrast with other sense perceptions, however, as Albertus Magnus (following Aristotle) records in *De animalibus*: 'concerning the sense of touch, and taste (insofar as it is a sort of touch), it is clear to see that the heart is the first to feel'.[27] *On the Properties of Things* elaborates, 'taast and gropinge, beþ more in þe herte, and þerfore þey beþ of þe beynge of þe best and demeþ more opunliche of þinges þat he feliþ and knoweþ' (1, 119). This begins to suggest that taste and touch penetrate more deeply into the body interior: the 'open' properties of taste and touch, and their 'felt' encounter with objects, implicate them in a distinct mode of knowing with a particular affinity with the heart–soul system. It is not simply that taste and touch are more felt, however, but that they also bring about more material change. In the *Summa theologiae*, Aquinas makes a distinction between natural and supraphysical change in the body as a result of sensory perception. In the process of vision, he asserts, only supraphysical change occurs: that is, 'the form of the source of change is received in the subject of change supraphysically, the way the form of a colour is in the eye'. In contrast, in touch and taste, in addition to supraphysical change, natural change also occurs: that is, 'the form of the source of change is received into the subject in a physical way, as heat is absorbed by something being heated'. As a result, taste and touch thus 'transcend matter least'.[28] This, of course, provides physiological grounds for ranking taste and touch as the least spiritual of the senses, or as those most in need of guarding. Yet, this potential of taste and touch – to effect material and physical change in the body; to know its objects directly and inwardly; to 'feel' – also grounds its affective, moral and spiritual possibilities. The natural change wrought through sensation (for example, the warmth of the skin after a warm object has touched it) not only has moral implications (for example, the desire to experience the warmth of contact with another body) but also creates supraphysical possibilities: a touch or a taste of something substantially good – a relic of a holy person, a stone or plant endowed with natural virtue – might mediate something of those sacred or health-giving qualities into the body. Woolgar thus summarises: 'Virtues and holiness might also make a considerable impact through touch or general proximity: this was one of the most common ways by which moral or intangible qualities might pass between beings or to and from objects.'[29]

On the Properties of Things continues to explain more particularly that the organs of touch 'holdiþ þe more strongliche þe impressiouns and prentinges of þingis þat plesiþ oþir greueþ' (1, 120). Touch (and taste as a kind of touch) especially mediates and registers pleasure and pain. Moreover, the heart, the nerve-filled flesh and skin, the mouth – those instruments of touch – hold the likeness of things *more strongly* than the other organs of sense. Bartholomaeus's reference to 'impressiouns' and 'prentinges' connotes, on the one hand, the effect of (pleasurable and painful) pressure wrought by touch or taste on the external surface of the body, on the lips or in the mouth.[30] On the other hand, it connotes the internal cardial and cerebral processing of sense perceptions: taste and touch stamp a 'likeness' and produce a feeling in the heart and the 'ymaginacioun'. Things touched and tasted thus make deeper indentations on the body surface and the body interior and leave their traces for longer.[31] As a result, in contradistinction to (or, at least, in differing ways from) the other senses, taste and touch instantiate and operate within multiple temporalities in the body – that is, they continue to act at a distance after contact has ceased. A thirteenth-century Provençal love legend, *Flamenca*, exemplifies this difference as one of the degree of 'sotilnes' and 'boistousness' inherent in the senses. Thus the narrator relates how the eyes constitute a pure passageway of love to the heart (which here is established as the dwelling of the reasonable soul): 'But the mouth cannot prevent itself, while kissing, from keeping a little of the pleasure for itself before some of it reaches the heart.'[32] Iterating the physiology of taste and touch, which are more deeply rooted in the body, the pleasure experienced through kissing is caught up, delayed in the material of the body, in the lips and mouth. To kiss gratifies and satiates the appetite of the flesh and of the body, not just the longings of the soul.

Thus, while all the senses as gateways into the body need vigilance, taste and touch are understood as particularly liable to effect crossings over from the external world to the interior body. *Pastoralia* draws on this sensory physiology in thinking about the ways in which taste and touch foster human inclination to sin. In the thirteenth century, the Dominican William Peraldus, for example, takes up an understanding of the material, 'felt' difference between the senses to particularise the influence of taste and touch in shaping vice and virtue in his *Summa de vitiis*. He writes:

> the pleasures that occur through touch and taste are greater than those that occur through the other five senses. And the *inclination to the actions and pleasures stimulated through these two senses* is greater than that stimulated through the other three. Likewise, the vices that occur in respect to the actions and pleasures of these two senses are more dangerous.[33] (my emphasis)

Within a pastoral context, the natural philosophers' emphasis on the embodied, felt, material qualities of taste and touch explains their particular implications for behaviour: Peraldus's description suggests a stronger link between the sensations of taste and touch and the inclination to vicious or virtuous action. As Michael Camille notes, the kiss always leads somewhere else: in its negative aetiology, the kiss, seeded in sight and ending in touch, is implicated in a specifically downward progression, morally as well as physically.[34] Indeed, 'boistous' – that is, earthy – taste and touch themselves incline naturally towards 'boistous' objects: they therefore have a greater pull down to the earth and to material encounters (food, other bodies, etc.).

In its dependency on direct contact with objects in order to sense and to know them, and through its role in bringing objects into the body, the mouth is peculiarly implicated in acts that bring about deep material and physiological change in the body. What heightens the material pull of taste and touch mediated through kissing, however, is that kissing another human mouth (unlike eating food or touching the earth) at once stems from within and from without the individual, potentially involving the reciprocal agency – or the physiology of 'inclination to actions' outlined by Peraldus – of multiple subjects. It is this externality to which Henry of Lancaster's description of kisses draws particular attention in his confessional treatise *Le livre de seyntz medicines*. In listing the sins of his mouth, which he allegorises as wounds, Henry asserts that the third wound was caused by 'peccherouses beisers' (sinful kisses); these he calls 'pardehors, car ausi sont ils pardehors la bouche' (outside, because they are also outside the mouth) but 'entrez en l'alme parfond' (enter into the depths of the soul): kisses come from outside the body but traverse its boundaries and penetrate to the soul.[35] Regulation of kissing is therefore of pressing pastoral concern. As the author of *Of Shrifte and Penance* explains: 'Ichul telle ʒow of kyssynge, syth þer cometh so muche harme of touching.' While the author permits a man to kiss his mother, sister and wife, the prohibition largely concerns cross-gender kissing – the implication is that no other kind of woman should be kissed, because 'He þat ofte kysseth may sone go to þe devele.'[36] In the same way that *On the Properties of Things* outlines the potential for material and physiological change through taste and touch, kissing in the *Livre* as in the pastoral tradition brings about modifications in the self.

Two particular spiritual substances centred in the mouth – saliva, which conveys the flavours of things tasted into the organs of sense, and breath – further bear out the way in which the mouth naturally performs spiritual transformations. Saliva is central to the operation of the sense of taste. Defined in *On the Properties of Things* as a 'fleumatik humour ibred in þe kinde veynes of þe tonge' (1, 209), saliva is a product of the digestion process – rarefied food – which, as *spiritus*, carries out the virtues of soul in the body.[37] In the mouth, saliva acts on food in order to make it digestible, but it is also the 'mene bytwene þe wit of taast and þe þing þat is itasted'. It thus mediates between the sense of taste and the object tasted by taking a likeness of it into the sinews. It does so through undergoing mutation: in the act of tasting, saliva 'is ichaungid aftir þe qualite of þe sauour of þing þat is itastid' (1, 209). In other words, saliva is itself transformed into the inherent attributes of the 'sauour' of the substance tasted. The mouth's physiology thus naturally models the way in which objects encountered through taste and touch alter the material of the body and convey something of the quality of those objects into it.

This transformative power of saliva, however, in particular humoural conditions, can extend well beyond the individual to other bodies.[38] Albertus Magnus records in *De animalibus*, for example, that the saliva of a fasting man can heal 'abscesses when smeared on them and removes spots or scars'. So too, Albertus notes, can saliva be infectious or deadly: a wound received from an arrow touched to the mouth of a fasting person is infectious; the saliva of a fasting man put in the wounds of serpents and scorpions will kill them.[39] The power of saliva to infect and even kill, as Bartholomaeus explains (citing Haly Abbas) in *On the Properties of Things*, derives from its 'rawnesse': 'For rauȝ humour imellid [mixed] wiþ blood þat haþ parfite digestioun is contrarye þerto in his qualite and disturbiþ temperament þerof' (1, 210). Since abstaining from food affects the ability of the body to digest food and transform it into humours and *spiritus*, the saliva of a fasting man is 'rauȝ', that is, incompletely digested or unrefined (*MED*, s.v.). When mingled with blood, which has, on the contrary, been perfectly digested, the complexion of the body is altered to detrimental effect.

These kinds of ideas about the power of saliva do not remain the preserve of learned natural philosophy. John Trevisa's translation of Ranulf Higden's *Polychronicon* notes, 'There be men the towche or spatelle [spittle] of whom is medicinable ageyne serpentes and styngenge of theyme.'[40] It is also found in popular works of vernacular theology, as Mirk's sermon for Quadragesima (the first Sunday of Lent) demonstrates:

> os clerkus techon, þe spytell of a fasting mon schal slene a neddur [an adder] bodyly. Þan moche more it schall sle þe myght of þe olde neddur, þat is þe fend of helle, þat come to Eue in paradyse in lyknesse of a neddur to tempton hur of glotonye, of veyne glory, and of couetyse.[41]

Saliva acts on both the natural world (adders) and, through fasting, on the supernatural (the devil himself). Something of this transformative power of saliva also underlies its use as a figure for how the devil can penetrate

Christian bodies and souls through sin. *Book for a Simple and Devout Woman* instructs, for example, that:

> He þat fouleþ his mouþe wiþ synful speche, lodliche [abhorrent] þyngus þe fende wiþ him doþ. Forsoþe, he sofreþ þe fende to spete in his mouþe, and ho þat deliteþ him in ydul wordus þat mow kyndli synne, he ȝeueþ þe fende leue to nestele in his mouþe.[42]

Sinning with your mouth is like letting the devil spit in it; or worse, it is like letting him snuggle up inside it. As these examples show, both medical and pastoral understandings of saliva reinforce the perception of the mouth as a locus for physical and spiritual transformation, where encounters might have the power not only to traverse the exterior and penetrate to the interior, but also to traverse earthly and spiritual realms.

Similar properties inhere in breath. As Aelred reflects in *De spirituali amicitia*, since life ceases when breath ceases, breath seems to partake in some way in the nature of the soul: in exchanging breath, kissing therefore causes a reciprocal spiritual change in those who kiss. The association of soul with breath persists even as it is dismissed through the widespread transmission of Isidore's *Etymologies*, where he notes (and corrects) the pagans' derivation of the term 'soul (anima)' from 'the assumption that it is wind ... because we seem to stay alive by drawing air into the mouth'.[43] As *On the Properties of Things* records, in the schema of the tripartite soul breath is the 'vertu of lif' governed by the spirit *vitalis* in the heart (1, 104–5). Vincent of Beauvais records in the *Speculum naturale* that air drawn in through the mouth is required both to cool the life-giving heat in the heart, as well as to purify it.[44] In the process of breathing, two different substances are involved: one made in the body (the *vitalis*) and the other drawn into the body (air) from outside it. When brought into the body, air is acted on in the mouth in order to make it ready to be received by the heart, in the same way that food and drink are in order to make them suitable to be received in the stomach. Thus *On the Properties of Things* records that: 'þe aier and breþ', drawn into the mouth in conjunction with the 'spiritual' members (heart, lungs, etc.), 'is amendid and ipurid and made sotile þerinne, and is so isent by þe woosen [pipes] of þe longes [lungs] to kele [cool] þe herte' (1, 201). Trevisa's 'amendid' translates the Latin 'imutatur' (*Lewis & Short*, 'to change, alter, transform'): the mouth transforms what is brought into it, purifying 'aier and breþ' and making them more 'sotile' (rarefied). The materials of the mouth are not only subject to alteration, but themselves transform things brought into the body.

Breath and air, of course, are associated with not only the mouth but also the nose. As *On the Properties of Things* explains, air inhaled through the nose conveys smells to the fleshy 'gobettis' hanging in the nostril, from whence a likeness is sent to the brain (1, 115). But so too might breath have a smell. With the nose we perceive 'smellinge and spiritual þinges and demen bitwene swete and stynkinge' (1, 192). Things which are 'stynkinge' might also be infectious (as is the breath of lepers, which 'stenkiþ and infectiþ oþir'). In this regard, the powers of smell are not analogous with touch, but rather with an aspect of taste – as Aristotle observes, 'there is an analogy between smell and taste ... the species of tastes run parallel to those of smells'.[45] In *The Canterbury Tales*, the Manciple makes the Cook's breath a diagnostic tool – announcing that it 'ful soure stynketh: / That sheweth wel thou art nat wel disposed' – but also a social problem: 'Thy cursed breeth infecte wole us alle.'[46]

The medieval medical and cosmetic tradition is thus also committed to facilitating the sweet savour of mouths. Medieval texts belonging to the *Trotula* tradition of medicine provide recipes for sweetening a woman's breath: 'let her chew each day fennel or lovage or parsley, which is better to chew because it gives off a good smell and cleans gums and makes the teeth very white'.[47] Sweet breath is therefore (potentially) an aid to *luxuria*:[48] Absolon famously chews 'greyn and lycorys' to smell sweet;[49] Venus's intercession on behalf of the lover in a Middle English translation of *The Romaunt of the Rose* declares, 'His breth is also good and swete, / And eke his lippis rody, and mete / Oonly to pleyen and to kisse'.[50] The fourteenth-century preacher's handbook *Fasciculus morum* recounts the well-known exemplum of Bilia (to which Chaucer alludes in 'The Franklin's Tale'), which plays upon this notion of the mouth's smell-as-taste.[51] Bilia's husband suffers from halitosis and so his breath, mouth and teeth smell horribly. On discovering this, he reproves his wife for not warning him about it so he could have it treated medically. Bilia answers, ' "I would certainly have told you so, but I thought all men's mouths smell that way." She had obviously never tasted another man's mouth!'[52] The exemplum thus draws upon the perception of the inherent (though not always pleasant) taste of mouths, as well as the analogy of smell and taste, to teach a lesson about continence in kissing.

The mouth's threshold status is further sensitised by the widespread belief that the soul leaves the body through the mouth in death. Underscoring the association of the soul with breath, Aquinas notes in the *Summa theologiae*: 'Take breathing away and the union of soul and body breaks up.'[53] These natural correlations ground supernatural possibilities: if the soul leaves the body through the mouth, then the mouth might also be the site at which the invisible and unseen world does battle for the soul. Exempla found in sermon collections such as Mirk's *Festial* thus describe the ways in which the souls of sinners might be dragged out of the body through the mouth with hooks. One *narracio* in the *Festial* records a vision granted to a hermit in which two fiends are seen seated at the head of a dying man 'with too [two] brennyng ewles [hooks] þraste into hys þrotte [throat], rakyng aftyr þe soule'.[54] The vernacular homily collection *Of Shrifte and Penance* similarly records the example of a monk who, appearing to fast in order to feign righteousness in life, is tormented by a dragon in death who binds him with his tail and 'put his hede in my mowht. He drawyt owt my sovle, nevre more I schal nat speke.'[55] The close association of the soul with breath, on the one hand, and the mouth as the exit for the soul in death, on the other, suggests just what might be at stake in exchanging breath in a mouth-to-mouth kiss.

Each of these 'kynde' examples – of the senses of taste and touch, saliva and breath – characterises the body's physiology as an 'open process'; one, in Woolgar's words, 'which enabled tangible qualities, and, indeed, spiritual or intangible qualities to be passed from one party or object to another'. Reading between natural philosophy, medicine and *pastoralia* suggests that, in both learned and popular traditions alike, the mouth is understood as a locus of material and spiritual transformation. The close readings of *Piers Plowman* and pastoral texts that follow assume that these 'kynde' properties of the mouth form part of the understandings of the kiss in these works. As a taste and touch, a kiss makes deep indentations in the interior body; it mediates pleasure that is caught up and delayed in the material of the body; and it continues to act at a distance. Part of the power and danger of the kiss also lies in the possibility for the exchange of saliva and breath to occur through it: saliva is transformed into the likeness of that which is tasted, but also has the potential to heal or to kill; breath conveys the core of the individual within it, binding body and soul together, but also, when conveying 'stynkinge' odours, has the potential to infect. While the kiss shares in these natural properties of the mouth, at the same time it is also in some ways superfluous to them: it arises out of and in response to natural needs and desires, but is, as Camille argues, surplus.[56] In *Piers Plowman*, Haukyn's kiss is a taste: it is situated in, but is also surplus to, both the sensory structure of desire and the gustatory system necessary to sustain life. The kiss thereby epitomises the very human, materialised experiences of desiring and sinning that arise from being-in-the-world. As such, Haukyn's debased 'taste' is a symptom of his sensory pathology and his failure to learn the lessons offered by the *via positiva*. The drive downward into the body evinced by Haukyn's kiss, moreover, exposes the problem of misdirected ends. The kiss is multidirectional: it can move the human into the realm of the spiritual as well as extend out into the world or, in Haukyn's case, back down into the body.

Haukyn's Taste for Mouths

Haukyn makes his appearance in Passus XIII–XIV of the B-text of *Piers Plowman*. After the feast of Conscience, where Langland has put to the test the literal and figurative connections of eating and knowing, Conscience and Patience (observed by the dreamer) set out on pilgrimage. They encounter Haukyn, who tells them he is a 'waferer' (*MED*, s.v. 'a maker or purveyor of wafers'). Haukyn's profession – providing bread as 'liflode', but also the eucharistic wafer – signals that this passus will continue to test the material and spiritual meanings of food and of materiality. Seen by many critics to mirror the dreamer and to echo and replay themes raised by Piers the Plowman (recalling both the ploughing of the half-acre and the pardon scene, for example), Haukyn is commonly seen as 'mundane', 'vigorous and earthbound' and as a psychosomatic unity – in other words, human.[57] As Carruthers remarks, 'the self-images Will has met before, like Thought, have been particular faculties, split off from the complete individual soul. Haukyn is a complete self; it is crucial for Will to perceive him wholly.'[58] Another way of putting this is to say that it is important for the dreamer (and, so, us as readers) to perceive Haukyn as wholly embodied, as body and soul.

Haukyn's manner of reading the world, of learning through experience and through his sense perception, leads to an insistent materialisation and literalising of 'liflode' (those things necessary for life) and matters of faith and religious doctrine. Haukyn reads spiritual and symbolic things literally and materially: he has, he claims, provided 'payn [bread] for the Pope' but 'hadde nevere of hym' (B.XIII.244–5). He seeks seals that are salves for pestilence (249) and pardons that can 'lechen [cure] a man' (254). His complaint points up the lack of food and of bodily health that he and others like him experience, a lack which religion does not seem to him to satiate since it provides neither a blessing which destroys 'bocches' nor real bread for the hungry (B.XIII.250–4). In essence, Haukyn employs an everyday discourse about the care of the body, about the experience of sin as a pathological affliction and the difficulty of living in the world and not sinning: ' "So hard it is," quod Haukyn, "to lyve and to do synne" ' (B.XIV.322). The episode sets out to re-educate Haukyn by helping him properly understand the relationship of his body and his tripartite soul, to revalue hardship and suffering, and to use his sense perception for spiritual and not only earthly ends. In so doing, it revisits and reframes the dreamer's experience in the previous passus, where the dreamer had watched the doctor of divinity fill his gorge with costly dishes, while he and Patience ate scriptural quotation. In Passus XIII, Conscience and Patience now seek to teach Haukyn how to extrapolate knowledge from the created material world in order to understand God and the spiritual economy, to move from real bread to spiritual bread.[59] Thus Patience's promise to 'purveie thee paast' without plough or grain is at first met with scorn before Haukyn understands how the *Pater noster* might in fact be his 'liflode' (B.XIV.29–36). Consequently, in the example of Haukyn we see the making and the unmaking of self-knowledge – as John A. Alford observes, Haukyn's 'warped vision of himself is shattered in an utterly demeaning confession'.[60] In the process of the dreamer's observations, Conscience's and Patience's sermons and his own confession, Haukyn (and so the dreamer and the reader) learns about the whole man: the body, the interior body and the soul, the last of which is represented by Haukyn's 'coat' (B.XIII.314–15). The soul-coat turns Haukyn's inside out – a garment (very often a way of thinking about the exterior body, about skin) is inverted as an image and made to represent the immaterial and inner soul. This episode thus enacts the 'interchange of inside and outside surfaces', which, as Elaine Scarry posits, 'requires *not* the literal reversal of bodily linings but the making of what is originally interior and private into something exterior and sharable and, conversely, the reabsorption of what is now exterior and sharable into the intimate recesses of individual consciousness'.[61] By having that which is normally hidden exposed to the scrutiny of Conscience, Patience and the dreamer, Haukyn comes to a new self-awareness, which (in an optimistic reading of the passus) he uses to construct a new sense of self.

This new self, however, fundamentally requires the re-education of his senses, for Haukyn's reifying is the result of the pathology of his sensory processes. In documenting the ways in which Haukyn senses, Langland reveals the sensory structure of sinful, earth-driven desire. Prior to Haukyn's confession, the dreamer describes how Haukyn pretends outwardly to be something he is not, bragging and boasting – he makes out he is 'an ordre by hymselve – / Religion saunz rule' (285–6),[62] and:

> In likynge of lele lif and a liere in soule;[63]
> With inwit and with outwit ymagynen and studie

As best for his body be to have a bold name;
And entremetten hym over al ther he hath noght to doone;
Wilnynge that men wende his wit were the beste,
Or for his crafty knonnynge or of clerkes the wisest. (B.xiii.288–93)

The catalogue of his self-aggrandisement continues: Haukyn wants people to think he is the 'lovelokest' to look on, the cleanest liver, the 'most sotil of song'; he boasts of things he has never seen and things he has never done; he seeks in all things to 'plese the peple and preisen hymselve', and so on (B.xiii.295–313). This establishes some important components of Haukyn's 'wholism'; his worldly (pre)occupations involve both his 'inwit' (the cerebral faculties, including *ymaginatiua, estimatiua* and *memoratiua*) and his 'outwit' (the sense organs) – in other words his sensible soul, the second and medial virtue of the soul in the tripartite system. The sensing part of Haukyn's body – that which ultimately makes him (a desiring) human – is committed to 'ymagynen' and 'studie'. 'Ymagynen' is, of course, reliant on those impressions and imprints previously made by sense perception in his brain. 'Studie' in turn conveys Haukyn's pursuit of knowledge, his mental effort as well as his physical activity:[64] his whole body–soul aims to attain what he thinks is 'best for his body be to have a bold name', that is worldly reputation for (to take up Schmidt's gloss) 'sexual prowess'.[65]

   Like the dreamer ('Ac for thyn entremetynge here artow forsake', B.xi.414), like Adam ('Ac when he mamelede aboute mete and entremeted to knowe', B.xi.416), Haukyn 'entremetten hym over al ther he hath noght to doone'. He meddles in matters that are not his concern, wanting to be thought witty, knowledgeable in crafts or the wisest 'of clerkes'. Reginald Pecock's *Repressor of Over Much Blaming of the Clergy* (c.1449) provides a further, illuminating gloss on the verb: just as it would have been praiseworthy if Adam and Eve had 'forborne the eting of the appil in Paradise', Pecock observes, so likewise would it have been 'good and preiseable if thei hadden forborn the *entermeting* which thei maden aboute the appil in it *biholding, handling, taasting, ymagynyng, and questiouns theraboute moving*' (my emphasis).[66] Adam and Eve's 'entermeting' about the apple, Pecock clarifies, included looking, touching, tasting, imagining and asking questions about it. Adam and Eve's 'entermeting' has everything to do with the sensing body and with a mode of inquiry into objects in the world in which the entirety of thought is set. Interfering, reifying, Haukyn likewise sets his senses, his imagination, his thought and reason in the (element) earth – in worldly reputation, in his body and in other bodies – and, accordingly, the knowledge he seeks and gains is not spiritual but material and sexual.

Conscience thus observes just how dirty Haukyn's (soul-)coat is. Haukyn turns around, noting the patches, creases and stains caused by the likes of wrath, wicked will, envy, lying, quarrelling, gossiping, slandering and cursing. As the passus continues, the ways in which Haukyn's sinfulness and suffering derive from the misuse of his senses is made even more explicit. Among the many (and largely oral) transgressions that the dreamer observes in Haukyn is his seduction of women – an act which engages his sensible soul, his desiring and sensing faculties, but with the wrong *telos*. Thus the dreamer recounts how he waited 'wisloker' (diligently, intently) and looks even more carefully at Haukyn's coat, seeing that it is 'soilled'

> With likynge of lecherie as by lokynge of his eighe.
> For ech a maide that he mette, he made hire a signe
> Semynge to synneward, and somtyme he gan taste
> Aboute the mouth or bynethe bigynneth to grope,
> Til eitheres wille wexeth kene, and to the werke yeden. (B.xiii.344–8)

Sin proceeds in a downward movement from sight to taste and finally to touch. Langland thus invokes a schema which equates the materiality of taste and touch, not with its spiritual possibilities, but with sinful bodily pleasure. Langland's elucidation of lechery follows a fivefold development, (1) 'lokynge' of eye, (2) making signs 'semynge to synneward', (3) tasting, (4) groping and, finally, (5) 'werke'. The cerebral process implied in this movement through the stages of lechery (conveying a downward bent from eyes to mouth to 'bynethe') is as follows: the sense perception of sight (knowing at a distance) brings a likeness of another body, making an impression in the *ymaginatiua* in the brain, from whence it is sent to the heart. Having been judged (determined to be preferable or repulsive), the desire of the soul, which has been whet by the sense image, is externalised by the mouth first in speech and then in seeking out contact, tasting and testing through kissing and embracing (knowing directly, in and by the body) and finally 'the deed' itself. The dreamer's description of Haukyn's 'likynge of lecherie' (echoing Trevisa's rendering of the habit-forming 'lykyng' which leads to lechery in *De regimine principum*) follows the fivefold pattern of cause and effect established in the pastoral tradition. *Speculum vitae*, for example, describes the aetiology of lechery in the outer senses as a progression from sight to touch: from 'fole sight of eghe', 'speche of wordes sleghe', to 'fole touchyng with hande', followed by 'kyssyng', until 'sone þe litcherous [lecherous] dede folwes þan / To whilk þe fende þus ledes a man'.[67] Similarly, *Book for a Simple and Devout Woman* records: 'as Seynt Gregor seiþ: "Firste wiþ foule lokynge, siþþen [next] wiþ foule speche, siþþen wiþ foule nyȝynge [touching] and after wiþ foule kessynge and after to þe foule forboden dede. And echon of þese oþer norscheþ [feeds, fosters] and makeþ wey to oþer".'[68]

Haukyn's kiss – like those of the habitual lecher of the pastoral tradition – is somewhat buried in and among all the other sensory and signifying activities, and this is precisely the point: the kiss, in Langland's account, cannot be detached from its multisensory milieu. What Langland describes here is the very system of sensing that structures desire, in which the kiss marks both the consummation of desire – direct, firsthand – and yet inclines Haukyn on, to groping beneath, to sex ('werke').

Langland does not describe Haukyn's act as a kiss but rather as a taste: 'somtyme he gan taste / Aboute the mouth or bynethe bigynneth to grope'. By designating kissing as tasting, the expression of sexual desire (for another body) is located as part of the broader discourse in the poem of experiential, 'kynde knowyng', reiterating the connection of tasting with knowing, but also raising the problem of misdirected ends (the tasting which causes surfeit, gluttony, *scientia* and also lechery). Firstly, the kiss as a taste catenates with eating – reminding us of its source of origin in the vegetable part of the soul. Secondly, the kiss as taste directs, as eating does, down into the body – it leads, in Camille's terms, somewhere else. Finally, the simultaneity of Haukyn's tasting with the mouth and groping 'bynethe' provides a counterpart to, and a perversion of, the spiritualised modes of taste and touch the poem elsewhere deploys.

The sense that kissing is like eating is borne out elsewhere in medieval literature – in the signs that presage Absolon's own misdirected kiss in Chaucer's Miller's tale, for example. Absolon's kiss raises issues of disgust associated with kissing body parts implicated in purgation and digestion, as well as the problem of the conflation or substitution of mouth with anus.[69] (Indeed, as Camille reminds us, the very word *osculum*, in fact, gestures towards the 'cul', the anus.)[70] Hopeful that he is soon to succeed in wooing Alison, Absolon notices some good omens: 'My mouth hath icched al this longe day; / That is a signe of kissyng atte leeste. / Al nyght me mette [dreamed] eek I was at a feeste.'[71] The *MED* glosses 'yicchen' (s.v.) as 'To feel an itch', 'to produce itching', '*fig.* to feel craving or desire'. Similarly, On the Properties of Things records of the melancholic humour that 'it is an help þat it be moche in þe mouþ of þe stomak to make it þicke and make it *icche*, and so to make hungur and desire of fedinge' (1, 160, my emphasis). Physiologically speaking, itching is a bodily signal arising from the mouth of the stomach to incite appetite and cause the human to search out food. Relocated (or directed from the stomach) to the mouth, Absolon's itch is a physical impulse causing him to seek out a different kind of food to satiate his feeling of hunger. But Absolon kisses, of course, not Alison's mouth but her genitals, thereby exposing – making visible and literalising – the kiss's physiological drive downwards that is always already at work, just as it is in Haukyn's taste.

The kiss is thus a taste, but tasting itself is part of the physiology and pathology of kissing: certain kinds of eating lead to certain kinds of kissing. The medieval understanding that lechery is fostered by prior consent to excessive appetite for real food is pervasive in *Piers Plowman*, which insistently forges the connection between desire for food and desire for bodies. Thus, Holy Church in Passus 1 demonstrates how quickly need can run over or slip into excess through the example of Lot who, because of his 'likynge of drynke', commits incest (B.1.27–34). Elsewhere, Langland instances the fraudulent beggars who go to bed in gluttony and rise with 'ribaudie' (B.Prol.43), and those who sup on fast days and then go to bed and 'breden as burgh swyn' (B.11.93–9). Excessive eating will foster the physiological conditions (and, perhaps also, in idling around the dinner table or sitting in the tavern, the physical circumstances) for lechery. Thus *Dives and Pauper* advises that, in addition to vigilance over the five senses, the prophylactic for lechery is 'resonable abstinence fro mete & drynke & for to flen deynte metis & deynte drynkys & to flen glotonye as mest begynnynge & mene to lecherye'.[72] Mirk similarly warns that man is led 'into gloteny by surfet [overindulgence] of diuers metus and drynkus; into lechery þat scheweth [follows] alway gloteny'.[73] The kiss here is firmly rooted in the body and its physiology: it arises out of its material needs and conditions. It is thus care of the self – daily regimen and diet, as well as devotion – that will order and regulate kisses and direct them towards noble ends.

In Haukyn's kiss we also see a further aspect of the paradox of the 'tasty' knowing that has demarcated both *sapientia* and Adam's sin of epistemophilia in *Piers Plowman*.[74] Haukyn's movement, from tasting the maid's mouth (with his own) to groping her 'bynethe', mirrors that of Adam tasting with his mouth and covering up his genitals. The verb 'to grope' in Middle English is, like 'to taste', a mode of investigating, probing and testing.[75] It has likewise peculiarly heightened spiritual connotations, as Passus XIX demonstrates: '[Christ] took Thomas by the hand and taughte hym to grope, / And feele with hise fyngres his flesshliche herte' (B.XIX.170–1). 'Gropinge' at this point in *Piers Plowman* is a liminal act which transgresses bodily boundaries, penetrates and explores the interior body in order to gain access to spiritual revelation or faith in the risen Christ.[76] Groping is therefore another act which is debased by Haukyn's materialisation of taste and sex and which he implicates with an 'unkynde', unnatural body knowledge; as Patience perceives, Haukyn's coat is dirty 'thorugh coveitise and *unkynde desiryng*' (my emphasis, B.XIII.356). It is the mouth that both mediates Haukyn's search for knowledge and acts as a signifier of (and precursor to) sin. The role of taste and touch as faculties of epistemology and discernment is an important part of the mouth's physiology, but Haukyn applies them as modes of making judgements and learning about the world and about people while remaining ignorant about himself. Retaining but perverting the sense of tasty knowledge as that which is felt (direct, present to the body), Haukyn tastes to effect his lustful, sinful, but all too human desire. Tasting as a sapiential mode in the poem is debunked; it becomes transgressive and is made subject to a downward drive away from God and into the genitals.

The kiss in *Piers Plowman* is situated in a dizzying network of sensing and sign-making. Founded in pastoral understandings of the physiological circumstances that give rise to kissing, Langland's kiss is thus revealed as embedded in the vegetable and sensible faculties of the soul. As such, the kiss belongs to the spectrum of both natural bodily need and the natural means of experiencing and learning about the world. But Haukyn's mode of reading and of using his senses, like that of the swine or the 'rude and boistous' man who is busy about his 'bely joye', both goes beyond need and is reifying; it leads to a travestying of the epistemological potential of the mouth, of taste, touch and 'food'. As a result, the material leads Haukyn to a misapprehension of the spiritual and to a comfortless understanding of Scripture and Christian doctrine.

In contrast, in the Middle English accounts of Judas's kiss of betrayal, the kiss shares in the properties of the mouth and in the sensory qualities of taste and touch: it makes and takes impressions; it effects material changes in the body, which penetrate the heart deeply; it makes exterior what is interior; it continues to act at a distance, even once contact has ceased, thereby instantiating multiple temporalities within the body. In so doing, these osculatory encounters take kissing to the edges of the human and highlight the liminal, ensouled nature of the zone of the kiss. Emphasising spiritualised understandings of the kiss – as effecting both the exchange of bodily *spiritus* and the union of souls, and as the material expression of interior thought and intention – kisses in the *Festial* further expose, as Haukyn's does, the problem of misdirected ends.

Kisses of Betrayal

The sermon for the feast of St Matthew (or Matthias) in Mirk's *Festial* describes the betrayal of Christ by Judas, who kisses Christ to identify him to the Roman soldiers. Falling into despair after betraying Jesus, Judas hangs himself with 'þe grenne of a roppe':

> So be ryght dome þat þrote þat spake þe wordys of trayturye aȝeynus hys Lorde, þat same þrote was strangullyd wyth a roppe. For he wold a sayde mony ele [evil] wordus be hys Lorde aftur hys deth þat dude so foule be hym yn hys lyue. And for þe fende mythe notte drowen hys sowle owte be hys mowthe, þat hadde cussid þe mowthe of God so late beforne, he braste hys wombe and schedde oute hys guttys, and þat way drewe oute hys sowle and bare hit into helle.[77]

Following the 'just judgement' typical of exempla, in which bodily punishments are experienced in the sinning body part, Judas's throat is strangled with the 'grenne [noose]' of a rope in return for the treasonous words that arose from it.[78] Furthermore, the devil is able to carry off Judas's soul – not through his mouth 'þat hadde cussid þe mowthe of God so late beforne' – but only through his stomach. Kissing Christ has materially altered Judas's mouth: the devil cannot now touch it. The 1439 Middle English *Gilte Legende* version draws out (more closely following the source than Mirk's truncated version) the causal effect of touch: 'And the mouthe was defended that there shulde nothing passe ther, for it was not sitting that the mouthe shulde be so horribly defouled that hadde so late touched so blessed and so holy a mouthe of Crist.'[79] Christ's kiss thus exemplifies the way in which touch enables, in Woolgar's words, 'tangible qualities, and, indeed, spiritual or intangible qualities' to be passed between bodies.

What might also be at stake in Judas and Christ's kiss, however, is another bodily substance: saliva.[80] Indeed, just such a possibility arouses medieval Christian horror at accounts of Jews spitting on Christ in the Buffeting.[81] *The Book of Margery Kempe* details a meditation in which, having seen Judas's kiss of betrayal, Margery 'beheld wyth hir gostly eye the Jewys puttyng a cloth beforn owr Lordys eyne, betyng hym and bofetyng hym in the hevyd and bobyng [striking] hym beforn hys swete mowth … Thei sparid not to spittyn in hys face in the most schamful wise that thei cowde.'[82] The possibility that in kissing saliva is exchanged might also inform, not only the horror felt at Judas's betrayal of Christ, but also something of the powerful effect Christ's kiss has on Judas's mouth. In either case, the kiss, in continuing to act once contact has ceased, has a supernatural effect on the natural body; but, as we have seen, the *a priori*

possibility for such material transformation already inheres in the sense
of touch. To recall *On the Properties of Things*: those things felt by touch
'makeþ mo chaunginges þanne þinges þat beþ ifelid by oþir wittis' (1, 120).
In kissing Christ, Judas takes a likeness of the very substance of Christ's
(divine) body into his own and is accordingly materially altered. (In this
sense, to kiss Christ is an act akin to partaking of the Eucharist, which
similarly has a supernatural effect on the body of the communicant.)[83]

An emphasis on the way in which the touch wrought by a kiss makes
material change and instantiates temporal alterity within the body (by
leaving its trace long after the touch itself) appears widely in medieval
commentaries on, and exemplary narratives about, Judas's betrayal. *Dives
and Pauper*'s account of Judas begins by stressing the greed – the desire for
money – that first motivates the betrayal:

> For coueytise Iudas solde Crist, Goddis sone, for þretty penyys and
> betraythyd hym, and aftir he wente & heng hymself til hys bely brast, and
> þer þe deuyl þat was in hym fleyy out and bar hys soule with hym to helle.[84]

The devil, this time already imagined as dwelling inside Judas, leaves
conveniently with Judas's soul through the hole made by his stomach
bursting open. For Diues, the rich man listening to Pauper's retelling of
this scriptural episode, however, this unnatural exit raises questions. Diues
asks, 'Why wente þe fend nout out of hys mouth?' Recalling the kind of
'lewed' questions provoked by the Genesis narrative of Adam and Eve,
who covered not their mouths (which sinned) but their genitals, Diues's
question testifies to the popular understanding that the soul in death exits
the body through the mouth. It also makes the mouth an opportunity
for exegesis. Pauper replies: 'For his mouth hadde touchyd Cristis mouth
whan he kyssyd Crist in gyle and seyde, "Heyl, Maystyr".'[85] Pauper thus
offers the same aetiology as *The Gilte Legende* and the *Festial* do: the kiss as
a touch has had a material effect. However, Pauper's answer further raises
the problem of the kiss as a bodily sign: Judas kissed 'in gyle', thereby
perverting the natural model in which to kiss is a form of bodily language –
the external expression of interior affection and intention – that brings
about the exchange of breath and the union of minds and souls.

Patristic writings, as we have seen, are explicit about the kind of
physiological dysfunction that characterises Judas's betrayal. In a healthy
body, 'what the lips do, says Augustine, the hearts of those who kiss should
do, that is, join with the lips and heart of the one who is kissed'.[86] In this
way, kissing is like not just eating but also speaking and thinking. The
external body, in other words, should express and perform the interior.

The problem with the postlapsarian body is its potential for multivocality, to say and do one thing outwardly and mean something very different inwardly. This discrepancy between the heart and the lips of Judas is taken up elsewhere in fourteenth-century pastoral literature. *Of Shrifte and Penance*, for example, records:

> 'Whanne þe schrewe spekyt, he swetyth his lippes and mekyth his voice, but his herte schal þenke how he may schynde ȝow [harm you].' So dede þe cursed Iudas ... First he grette hym mekely and aftur he kyste hym, whanne his herte was ful of venym.[87]

Judas makes his lips 'sweet' – tasty – but his heart is full of venom. Similarly, *Handlyng Synne* (citing Solomon) says of the backbiter, that ' "Hys lyppes ... he shal make swete" ' while he plots evil: 'So dede þe treytur, fals Iudas', who first greeted Christ '& gan lagh, / And seþen hym keste þat alle men sagh. / And yn hys herte was tresun bold.'[88] Judas's kiss is thus interpreted, with Augustine and Ambrose, as no kiss at all. Mirk notes in the sermon material for Maundy Thursday that: 'Þis day is no pax ȝeven at masse. For Iudas trayed Cryste þis nyȝte wyth a cusse.'[89] The kiss in the liturgy of the Mass is a sign, not only of the unity of the Christian community, but also of the Incarnation – the union of God with man. Judas's guileful kiss, however, becomes instead the sign of the irreparable disjunction – of heart and lips, and of Judas from the Christian community and from the body of Christ. The effect of Judas's kiss – the bursting open of his stomach – reveals the dysfunction of his interior body, of the system in which the intentions and thoughts of the heart (and thus of the soul) are materialised and expressed. By opening up his body, Judas's kiss is shown to be dissembling, the rupture between his lips and his heart – the presence of competing impulses and conflicting discourses within the body itself – is exposed.

The example of Judas demonstrates the ability of the kiss to extend beyond the realm of the natural. The mouth in the act of kissing is characterised as a liminal domain, which itself does not cross over but effects (multidirectional) crossings over. Mirk's *Festial* also imagines an encounter with a diabolical other through the conjoining of lips. The *Sermo de nupcijs* (on the sacrament of marriage) contains a homily on adultery, warning against breaking the marriage oath, which not only exemplifies the harm that comes of kissing, but also invites comparison of the adulterous kiss with Judas's. In Northampton, so the sermon relates, there was an eleven-year-old child that was 'syk in a pestelens and was in a transon [a trance]'. When he awakes he tells of many wonders. A local man, who was secretly committing adultery, decides to visit this child. On his way he meets the devil disguised as his 'lemman [lover]'; he kisses her and then goes on his way until he comes across the child. This child possesses supernatural knowledge of the man's adultery and makes him this warning:

> 'Syr, ... þou farust ful ylle, for þou haste a lemman vndur þi wyf aȝeynus Goddys lawe, þe wyche þou wendust [believe] þat þou haddust cussud in þe way hydurwarde, bot it was a fende lyk to hur, and hath wyth þat cusse sette a kanckyr in þi lypp þat schal ete þe into þe herte-coll, but þou amende þe.' But for þis man toke hys wordes bot for a fantasye, þis kanckur quikkonod and ete hym os he sayde, and dyud þeron.[90]

The man, not believing the warning, makes no effort to amend himself; so the 'kanckyr' the devil implants in his lip through kissing him 'quickkonod' and he dies. This exemplum makes clear the consequences, warned of so often in *pastoralia*, of kissing – literalising the claim of *Of Shrifte and Penance*, for example, that 'þe devel trowyth to haue þe soule of hym þat folyly [lasciviously] toucheth a woman.'[91] In the *Festial*, kissing carries the possibility of contagion and disease but also of wounding: through the kiss the adulterer has caught (though he does not credit the spiritual aetiology) a 'kanckyr' in his lip. Kissing has, as the Judas exemplum makes equally clear, physical as well as spiritual consequences. The *MED* glosses 'canker' as: 'A cancer; carcinoma; also, an ulcerated non-malignant tumor, a spreading ulcer'; 'ulceration of a wound'; 'a sore in the mouth'. This canker will eat into the 'herte-coll' – that is the chamber of his heart – unless the adulterer confesses.[92] One manuscript variant of the *Festial* gives instead 'þrote-boll', which refers variously to 'the epiglottis', 'the larynx' or 'the Adam's apple' (*MED*, s.v.).

    Not just a taste, then, to kiss here is also to bite into and to be bitten. Odo of Cheriton, the thirteenth-century English preacher and fabulist (d.1247), demonstrates the dangers of kissing a woman in his *Summa de poenitentia*, similarly suggesting the contagiousness of kissing, but this time using the specific image of an apple:

> If anyone bites into a very beautiful fruit and discovers a worm within, at once he will spit it out. The delicious fruit is a beautiful woman. He who embraces such a woman tastes this fruit. But he should consider the worm, that is, the devil, or sin hiding in the apple and at once through confession he should hurry to spit it out.[93]

Confession – spitting out sin like a wormy piece of apple – would remedy the corruption that otherwise would follow from lecherous kisses, just as it would remedy the 'kanckyr' in the adulterous man's lip. Odo's moralising about and stigmatising of the kiss recalls the Genesis narrative, recasting again the nexus of eating and knowing: to kiss a woman is like biting an apple.[94] Similarly, Mirk's homily of the adulterous man betrays an anxiety that the consequences of kissing might be the removal of the defences of the body (lips, teeth), an act which allows things unbidden and unknown to enter in. Mirk's description of the progress of the canker to the heart recalls the passage of sense perceptions to the heart by the mouth through the sinews: 'heart' here does not just symbolise an immaterial soul but is a material bodily organ. Kissing brings about the decay, not just of the adulterer's soul, but also of his body. The effect of the kiss between the devil and the adulterous man (like that between Christ and Judas) both continues to act at distance and begins the disintegration of self, eroding the adulterer's boundedness.

The adulterer's encounter with the devil in disguise further discloses the liminality of the mouth: the kiss can extend not just into the world, but also into hell, with which, since it is popularly represented as a mouth, there is a heightened connection. Thus *Fasciculus morum* cites Bede's dictum that: ' "He who kisses a whore is knocking at the door of hell." Surely, if one takes delight in the sign, the door is opened with the deed. Therefore the kisses of a whore can be compared to the kiss with which Judas sold Christ and betrayed him to the Jews.'[95] The distinction between the kiss motivated by lust for sex and that by the desire for thirty pieces of silver is here collapsed: both open up the human to moral, and ultimately physical, dissolution.

The identification of the mouth as a bodily orifice that borders on hell similarly pervades the Parson's discussion of the seven deadly sins in the closing tale of *The Canterbury Tales*. Expounding the same fivefold structure of lechery experienced by Haukyn in *Piers Plowman*, the Parson gives kissing as the fourth and penultimate stage:

> trewely he were a greet fool that wolde kisse the mouth of a brennynge oven or of a fourneys. / And moore fooles been they that kissen in vileynye, for that mouth is the mouth of helle; and namely thise olde dotardes holours [lechers], yet wol they kisse, though they may nat do, and smatre [defile] hem.[96]

If it is foolish to kiss the mouth of a furnace, more so is it to kiss another mouth in 'vileynye' (that is, lasciviously). Lechery transforms human mouths into hellmouths. Kissing is multidirectional. It extends the human both into the corporeal and into the unseen tortures of hell.

The transference between the human mouth, the mouth of the devil (or devils) and the entranceway to hell is predicated first on the mouth's analogy to a door or gateway, leading in and out of the body, and secondly on the action of swallowing.[97] Thus Margery Kempe, when unable to confess her sin during a period of illness after childbirth, is tormented by spirits, seeing 'develys opyn her [their] mowthys al inflaumyd wyth brennyng lowys [flames] of fyr as thee schuld a swalwyd hyr in'.[98] And the Manciple, whose tale precedes the Parson's, mocks the Cook who (with his sour breath) 'ganeth [yawns]' as if he would 'swolwe us anonright right'. Vulnerable to letting the devil in ('Hoold cloos thy mouth,' the Manciple warns, 'The devel of helle sette his foot therin!'), the Cook's yawning mouth also recalls the popular iconography of hell in visual art and in dramatic representations of the Harrowing of Hell and the Last Judgement.[99]

The analogical and figurative possibilities of the kiss, as an entrance to hell or heaven, go far beyond the model provided by human physiology. However, natural knowledge about the mouth and about the relationship of the tripartite soul to the body provides a crucial framework for recognising the multiplicity and multidirectionality of the kiss in medieval contexts. Understood as part of the category of 'kynde', the kiss is shown to be embedded in medieval sensory epistemology. The medieval kiss – not just as a sign, but as a complex sense – shares in the physiology of tasting and eating, and extends into speaking and signifying. As Haukyn, Absolon and the pastoral tradition show, the kiss is rooted in the vegetable and sensible drives of the soul: attitudes towards food have consequences for the *telos* of kissing and for the kinds of transactions kissing performs. The pastoral concern with the kiss is coloured by an understanding that certain kinds of eating lead to certain kinds of kissing: too much food or drink results in the surplus of kissing. The kiss thus arises from and within a complex sensory structure of desire and appetite, which when oriented towards God leads to spiritual union, but when directed into the body and the earth perverts the mouth's modes of knowing and destabilises its capacity to function as a sign.

Kissing (as well as tasting and groping through kissing) potentially involves a loss, a bodily transaction that is costly and deadly. In the *Festial*, the kiss provides Mirk with the opportunity to demonstrate what might arise from contact between natural and supernatural bodies. Both Judas and the adulterous man variously encounter the divine and the diabolic other at the threshold of their mouths, an encounter that ultimately leads to their loss of bodily wholeness and of the hope of salvation. These kisses, then – impressing deeply and penetrating the body interior – continue to act at a distance long after contact has ceased. As such, they pervert the spiritual model whereby the kiss, through the exchange of breath, mingles souls and minds. Moreover, they also pervert the kiss's incarnational logic expressed by both Augustine and Bernard: the superlative sign of the union of Christ and man becomes the means of their irreparable disjunction and separation. The consequences of the osculatory encounters of Judas and the adulterous man expose the interior dysfunction that leads to sin and to damnation (greed is rooted in the body, lust in the heart). The downward drive of the kiss, as it does for Haukyn, reveals the problem of what happens when the body and the natural are misread, when the human fails to progress from the visible and material to the unseen and spiritual. The kiss in late medieval vernacular theology cannot be detached from its multisensory milieu or from its interior physiology and physical effect. To kiss is a mode of experiencing and knowing that is thus fraught with anxiety, since the material and physical changes wrought through taste and touch, through saliva and breath, establish the mouth as a locus for self-modification, but also as an active agent through which other bodies and objects in the world can be made and unmade.

CHAPTER 5

Surgical Habits

The late medieval habit of reading between works of vernacular theology and vernacular medicine arises out of a profound understanding of the interrelation of body and soul. It gives to the care of the self – of the body and soul as a related whole – a particular importance in guides to spiritual health and in poetic explorations that ask questions about how to do well while living in the world. Understood to cultivate ethical dispositions, regimen, diet and remedies for the body's pathologies also provide aetiologies of vice or virtue, as well as models for spiritual remedies. As a result, everyday embodied experiences are valued within vernacular theology as sites for spiritual learning. This chapter looks to the experience of medical care in late medieval England, and to medical descriptions of the passions of the mouth and their remedies, to show how medical interventions in the mouth – filing or extracting teeth, trimming back superfluous flesh of the gums or lips – offer medieval authors and readers powerful ways of thinking about the ethics of speech. In so doing, it focuses on a set of discourses – of spiritual discipline, grammatical *habitus* and penitential practices – that are situated at the intersection of learned, Latinate traditions and vernacular, popular medical learning. At the centre of these discourses lie oral surgical remedies and the figure of the barber-surgeon, who appears, unexpectedly, as a figure for the monastic superior and for the personifications of Grammar and Penance. The analogy of the barber-surgeon's crafts to these clergial disciplines derives in part from the literal connection posited in medicine between properly shaped teeth and the capacity to speak well. In their Middle English iterations, however, the surgical potency attributed to confessional speech is made to ask difficult questions about the limits of this kind of understanding of the material basis of the ethical self.

Reading between evidence for medical practice in later medieval England, the vernacular textual tradition that delineates surgical practice in relation to the mouth and pastoral works, such as the Middle English translation of *The Doctrine of the Hert* and Mirk's *Festial*, this chapter first establishes the role of the barber-surgeon in the medieval care of the self. In its concern with the superfluous matter made in the body, the barber-surgeon's craft parallels the pastoral concern with the superfluity of sin. The barber-surgeon thus figures in Middle English *pastoralia* as a figure for the processes of spiritual correction and of penitential preparation for receiving the Eucharist. More than just analogy, however, these texts also suggest that the work of the barber-surgeon – trimming hair, paring nails and dealing with apostemes and protuberances on the skin – facilitates the work of the confessor. The ways in which the actions of shaving and shearing the exterior body parallel and perform spiritual shaving and shearing are drawn even closer in the context of the mouth. As the specialist practitioner of dentistry, the barber-surgeon cleans, scrapes and pulls teeth; files and shaves the teeth and tongue; and works to correct speech impediments. The hygienic and surgical care of the mouth provides particularly close analogy with confession, but is also literally understood to facilitate properly formed speech. As a result, the analogical level of these surgical figures is continually destabilised: 'surgical' intervention (in its broadest sense) in the body has spiritual effects. The barber-surgeon's craft therefore underscores the way in which the care of the body and its material shaping is understood in the medieval period to influence and cultivate virtuous or vicious habits.

Middle English translations of surgical treatises such as those of Guy de Chauliac and Lanfrank evidence a particular concern with deformities or pathologies that might affect the mouth's two offices of eating and speaking, and so also with preserving teeth. This chapter establishes the oral surgical lexis – of scraping, shaving, filing, 'fretynge' and 'frotynge' (forms of abrasive rubbing) – that catenates with both grammatical and confessional discourses. It is the same oral deformities detailed in surgical texts that Grammar is figured as correcting in the allegorical tradition of the trivial arts. Following Martianus Capella's *De nuptiis philologiæ et Mercurii*, writers such as Baudri de Bourgueil, John of Salisbury and Alan of Lille imagine Grammar performing treatments with her file on the mouths of children. This surgical correction of the mouth through the acquisition of the rules of Latin grammar is a central part of *habitus* – the prerequisite for monastic and clerical models of virtue acquisition. The tradition of Grammar underscores both the bodily basis of medieval epistemology and its implication with practices of the care of the self: the repetition central to learning Latin mirrors and parallels the repetitions of teeth-cleaning and, before that, of rubbing the teeth, tongue and gums of the infant.

Vernacular theological and natural philosophical traditions also disclose a 'kynde' understanding of the surgical properties and effects of speech. The reform initiated through the Fourth Lateran Council, which institutes yearly oral confession for the laity and in part motivates the translation drive, makes the instruments of spiritual discipline, as well as the theological and monastic theories of virtue acquisition, available to illiterate and lay readers (even if in limited, contested ways).[1] *The Book of Vices and Virtues* (and pastoral works like it) thus makes clerical tools of spiritual discipline available in English; it also describes a virtuous *habitus* that transforms (lay) tongues into files which shape (vernacular) speech. In a confessional context, the same lexis of filing, scraping and shaving is taken up to explain the way in which the threefold stages of penance reform and remake the self. The second part of the chapter turns to two Middle English examples which offer hybrid allegories of confession in which the mouth becomes the site of oral surgical intervention in order to reshape the self – or perhaps merely to attempt to alleviate physical suffering. In John Lydgate's translation of *The Pilgrimage of the Life of Man* the corrective process of speaking a confession described by Dame Penance invokes the oral surgical treatment prescribed for tooth-worm in the Middle English surgical tradition. The personification of Dame Penance herself borrows from and recollects the figure of Lady Grammar. Just as filing the teeth and cleansing the tongue figure the effects of grammatical speech on the morals and mind of the student, so does scraping the teeth figure the cleansing, healing effects of speaking a confession. The second example is that of Envy in *Piers Plowman*, who exemplifies the problem of (lay, vernacular) bodies habituated to sin. Through Envy, Langland calls into question the potential for sinful bodies to acquire virtuous *habitus* – grammatical or otherwise: are the surgical effects of confession efficacious in bodies accustomed to sin? Or might the surgical properties of speech finally destroy the self rather than restore health? Envy's confession questions the extent to which physical care of the self has the power to reform the soul and warns against the dangers of too literal an understanding of the way in which the material acts on the spiritual.

Barber-Surgeons and Pastoral Care

The analogies of confessor to physician, penitent to patient and sin to sickness are familiar ones – both to confessional handbooks and literary representations of confession as well as to recent scholarship on medieval religious practices.[2] Canon 21 of the Fourth Lateran Council explicitly invokes the analogy in setting out the priest's role in confession: 'the priest must be prudent and cautious, so that in the manner of an expert physician he may pour wine and oil on the wounds of the injured person'.[3] Middle English *pastoralia* takes up and extends these analogies, in ways that clearly show that the reach of pastoral care includes real bodily sickness as well as the soul. *The Book of Vices and Virtues*, for example, records that sin 'is ariȝt gret seknesse, and þe schrift is þe medicine', but also that both 'wikked humores' in the body and 'wikked tecches [vices]' in the heart need to be driven out to restore a person to spiritual health.[4] Medieval healthcare, however, was administered by a spectrum of practitioners ranging from physicians and surgeons to barbers, midwives and apothecaries.[5] In London, barbers and surgeons were organised under separate guilds; elsewhere, according to Carole Rawcliffe, 'there was no overt demarcation between the two groups at least for organisational or administrative purposes'.[6] Such separation, where it occurred, however, did not preclude barbers from undertaking surgical procedures. Under the London Barbers' guild structure were two crafts: 'barbery proper', practised by 'Barbitonsures' and defined as that concerned with phlebotomy and tooth-drawing; and barber-surgery (though this is not a medieval term), practised by 'Masters of the Barbers exercising the faculty of Surgery'. Surgeons (distinct again from barbers 'exercising the faculty of surgery') remained a relatively elite and small group – with numbers sometimes fewer than twelve and no more than twenty in the guild.[7] Barbers proper and barbers practising surgery, which I mainly refer to under the catch-all term 'barber-surgeon', had particular responsibility for shaving, bloodletting and dental procedures such as tooth-drawing.[8] Outside Cambridge and Oxford, the numbers of barber-surgeons in the fourteenth century in fact far outweighed numbers of physicians: the 1381 Lay Poll Tax returns for York, for example, record eighteen barbers, but just one physician.[9] On this evidence, the ordinary medieval man or woman would more rarely encounter a physician but was likely to have been rather better acquainted with his or her local barber-surgeon. Identifying 'the surgeon's rapid emergence as a figure of literary significance in the fourteenth century', Jeremy Citrome documents, in a number of Middle English examples, the transformation of the surgeon 'into both religious metaphor and psychological agent'.[10] Citrome's study sheds particular light on the transference of the surgeon's treatment of wounds to the confessor's cure of the soul, both of which might require a corrective or punitive form of wounding as much as a process of healing.[11] However, on the cultural impact of the barber-surgeon's more mundane crafts of shaving, tooth-pulling and teeth-cleaning, Citrome is wholly silent. Yet, the hygienic and surgical care of the mouth (in which physicians, surgeons and barbers might all variously be implicated) provides a powerful analogy for the work of pastoral care, and especially for confession in the late medieval period. More than just analogy, however, the barber-surgeon's work of shaving hair, paring skin and flesh, and filing teeth plays a crucial role in keeping the body's form and physiology in check and, thus, in turn, in facilitating virtuous living and spiritual fitness. More particularly, in its concern with the superfluities of the body, the barber-surgeon's craft works to correct the vitiations of regimen and diet and of unregulated eating and drinking. In his concern with the pathologies of the mouth, the barber-surgeon works to maintain the mouth's two primary offices: its capacity to eat and also to speak.

The barber-surgeon's attentiveness to the skin's surface and the body's superfluities arises in part from the medieval adherence to the theory of humours and the importance of humoural balance. As *On the Properties of Things* discloses (following Galen), 'þe body renneþ, lykeþ [leaks], and droppiþ, as in swetynge, spettinge, and oþir suche' (I, 148). Thus food and drink are needed to restore what is lost in the body.[12] Hair, nails and teeth are the by-products of the last part of the digestion process, which works to restore the body. Formed from humours that transgress the edges of the body, hair, nails and teeth are necessarily subject to trimming, cutting and paring. So, Bartholomaeus records that teeth are humours pushed to the boundaries of the body;[13] nails, like hair through the pores of the skin, pass the end of the fingers and 'þere þe fumositees [fumes] entreth and ben idryed outward by þe aier, and chaungiþ into substaunce of nayles' (I, 226–7). If humoural imbalance occurs in the body through excess consumption or abstention, however, food is imperfectly digested and so 'apostemes' (any morbid swelling or inflammation) develop.[14] Similarly, if any of the four humours are out of balance – moisture, dryness, heat or coldness, which precipitate rottenness, cracking, swelling or hardness respectively – protuberances form at the margins and boundaries of the body, as *On the Properties of Things* relates:

> [when] hete is feble and may not defye it [food] nouþir make þerinne parfite digestioun nor waste it at þe fulle, it lediþ þat moisture vndefied now to þe ouere parties and now to þe neþere. And whanne þis sendinge is igedred, it is cause of diuers eueles ... (I, 145)

When there is not enough heat in the body to digest food perfectly, undigested 'moisture' is drawn to the body's extremities, causing 'diuers eueles'. Since the physiological processes of assimilation and purgation are imperfect, the quest to maintain human form requires intervention in the body. The three crafts (or 'operations') of surgery, as Guy de Chauliac recounts, are: 'to loose þat is contynue' through bloodletting and 'garsynge' (scarification); 'to ioyne þat is departed' through healing wounds and fractures; and 'to kut of þat is to moche', such as 'postomes [apostemes]' or 'kernellis [a swollen gland or pathological lump or growth]'.[15] This third aspect – cutting off that which 'is to moche' – is part of a general medical project, akin to shaving hair, bloodletting and drawing teeth, which is concerned with superfluous bodily material and which works to remedy the body's propensity to overspill its own bounds.

If the body's ability to digest and assimilate food is naturally subject to a gradual decline, so too, as earlier chapters explore, is it compromised by eating habits: excessive eating of rich food fosters the physiological circumstances for sin, but such sin might also manifest itself in excrescences and protuberances on the surface of the body and on the inside of the mouth. Eaterly attitudes underlie human disposition to vice or virtue, but also to swellings, lumps, growths and blemishes. The barber-surgeon, concerned with the external surface of the body, with the skin and its convexities, acts to remove superfluities and aberrations in bodily form. In the same way, the goal of the confessor is to pare away the superfluous matter created by sin – both on the invisible material of the soul and in sin's psychosomatic manifestation in the body. To some extent these are therefore complementary activities: the barber-surgeon (as well as the physician) is in league with the confessor. Both are vital agents in maintaining spiritual and bodily health in the Middle Ages. Confessor and surgeon sometimes might even have been the very same figure, despite prohibitions against the religious shedding blood.[16] John Ottryngton, Chaplain of St John's Ouse Bridge in York, for example, appears in the records 'accused before the Dean and Chapter court in 1424 of practising surgery, including incision of women's breasts'.[17]

The fifteenth-century Middle English translation of the thirteenth-century *De doctrina cordis* – a 'devotional bestseller' – provides a striking example of the convergence of pastoral care and the craft of barber-surgery.[18] Chapter 5 of *The Doctrine of the Hert* treats 'How and in what wise a mynche [nun] shuld yif [give] here hert to God be þe yifte of counseyle', and explains what it means for a nun to submit herself in perfect obedience to her superior. To do so, it takes up the terms of the craft of barber-surgery:

> ¶ It shuld fare be a cloystrer [a monastic] þat is undir obedience as it doth with a man þat is schave under a barbouris rasoure. ¶ Thou wost wel: he þat sit under a rasoure he suffreth þe barbour to turne his hede, now on þe to

side, now on þe toþer syde, now he suffreth him to opyn his mowth, and
now for to lefte up his chyn, and al þis he suffreth lest he be hurte of þe
rasoure yif he stroglid.

¶ Right so shuld a cloystrer do. As longe as þou art under þe governaunce
of þi sovereyn in religioun, so longe þou art under þe hondes of a barboure
for to schave away þi synnes. Be not rebel ne stryve not under þe rasour
of correccioun, but suffre it lowly be it never so scharp, lest þou be hurt
grevously in soule be þin unobedience.[19]

The 'cloystrer', then, should submit to her superior as a man does to a
barber-surgeon – or to his razor – when his beard and head are shaved.[20] The
analogy is drawn out in vivid, experiential detail: the physical manipulation
of the head tilted first one and then the other way, the opened mouth,
the lifted chin. As such, both processes – being shaved and submitting
to religious governaunce – are understood as forms of correction that are
not entirely comfortable for its subjects, and not entirely without risk: the
razor is sharp.[21] The 'cloystrer' and the barber's patient should therefore
submit without resistance. In this Middle English translation, however,
the analogy is unstable: 'As longe as þou art under þe governaunce of þi
sovereyn in religioun, so longe þou art under þe hondes of a barboure for to
schave away þi synnes.'[22] It is, of course, the superior's task metaphorically
to shave away sins, but the syntax makes possible that it might also literally
be the barber's.

John Mirk's *Festial* similarly demonstrates the implication of the craft
of barber-surgery in pastoral care. Mirk's explanation (provided to spare
priests from shame when 'lewed men, þe wyche beth of many wordus and
prowde in here wytte, wollon askon prestus diuerse questions of þinggus
þat towchon þe seruice of Holy Chirche') of the traditions surrounding
Schere Þursday (that is, Maundy Thursday) in the *Festial* demonstrates that
the craft of barber-surgery mirrors, but also facilitates, spiritual processes.[23]
Drawing on the authority of John Beleth ('as Ion Belette telluth and
techuth'), Mirk explains:

on Schere Þursday a man schal dodun [shave] his heued and clypponde his
berde, and a prest schal schaue his crowne, so þat þere schal no þinge bene
betwene Gode almython and hym. He schal also schauen þe herus of his
berde, þat cometh of superfluite of humeres of þe stomak, and pare þe nayles
of his handes, þat cometh of superfluite of humerus of þe herte. So þat ryȝte os
we schauyn and scheron away þe superfluite of filthe withowtyn, so we schalle
schauon and scheron away þe superfluite of synne and off vices withineforthe.[24]

Shaving off the superfluous filth on the exterior body mirrors – operates
in parallel with – the shaving of the superfluities of sin from the interior.

Both actions are necessary to prepare the Christian to receive the body of Christ in the form of the host as part of the Easter liturgy. Exemplifying the confluence between medicine and religion emerging in vernacular theology in this period, Mirk retains Beleth's explanation of physiology in glossing spiritual practices, not dismissing as irrelevant the detail that it is specifically the superfluity of the stomach which produces facial hair and that of the heart which produces nails. The stress in Beleth's twelfth-century *Summa de ecclesiasticis officiis*, however, is on the way in which shaving hair and trimming nails act as a reminder – it 'signifies that' ('significat quod') we ought to 'trim back the faults and sins which are superfluities in us'.[25] Mirk's Englishing instead implies they are complementary, indeed, parallel actions. The physical act of paring away bodily superfluities itself is necessary, in conjunction with confession, to rid the body of sin and make it fit for devotion: 'schauon' (to shave) and 'scheron' (to shear) are actions – including scraping, chafing, paring, polishing, shaving, cutting into and cutting off – that are to be performed both on the body and on the soul.[26]

I have gone to such lengths to set up some of the ways in which barber-surgery is implicated in spiritual work – as preparation for participation in liturgical performance and for consuming the host; as a means of figuring the process of cleansing and regulating the soul – because it underscores the way in which the physical care of the body and its material shaping are imaginatively, as well as literally, implicated in shaping Christian identity and cultivating virtuous habits. As medieval surgical treatises and encyclopaedias also show, shaving and shearing take on more specific connotations in the mouth itself, and in ways that have very specific implications for properly formed speech and for understanding how utterances have material and spiritual consequences. As allegories and analogies for thinking about the processes of speaking and confessing, common oral remedies and the daily practices of washing and cleansing the mouth – whether performed by medical practitioners or delineated in the textual tradition – destabilise the allegorical level on which they at first operate, since they also have a real effect on these cognitive processes and spiritual practices.

Oral Surgery

Further to shaving and paring the body's surface, the barber-surgeon is the specialist practitioner of oral surgery.[27] Oral hygiene, tooth-drawing and treatments for diseases of the mouth are the common stuff of remedy books and also, by the fourteenth century, of vernacular medical and surgical manuals. Thus, fourteenth-century Middle English receipt books record remedies for: 'vermibus in dentibus' (tooth-worm), 'ȝelow [yellow] and stynkyng teþe', 'touþ-ache', 'cancre in þe teth', stinking breath, speech impediments, blisters and 'waggyng of teth'.[28] Surgical treatises such as Guy de Chauliac's, as well as encyclopaedias such as Vincent of Beauvais's, provide detailed descriptions of treatments for the mouth's pathologies. The textual basis for oral surgical knowledge in this period is in large part indebted to the late tenth-century encyclopaedic medical treatise (the *al-Tasrif*) of Albucasis (Abu al Qasim al Zahrāwī), a surgeon from Cordoba. Book 30 of the *al-Tasrif*, which circulated independently from the rest of the treatise, deals specifically with surgery and was known through Gerard of Cremona's twelfth-century Latin translation, the *Liber Alsaharavi de cirurgia*.[29] Widely influential, Cremona's *Liber* was also translated into medieval vernaculars and drawn on in particular by Italian and French surgeons.[30] Guy, for example, substantially derives his knowledge of dentistry, as well as his illustrations of surgical instruments, from Albucasis.[31]

The textual tradition of oral surgery betrays a particular concern with deformities or diseases that might diminish the powers of the soul that operate through the mouth and its parts. Remedies thus include cutting the strings under the tongue if they are hindering speech because they are too tight: 'þe cure of þe þrede or of þe ligament drawynge þe tonge is kyttynge by þe brede [crosswise] til þat þe tonge be lousede fro his wiþhaldynge, as Albucasis saith'.[32] While cutting a ligament is recommended in this instance, the majority of the remedies prescribed in surgical treatises take the closely related forms of scraping, shaving, shearing, filing and rubbing. Thus, in the instance of a tooth full of filth, worms and holes, Guy recommends that, if washing the mouth has had no effect, a process akin to shaving be tried:

> If thise [washing and gargling] avayle not forsoþe, rowme it wiþ a shauynge knyf, and make a way þerto þat mete be noght wiþholden in the hole. And if þis availe not, brenne it. And if it be nede, drawe it out.[33]

To 'rowme' is to scrape or bore out the decayed matter from the tooth with a razor-like shaving knife. In the event this does not cure the problem, then the tooth should be cauterised ('brenne it') and, if necessary, extracted ('drawe it out').[34] Similarly, in the case of discolouration, if washing and 'frotynge' (rubbing) have failed to clean them, the teeth should be scraped or shaved: 'for þat þere were hardenede filþes, schaue hem with schauynge knyfes and wiþ spatures [cutting instruments]'.[35] These procedures are likewise derived from Albucasis, whose recommendation to scrape the rough, blackened scales that collect on the inner and outer surface of the teeth and on the gums becomes a medieval medical commonplace.[36] Archaeological remains from York provide evidence that these kinds of treatment were carried out: three skulls excavated from the cemetery of the Gilbertine Priory of St Andrew in Fishergate showed 'a polished appearance on the teeth and abrasion of the enamel on their external surface, probably indicating regular cleaning of the teeth during life'.[37] Encyclopaedias and surgical treatises attest that the tongue as well as the teeth might be subject to a form of scraping, as a fifteenth-century surgical treatise (after 'saint William of Touke', an unidentified authority) extant in London British Library MS Sloane 563, records: 'ffor filthe abowte þe teth þat cometh ofte tyme of þe stomake And clevith on þe tongue and so þe teth ben foule shave [scrape] þe tongue wiþ trene [wooden] knife made of hasell'.[38]

As recommended in the Latin and vernacular translations of the *al-Tasrif*, when there are too many teeth or when teeth are overgrown they too should be shaved and filed down or extracted.[39] Albucasis further urges the surgeon to carry out the filing of the tooth gradually over a number of days so that the tooth is not loosened.[40] Repeating this lore, Guy records: 'If þe toþe were encresede ouer kynde, even it, and playn it sliely [cautiously] with a file, and move it nou3t.'[41] Albucasis further instructs that if a tooth is broken and causes pain when speaking it should be filed down until the 'tooth is smooth and neither injures the tongue nor hinders speech'.[42] Mediating Albucasis's instructions on overgrown teeth, Vincent advises variously in the *Speculum doctrinale* that the tooth should be extracted with a pair of forceps ('cum forcipibus extrahatur'), or, if another tooth would be affected, levelled with a file ('si quid superfuerit lima explanetur').[43] Vincent further records, 'if any of the teeth is larger than is proper, which will be clearly ugly, it is necessary to correct it with a file, and remove what is superfluous, whereby it should be made equal to the other ones, corresponding in proportion'.[44] Such filing, then, might also be carried out on aesthetic grounds.

In the case of dead flesh in the mouth, 'fretynge' (*MED*, s.v. 'freten' (v.), 'to file or scrape', 'rub to pieces') and 'frotynge' (*MED*, s.v. 'froten' (v.), 'to rub', 'to polish') are commonly prescribed – actions that imbricate with those of scraping or filing.[45] The remedy for 'fetore oris' (stench of mouth) outlined in *On the Properties of Things*, for example, dictates that when rotten teeth are the cause they should be extracted, but when rotten gums are they should be 'ifrotid and iclansid' with medicines, and the roots likewise 'frotid and iclensid' with powders and honey (I, 370). In the case of discoloured teeth, Lanfrank advises the teeth and gums should be 'froted' with a medicinal powder.[46] In a section on remedies for toothache, Guy records a recipe ('Take of mercurye, of peritorye [a medicinal plant] menely [moderately] brent', etc.) which he instructs should be applied by 'frotyng': 'frote þe rootes of þe tieth and of þe gomes, of moyste gomes and nouȝt of drye gomes'.[47] 'Frotyng' is not, however, simply an abrasive method of cleansing a part of the mouth; it is also, for example, a means of drawing superfluous humours from the body. Thus Guy advocates 'wasshynges of þe mouthe or frotynges of þe tonge' as part of the tripartite therapy for 'wlaffyng' (that is, stammering or stuttering), which is caused by excessive moisture.[48] Elsewhere in the *Cyrurgie*, 'frotyng' is the means by which the humours causing a swollen tongue can be led out of the body (through spitting); 'ranula' – an abscess under the tongue 'lettynge [hindering] his [its] werke' – similarly should first be treated with 'rubbynge and frotynge' medicines.[49] The Middle English translation of Gilbertus Anglicus's medical writings prescribes 'frotyng' as a means of diagnosis as well as remedy: in order to diagnose whether the gums are the cause of stinking breath, 'frote and rubbe þy gummes with þi fyngir and þy mouþe wil stynke'. In which case, 'if þer be eny roted flesshe, let freten it awei and þen hele it vp'.[50] Like Absolon, the parish-clerk-cum-barber-surgeon in 'The Miller's Tale', who 'rubbeth now, who froteth now his lippes / With dust, with sond, with straw, with clooth, with chippes', medieval care of the mouth commonly requires abrasive treatment.[51] Instructions to barber-surgeons to employ 'fretynge' and 'frotynge' variously indicate: rubbing or scraping the gums, lips, tongue or palate of the mouth in order to remove dead or diseased flesh and growths (such as epulis and ulcers); an abrasive method of cleaning and polishing the teeth or gums; and a technique for applying medicines via the mouth, especially to draw out excess or corrupt humours.

The removal of teeth, however, is always prescribed as a last course of action, because of the dangers inherent in the process, but also because of its implications for speech and for reason. The presence of teeth is associated with an ability to discern good from evil, with participation in rational society and with appetite. Their loss thus has wide-ranging implications for human status. As the *Cyrurgie* outlines, every attempt should be made to save a tooth loosened – either by a blow, by 'lubrifieng' (which makes the sinew 'sliddry') or by 'fretynge' (which loosens the flesh of the gums) – through withdrawing nourishment to reduce excess moisture, or by bloodletting and binding. The patient in turn is instructed to avoid eating hard foods and to 'lesse [reduce]' his speech.[52] MS Sloane 563 observes, in cases of toothache, that only after first making a 'ruptory' behind the head to let blood from an artery in the temple, and thereafter trying cautery, should extraction be resorted to: 'þe laste remedy of alle is to drawe owte þe tothe'.[53] What might in part lie behind this anxiety about pulling teeth is their physiological connection with the substance of the brain. The *Prose Salernitan Questions* record the example of the philosopher at Delphi who died after having a tooth drawn: since teeth are formed from the overflow of the substance of the brain and the marrow of the eyes or cheekbones, drawing a tooth might cause the substance of the brain to be drawn out with it.[54] Thus, in Guy's instructions for 'pullynge vp of tieþ by þe rootes', he urges that, after having 'þe pacient putte bytwene þe legges in a clere place', the barber-surgeon should 'vnhelle [uncover] þe roote of þe tothe al aboute, and move it slyly and fully þat no schrewed [corrupt] siknesse come to the tieth of þe ey3e or of þe bone of þe iawe'.[55] This movement must be done with care because of the risk, recalling the fate of the philosopher at Delphi, of disrupting humoural matter 'of þe ey3e or of þe bone of þe iawe' into the teeth, thus bringing further sickness. At most, tooth extraction can lead to death; at the least it can diminish the ability of the human to think and to create and craft speech.

The dictates of surgical texts and encyclopaedias for the care of the mouth and its parts thus have as their goal, alongside mitigating unsightly teeth and the social embarrassment of bad breath, the promotion of the work of eating and the preservation, even improvement, of the capacity to speak. In cataloguing the varied treatments for the passions of the mouth, these medical texts remind us not only that disease and deformity in the mouth have implications for the action of eating and speaking, but also that the painful experience of toothache, or an ulcerated tongue or gums, might punctuate meal times or interrupt the repetitions of prayer in daily devotions. As such they are part of the spectrum of experience of the everyday body. In his *Confessions*, Augustine recounts a time when he experienced 'the agony of toothache', in which 'the pain became so great that I could not speak'. When he asks (through a written note) his friends to pray on his behalf the pain vanishes, leading Augustine to recognise both 'the sting' of God's 'lash', as well as the swiftness of his mercy.[56] Medicalised descriptions likewise point to the painful, embodied conditions of which they are the symptoms – conditions that might, as they do for Augustine, be embedded in the processes of coming to self-knowledge and knowledge of God.

If oral treatments have literal consequences for forming speech and for rational thinking, the surgical lexis of scraping, shaving, shearing, as well as 'fretynge' and 'frotynge', is also taken up to think about the *effects* of speaking, whether of 'speaking well' (through grammatical speech or in confession) or of 'speaking badly' (lying, backbiting or other sins of the tongue). Treatises on grammar display an understanding of the surgical power of speech to shape human form and Christian identity. The surgical lexis, in turn, blends with an ethical and spiritual vocabulary for thinking about the effects of sin and the process of confession and reformation, as we see in *pastoralia* and devotional poems that articulate the deleterious effects of speech (destroying the self and maiming others), as well as its corrective power through confession in surgical terms.

Learning to Speak Well: Grammar and Surgery

Among the various traditions – scientific, philosophical, biblical and pastoral – in which the organs of speech become surgical instruments and speaking becomes a surgical act, the trivial arts provide the most sustained and developed allegory in which the corrective, reforming potential of speaking well (i.e. grammar) is figured in explicitly surgical terms. Grammar and dentistry are in fact logical counterparts, for just as grammar facilitates speaking well, aspects of dental surgery (in theory) work to correct physical impediments to speech. A twelfth-century poem, *Ad adelam comitissam*, composed by Baudri de Bourgueil for William the Conqueror's daughter, points to this close association of grammar and medicine, speech and surgery, in medieval thinking.[57] In his poem to Adèle, Baudri describes her chamber in which, surrounded by richly tapestried walls, the statue of Grammar stands along with other representations of the trivial arts:

> The statue of Grammar brilliantly shone at the side of her sister;
>   Rhetoric's neighbour and friend within the trivial arts.
> She held an eight-part tool, a kind of coarse-toothed file,
>   Which, in her healing hands served to polish rough teeth.
> With her medicinal shears she'd cut back the lips she judged faulty,
>   Quickly fill in the cut, trim the wound's edges with care.
> Tending the wound she would smear it with a particular powder:
>   Made from the cuttlefish's ink, or from the fire's black soot.
> For it's her duty to train and improve the mouths of young children,
>   And to soften and smooth all that sounds awkward or shrill.[58]

In *Ad adelam*, Grammar files the teeth of children and trims their lips. Her eight-toothed file ('limam') and her shears ('forpicibus') represent the rules that govern language; so too are they instruments pertaining to the craft of barber-surgery.[59] Grammar's instruments are labile images. On the one hand, her shears are a tool used by the teacher-cum-surgeon, who acts on the material of the body, suggesting an intervention in the mouth by an external agent. On the other hand, they are the speaker's own lips which clip and cut words. Likewise, the file wielded by Grammar becomes a part of the very anatomy of the body it acts upon – an internal, natural organ that works on the materials of speech, on air, sound and voice. In other words, the tongue both should be filed and is itself a file.

Baudri's conception of grammar is derived from Martianus Capella's fifth-century work *De nuptiis philologiæ et Mercurii*. Capella's description of Grammar as a 'physician' with a file 'divided into eight golden parts' with which 'by gentle rubbing she gradually cleaned dirty teeth and ailments of the tongue' gains widespread currency in the medieval period.[60] John of Salisbury's (1159) *Metalogicon* repeats Martianus's description of Grammar 'with a knife, a rod, and the ointment case carried by physicians. She uses the knife to prune away grammatical errors, and to cleanse the tongues of infants as she instructs them.'[61] Holding a rod, John's Grammar physically disciplines as well as surgically corrects children. In the *Anticlaudianus* (c.1182), Alan of Lille similarly depicts Grammar – one of seven maidens enlisted to correct the defects of man – holding a file in one hand, with which she 'cleans the tartar from the teeth'. If 'one tooth strays from the rest of the row, she cuts the outgrowth back to normal'. She 'teaches infants to speak, looses tied tongues and shapes words in the proper mould'.[62] The varying oral surgical treatments these personifications perform – polishing rough teeth with a file; rubbing dirty teeth clean; cutting the strings that restrict the tongue; filing back overgrown teeth – all find their counterparts in received surgical tradition and, arguably, in practice. Learning to speak Latin is imagined as an oral surgical procedure. Soo too do these texts implicate learning to speak well through grammar with the remedial medical work of forming and shaping the child's mouth, teeth and tongue.

Grammar's concern with training and moulding the child's mouth recalls the instructions in regimen for infants to rub the teeth, tongue and gums to encourage both the growth of teeth and the onset of speech, as well as the ability to eat 'mete' instead of drinking milk.[63] So too does it accord with the correlation of the appearance of permanent teeth with the onset of an ability to discern good and evil and with the entry into pedagogical structures – that is, in other words, to begin to learn Latin and to cultivate a virtuous *habitus*. As Katharine Breen summarises: 'as the first subject of formal study, and a learned language with clearly articulated rules, it [grammar] was thought to shape the mind linguistically and morally from the very first repetitions of *do, das, dat*.[64] If grammar is the paradigmatic *habitus*, it is markedly medicalised and embodied. It therefore bears out not only the bodily basis of medieval theories of virtue acquisition, but also the fundamental role of regimen and medicine – that is, of the care of the self – to them. Rita Copeland observes that grammar

> is the most physically embodied of the *trivium* arts (with its emphasis on tongue and mouth for pronouncing words, and the formation of letters inscribed on parchment or wax by fingers correctly holding pens), it is also enacted in and through the bodies of the students learning its rules.[65]

Classroom teaching in general and learning Latinate habits in particular are peculiarly embodied practices in medieval contexts.

This association of oral surgery, physical discipline and education reappears in university initiation rituals, where, in addition to the teeth being filed, the initiate is also made to confess his sins, as he is in *The Manuale Scholarium* (a late fifteenth-century German handbook comprising Latin dialogues).[66] Both Marie-Christine Pouchelle and Jacques Le Goff suggest that these rituals originate much earlier in the medieval period and were practised more widely in Europe.[67] While there is not comparable evidence from England, Ruth Mazo Karras notes that 'shaving also appears in the records of New College, Oxford, from 1400; it was apparently a "vile and horrible" ritual inflicted upon new masters of arts the night before their inception'.[68] In the *Manuale*, the initiate (or *bejaunus*) is described as rude, unlearned, stinking like a beast, bearing horns and having 'teeth, sticking out in both directions from his jaw'. Furthermore, the initiate cannot speak properly, but rather mumbles and stammers. Thus, the problem of badly formed, overgrown teeth raised in the medical tradition is displayed with exaggerated and animal effect. A 'physician' is summoned and he applies a salve to the initiate's mouth and nose and then saws off his horns. Next, the physician takes up some forceps and extracts the initiate's teeth; a sharp razor is used to shave his beard and then he is made to confess to outrageous crimes.[69] This ritual rids the initiate of his bestiality and effects a process of smoothing, filing and shaving away his superfluities – namely, the excrescences and protuberances of the everyday and unlearned body.

As a parody of confession, this ritual must also reveal something about the perceptions of confession itself; confession works towards producing a body (and soul) unmarred by the deformities and superfluities of sin. In both parodic and serious contexts, speaking enacts a procedure that is articulated in terms of the craft of dentistry and barber-surgery. These examples of the regulating effects of the speech of those acted on not only by surgery but also by formal pedagogical structures raise the question, however, of whether such surgical benefits extend to lay, vernacular teeth and tongues as well.

Vernacular Habits

The Latinate figure of Grammar borrows from the (rude) craft of barber-surgery to figure the close nexus of (grammatical) speech and ethics. In so doing, the analogy of Grammar to the barber-surgeon simultaneously discloses a closer, literal connection between properly shaped, clean teeth and a freely moving tongue, on the one hand, and the capacity to speak well, on the other. The ethical project in which grammar is implicated is, of course, first and foremost a Latinate one, and the body it acts upon a male one. However, medieval understandings of the material basis and effects of speaking, which underpin Grammar's surgical effects, are themselves the 'kynde' attributes described in vernacular natural philosophy and theology: the lips are thin and subtle, *On the Properties of Things* observes, in order to move easily, but also 'to forkutte þe aier' (1, 199); the tongue is 'ischape as a swerd' (1, 208); teeth 'ben able to kerue al þing, and alle þing þat þey fongiþ [receive] þei brusiþ and bitiþ atwynne' (1, 202). Such descriptions resonate with the figural explanations of how corrective speech might act, as it does in Hebrews 4:12, as a sword piercing the heart or cutting through sin.[70] Sinful speech – like the barber's razor – also wounds and harms. *Speculum vitae* describes the 'felounes' (evildoers) 'Whase tunges er mare sharpe bytande / Þan any rasour in barbours hande'.[71] Chaucer's 'Manciple's Tale' likewise exemplifies the deadly effects of an unrestrained tongue. Moralising the fate of the crow who tells Phebus of his wife's adultery, the Manciple ventriloquises his mother's teaching – teaching that draws on the natural example of the mouth's physiology, as well as on Solomon, the Psalmist David and Seneca – to warn that a 'rakel' (that is, rash or rebellious) tongue works to destroy friendship just as 'a swerd forkutteth and forkerveth / An arm a-two'.[72] The work of grammar (which is performed both externally, through pedagogy, but also internally once acquired), then, is to mould and shape mouths and to rein in the tongue under reason. But so too, since the tongue without regulation becomes a deadly weapon, is the training of 'rude' and 'boistous' mouths the objective of pastoral care. As Middle English *pastoralia* makes clear: lay, vernacular tongues, like Latinate ones, when governed by reason can also file words and govern and shape the ethical self.

In a section on the gift of 'cunnyng' (knowledge) and its corresponding virtue, that of 'equyte' (measure, temperance), *The Book of Vices and Virtues* outlines for its lay (as for its clergial) readers a model of the co-ordination of the rational part of the soul with its lower appetites and with the body. It is this co-ordination that enables the 'equyte' that, in turn, leads to good self-governance, virtuous dispositions and filed speech – in other words, a virtuous *habitus*. Such 'equyte' should result from the childhood teaching of the Manciple's dame, and would have spared Phebus's crow. The heart, it explains, has two sides: understanding and will are in one side; reason and affection in the other. When these two sides accord, they 'maken a swete melodie and wel faire seruice'. The particular offices of reason are outlined as fourfold: 'to enquere', 'to juge', 'to þenke wel on' and 'to schewe þat sche vnderstont bi word'.[73] The logical result of inquiry, judgement and careful consideration is the expression of reason in speech. This process 'makeþ þe resoun speke bi mesure and gladliche be stylle and not speke gladliche, so þat þe word mowe sunnere come to þe *vile* þan to þe tonge'. In ways not unlike those modelled by Grammar, the material word is here subject to a process of filing by the tongue. The perception of the tongue as a file (or of the substitution of the tongue with a file), in this case drawing on Gregory the Great, is a commonplace one in Middle English contexts. *On the Properties of Things* thus reveals a similar catenation (likewise citing Gregory):

> Gregor seiþ þat þe mouþe is closed and iclippid with many kepinges and wardes, as wiþ teeþ and lippis, þat by so many meenes þe witte and þe soule may deme and auyse what he schal speke, þat þe word may raþir *passe by þe fyle þan by þe tonge*. (1, 200, my emphasis)

Armed with the faculty of judgement – in the mouth, between its teeth – the tongue is transformed into a file, which subjects speech to painful but beneficial smoothing and cleansing, just as the barber-surgeon files the tongue and teeth and just as Grammar does. *The Book of Vices and Virtues*, however, continues that words should come 'to þe vile', so

> þat sche be weye to loke þat sche be good as moneye & asayed, as Salamon seiþ; þat is to seye þat þe wordes ben as good matere as of good metal, and of good schap, þat is to seyn and to speken in good wise, and þat it haue his riȝt wiȝt [weight] and his riȝt noumbre.[74]

Here, mixing the authority of Gregory with Solomon (Ecclesiastes 5:2), the image of the tongue as a file evokes, not surgery, but filing metal coins: in either analogy, however, words must be filed and tested.[75] This reminds us that figures and metaphors rarely (if ever) signify singly or uniformly, but multiply: measured, reasoned speech is like surgical filing, like filing metal, like testing money.

This vernacular pastoral model for virtue acquisition shares with the grammatical habit the understanding of the tongue as a file. In a confessional context, these perceptions about speech and the instruments of speech become part of a characteristically medieval ethical project to which the everyday body is subject, and suggest a nexus between epistemological practices, speech-acts and bodily form. The vocabulary of scraping, shaving, filing and 'fretynge' – found in surgical treatises and allegories of grammar alike – becomes a fitting mode of understanding the effect of confession (as well as what happens when a subject *does not* confess), which not only cleanses and reshapes the soul but also erases the material as well as the invisible evidence of sin. As *Ancrene Riwle* observes, 'shrift hit schrapeþ'.[76] In the same vein, Mirk teaches in the sermon for the second Sunday of Lent in the *Festial* that 'Lenton is ordeynod only for to schow[r]on' – that is, to scour, to polish – 'and to clenson ʒoure conscience of alle maner ruste and fylthe of synne þat he is defouled inne'.[77] *Book to a Mother* instructs the penitent to 'scrape it [sin] out wiþ sorew of herte and schrift of mouþe and satisfaccioun'.[78] Literal, material scouring and scraping therefore facilitates spiritual scraping and paring, both accompanying and figuring it. Here too the figure is labile. Confession makes recourse to multiple analogies: confessing is like scraping parchment, like scouring metal, but also, as I discuss below, like having your tongue filed, your teeth scraped, like sweeping your mouth out with a broom, like breaking pots or like self-harming.

The *disciplina* of the repeated act of penitence is, of course, the primary means of cultivating virtue and self-reformation in the laity. As Nicole Rice emphasises, in the penitential practices that develop after the Lateran Council of 1215, 'the penitent having expressed contrition for sin, was required to accuse herself and then … reform her own dispositions to produce a reformed self'.[79] The vernacularisation of pastoral literature, first intended to aid unlearned parish priests, makes clerical forms of spiritual discipline increasingly accessible to the laity; confessional practice seeks to redress and mitigate the problem of repeated habitual sin in the Christian community at large. According to Breen, an important difference between vernacular imaginings of *habitus* and their Latinate counterparts is that Middle English authors such as Mirk and Langland are engaged in thinking through how to make virtue accessible to a community already engrained in the habits of sin.[80] In this context, if the threefold sacrament of penance – working contrition in the heart, confession in the mouth and satisfaction in deed – is its fundamental vehicle, its efficacy is also often questioned.

Two Middle English examples – those of Dame Penance in the *Pilgrimage* and of Envy in *Piers Plowman* – demonstrate the ways in which late medieval penitential and confessional allegories offer vernacular versions of the clergial models of *habitus*, sharing with them an understanding of the surgical effects of both learning to speak and the process of speaking, as well as a literal and figurative understanding of the tongue as an instrument of ethical action and correction. In the *Pilgrimage* the allegorical tradition of Grammar is written into the attributes of Dame Penance. Here, the corrective process of speaking a confession, as well as the deleterious effects of sinful speech, is imagined as oral surgical treatments. Reading Middle English confessional discourses through the lenses of the craft of barber-surgery, on the one hand, and the authoritative figure of Grammar, on the other hand, discloses both the inherently surgical nature of speech-acts and the ethical project by which 'speaking the self' and modifying the mouth transforms the body but also (re)constructs human identity.

Dame Penance

At the point that Dame Penance enters the scene in *The Pilgrimage of the Life of Man*, Grace Dieu has been teaching the Pilgrim about the sacrament of the altar. The Pilgrim has thus witnessed the bread turned into raw flesh, listened to the confusion of Reson at how this could be, and seen the anger of Nature at this transgression of her laws turn to humble repentance. Now the Pilgrim, having observed Moses serve the crowd 'releef' (a meal) at his 'borde' (the altar), sees two ladies come among the people, one of whom is revealed to be Dame Penance (the other is revealed later to be Charity). Dame Penance holds a hammer in one hand, a broom ('bysme') in her mouth and a rod ('yerde') in her other hand. Drawing curious gazes from the pilgrims gathered at Moses' altar, she undertakes to educate them in her allegorical significance. Recalling the maidens of allegories of the seven liberal arts, the capacious allegory of Dame Penance here incorporates and expands upon the attributes of Lady Grammar. Dame Penance uses her rod, we are told, 'To skouren [scour, polish, beat] chyldern' (4011). She is thus also 'off scolys a maystresse, / Chyldren, in ther wantownesse, / Affter ther gyltys to chastyse' (4475–7). The children she disciplines and trains in school can be any age from twenty to one hundred (4481–2).

The lifelong work of educating these intemperate sinners is that of penance, which is performed through three stages, each of which is represented by one of Dame Penance's instruments: the hammer is contrition, which is used on the heart; the broom is confession and works in the mouth; and the rod is satisfaction performed externally through the penitent's deeds. As Lisa H. Cooper remarks, these are standard tools, but '[Dame Penance's] explanation of what she does with them blurs the distinction of the inner and outer self'.[81] Dame Penance with her tools – like Grammar with her file – is an ambiguous and labile figure; she is, at once, external to and inside the Pilgrim, both the figure of the confessor and of the confessant. Her function, Dame Penance claims, is to clean the inner man 'Off allë fylthe & al ordure [filth]' (4060), for which purpose she holds the hammer and the broom (4063–5).[82] In the same way that Mirk explains the Maundy Thursday practices of shaving the hair and beard and clipping nails in the *Festial*, Dame Penance establishes this kind of introspection as a necessary precursor to participation in the meal that Moses distributes from the altar: she is the 'porteresse [door-keeper]' (4577) and 'trewë chaunceler [chief officer]' (4580) of this 'releff', which is 'trewë ffoode' (4589). No man may touch it if he has not first been chastised by her rod and hammer and swept with her broom. Firstly, then, Dame Penance uses the hammer of contrition to beat the sinner's heart. This painful process softens the hardened filth in the heart, which, when flushed out through the penitent's tears, Dame Penance washes with a 'lyë strong' (4140). Thus, in this domestic allegory, Dame Penance is a 'lavendere' (a laundress). Next, she explains that her hammer acts on the sinful man as it would on pots (4159–69). The pot of sin, full of hardened filth, must be broken and each shard scraped clean (4201) by considering all the circumstances of each sin. In this pot, Dame Penance warns, a worm is engendered that gnaws away 'vp-on hys mayster' (4282–3) if it is not dealt blows by the hammer. At this point, Dame Penance reveals that she is also a 'lavendere' (a laundress) 'chaumberere' (a chambermaid) and the Pilgrim's body is a domestic space (4151–2).[83] Once sin has been hammered, the broken shards are swept out with Dame Penance's broom through a gate that leads out of the building. There are, she clarifies, in fact six gates in the building, just as there were six gates in Nehemiah's city (Nehemiah 2–3). At this stage, the literal, anatomical meaning of the multivalent allegory is now revealed to be the body of man. Five gates, through which filth

can enter the building, are disclosed as anatomical referents – they are the
five senses:

> 'And by thys fyvë, day & nyht,
> Entreth in-to that mansïoun
> Al felthe & al corrupcyoun
> And al ordure (yt ys no doute),
> The wychë may nat comen oute
> Ageyn by hym in no manere.' (4400–5)

If filth enters daily into the body through these five sense organs, Dame
Penance asserts that there is only one exit through which the body can be
cleansed of this filth, namely and rather euphemistically through a 'sixth
gate':[84]

> 'ffor thys syxtë gate, in soth,
> Gret helthe & gret profyt doth;
> ffor yt maketh purgacioun
> Off al maner corrupcioun;
> …
> Thys gate ys callyd "the mouth off man".' (4411–20)

This sixth gate – the mouth of man – is as vital to the health of the
body through making 'purgacioun' as it is to the soul through making
confession. Given that the mouth itself, as the organ of taste, is one of
the five senses-as-gates through which filth 'may nat comen oute / Ageyn
by hym in no manere', as Dame Penance has earlier claimed, the reading
of the sixth gate as 'the mouth of man' rather than as his anus goes
somewhat against biology. It is, however, a slippage symptomatic of the
interchange and interorientation of mouth and anus. While laden with
legal and doctrinal connotations, the medical and physiological meanings
of 'purgacioun' are emphasised here: thus confession, as Dame Penance
continues, is the means by which 'men putten oute. / Who that wyl with-
Innë be Clene off al dishoneste, / To purge hym clene, as he best kan'
(4416–20). Notably, the body imagined here lacks an anus; the mouth
is one of five gates wherein filth enters but is, as the sixth gate, the *only*
exit for filth out of the body. Indeed, an anus would not fit Deguileville's
penitential model – which progresses from heart to mouth to deed – and
the only exit for sin in this body system is therefore back through the
mouth. Speech, issuing as excrement or vomit from this oro-anal orifice,
purges the body from the excesses and impurities of sin that have entered
it through the five senses.

Next, Dame Penance also reveals that the broom she holds in her mouth between her teeth is, in fact, her tongue: 'my bysme, that al thys [purging] doth, / Ys myn ownë Tonge, in soth, / Wher-with I swepe & make al wel' (4439–41).[85] With this tongue-as-broom, 'I cerche ech Angle & ech corner; / Euery hoolë, gret & smal, / I remewe, in éspecial, / Clene with-outen & with-Inne, / The fylthe of euery maner synne; / Caste hem out, & sparë nouht' (4444–9). The scouring performed with the tongue-as-broom is, of course, introspection expressed as confessional speech. Henry of Lancaster's *Le livre de seyntz medicines* – contemporary with Deguileville's second recension of the *Pilgrimage* – bears out similar perceptions of the mouth. Here, confession is shown to cleanse the soul in the same way that the tongue cleans the mouth:

> very sweet Lord, have mercy on me and give me grace to be able to heal the vile wound of my mouth with my tongue, and to clean the ordure that is therein with my tongue; that is to say, to immediately confess the vile sins of my mouth [along] with all the others [i.e. sins] though true confession [and] with sorrow of heart. And if I may in this way cure the wickedness of my mouth with my mouth, a very great favour, sweet Lord, would you do me [if you could] so soon and so easily heal [me].[86]

Just as the tongue helps to heal the mouth and, through 'frotynge' and 'scraping', clean the teeth, so does the tongue clean the mouth and soul of its sin in the process of speaking a confession. Dame Penance's ambiguous position (like Grammar's) makes her tongue that of correction (i.e. the confessor's), but also the Pilgrim's own when put to the task of penitential introspection and confession. Having laid bare the literal sense of the allegory – Penance occupies not a room in a house but the Pilgrim's mouth; her broom is not a broom but the Pilgrim's own tongue – the anatomical sense continues to show through the domestic allegory like a palimpsest.

From the perspective of this anatomical and medical register, the preceding allegory of contrition in Deguileville's poem can now be read over again, with the literal meaning of the mouth and its parts showing through its allegorical referents. The hammer breaks the pot of sin and the tears of contrition draw the filthy pieces of pot into the mouth – as Dame Penance asserts, 'fyrst off allë I begynne / To drawe the felthë hyd with-Inne / Out, to make yt shede a-brood, / Wych with-Inne so long a-bood' (4175–8).[87] Notably, the etymology of contrition underlies this process of breaking the pots: *contritio* (from *con* and *tero*), as described by Thomas Tentler, means 'a breaking up, or a smashing of something breakable into its smallest parts, as if all at once it were completely pulverised'.[88] Relocating sin from the heart to the mouth, the broken shards of pots become like teeth which must 'be cerchyd wel /

Touchynge hys ordure euerydel, / And yscrapyd clene a-way' (4199–201).
Evoking the technical procedures of barber-surgery – as the *Cyrurgie* records,
to remove 'hardenede filþes' from the teeth the barber-surgeon should 'schaue
hem with schauynge knyfes' – Dame Penance's scraping and the barber-
surgeon's shaving are homologous activities. In the speech-act of confession,
the tongue-as-broom scrapes and files pots-as-teeth in the mouth.

The reading of the broken shards of pot as teeth is reiterated by the
condition that afflicts them:

> Thys, the werm of conscïence,
> Wych hath hys teht by vyolence
> Hardere (who that lookë wel,)
> Than outher Iron outher stel;
> Wonder cruel, ay fretynge,
> And ryht perillous in percynge. (4273–8)

The fretting of the worm of Conscience mirrors medical descriptions of
the pathological condition known as tooth-worm. *On the Properties of
Things* records that 'wormes brediþ in þe cheke teeþ of rotid humours þat
beþ in þe holou3nes þerof, and þis is iknowe by icchinge and tikelinge,
and contynual dikkinge [boring, i.e. of worms] and þurlinge [piercing],
and by stenche þat comeþ þerof, and in many oþer wise' (1, 371). The
Cyrurgie devotes a whole section to this condition, the rubric of which
elaborates: 'Of filþe, of wormes and of fretynge and of persynge of the
tieth', recalling the very lexis of 'wormes', 'fretynge' and 'percynge' found in
the *Pilgrimage*.[89] Moreover, the *Cyrurgie's* remedy for tooth-worm parallels
the remedy of penance prescribed. Firstly, the *Cyrurgie* makes recourse to
medicinal treatments such as mouthwashes and gargles; thus the diseased
tooth should 'be wasshed with water ardaunt [*MED*, s.v. 'an alcoholic
distillate'] or with wyne'. Similarly, in the first stage of penance, as the
Pilgrimage describes, tears of contrition act like a mouthwash and soften
the 'indurat [hardened]' (4070) sins and make them 'souple, nesshe [soft],
and tendre' (4073). Next, the *Cyrurgie* advises that 'if thise [mouthwashes]
avayle not forsoþe, rowme it wiþ a schauynge knyf' – and 'rowme' (as
we have seen) is a word, like scrape and shave, meaning 'to scrape out (a
hole), ream out'.[90] Likewise, in the second stage of penance (in which the
conscience must be thoroughly scoured), the Pilgrim's pots-as-teeth are to
be 'cerchyd wel' and scraped clean by the tongue. Going to confession –
for Lydgate's toothache-prone reader – might thus evoke the experience
of having one's mouth washed and one's teeth literally scraped by the
barber-surgeon.

Dame Penance is a hybrid allegory: she is a laundress, a chambermaid, a schoolmistress. Like Grammar, so too is she a barber-surgeon. Both external to (in the form of a confessor) and inside the penitent (as the penitent's own tongue), penitential speech washes the soul as a cloth, or breaks sins as pots or scours them clean like teeth. As a model for thinking about how the process of self-reformation works in those in whom sin is hardened, the heterogeneity of the allegory – washing clothes, cleaning pots, curing toothache – fully occupies the register of the everyday and the experiential as (repetitive) sites for learning to 'do well'. It also accommodates within it a spectrum of bodily states and conditions, each of which requires forms of the care of the self: the dirty clothes in need of washing; the healthful body in which purgation is necessary; the suffering body that induces tears; the diseased body in which a worm festers. Reading between penitential and medical practice, the literal sense of Dame Penance's allegory suggests the ways in which the mouth forms the material basis for bodily and spiritual reform. So too does it suggest, with *The Doctrine of the Hert* and the *Festial*, that the confessor is in league with the barber-surgeon.

Dame Penance is closely related to Lady Ryghtwysnesse in the poem, who is instead a smith but similarly holds a file, this one 'callyd "Correccïoun"', with which she files sins down to the root so that no rust can remain or 'kankren' there (15,706–10): 'She skoureth yt a-way so clene, / That noon ordure may by sene' (15,711–12). 'Kankren' (*MED*, s.v.) means to corrode, but also 'to cause (a part of the body) to become cancerous', or 'to make an ulcer in a tooth'. Ryghtwysnesse, the Pilgrim learns, files the saw that the deadly sin of Wrath holds in his mouth. Designed to correct him, so engrained is Wrath's habitual sin that it only sharpens his saw, so that any time he prays or says the *Pater noster*: 'Thanne I sawhe my-sylff a-way / ffrom the hooly trynyte' (15,742–3). Demonstrating the deleterious effects of vicious speech – when the heart does not accord with the mouth in prayer – the *Pilgrimage* also shows the bivalent potential of the tongue as a file, to either reform the self or destroy it. Langland's Envy – like Wrath – is an example (in Breen's words) of the effects of 'repeated physical and emotional acts'.[91] Langland's personification of Envy similarly stages confession as a surgical process that takes place in and on the mouth with uncertain effect.

Envy

Passus v of *Piers Plowman* presents a dream vision in which the dreamer returns to the field full of folk (seen first in the Prologue) and observes Reson preaching to the people, urging them to reform their social and personal behaviour. Repentance then takes up the 'teme' (the sermon text and theme) and proceeds to lead an allegorical parade of the seven deadly sins through a series of confessions. The deadly sins are, as scholars have often pointed out, models of habitual sin – engrained, lifelong habits that are likely impossible to break. As Breen summarises: 'Langland's sins seem to have produced themselves over their own lifetimes through their repeated physical and emotional acts.'[92] Envy suffers in ways which encyclopaedic and medical texts identify with both humoural imbalance and indigestion caused through either excess or lack of food; he is 'pale as a pelet [a stone ball], in the palsy he semed' (B.v.77), and his body is 'to-bollen [swollen] for wrathe, that he boot [bit] hise lippes' (B.v.83). The 'palsy' might variously be a form of paralysis or an attack of tremors.[93] Similarly, the pastoral tradition commonly gives the aetiology and symptoms of the seven deadly sins real bodily sicknesses. Thus, *The Book of Vices and Virtues* outlines the threefold effect of envy: 'þis synne first enuenymeþ [poisons] þe herte & after þe mouþ and after þe dedes', causing sleeplessness and depressive behaviour.[94] Wrath likewise causes torment in soul and body, and it even sometimes 'bynemeþ [deprives]' a man of 'mete and drynke', causing him to fall into a fever or such sorrow that it brings on death.[95] In *Piers Plowman*, the causes of Envy's sickness are his many verbal transgressions which have been his diet, and include 'chidynge', 'chalangynge' and 'bakbitynge and bismere [derision]' (B.v.87–8) through which many a 'lif and lyme' have been lost (B.v.98). Envy's confession therefore attests to the physical potency of vicious speaking. The C-text makes even clearer Langland's perception of the surgical action inherent in speech: Envy here confesses to having 'Venged me vele tymes other vrete myself withynne / Lyke a schupestares sharre'.[96] His envious condition causes him either to take revenge or to 'fret' ('vrete') – that is, in this instance, to cut – himself within like a pair of shears does. A 'shupestare' might be a dressmaker or a female barber, which suggests the tantalising possibility that Langland here is referring to barber's shears.[97] In speaking well, the tongue – like Grammar – as a pair of shears prunes and regulates the mouth; in speaking badly the tongue destroys and maims bodies, as the Latin quotation Langland cites immediately following suggests: 'The sons of men, their teeth are weapons and arrows; and their tongue a sharp sword' (Psalm 56:5).[98] As a result of the sins of his tongue (and his immoderate diet), Envy complains:

> 'And thus I lyue loveless like a luther [fierce] dogge
> That al my body bolneth [swells] for bitter of my galle.
> I myghte noght ete many yeres as a man oughte,

For envye and yvel wil is yvel to defie.
May no sugre ne swete thyng aswage my swellyng,
Ne no diapenidion dryve it from myn herte,
Ne neither shrifte ne shame, but whoso shrape my mawe?' (B.v.117–23)

Because envy and evil will are difficult to 'defie' – that is, to digest, assimilate into the body or defecate from it, but also difficult to renounce – Envy is unable to eat.[99] Sins like undigested food are blocking Envy's body – preventing eating, purging and confessing. The remedy of confession that Envy attempts to make follows a clinical model not unlike that discernible in the allegory of Dame Penance. Envy's symptoms are described and diagnosed and then a 'prescription' is outlined, firstly for medicinal therapy and finally for surgery to deal with the excess matter or sin built up in his body.[100] The attempted cure first makes recourse to the 'commune' instruments of medicine – sugar, sweet things, 'diapenidion [a sweet drug]'[101] – and progresses to the more extreme measures of surgery or 'mawe-shraping'. Perhaps fallen victim to the confessional dangers of scrupulosity, Envy questions the efficacy of his speech and the power of confession (and, by extension, of medicine) to adequately cleanse his body of sin (or sickness) unless someone 'shrapes' his 'mawe'.[102] This sense is borne out in the A-text, which omits the question 'whoso shrape my mawe', but wonders: ' "May no sugre ne swet þing swage it an vnche, / Ne no dyapendyon dryue it fro myn herte. / 3it shrift shulde, it shope a gret wondir." '[103] If medicine will not drive envy out of him, it would be a great wonder if confession did.

The *MED* glosses 'shrapen' as 'to scrape' or 'to scratch' (and so it belongs to the same vocabulary as 'filen', 'scrapen', 'schauen' and 'rowmen') and the noun 'mawe' as 'stomach'. But scraping the *stomach* fits neither the oral surgical model nor a confessional one.[104] If this is indeed a surgical reference, it is difficult to maintain Envy's 'mawe' is his stomach; surgery is always the last resort in medicinal remedies, and surgical treatises in fact warn against any form of cutting into the viscera because of the potentially fatal consequences. However, as the *Cyrurgie* makes clear, scraping takes on specific medical connotations when put in the context of the mouth. Oral surgery works to file and scrape the teeth; the act of speech, and in particular that of confession, similarly works to scrape the hardened filth of sin away and to file down signs of man's bestial excess. 'Mawe' might therefore be better read as 'mouth' (or at least as a mouth as well as a stomach); indeed, the *MED* suggests that the noun 'mawe' also signifies the 'jaws', 'throat' and 'gullet'.

The Shipman's use of the word 'mawe' in the epilogue (found in some manuscripts) to the Man of Law's tale in *The Canterbury Tales* also suggests the use of the noun to refer specifically to the mouth. The Host at this point in the *Tales* has invited the Parson, 'for Goddes bones', to speak next. The Parson's reproof (what ails a man that he swears so sinfully?) smacks, as the Host points out, of Lollardy: the company should thus expect a 'predicacioun' – that is, a sermon. The Shipman, however, objects to hearing the suspect Parson preach or teach, instead proposing:

> 'My joly body schal a tale telle,
> And I schal clynken you so mery a belle,
> That I schal waken al this compaignie.
> But it schal not ben of philosophie,
> Ne phislyas, ne termes queinte of lawe.
> Ther is but litel Latyn in my mawe!'[105]

The Shipman reveals himself here to be politically 'lewed', deliberately unclergial in his rejection not only of vernacular theology, but also of 'philosophie' (a term that encompasses learning in general, as well as natural philosophy and science), 'phislyas' (a garbled technical term probably referring to the science of medicine) and 'termes queinte of lawe' (legal terms). As Christine F. Cooper observes, this epilogue 'essentially shuts down the possibility of Latin translation'.[106] There is, the Shipman claims, little Latin in his mouth. In showing the project of vernacularisation to be a contested one (even among the laity), the Shipman also casts doubts about the availability of a Latinate *habitus* – in part instilled by language, through the rules of grammar, between the teeth and on the tongue – to unshaped, vulgar 'mawes'.[107]

The reading of Envy's 'mawe' as mouth in *Piers Plowman* is further borne out by the sacrament of penance itself, which, as the *Pilgrimage* amply demonstrates, entails a logical progression from heart to mouth to deed. The medicinal remedies of sugar and 'diapenidion' – like contrition and mouthwashes – should work to drive the sins and sickness lodged in Envy's heart out from his body. But the second stage of shrift and shame requires that such filth be driven from the heart to the mouth from where it can be purged in confession. A biological logic, on the other hand, would direct this undigested, sinful matter down to the anus. Perhaps conflating, as Dame Penance does, his mouth with his anus, Envy may be seeking the skills of a barber-surgeon to scrape his mouth in order to ensure the efficacy of his confession. Envy, however, is thinking, as Haukyn does, too much about his body. Instead of seeking a cure for his spiritual sin, he wants a remedy for its physical symptoms. He is reading the natural – the relationship between the material and the spiritual, body and soul – too literally, too materially. As a result, he has failed to extrapolate the spiritual truth from the material explanation of the way shrift 'schrapeþ' and so remains in ignorance about himself and about God. Envy's confession therefore raises questions about vernacular understandings of the way in which the material acts upon the spiritual, and of the way in which texts such as *The Doctrine of the Hert* and Mirk's *Festial* understand that physical care of the body has the power to reform the soul.

The barber-surgeon's crafts – shaving and shaping the body, scraping and cleaning teeth – provide a framework for understanding confessional as well as pedagogical processes, demonstrating an ambiguous distinction between the material and spiritual: speaking acts materially on the body; surgery might act immaterially on the soul. The late medieval insistence on oral confession suggests that the physical, material act of 'speaking a confession' has intrinsic physical, moral and spiritual value that we would do well to pay attention to. Reading between medieval textual traditions and practices, the example of oral surgery demonstrates the ways in which medicine provides a form of commentary on, or gloss for, vernacular theology; it also directs us to a discourse of the care of the self in which material bodily practices are understood to have ethical and spiritual effects. As the examples in this chapter make clear, as do those explored throughout this book, this discourse fully occupies the register of the everyday: it takes in the mundane habits of washing, eating and drinking. Medical interventions in the body in the Middle Ages, in Foucault's terms, 'define ... a way of living, a reflective mode of relation to oneself'. An understanding of biology and medicine is bound up with concerns, not only of everyday care, but of spiritual good and eternal life. Injunctions to rub the gums, scrape the teeth, shave the tongue or trim the hair are thus instruments of *habitus*, 'capable of instilling a whole cosmology, an ethic, a metaphysic'.

The slippage between the material and the spiritual which this book traces is the basis both of the power of the natural and of the recuperation of everyday experience in late medieval thinking. As the example of Dame Penance shows, material practice and literal readings of the mouth are peculiarly powerful in the reconstructive work of medieval penance. But while vernacular theology points to the centrality of 'kynde' knowledge about the mouth to understanding sin and salvation, so too does it point to the dangers inherent in it. Just as we might misread the created world or misdirect the mouth's *telos*, so too might we misunderstand the relationship of body and soul, seeking a physical cure for a spiritual ill: like Envy, we might take the material too literally. These cautions notwithstanding, we have perhaps been too ready to discredit the material bases of late medieval spirituality. Taking these material bases seriously discloses the importance of the human mouth and its physiology in medieval answers to questions about what it means to be human, just as it discloses the mouth's centrality to medieval discourses of physical, ethical and spiritual good.

Notes

Introduction: Everyday Mouths

1 Pierre Bourdieu, *Outline of a Theory of Practice*, trans. Richard Nice (Cambridge University Press, 1977; repr. 2007), p. 94.

2 The tendency of theory to dissolve bodies into language or metaphor has been criticised, for example, by Florike Egmond and Robert Zwijnenberg (eds.), *Bodily Extremities: Preoccupations with the Human Body in Early Modern European Culture* (Aldershot: Ashgate, 2003). They remark that the ways in which the body is viewed in literary sources 'regularly leads to the strange phenomenon of bodies being reduced to text and metaphor alone, losing their principal characteristic of physicality' (p. 2). Cf. Caroline Walker Bynum, 'Why All the Fuss about the Body? A Medievalist's Perspective', *Critical Inquiry* 22 (1995): 1–33, which cites the observation that in so much scholarship the body 'dissolves into language. The body that eats, that works, that dies, that is afraid – that body just isn't there' (1).

3 For the standard account of 'vernacular theology', see Nicholas Watson, 'Censorship and Cultural Change in Late-Medieval England: Vernacular Theology, the Oxford Translation Debate, and Arundel's Constitutions of 1409', *Speculum* 70 (1995): 822–64 (823 and n. 4), but also Vincent Gillespie, 'Vernacular Theology', *Oxford Twenty-First Century Approaches to Literature: Middle English*, ed. Paul Strohm (Oxford University Press, 2007), pp. 401–20, which offers a revision of scholarly accounts of vernacular theology, in particular Watson's. The importance of French or Anglo-Norman translation for 'vernacular theology' has also been advanced in recent scholarship. See, for example, the essays collected in *Language and Culture in Medieval Britain: The French of England c.1100–c.1500*, ed. Jocelyn Wogan-Browne and others (Woodbridge: York Medieval Press in association with Boydell Press, 2009).

4 For the late medieval engagement with Nature, see M.-D. Chenu, O.P., *Nature, Man, and Society in the Twelfth Century: Essays on New Theological Perspectives in the Latin West*, trans. and ed. Jerome Taylor and Lester K. Little (University of Toronto Press, 1997); see also Hugh White, *Nature, Sex, and Goodness in a Medieval Literary Tradition* (Oxford University Press, 2000), and his references to the major scholarship on Nature, pp. 1–7; Edward Grant, *The Nature of Natural Philosophy in the Late Middle Ages* (Washington,

DC: Catholic University of America Press, 2010); Steven A. Epstein, *The Medieval Discovery of Nature* (Cambridge University Press, 2012); and Kellie Robertson, *Nature Speaks: Medieval Literature and Aristotelian Philosophy* (Philadelphia: University of Pennsylvania Press, 2017).

5 For the interpretations of Langland's term, 'kynde knowyng', see Mary Clemente Davlin, '*Kynde Knowyng* as a Major Theme in *Piers Plowman* B', *Review of English Studies* ns 22 (1971): 1–19 (esp. 1 n. 1).

6 On *via positiva* and its debt to St Paul and St Augustine, see Alastair Minnis, 'Medieval Imagination and Memory', *The Cambridge History of Medieval Literary Criticism*, Volume II: *The Middle Ages*, ed. Alastair Minnis and Ian Johnson (Cambridge University Press, 2005), pp. 239–74 (pp. 258–60).

7 For the tradition of *experientia* and its connection with 'kynde', see Nicolette Zeeman, 'The Condition of *Kynde*', *Medieval Literature and Historical Inquiry: Essays in Honor of Derek Pearsall*, ed. David Aers (Cambridge: Brewer, 2000), pp. 1–30 (e.g. p. 9, and the discussion of Trajan, p. 11). For further definitions of *experientia* (trial, testing, experience, the inner workings of the mind, etc.), see Nicolette Zeeman, '*Piers Plowman' and the Medieval Discourse of Desire* (Cambridge University Press, 2006), e.g. p. 167; see also pp. 1, 38–63, where she explores sin, suffering and the natural, as well as 'the consequences for human life if sin brings its own rewards'.

8 Bourdieu, *Outline of a Theory of Practice*, p. 94; Mary J. Carruthers, *The Book of Memory: A Study of Memory in Medieval Culture* (Cambridge University Press, 1990), p. 68. Here Carruthers is quoting Theodore Tracy.

9 Mikhail Bakhtin, *Rabelais and His World*, trans. Hélène Isowlsky (Bloomington: Indiana University Press, 1968), p. 281.

10 See, for example, Angelina Keller, 'Grotesquely Articulate Bodies: Medicine, Hermeneutics and Writing in *The Canterbury Tales*', *Fleshy Things and Spiritual Matters: Studies on the Medieval Body in Honour of Margaret Bridges*, ed. Nicole Nyffenegger and Katrin Rupp (Cambridge Scholars Publishing, 2011), pp. 79–124. See also Liz Herbert McAvoy and Teresa Walters (eds.), *Consuming Narratives: Gender and Monstrous Appetite in the Middle Ages and the Renaissance* (Cardiff: University of Wales Press, 2002), e.g. p. 9.

11 Bakhtin, *Rabelais and His World*, p. 19.

12 David Williams, *Deformed Discourse: The Function of the Monster in Mediaeval Thought and Literature* (University of Exeter Press, 1996), p. 16.

13 Michael C. Schoenfeldt, *Bodies and Selves in Early Modern England: Physiology and Inwardness in Spenser, Shakespeare, Herbert and Milton* (Cambridge University Press, 1999), pp. 14–15. Schoenfeldt suggests that the classical body, informed as it is by Galenic humoral theory, 'demands not the seamless corporeal enclosure that Bakhtin identifies with the classical body but rather the routine excretory processes that he displaces onto lower-class festivity' (p. 14).

14 Michel Foucault, *The History of Sexuality*, trans. Robert Hurley, 3 vols. (London: Penguin, 1990), III, 99–100. Schoenfeldt suggests this is a point of departure from Foucault's earlier thinking on control and bodies, *Bodies and Selves*, pp. 12–13.

15 See Caroline Walker Bynum, *Holy Feast and Holy Fast: The Religious Significance of Food to Medieval Women* (Berkeley: University of California Press, 1987), e.g. pp. 2, 5, 245. This influential line of thinking, which Bynum associates in particular with women's spirituality, has received some criticism and revision. See David Aers and Lynn Staley, *The Powers of the Holy: Religion, Politics, and Gender in Late Medieval English Culture* (Philadelphia: Pennsylvania State University Press, 1996), e.g. p. 3.

16 See, for example, Caroline Walker Bynum, 'The Female Body and Religious Practice in the Later Middle Ages', *Fragmentation and Redemption: Essays on Gender and the Human Body in Medieval Religion* (New York: Zone Books, 1991), pp. 181–238.

17 See Sarah Beckwith, *Christ's Body: Identity, Culture, and Society in Late Medieval Writings* (London: Routledge, 1993), which describes Franciscanism, affective piety and representations of Christ's body (e.g. pp. 52–5). See also Bynum, *Holy Feast*, which discusses food practices and female piety, and Miri Rubin, *Corpus Christi: The Eucharist in Late Medieval Culture* (Cambridge University Press, 1991), for eucharistic piety specifically.

18 On 'affect', see, for example, Sarah McNamer, *Affective Meditation and the Invention of Medieval Compassion* (Philadelphia: University of Pennsylvania Press, 2010); cf. the History of Emotions (1100–1800) project led by Stephanie Trigg, funded by the Australian Research Council. On objects, see, for example, Tara Hamling and Catherine Richardson (eds.), *Everyday Objects: Medieval and Early Modern Material Culture and Its Meanings* (Farnham: Ashgate, 2010).

19 Caroline Walker Bynum, *Christian Materiality: An Essay on Religion in Late Medieval Europe* (New York: Zone Books, 2015), p. 32. See further Susan Signe Morrison, *Excrement in the Late Middle Ages: Sacred Filth and Chaucer's Fecopoetics* (New York: Palgrave, 2008), where she asserts that 'the lowest of matters – excrement – matters' (p. 2).

20 For an exemplary discussion of medieval multisensoriality in connection with material culture, see Richard G. Newhauser and Arthur J. Russell, 'Mapping Virtual Pilgrimage in an Early Fifteenth-Century *Arma Christi* Roll', *The Arma Christi in Medieval and Early Modern Material Culture, with a Critical Edition of 'O Vernicle'*, ed. Lisa H. Cooper and Andrea Denny-Brown (Farnham: Ashgate, 2014), pp. 83–112. See more generally, Richard G. Newhauser (ed.), *A Cultural History of the Senses in the Middle Ages* (London: Bloomsbury, 2016); and Mark M. Smith, *Sensing the Past: Seeing, Hearing, Smelling, Tasting and Touching in History* (Berkeley: University of California Press, 2007).

21 Karl Steel, *How to Make a Human: Animals and Violence in the Middle Ages* (Columbus: Ohio State University Press, 2011). For other recent work in this area, see also Susan Crane, *Animal Encounters: Contacts and Concepts in Medieval Britain* (Philadelphia: University of Pennsylvania Press, 2012).

22 See, for example, Irina Metzler, *Disability in Medieval Europe: Thinking about Impairment in the High Middle Ages, c.1100–c.1400* (London: Routledge, 2006); and Joshua R. Eyler (ed.), *Disability in the Middle Ages: Reconsiderations and Reverberations* (Farnham: Ashgate, 2010).

23 Michael Lambek and Andrew Strathern (eds.), *Bodies and Persons: Comparative Perspectives from Africa and Melanesia* (Cambridge University Press, 1998), p. 5. For the interest in 'embodiment' in medieval studies, see Suzannah Biernoff, *Sight and Embodiment in the Middle Ages* (Basingstoke: Palgrave, 2002), pp. 23–6.

24 Felicity Riddy acknowledges the impetus provided by the 'embodied turn' in sociology and anthropology for thinking about everyday practice and experience in 'Looking Closely: Authority and Intimacy in the Late Medieval Urban Home', *Gendering the Master Narrative: Women and Power in the Middle Ages*, ed. Mary Carpenter Erler and Maryanne Kowaleski (Ithaca: Cornell University Press, 2003), pp. 212–28 (p. 216). See also Henri Lefebvre, *Everyday Life in the Modern World*, trans. Sacha Rabinovitch (London: Allen Lane, 1971); Bourdieu, *Outline of a Theory of Practice*; and Michel de Certeau, *The Practice of Everyday Life*, trans. Steven Rendall (Berkeley: University of California Press, 1984).

25 Felicity Riddy, 'Temporary Virginity and the Everyday Body: *Le Bone Florence of Rome* and Bourgeois Self-Making', *Pulp Fictions of Medieval England: Essays in Popular Romance*, ed. Nicola McDonald (Manchester University Press, 2004), pp. 197–216 (pp. 207–8).

26 Ibid., p. 210.

27 I have chosen to follow medieval texts in primarily referring to the male body and to that broader category 'man'. In so doing, as some of the examples treated will make clear, the question of how to account for women's experience and women's bodies is sometimes explicitly or implicitly raised (see, for example, the discussion of the analogy of a barber shaving a man in a text adapted for women readers, Chapter 5, pp. 149–50).

28 On vulnerability and disability, see Jackie Leach Scully, 'Disability and Vulnerability: On Bodies, Dependence, and Power', *Vulnerability: New Essays in Ethics and Feminist Philosophy*, ed. Catriona Mackenzie, Wendy Rogers and Susan Dodds (New York: Oxford University Press, 2014), pp. 204–21.

29 Science and medicine were, in fact, in the 'vanguard of vernacularisation' in the later fourteenth century. Linda Ehrsam Voigts and Patricia D. Kurtz, compilers, *Scientific and Medical Writings in Old and Middle English: An Electronic Resource*, CD-ROM (Ann Arbor: University of Michigan Press, 2000) lists around 200 fourteenth-century items and nearly 8,000 fifteenth-century items. See also Päivi Pahta and Irma Taavitsainen, 'Vernacularisation of Scientific and Medical Writing in its Sociohistorical Context', *Medical and Scientific Writing in Late Medieval English*, ed. Päivi Pahta and Irma Taavitsainen (Cambridge University Press, 2004), pp. 1–22 (p. 11).

30 There is growing scholarly recognition of the importance of the relationship between medieval medical and religious discourses. See, for example, Virginia Langum, *Medicine and the Seven Deadly Sins in Late Medieval Literature and Culture* (New York: Palgrave, 2016); and the essays in the collection *Medicine, Religion and Gender in Medieval Culture*, ed. Naoë Kukita Yoshikawa (Cambridge: Brewer, 2015).

31 See Päivi Pahta and Irma Taavitsainen, 'Vernacularisation of Medical Writing in English: A Corpus-Based Study of Scholasticism', *Early Science and Medicine* 3 (1998): 157–85 (160).

32 Peter Murray Jones, *Medieval Medical Miniatures* (London: The British Library, 1984), p. 32. The same claim is made by Faye Marie Getz, 'Charity, Translation, and the Language of Medical Learning in Medieval England', *Bulletin of the History of Medicine* 64 (1990): 1–17 (5).

33 Getz, 'Charity', 9.

34 Julie Orlemanski, 'Jargon and the Matter of Medicine in Middle English', *Journal of Medieval and Early Modern Studies* 42.2 (2012): 395–420 (398).

35 On this reading habit, see further my 'Books and Bodies: Ethics, Exemplarity and the "Boistous" in Medieval English Writings', *NML* 14 (2012): 95–125.

36 Judson Boyce Allen, *The Ethical Poetic of the Later Middle Ages: A Decorum of Convenient Distinction* (University of Toronto Press, 1982).

37 On this manuscript compilation, and the notion of complementarity, see Jean-Pascal Pouzet, '"Space this Werke to Wirke": Quelques figures de la complémentarité dans les manuscrits de Robert Thornton', *La Complémentarité: Mélanges offerts á Josseline Bidard et Arlette Sancery a l'occasion de leur départ en retraite*, ed. Marie-Françoise Alamichel (Paris: AMAES, 2005), pp. 27–43.

38 R. Allen Shoaf, *Chaucer's Body: The Anxiety of Circulation in the 'Canterbury Tales'* (Gainesville: University of Florida Press, 2001), p. 21.

39 This medieval reading habit is cognate with but distinct from medieval theories of reading as healing or hygienic, or as a form of self-diagnosis (though it can accommodate both of these). In this vein, Glending Olson's *Literature as Recreation in the Later Middle Ages* (Ithaca: Cornell University Press, 1982) is seminal. Louise M. Bishop develops the notion of material reading in *Word, Stones, and Herbs: The Healing Word in Medieval and Early Modern England* (New York: Syracuse University Press, 2007). See also Rebecca Krug, '*Piers Plowman* and the Secrets of Health', *Chaucer Review* 46.1/2 (2011): 166–81, where she takes up the notion of 'sickly reading'. Suggesting the influence of *regimen sanitatis* on *Piers Plowman*, Krug identifies reading as a practice that 'enables personal transformation' (167), providing readers with the means to analyse their own physical condition (174).

40 Carole Rawcliffe, *Sources for the History of Medicine in Late Medieval England* (Kalamazoo: Medieval Institute Publications, 1995), asserts, 'we may certainly assume that the more affluent, book-owning classes were quite well informed about the way their bodies worked (or were believed to work), not least because of the pervasiveness of ideas and terminology that went far beyond the pages of the *regimen sanitatis*' (p. 30). The connection with *pastoralia* is also raised by Jeremy J. Citrome in *The Surgeon in Medieval English Literature* (New York: Palgrave, 2006), where he suggests that 'the careful assembly in many confessional manuals of extant surgical knowledge bespeaks an awareness among priests and parishioners alike of, at the very least, the rudiments of practical medical treatment' (p. 9).

41 William Langland, *The Vision of Piers Plowman: A Critical Edition of the B-Text Based on Trinity College Cambridge MS B.15.18*, ed. A. V. C. Schmidt, 2nd edn (London: Dent, 1978), B.1.36–7. (Further references to this edition are given after quotations in the text.)

42 *Dives and Pauper*, ed. Priscilla Heath Barnum, EETS 275, 3 vols. (Oxford University Press, 1976), I/i, 129. Cf. 'Also sumtyme oon is enclynyd to synne more þan anothir, for he was conseyuyd and begetyn in more synne þan anothir' (p. 128).

43 The concept of *habitus* is drawn on broadly in *Middle English Mouths* – sometimes to invoke the specific, formal theories of virtue acquisition, as well as to express the more general medieval belief in the influence of the 'use' of the body on ethical and spiritual status.

44 For the notion of *habitus* in the medieval period, see Cary J. Nederman, 'Nature, Ethics, and the Doctrine of "Habitus": Aristotelian Moral Psychology in the Twelfth Century', *Traditio* 45 (1989/90): 87–110; Marcia L. Colish, '*Habitus* Revisited: A Reply to Cary Nederman', *Traditio* 48 (1993): 77–92.

45 Bourdieu notes the range of meaning encompassed by the term 'disposition': the '*result of an organising action*', '*a way of being, a habitual state* (especially of the body)' and 'a *predisposition, tendency, propensity*, or *inclination*', *Outline of a Theory of Practice*, p. 214 n. 1.

46 For the relationship between *natura* and *habitus*, see Bernard Ryosuke Inagaki, '*Habitus* and *Natura* in Aquinas', *Studies in Medieval Philosophy*, ed. John F. Wippel (Washington, DC: The Catholic University of America Press, 1987), pp. 159–76.

47 Thomas Aquinas, *Summa theologiae*, ed. Thomas Gilby, 61 vols. (London: Blackfriars, 1964–81) 1a.1.9 (pp. 33, 35).

48 See, for example, Biernoff, *Sight and Embodiment*, p. 1. Stephen G. Nichols in his prologue to *Rethinking the Medieval Senses: Heritage, Fascinations, Frames*, ed. Stephen G. Nichols and others (Baltimore: The Johns Hopkins University Press, 2008), ascribes to sight and hearing only an important role in the formation of the individual, 'morally, intellectually, and ... in indoctrination to the faith' in the medieval period (p. vii).

49 See, for example, Aristotle, *De anima*, trans. J. A. Smith, *The Complete Works of Aristotle: The Revised Oxford Translation*, ed. Jonathan Barnes, Bollingen Series 71, 2 vols. (Princeton University Press, 1984), I, 641–92 (665–7). For the early patristic tradition, see Saint Ambrose, *Hexameron, Paradise, and Cain and Abel*, trans. John J. Savage, The Fathers of the Church 42 (New York: Fathers of the Church, 1961), pp. 257, 272–3.

50 Cited in Dallas G. Denery II, *Seeing and Being Seen in the Later Medieval World: Optics, Theology and Religious Life* (Cambridge University Press, 2005), p. 5.

51 A. C. Spearing, *The Medieval Poet as Voyeur: Looking and Listening in Medieval Love-Narratives* (Cambridge University Press, 1993), p. 5.

52 Carolyn P. Collette, *Species, Phantasms, and Images: Vision and Medieval Psychology in 'The Canterbury Tales'* (Ann Arbor: University of Michigan Press,

2001), p. 1. See further Dana E. Stewart, *The Arrow of Love: Optics, Gender, and Subjectivity in Medieval Love Poetry* (London: Associated University Presses, 2003), at p. 13 for example.

53 Denery, *Seeing and Being Seen*, p. 7.

54 See, for example, Martin Jay, *Downcast Eyes: The Denigration of Vision in Twentieth-Century French Thought* (Berkeley: University of California Press, 1993), p. 152.

55 Other important work that focuses on taste and touch includes: Mary J. Carruthers, *The Experience of Beauty in the Middle Ages* (Oxford University Press, 2013), as well as 'Sweet Jesus', *Mindful Spirit in Late Medieval Literature: Essays in Honor of Elizabeth D. Kirk*, ed. Bonnie Wheeler (New York: Palgrave, 2006), pp. 9–19. On the call to rethink touch, see Fernando Salmón, 'A Medieval Territory for Touch', *Studies in Medieval and Renaissance History*, 3rd Series 2 (2005): 59–81 (60). See also Constance Classen, *The Deepest Sense: A Cultural History of the Sense of Touch* (Urbana: University of Illinois Press, 2012).

56 See Biernoff, *Sight and Embodiment*.

57 Cf. modern thinking, e.g. that of Hans Jonas, summarised by Jay, that vision is 'intrinsically less temporal than other senses' and so 'tends to elevate static Being over dynamic Becoming', *Downcast Eyes*, p. 24.

58 M. C. Seymour and others (eds.), *On the Properties of Things: John Trevisa's Translation of Bartholomaeus Anglicus 'De Proprietatibus Rerum'*, 3 vols. (Oxford: Clarendon, 1975), I, 172, cf. I, 108, lines 4–10. (Further references to this edition are given after quotations in the text by volume and page number.) Cf. the Latin text, which describes the sense of sight as *subtilis* and the sense of taste as *grossus*, Bartholomaeus Angelicus [Anglicus], *De rerum Proprietatibus* (Frankfurt: Minerva 1601; repr. 1964), p. 70.

59 *MED*, s.v. 'sotil': 'Of a person, the intellect, etc.: penetrating, ingenious, perspicacious; sophisticated, refined; of the sight, sharp, keen'; 'Of a substance, human body, etc.: not dense, light'.

60 Elaine Scarry, *The Body in Pain: The Making and Unmaking of the World* (Oxford University Press, 1985), p. 165.

61 *MED*, s.v. 'boistous': 'Of things: big, sturdy, coarse; big (blossoms); huge (cross, nail); clumsy (shoes); sturdy (ship, weapons, etc.); coarse (fabric); rough, coarse (food)'; 'Partaking of, or dominated by, the "element" earth; gross, coarse, opaque (object); "earthy" or crude (sense); "thick" (blood).'

62 Aristotle also understands smell to have some analogy with taste. See further the discussion on p. 128.

63 The peculiar importance of the mouth and the senses of taste and touch for the everyday body is also suggested in socio-anthropological thought, for example, Certeau, *The Practice of Everyday Life*, see pp. xix, 36–8. Offering a critique of 'panopticism' (the alignment of knowledge, vision and power), Certeau here posits a diminished capacity for (fore)sight in the everyday body; rather it experiences at close quarters, in the process of moving and living.

64 Robert von Fleischhacker (ed.), *Lanfrank's 'Science of Cirurgie'*, EETS os 102 (London: Kegan Paul, Trench, Trübner, 1894). There are two different Middle English translations extant. For the dates of the Middle English translations, see Bryon Grigsby, 'The Social Position of the Surgeon in London 1350–1450', *Essays in Medieval Studies* 13 (1996): 71–80.

65 Margaret S. Ogden (ed.), *The Cyrurgie of Guy de Chauliac*, EETS 265 (London: Oxford University Press, 1971). For an overview of the *Cyrurgie's* structure, see Cornelius O'Boyle, 'Surgical Texts and Social Contexts: Physicians and Surgeons in Paris, c.1270 to 1430', *Practical Medicine from Salerno to the Black Death*, ed. Luis García-Ballester and others (Cambridge University Press, 1994), pp. 156–85 (pp. 176–9). There are six extant Middle English manuscripts (two complete), the earliest of which is dated (though there is some disagreement) to the end of the fourteenth or to the early fifteenth century. On the translations, see G. R. Keiser, 'XXV. Works of Science and Information', *A Manual of the Writings in Middle English, 1050–1500*, ed. Albert E. Hartung and others, 11 vols. (New Haven: Connecticut Academy of Arts and Science, 1998) x, 3636–48. Cf. Björn Wallner (ed.), *The Middle English Translation of Guy de Chauliac's Anatomy* (Lund: CWK Gleerup, 1964), pp. vii–ix.

66 Ten copies of *De proprietatibus rerum* were bequeathed to Oxford and Cambridge colleges in the fourteenth and fifteenth centuries, and there is evidence for its use both as a chained and a distributed book that scholars were expected to use in their studies. Sue Ellen Holbrook, 'A Medieval Scientific Encyclopaedia "Renewed by Goodly Printing": Wynkyn de Worde's English *De Proprietatibus Rerum*', *Early Science and Medicine* 3 (1998): 119–56 (123–7).

67 Michael W. Twomey, 'Towards a Reception History of Western Medieval Encyclopaedias in England before 1500', *Pre-Modern Encyclopaedic Texts: Proceedings of the Second COMERS Congress, Groningen, 1–4 July 1996*, ed. Peter Binkley (Leiden: Brill, 1997), pp. 329–62 (p. 362). Twomey notes its influence on a number of English works, p. 360. See also A. S. G. Edwards, 'Bartholomaeus Anglicus' *De Proprietatibus Rerum* and Medieval English Literature', *Archiv für das Studium der neueren Sprachen und Literaturen* 222 (1985): 121–8; and E. Ruth Harvey, 'The Swallow's Nest and the Spider's Web', *Studies in English Language and Literature: 'Doubt Wisely': Papers in Honour of E. G. Stanley*, ed. M. J. Toswell and E. M. Tyler (London: Routledge, 1996), pp. 327–41, gives evidence for encyclopaedic knowledge in *Piers Plowman*.

68 Edwards writes, 'it is clear that after its completion sometime around the middle of the thirteenth century, the work established itself as *the* standard medieval encyclopaedia', 'Bartholomaeus Anglicus', p. 121. On the importance of the *Speculum maius*, see Monique Paulmier-Foucart, with Marie-Christine Duchenne, *Vincent de Beauvais et le Grand miroir du monde* (Turnhout: Brepols, 2004).

69 *Speculum vitae* is a northern verse translation of the *Somme le roi*, extant in around forty manuscripts); *The Book of Vices and Virtues* is a prose translation of the *Somme*, extant in three manuscripts; and *Book for a Simple and Devout*

Woman is an adaption of *Somme le roi* and William Peraldus's *Summa de vitiis et virtutibus*, made perhaps for a laywoman, and extant in two manuscripts.

70 Fiona Somerset, *Clerical Discourse and Lay Audience in Late Medieval England* (Cambridge University Press, 1998), p. 13. Somerset summarises that ' "clergie" is used to mean "learning" and even "body or field of knowledge" as well as to refer to persons of clerical status'. Zeeman, *Discourse of Desire*, argues that 'clergie' in *Piers Plowman* refers primarily to 'Christian teaching and its texts' (p. 132).

71 For the audience of the poem, see Anne Middleton, 'The Audience and Public of *Piers Plowman*', *Middle English Alliterative Poetry and Its Literary Background: Seven Essays*, ed. David Lawton (Cambridge: Brewer, 1982), pp. 101–23 (p. 104).

72 David Aers, *Beyond Reformation? An Essay on William Langland's Piers Plowman and the End of Constantinian Christianity* (University of Notre Dame Press, 2015) offers a lucid account of Langland's response to the moral challenges of dechristianisation in relation to the C-text. See, for example, pp. 64–5, 83–103 on *habitus*.

73 Rebecca A. Davis, ' "Save man alone": Human Exceptionality in *Piers Plowman* and the Exemplarist Tradition', *Medieval Latin and Middle English Literature: Essays in Honour of Jill Mann*, ed. Christopher Cannon and Maura Nolan (Cambridge: Brewer, 2011), pp. 41–64 (p. 42). Cf. James Simpson, 'The Role of *Scientia* in *Piers Plowman*', *Medieval English Religious and Ethical Literature: Essays in Honour of G. H. Russell*, ed. Gregory Kratzmann and James Simpson (Cambridge: Brewer, 1986), pp. 49–65 (p. 65); Zeeman, 'The Condition of *Kynde*', pp. 7–8, 21.

74 Zeeman, 'The Condition of *Kynde*', pp. 1–2.

75 A. V. C. Schmidt, ' "Elementary" Images in the Samaritan Episode of *Piers Plowman*', *Essays in Criticism* 56 (2006): 303–23.

76 Rosanne Gasse, 'The Practice of Medicine in *Piers Plowman*', *Chaucer Review* 39.2 (2004): 177–97 (179); Bishop, *Words, Stones, and Herbs*, p. 6. See also Krug, '*Piers Plowman*', for the influence of the *regimen sanitatis* tradition on *Piers Plowman*.

77 Deguileville wrote the first recension of *Pèlerinage de la vie humaine* in 1331. It is part of a trilogy with poems on pilgrimages of the soul (1355) and of Jesus Christ (1358). The trilogy is published in J. J. Sturzinger (ed.), *Le Pèlerinage de Vie Humaine de Guillaume de Deguileville*, Roxburghe Club 124 (London: Nichols, 1893). There are two Middle English versions of the *Pèlerinage de la vie humaine*: the later is Lydgate's; the earlier is an anonymous prose version of the first recension, Avril Henry (ed.), *The Pilgrimage of the Lyfe of the Manhode*, EETS os 288, 292, 2 vols. (London: Oxford University Press, 1985–8). The influence of Deguileville's trilogy, and particularly of the *Vie*, on both Chaucer and Langland has long been attested. See, for example, Joseph M. Keenan, 'The Cistercian Pilgrimage to Jerusalem in Guillaume de Deguilville's *Pèlerinage de la Vie Humaine*', *Studies in Medieval Cistercian History II*, ed. John R. Sommerfeldt, Cistercian Studies Series 24 (Kalamazoo: Cistercian

Publications, 1976), pp. 166–85 (p. 167). For the influence on Langland, see J. A. Burrow, *Langland's Fictions* (Oxford: Clarendon, 1993), in which Burrow gives the view that 'Langland knew the whole of Deguileville's trilogy' (p. 114).

1 Natural Knowledge

1 W. Nelson Francis (ed.), *The Book of Vices and Virtues: A Fourteenth Century English Translation of the Somme le roi of Lorens d'Orléans*, EETS os 217 (London: Oxford University Press, 1942), pp. 276–7. See Francis's introduction on the English manuscripts and their relation to the French source, the *Somme le roi*, pp. i–xxvi. See also Kiril Petkov, 'The Cultural Career of a "Minor" Vice: Arrogance in the Medieval Treatise on Sin', *Sin in Medieval and Early Modern Culture: The Tradition of the Seven Deadly Sins*, ed. Richard G. Newhauser and Susan J. Ridyard, York Medieval Press (Woodbridge: Boydell and Brewer, 2012), pp. 43–65 (p. 55 n. 29) for bibliography and a recent assessment of Francis's edition.

2 This essentially Aristotelian observation is repeated, for example, in Vincentius Bellovacensis [Vincent of Beauvais], *Speculum Quadruplex sive Speculum Maius*, Volume 1: *Speculum Naturale* (Douai: Bibliotheca Mundi, 1624; repr. Graz, Austria: Akademische Druck -u. Verlagsanstalt, 1964), xxiii, c.1656. [Hereafter *Speculum naturale*. References are given by book, chapter and column number. All Modern English translations from this text are my own.]

3 *MED*, s.v. 'sobrenesse', 'Moderation in desires or actions, prudent living; moderation in regard to food and drink, habitual temperance, sobriety'.

4 For the phrase 'kynde is of litle sustenaunce', the French *Somme le roi* gives 'car nature est de petit soutenne e par trop de viande est souvent abatue', i.e. 'is sustained by little food [and through too much is often overthrown]'. Ralph Hanna gives the French and Modern English gloss in his commentary to his edition, *Speculum Vitae: A Reading Edition*, EETS os 331–2, 2 vols. (Oxford University Press, 2008), ii, 626.

5 It continues: 'Holi Writ' teaches 'in many maneres and bi many ensaumples', as those who know Scripture and saints' lives can attest; 'alle creatures' teach (as Solomon says) because their behaviour is measurable, see Francis (ed.), *Book of Vices and Virtues*, p. 277. Cf. Hanna (ed.), *Speculum Vitae*, ii, 495–6 for the parallel passage.

6 Francis (ed.), *Book of Vices and Virtues*, p. 277.

7 Edwin D. Craun, 'Aristotle's Biology and Pastoral Ethics: John of Wales's *De Lingua* and British Pastoral Writing on the Tongue', *Traditio* 67 (2012): 277–303 (282).

8 Zeeman, 'The Condition of *Kynde*', p. 1.

9 For Mirk's pastoral programme, see Susan Powell, 'John Mirk's *Festial* and the Pastoral Programme', *Leeds Studies in English* ns 22 (1991): 85–102. On the relationship of 'natural' knowledge to taught in *The Pilgrimage of the Life of Man*, see Susan Hagen, *Allegorical Remembrance: A Study on 'The Pilgrimage of the Life of Man' as a Medieval Treatise on Seeing and Remembering* (Athens: University of Georgia Press, 1990), p. 50.

10 For the 'twelfth-century renaissance', see Chenu, 'Nature and Man', pp. 1–48; Jacques Le Goff, *The Birth of Europe*, trans. Janet Lloyd (Oxford: Blackwell, 2005), pp. 75–6, 128–9 (on encyclopaedias), and 216 for bibliography; and Jacques Le Goff, 'What Did the Twelfth-Century Renaissance *Mean*?', *The Medieval World*, ed. Peter Linehan and Janet L. Nelson (London: Routledge, 2001), pp. 635–47.

11 On the status of the body as commentary, see Alastair Minnis, *Medieval Theory of Authorship: Scholastic Literary Attitudes in the Later Middle Ages*, 2nd edn (Aldershot: Scolar Press, 1984, 1988), p. 72; on learning through the senses, see my 'Books and Bodies', pp. 99–104.

12 See Boyd H. Hill, Jr, 'The Grain and the Spirit in Mediaeval Anatomy', *Speculum* 40 (1965): 63–73, which notes that the Council of Vienne (1311), for example, 'declared that the soul is the form of the body. However, it was not said to be *immediately* so' (69). For an overview of medieval thinking on the soul, see Dag Nikolaus Hasse, 'The Soul's Faculties', *The Cambridge History of Medieval Philosophy*, Volume 1, ed. Robert Pasnau (Cambridge University Press, 2010), pp. 305–19. As Hasse observes, in the earlier medieval period Augustine's understanding of the soul as 'an indivisible unity' was influential on Christian thinkers. With the influx of Classical and Arabic sources 'the discussion changes' (p. 306). See also Pamela M. Huby, 'Soul, Life, Sense, Intellect: Some Thirteenth-Century Problems', *The Human Embryo: Aristotle and the Arabic and European Traditions*, ed. G. R. Dunstan (University of Exeter Press, 1990), pp. 113–22.

13 Nancy G. Siraisi summarises the late medieval understanding of the soul and the influence of Aristotelian and Galenic traditions in *Medieval and Early Renaissance Medicine: An Introduction to Knowledge and Practice* (London: University of Chicago Press, 1990): she notes that later thinkers – following Avicenna (whose account was complicated by trying 'to reconcile the essentially incompatible views of Aristotle and Galen by allowing the heart a sort of overriding influence', p. 107) – introduced a 'conceptual hierarchy in which the heart ruled the brain in some ultimate or philosophical sense and the brain ruled the nervous system directly' (p. 81).

14 Seymour and others (eds.), *On the Properties of Things*, I, 96–7. This does not suggest, however, that Bartholomaeus believes in three separate souls in the body: plants only have a vegetable soul, so they have 'life' not movement or reason; animals have a sensible soul so they have life and movement, but not reason; man has a reasonable soul so has life, movement and reason: 'who þat haath þe soule *racionalis* haþ also *sensibilis* and *vegetabilis*, and folwiþ not aȝenward', I, 97.

15 Seymour and others (eds.), *On the Properties of Things*, I, 101. See further Siraisi, *Medieval and Early Renaissance Medicine*, p. 107: 'Aristotle generally taught that the heart, the source of heat and life, ruled the entire body; the Galenists taught that the three principal members – heart, brain, and liver – each governed or provided the originating or ruling principal (*principium*) of

a separate group of organs and functions.' Whether the ultimate principal or principals was one or several, they were grouped into three distinct systems.

16 Compare Bartholomaeus's entries with Vincent's, *Speculum naturale*, for example, on the division of the soul, xxv.14, c.1661; the location of the soul, xxv.15, c.1675; and the union of body and soul, xxv.42, c.1681. Entries on the soul are extensive, however.

17 Jennifer Bryan, *Looking Inward: Devotional Reading and the Private Self in Late Medieval England* (Philadelphia: University of Pennsylvania Press, 2007), details seven different senses of 'interiority', including two which emphasise cognate material senses (e.g. pp. 62–74).

18 Matthew Milner, *The Senses and the English Reformation* (Farnham: Ashgate, 2011), pp. 25, 33. Milner gives a detailed outline of fifteenth-century discourses on the senses in a chapter on 'The Senses and Sensing in Fifteenth-Century England', pp. 13–53. See also Richard G. Newhauser's nuanced discussion of taste in 'John Gower's Sweet Tooth', *Review of English Studies* 64 (2013): 752–69, where he also reiterates the traditional division between those 'higher senses' (sight and hearing) involved in education and those 'lower' senses deemed rather less important (757).

19 Aristotle, *De anima*, Barnes (ed.), 1, 691, 692. Cf. 1, 691, where Aristotle explains that, 'An animal is a body with soul in it: every body is tangible, i.e. perceptible by touch; hence necessarily, if an animal is to survive, its body must have tactual sensation.' This Aristotelian position is repeated by Vincent (who cites Albertus Magnus); see, for example, *Speculum naturale*, xxv.23, c.1790. On Aristotle's account of the senses and touch in particular, see further Daniel Heller-Roazen, *The Inner Touch: The Archaeology of a Sensation* (New York: Zone Books, 2007), pp. 21–30.

20 This view is found in Hippocratic treatises, for example, and is repeated in Aristotelian works and later in Albertus Magnus's *De animalibus*, which records that when 'the twins or the single infant are no longer drawing sufficient nourishment and spirit through the veins of the umbilicus, then the fetuses are complete for leaving and the time for natural birth is at hand', *On Animals: A Medieval 'Summa Zoologica'*, trans. Kenneth F. Kitchell and Irven Michael Resnick, 2 vols. (Baltimore: The Johns Hopkins University Press, 1999), 1, 825; cf. 1, 787. Birth, in these accounts, begins as a quest for food and is driven by appetite. Cf. Vincent of Beauvais, *Speculum naturale*, xxxi.52, c.2331, for the views of William of Conches, 'Razi' (Rhazes) and Aristotle, among others, on the end of pregnancy. See also Päivi Pahta, *Medieval Embryology in the Vernacular: The Case of 'De Spermate'*, Mémoires de la Société Néophilologique de Helsinki 53 (Helsinki: Société Néophilologique, 1998), which records both Hippocratic and Aristotelian views (p. 45).

21 The phrase is Jacques Le Goff's, who describes in *Intellectuals in the Middle Ages*, trans. Teresa Lavender Fagan (Cambridge, MA: Blackwell, 1993), p. 50, the role of nature in 'Chartrian humanism' of the twelfth century: 'For the Chartrians, nature was first and foremost a life-giving power, perpetually creative, with inexhaustible resources, *mater generationis*. Thus was established

the naturalist optimism of the twelfth century, one of development and expansion.' In the Chartrian view, 'man was the object and centre of creation', and, as a rational being, the antithesis of the brute (p. 53).

22 Philip Lyndon Reynolds's study demonstrates that, by the thirteenth century, scholastic theologians in Paris 'recognise the intrinsic rationality and consistency of the natural order. From their point of view, it is nonsensical and even contradictory to say that the generation or growth of human bodies depends on miraculous intervention', *Food and the Body: Some Peculiar Questions in High Medieval Theology* (Leiden: Brill, 1999), p. 48. See further, on this desacralising of nature, Chenu, 'Nature and Man', pp. 14–15.

23 See further Reynolds, *Food and the Body*, p. ix. Cf. Caroline Walker Bynum who seeks to trace the impact of these changing ideas about the assimilation of food into the body and the resurrection of the body on medieval notions of identity in *Metamorphosis and Identity* (New York: Zone Books, 2001), e.g. pp. 22–8, and *The Resurrection of the Body in Western Christianity, 200–1336* (New York: Columbia University Press, 1995), e.g. pp. 13–14.

24 Seymour and others (eds.), *On the Properties of Things*, I, 97, 100.

25 Ibid., I, 104.

26 Cf. Vincentius Bellovacensis [Vincent of Beauvais], *Speculum Quadruplex sive Speculum Maius*, Volume II: *Speculum Doctrinale* (Douai: Bibliotheca Mundi, 1624; repr. Graz, Austria: Akademische Druck -u. Verlagsanstalt, 1964), XIII.143, cc.1259–60 on the stages of digestion. [Hereafter *Speculum doctrinale*. References are given by book, chapter and column number. All Modern English translations from this text are my own.]

27 For an outline of the development of the theological understanding of the assimilation of food into the body, see Reynolds, *Food and the Body*, esp. pp. ix, 1–19.

28 Geoffrey Chaucer, 'The General Prologue', *The Riverside Chaucer*, gen. ed. Larry D. Benson, 3rd edn (Oxford University Press, 1987), 1.153; 127–8; 130–1.

29 Chaucer, 'The Prioress's Tale', *The Riverside Chaucer*, ed. Benson, VII.493–4.

30 Ibid., VII.544–9; 572–3.

31 Deanne Williams, *The French Fetish from Chaucer to Shakespeare* (Cambridge University Press, 2004), observes that Chaucer 'mentions the mouth eight times in fifty-two lines, and when he is not talking about her [the Prioress's] mouth, he is talking about other openings such as her nose' (p. 39). She reads the Prioress's 'vigorous attention to removing bodily traces of bodily fallibility' as 'bourgeois anxiety' and evidence of 'the self-surveillance required to combat the body's potential to betray the truth of class identity' (p. 38). See also Morrison, *Excrement*, pp. 82–8 for a reading of excremental imagery in 'The Prioress's Tale'.

32 On the tale's antisemitism and the association of Jews with scatology, see further Kathy Lavezzo, 'The Minster and the Privy: Rereading "The Prioress's Tale"', *PMLA* 126.2 (2011): 363–82.

33 See Siraisi, *Medieval and Early Renaissance Medicine*, p. 107.

34 Fleischhacker (ed.), *Science of Cirurgie*, p. 162.

35 See further Seymour and others (eds.), *On the Properties of Things*, I, 99–100, 121–2. Cf. Vincent of Beauvais, *Speculum doctrinale*, XIII.47, c.1199, which records, following 'Razi' (Rhazes), the process of making *spiritus* in the liver, the heart and the brain.

36 Seymour and others (eds.), *On the Properties of Things*, asserts that 'withoute a sinewe comynge fro þe heed is no membre couplid to anoþir. But ȝif þe vertue is ilette þat comeþ by senewes fram þe heed by vice and corrupcion of sinewes, þe vnyte and þe ioynenge of al þe body tofalle' (I, 170).

37 David C. Fowler and others (eds.), *The Governance of Kings and Princes: John Trevisa's Middle English Translation of the 'De Regimine Principum' of Aegidius Romanus*, Garland Medieval Texts 19 (New York: Garland, 1997), p. 129.

38 Vincent of Beauvais, *Speculum doctrinale*, XIII.135, c.1255: 'Accidētia porro quæ actioni cerebri contingūt, ex incommodis quæ fiunt in ore stomachi, sunt alienatio mentis, obstupefactio, somni immersio, epilentia, & mania' [Further, the 'accidents', which are linked with the action of the sense (head/brain), out of the inconveniences, which happen in the 'mouth' of the stomach, are loss of reason, stupefaction, extreme lethargy, epilepsy and madness].

39 Fleischhacker (ed.) *Science of Cirurgie*, pp. 119–20.

40 Ogden (ed.), *Cyrurgie*, p. 481; see also Seymour and others (eds.), *On the Properties of Things*, I, 207–8, which records, for example, that 'Ratelinge [stuttering] men ben most itake, for to moche moisture of suche men þat is cause of ratelinge comeþ to þe stomak and makeþ ofte þe bowels slider and brediþ *diariam*, þat is "þe flux of þe wombe". So seþ Galien.'

41 Mary Macleod Banks (ed.), *An Alphabet of Tales: An English Fifteenth Century Translation of the Alphabetum Narrationum*, EETS os 126–7, 2 vols. (London: Kegan Paul, Trench, Trübner, 1904–5), II, 466–7. See also the example of a man who had robbed churches whose mouth turns into an anus in Jacobi a Voragine [Jacobus de Voragine], *Legenda aurea: vulgo historia Lombardica dicta*, ed. Theodore Graesse, 3rd edn (Bratislav: Guilelmum Keobner, 1890), p. 571. Trans. William Granger Ryan, *The Golden Legend: Readings on the Saints*, 2 vols. (Princeton University Press, 1993), II, 136.

42 Vincent of Beauvais, *Speculum doctrinale*, XIV.76, c.1330: 'Passiones quæ neruis ad linguam venientibus accidunt, aut fiunt in neruo per quem sensus est gustus, & sunt ipsius imminutio, & priuatio; (quod fit cum in ore nullum sentit homo saporem omnino) aut in neruis per quos verba fiunt, & motus, & hæ sunt linguę grauitas, verborumque priuatio.' [The pains which befall the nerves leading up to the tongue either occur in the nerve through which taste is 'felt', and they are the impairment and privation of it (what happens is that a man feels in his mouth no taste at all), or in the nerves through which words are formed, and movement, and these are the heaviness of the tongue, and the privation of words.]

43 Kitchell and Resnick (eds.), *On Animals*, I, 231. So too do the stomach and brain have a common boundary; when the stomach is functioning well, it aids the brain, 'but a bad stomach destroys [it]' (I, 231).

44 Ogden (ed.), *Cyrurgie*, pp. 142, 47.

45 Ibid., p. 47. Cf. Kitchell and Resnick (eds.), *On Animals*, 1, 258–9.

46 Ogden (ed.), *Cyrurgie*, p. 142; Fleischhacker (ed.), *Science of Cirurgie*, p. 152.

47 For other examples, see Ynez Violé O'Neill, *Speech and Speech Disorders in Western Thought before 1600*, Contributions in Medical History 3 (London: Greenwood Press, 1980), esp. pp. 123; 131–2.

48 On the materiality of medieval words, see further Bishop, *Words, Stones, and Herbs*.

49 See *MED*, s.v. 'menen 1', 1(a).

50 Barnum (ed.), *Dives and Pauper*, 1/ii, 217–18, see also the commentary, 11, 274. Cf. Robert Mannyng of Brunne, *Handlyng Synne*, ed. Idelle Sullens, Medieval & Renaissance Texts & Studies 14 (Binghamton: Medieval & Renaissance Texts & Studies, 1983), p. 68.

51 See *MED*, s.v. 'disposiciouns', 4 and 5; and s.v. 'passioun', 4.

52 The C-text has 'And þat seeth þe soule and sayth hit the in herte' (1.39) – i.e. 'tells you of it in your heart' – thus stressing the process as one of an internal dialogue, William Langland, *Piers Plowman: An Edition of the C-Text*, ed. Derek Pearsall (London: Edward Arnold, 1978).

53 Jill Mann, 'Speaking Images in Chaucer's *Miller's Tale*', *Speaking Images: Essays in Honor of V. A. Kolve*, ed. Charlotte C. Morse and Robert F. Yeager (Asheville: Pegasus Press, 2001), pp. 237–53 (p. 247).

54 There is also a sense that the stomach might 'speak' through its grumblings and the anus through its farts, a sense that is pertinent certainly in the 'confessions' of the seven deadly sins in *Piers Plowman*. See Williams, *Deformed Discourse*, on speech from the belly as deformed or monstrous, p. 143.

55 Francis (ed.), *Book of Vices and Virtues*, p. 47.

56 Ibid., p. 53. This particular body part dialogue appears commonly in pastoral literature in the tradition of the *Somme le roi*: see also Hanna (ed.), *Speculum Vitae*, 11, 432–3 (in this case, the debate is between God and various body parts); and F. N. M. Diekstra (ed.), *Book for a Simple and Devout Woman: A Late Middle English Adaptation of Peraldus's "Summa de Vitiis et Virtutibus" and Friar Laurent's "Somme le Roi"* (Groningen: Egbert Forsten, 1998), p. 261.

57 On the role of sensation in epistemology in the thinking of medieval authors such as Albertus Magnus and Thomas Aquinas, see further Hasse, 'The Soul's Faculties', pp. 318–19. Within a Christian context, which traditionally distrusts the senses, this natural philosophical emphasis on sensation as the basis of epistemology creates a paradox. On medieval distrust of the senses, see Richard G. Newhauser, 'Peter of Limoges, Optics, and the Science of the Senses', *Senses & Society* 5.1 (2010): 28–44 (e.g. 30).

58 Gilby (ed.), *Summa theologiae*, 1a.1.9 (pp. 33, 35). Cf. Carruthers citing Bernard of Clairvaux, *The Experience of Beauty*, p. 91, on the way human knowledge is created from natural psychological and sensory experiences.

59 Classical accounts drawn on in the Middle Ages do not necessarily allow a straightforward connection of taste to knowledge – see, for example, Carruthers, *The Experience of Beauty*, who notes: '*Gustus* is not allied in ancient psychology with intelligent judgement. Taste was considered to have no

direct connections to the brain at all, but only to appetite' (p. 108). However, I suggest that Aristotle's model of sensation and psychology, deeply influential in this period and largely assumed in this book, allows taste and touch to be situated in cognitive and intellectual systems.

60 The debate about the localisation of the reasonable soul in the body creates a doubling of the sensory and cognitive system. Aristotelians hold that the sensory perceptions mediated by the mouth and tongue are first received by the heart from where they would then repair to the brain. In the Galenic model, perceptions are received directly in the brain. For a description of the cardiosensory system, see Heather Webb, 'Cardiosensory Impulses in Late Medieval Spirituality', *Rethinking the Medieval Senses*, ed. Nichols, pp. 265–85. The biblical model also privileges the heart as the seat of the soul and the source of thought. See, for example, biblical passages such as Matthew 12:34, Mark 7:21 and Luke 6:45. See also Carruthers, *Book of Memory*, pp. 48–9, where Carruthers outlines the persistence of the metaphoric use of the heart for memory in the medieval period.

61 For further description of the brain and mental activity, see Seymour and others (eds.), *On the Properties of Things*, 1, 172–3; Fleischhacker (ed.), *Science of Cirurgie*, p. 113; Kitchell and Resnick (eds.), *On Animals*, 11, 940–3. The brain, its cells and its virtues receive extensive cataloguing in Vincent of Beauvais's *Speculum maius*, see, for example, *Speculum naturale*, XXVIII.40, cc.2018–19, and XXVIII.41, c.2019, etc.

62 Minnis, *Medieval Theory of Authorship*, p. 5. Minnis provides a useful overview of the four causes – the efficient (or motivating) cause, the material cause, the formal cause (or substance) and the final cause – and some of their medieval iterations, see, e.g., pp. 28–9, 76, etc. On Aristotle's scheme of the causes and its role in allowing 'pastoral writers to bridge the natural world and the ethical, to generate ethics out of the physical: the forms, functions, and final state of animals', see Craun, 'Aristotle's Biology', 280.

63 In contrast, in the case of touch: 'To make þis wit parfite þese þinges nediþ: þe cause efficient, doynge, and þat is þe springinge of þe spirit *animalis* to þe instrumentis of gropinge. Also a conuenient instrument and in twey maner. On is þe synewis þat comeþ from þe brayn and bringiþ þe spirit *animalis* to alle þe lymes. Þe seconde instrument is þe fleische in þe whiche ben iwrappid and ipi3t [rooted] þe synewis by þe whiche þe vertu of gropinge worchiþ … Þe þridde nediþ help of vttir worchinges so þat þe þing þat schal be igropid be ny3e [near] þe lyme of gropinge', Seymour and others (eds.), *On the Properties of Things*, 1, 119.

64 Fleischhacker (ed.), *Science of Cirurgie*, p. 112; Seymour and others (eds.), *On the Properties of Things*, 1, 117, 98.

65 Cf. Kitchell and Resnick (eds.), *On Animals*, 1: Albertus gives seven pairs of nerves arising from the brain (1, 179), and attributes the sense of taste to the fourth pair (1, 182). See further, 1, 185, for the nerves arising from the *nucha*.

66 Ogden (ed.), *Cyrurgie*, p. 46.

67 See further, on spittle, Carruthers, *The Experience of Beauty*, pp. 127, 129.

68 For comparable descriptions of the operation of taste through the sinews in the tongue taking a likeness of the object tasted and sending it to the brain, see Vincent of Beauvais, *Speculum naturale*, XXV.71, c.1820, where he cites both William of Conche and Hali Abbas on the operation of taste.

69 See Seymour and others (eds.), *On the Properties of Things*, I, 174.

70 Cf. Seymour and others (eds.), *On the Properties of Things*, I, 108. Cf. the Latin text, which describes the sense of sight as 'subtilis' and the sense of taste as 'grossus', Bartholomaeus Anglicus, *De rerum Proprietatibus*, p. 70.

71 On the meanings of 'sotil', see further Carruthers, *The Experience of Beauty*, p. 188.

72 On mediated and unmediated sense perceptions, see further Newhauser, 'John Gower's Sweet Tooth', 757, and on sight as a form of touch, see Biernoff, *Sight and Embodiment*.

73 Aristotle, *De anima*, Barnes (ed.), *The Complete Works*, I, 691.

74 Seymour and others (eds.), *On the Properties of Things*, I, 108. It continues: the office of each wit is to 'haue þe liknes and þe schap of þe obiectis. And what he fongiþ [receives] of þat he felith he presentiþ to þe inwit.' Cf. Vincent of Beauvais, *Speculum naturale*, XXV.10, c.1781 for a comparable description of the properties of the objects each sense acts upon.

75 *MED*, s.v. 'impressioun', carries the general sense of imprinting or indenting, as well as 'an image, a sensation, or an emotion produced in the mind, heart, soul, or senses'; similarly, s.v. 'prenting(e)', 'an image or impression produced in the mind or the senses'.

76 On material change effected through sensation, see Milner, *The Senses*, pp. 24–5; Carruthers, *The Experience of Beauty*, pp. 45–6. On Aquinas on this, see Neil Campbell, 'Aquinas' Reasons for the Aesthetic Irrelevance of Tastes and Smells', *British Journal of Aesthetics* 36.2 (1996): 166–76 (e.g. 169–70).

77 Newhauser, 'John Gower's Sweet Tooth', observes, for example, 'Although literary and philosophical texts conceive of the distance between the object of perception and the perceiver as an advantage, medical texts foreground taste as the superior sense precisely because it brings the object of perception into close contact with the body of the perceiver' (757).

78 See Campbell, 'Aquinas' Reasons', 171–2. Campbell notes (following Donald McQueen) this distinction is not one made in Aristotle's *Metaphysics* and so seems to represent Aquinas's own thinking here (172).

79 Vincent of Beauvais, *Speculum doctrinale*, XIII.131, c.1253: 'Et in tactu quidem fortiores sunt quàm in cæteris sensibus, quia crassior sensuum est, nec facile mutatur & alteratur in alicuius rei naturam, sed tarda quadam difficultate. Non enim passiones in eo celeriter operantur, propter ipsius crassitiem, quæ resistit ac prohibet.'

80 Cf. ibid., XIII.131, c.1253: 'Therefore sight because of the subtlety of its nature is more swiftly altered, in sensing [its] nature changes, as one may know, colour, and therefore great pleasure or pain does not befall it from the sense's nature.' [Visus itaque naturę suæ subtilitate citius alteratur, & in sentiti naturam

mutatur, scilicet colorem; & ideo non accidit ei magna delectatio vel dolor, ex sentiti natura.]

81 Fowler and others (eds.), *The Governance of Kings and Princes*, p. 69.

82 Thus, crucially, touch is understood to be the basis for 'common sense', which grounds 'consciousness' itself. On the Aristotelian basis for thinking about touch as the foundation of consciousness, see Heller-Roazen, *The Inner Touch*, pp. 35–41; and in medieval contexts, Elizabeth Robertson, '*Noli me tangere*: The Enigma of Touch in Middle English Religious Literature for and about Women', *Reading Skin*, ed. Walter, pp. 29–55.

83 The *Summa de saporibus* is edited by Charles Burnett, 'The Superiority of Taste', *Journal of the Warburg and Courtauld Institute* 54 (1991): 230–8. Burnett's edition of the text is provided in an appendix, 235–8. Cf. Carruthers, *The Experience of Beauty*, p. 129 for a brief discussion of *Summa de saporibus*, where she suggests Urso as the possible author and emphasises the text's claim for *gustus* 'as a reliable guide for investigating plainly and completely ("plene et perfecte") the causes of natural things and their complexions ... This is a full reversal of the Aristotelian and Baconian position assigned among the senses to *gustus*. The writer claims that taste is superior even to vision.' C. M. Woolgar, *The Senses in Late Medieval England* (New Haven: Yale University Press, 2006), asserts that the argument of *Summa de saporibus* 'would have found favour with many physicians' (p. 23).

84 Burnett (ed.), 'The Superiority of Taste', 236: 'Rerum naturae cognitio duobus modis habetur, experimento scilicet et ratione; experimento ut velocitate digerendi seu tarditate et pluribus aliis modis, de quibus nunc tractare non intendimus. Ratione vero rem experiendam diiudicante tribus modis rerum nature et proprietates cognoscuntur, scilicet sapore, odore, colore.' [All Modern English translations from this text are my own.]

85 Ibid. 'Solo ergo gustus proprie et principaliter ad rerum naturas investigandas pre ceteris sensibus est destinatus. Per eum enim plene et perfecte de rerum naturis vel complexionibus certificamur.'

86 Ibid., 237: 'Nam ad gustus instrumentum tota res gustanda secundum substantialem et grossam fumositatem et secudum totam substantiam rei et omnes proprietates pervenit et ei totaliter admiscetur. Unde melius ceteris rerum naturas comprehendit.'

87 Ibid. 'Ad linguam etiam sex veniunt lacerti a cerebro, per quos multus spiritus animalis venit. Ad instrumentum tamen odoratus duo tantum veniunt lacerti, quibus paucus spiritus animalis venit.'

88 The sense of 'spiritual' here refers to the amount of *spiritus* – virtue of soul – operating in it. This is therefore different to the tradition of the spiritual senses, which for some thinkers parallel the physical senses. See Gordon Rudy, *Mystical Language of Sensation in the Later Middle Ages* (London: Routledge, 2002); Carruthers, *Experience of Beauty*, pp. 127–8; and Paul L. Gavrilyuk and Sarah Coakley (eds.), *The Spiritual Senses: Perceiving God in Western Christianity* (Cambridge University Press, 2012).

89 *MED*, s.v. 'boistous'. For full definition, see the Introduction, pp. 12–13, and n. 61.

90 See Susan Powell (ed.), *John Mirk's Festial Edited from British Library MS Cotton Claudius A.II*, EETS 334–5, 2 vols. (Oxford University Press, 2009–11), I, 102; Schmidt (ed.), *Piers Plowman*, B.XI.3; and John Lydgate, *The Pilgrimage of the Life of Man*, ed. F. J. Furnivall and Katharine B. Locock, EETS es 77, 83, 92 (London: Kegan Paul, Trench, Trübner, 1899–1904), line 9,381. See also Pierre Courcelle, *Connais-toi toi-même. De Socrate à Saint Bernard*, 3 vols. (Paris: Études Augustiniennes, 1974–5) and J. A. W. Bennett, '*Nosce te ipsum*: Some Medieval Interpretations', *J. R. R. Tolkien, Scholar and Storyteller: Essays in Memoriam*, ed. Mary Salu and Robert T. Farrell (Ithaca: Cornell University Press, 1979), pp. 138–58, for the history and development of this tradition.

91 Joseph S. Wittig, '*Piers Plowman* B, Passus IX–XII: Elements in the Design of the Inward Journey', *Traditio* 28 (1972): 211–80 (211–12).

92 James Simpson, *Sciences and the Self in Medieval Poetry: Alan of Lille's 'Anticlaudianus' and John Gower's 'Confessio Amantis'* (Cambridge University Press, 1995), pp. 127–8.

93 Ibid., p. 127.

94 Wittig, '*Piers Plowman*', 221.

95 Caroline Walker Bynum, *Jesus as Mother: Studies in the Spirituality of the High Middle Ages* (Berkeley: University of California Press, 1982), p. 87.

96 Denery, *Seeing and Being Seen*; Bryan, *Looking Inward*, p. 8.

97 'Duplex est autem homo: interior et exterior. Interior homo anima, et exterior homo corpus', W. M. Lindsay (ed.), *Isidori Hispalensis Episcopi Etymologiarum sive originvm libri XX*, 2 vols. (Oxford: Clarendon, 1911) [hereafter *Etymologiae*], XI.i.6. Trans. Stephen A. Barney and others, *The Etymologies of Isidore of Seville* (Cambridge University Press, 2006), XI.i.6, p. 231.

98 Book III (entitled 'De anima racionali quoad nature simplicitatem et virium diuersitatem et operacionem in corpore', emphasising the work of the soul in the body), Seymour and others (eds.), *On the Properties of Things*, I, 91. Cf. Furnivall and Locock (eds.), *Pilgrimage*, which records that the inner man is 'the soule & the spyryt' (2501).

99 It is this reasonable part of soul which is the proper subject of Augustinian interiority, a notion which persists in the later medieval period. Thus it is in Bartholomaeus's catalogue of the rational soul that he includes the description of self-knowledge: 'And for þe reflexioun of himself vpon hymself he knowiþ himself, as þe philosofir seiþ; by seynge and vndirstondinge he knowiþ himself', Seymour and others (eds.), *On the Properties of Things*, I, 102. However, I suggest that there is another sense of interiority, also evident in *On the Properties of Things*, which also has currency in the later medieval period and which includes the body interior.

100 For a perceptive reading on how the recourse of this passage to both English and Latin terms turns it into a tool 'for self-knowledge, for the analysis of

one's own soul', see Katharine Breen, 'Langland's Literary Syntax, or Anima as an Alternative to Latin Grammar', *Answerable Style: The Idea of the Literary in Medieval England*, ed. Frank Grady and Andrew Galloway (Columbus: Ohio State University Press, 2013), pp. 95–120 (p. 98).

101 Edmund Colledge and James Walsh (eds.), *A Book of Showings to the Anchoress Julian of Norwich*, Studies and Texts 35, 2 vols. (Toronto: Pontifical Institute of Mediaeval Studies, 1978), II, 307.

102 Henry of Lancaster, *Le livre de seyntz medicines, the Unpublished Devotional Treatise of Henry of Lancaster*, ed. E. J. Arnould (Oxford: Blackwell, 1940), p. 86: 'jeo vous prie qe vous plese qe jeo peusse estre ensi defait et overt par devant vous, mon seignur et mon meistre, com sont ascuns devant ces surgens qe sont a ces escoles de Monpelers et aillours, qe quant un homme est mort par le droit de juggement, il lour est donee pur overir, a veoir et conoistre coment les veynes, les nerfs et les autres choses gisent dedeinz un homme et la manere. Douz Sire, ensi vorroie jeo estre overt pardevant vous, qe vous puissetz touz en apert veoir coment ma char et mes veynes et touz mes menbres sont pleyns de pecchés.' [All Modern English translations from this text are my own.]

103 Marie-Christine Pouchelle, *The Body and Surgery in the Middle Ages*, trans. Rosemary Morris (New Brunswick: Rutgers University Press, 1990), gestures towards such a claim in her exploration of Henri de Mondeville's anatomical and surgical treatise, see esp. pp. 187–9.

104 Katharine Park, 'The Life of the Corpse: Division and Dissection in Late Medieval Europe', *Journal of the History of Medicine* 50 (1995): 111–32 (114). For examples of the division of the corpse in England, see Elizabeth A. R. Brown, 'Death and the Human Body in the Later Middle Ages: The Legislation of Boniface VIII on the Division of the Corpse', *Viator* 12 (1981): 221–70.

105 Guy de Chauliac describes dissection, but also post-mortem external examination (Ogden (ed.), *Cyrurgie*, pp. 28, 406), and what might be the embalming or boiling of the flesh to transport bones (pp. 28, 413).

106 The Fünfbilderserie manuscripts state that arteries originate in a black grain in the heart and that *spiritus* also resides in the heart (see Hill, 'The Grain and the Spirit', fig. 2).

107 Mondeville's illustrations are reproduced in Mirko Dražen Grmek and Pierre Huard, *Mille ans de chirurgie en occident: Ve–XVe siècles* (Paris: Dacosta, 1966), figs. 104–9. Anatomical illustration, however, does not just occur in surgical and anatomical treatises but also in more properly natural philosophic works. A fourteenth-century manuscript of Albertus Magnus's *De animalibus*, for example, includes a depiction of an anatomy lesson, reproduced in John E. Murdoch, *Album of Science: Antiquity and the Middle Ages* (New York: Scribner, 1984), p. 233. For illustrations of flayed skin, and the example of St Bartholomew in particular, see Robert Mills, *Suspended Animation: Pain, Pleasure and Punishment in Medieval Culture* (London: Reaktion Books, 2005), pp. 80–2, 132.

108 Danielle Jacquart and Claude Thomasset, *Sexuality and Medicine in the Middle Ages*, trans. Matthew Adamson (Cambridge: Polity, 1988), p. 40.

109 Judy Ann Ford, 'The Autonomy of Conscience: Images of Confession in Mirk's *Festial*', *Renaissance and Reformation* 35.3 (ns 23.3) (1999): 5–27 (17).

110 Judy Ann Ford, *John Mirk's 'Festial': Orthodoxy, Lollardy, and the Common People in Fourteenth-Century England* (Cambridge: Brewer, 2006), p. 89. Cf. pp. 92, 99–100.

111 For a thorough and comprehensive account of the medieval sources and versions of the triumph exemplum, see Maura Nolan, *John Lydgate and the Making of Public Culture* (Cambridge University Press, 2005), pp. 184–255.

112 The triumph exemplum is glossed, in medieval contexts, according to both predominant traditions of self-knowledge. Some versions use it as part of a humility topos (Bernardine tradition) and others as part of the fickleness of Fortune (Aristotle via Boethius), see Nolan, *John Lydgate*, p. 224.

113 Mirk's invention of mouth-beating seems unremarkable to most other readers; Nolan, *John Lydgate*, for example, notes only that the *Festial* is 'very similar to the *Gesta [Romanorum]* account', p. 219 and n. 60.

114 Powell (ed.), *John Mirk's Festial*, I, 102. Cf. Susan Powell, 'A Critical Edition of the *Temporale* Sermons of MSS Harley 2247 and Royal 18 B XXV', 2 vols. (unpublished doctoral thesis, University of London, King's College, 1980), which records a later version of the *Festial* in which the mouth-beating topos also appears with the addition of the Latin as well as the corrupted Greek phrase: 'þere stode a man by hym in þe chare and bette hym on his mowthe ... saying þus to hym, "Anatho solitos, anatho solitos", id est, nosce teipsum, knowe þiself', II, 166. Bennett, '*Nosce te ipsum*', remarks: 'The Greek form of the phrase was corrupted by the early Middle Ages to *notis elitos*', p. 139 n. 2.

2 The Reading Lesson

1 Bourdieu, *Outline of a Theory of Practice*, p. 94.

2 Bakhtin, *Rabelais and His World*, p. 401.

3 Martha Bayless, *Sin and Filth in Medieval Culture: The Devil in the Latrine* (New York: Routledge, 2012), is a recent example; but see also Morrison, *Excrement*, for a nuanced discussion of the lower body and defecation.

4 Aristotle, *Historia animalium*, trans. d'A. W. Thompson, in Barnes (ed.), *The Complete Works*, I, 787. The notion of the *scala naturae* similarly reinforces this topographical hierarchy. On this, see further K. Robertson, *Nature Speaks*, where she notes that the notion of the *scala naturae* 'support[s] a stable moral order, a static hierarchy that allows for a transparent valuation of ontological categories in terms of their relative distance from God' (p. 56).

5 See further on man as microcosm, Chenu, 'Nature and Man', pp. 24–37. Cf. Vincent of Beauvais, *Speculum naturale*, XXIII.3, c.1653. The trope recurs frequently in *Speculum naturale*, see, for example, XXXI.3, cc.1560–1. The upright body of man is likewise a recurrent theme in *De animalibus*, see Kitchell and Resnick (eds.), *On Animals*, I, 237, 290, II, 957.

6　Mary M. Innes, trans., *The Metamorphoses of Ovid* (Harmondsworth: Penguin, 1955), p. 31. See also Steel, *How to Make a Human*, for a detailed discussion of the use of the Ovidian verses and the trope of the upright body as a characteristic dividing humans and animals, e.g. pp. 44–52.

7　Chaucer, *Boece*, in *The Riverside Chaucer*, ed. Benson, p. 466.

8　Phyllis Hodgson (ed.), *The Cloud of Unknowing and The Book of Privy Counselling*, EETS os 218 (London: Oxford University Press, 1944; repr. 1973), p. 113.

9　See further Dorothy Yamamoto, *The Boundaries of the Human in Medieval English Literature* (Oxford University Press, 2000), for a study that explores this propensity for human and animal identity to blur. See also Jeffrey J. Cohen, *Medieval Identity Machines* (Minneapolis: University of Minnesota Press, 2003).

10　K. Robertson, *Nature Speaks*, p. 289.

11　Within the extended discussion in the *Pilgrimage*, the role of Nature is acknowledged but subordinated to 'Grace Dieu'. Nature is thus figured as Grace Dieu's servant, and as one of her schools (along with the 'art of reasoning') through which she teaches, but without authority to limit the extent of Grace Dieu's powers (see Furnivall and Locock (eds.), *Pilgrimage*, pp. 83–101). Later, Aristotle appears as Nature's clerk to argue with Sapience about whether the logic-defying Eucharist is mere sophistry or truth (see further, pp. 145–57). On this, see further K. Robertson, *Nature Speaks,* for extended discussion of the controversy of Aristotle in the late medieval period, and both Deguileville's and Lydgate's pessimism about the powers of Nature. Robertson argues that here 'Nature is debarred from participating in the human world by her alignment with the nonrational world. Reduced to a figure of necessity, she can have nothing authoritative to contribute to the question of what is truly human' (p. 185). However, as I argue in this chapter, this 'natural' example of the denigration of Nature remains, in fact, a powerful teaching tool in the *Pilgrimage*.

12　For other medieval examples of this trope, see Arnau de Vilanova (c.1240–1311): 'A bent back (*dorsum incurvatum*) is the hallmark of those who indulge in worldly pleasures and always desire terrestrial things', cited in Joseph Ziegler, *Medicine and Religion c.1300: The Case of Arnau de Vilanova* (Oxford: Clarendon, 1998), p. 71. See also Bernardus Silvestris's twelfth-century work *The Cosmographia of Bernardus Silvestris*, trans. Winthrop Wetherbee (New York: Columbia University Press, 1973, 1990): 'Brute beasts plainly reveal the grossness of their faculties, their heads cast down, their gaze fixed on the earth; but man alone, his stature bearing witness to the majesty of his mind, will lift up his noble head toward the stars', p. 113.

13　Diekstra (ed.), *Book for a Simple and Devout Woman*, p. 282.

14　Ibid., p. 283.

15　Francis (ed.), *Book of Vices and Virtues*, p. 81.

16　Lynn Staley (ed.), *The Book of Margery Kempe* (Kalamazoo: Medieval Institute Publications), pp. 126–7.

17 On the education of the senses, see, for example, Richard G. Newhauser, 'The Senses, the Medieval Sensorium, and Sensing (in) the Middle Ages', *Medieval Culture: Fundamental Aspects and Conditions of the European Middle Ages*, ed. Albrecht Classen, 3 vols. (Berlin: De Gruyter, 2015), III, 1559–79 (e.g. pp. 1561–2).

18 Aristotle, *De partibus animalium*, trans. W. Ogle, in Barnes (ed.), *The Complete Works*, I, 1035. So too does the diaphragm act as a veil between the spiritual members (heart) and nutritive members (stomach), providing a physical barrier between the imagined high and low parts of the body. See further Kitchell and Resnick (eds.), *On Animals*, I, 257, II, 989.

19 Ralph Hanna (ed.), 'Henry Daniel's *Liber Uricrisiarum (Excerpt)*', *Popular and Practical Science of Medieval England*, ed. Lister M. Matheson (East Lansing: Colleagues, 1994), pp. 185–218 (p. 206). Broadly speaking, the *Liber* is, as Hanna describes, a translation of 'the Constantinian version of Isaac of Israeli's *De urinis*' along with other authorities (p. 189).

20 Ibid., pp. 206–7.

21 Ibid., p. 214.

22 Banks (ed.), *An Alphabet of Tales*, II, 466–7.

23 Kitchell and Resnick (eds.), *On Animals*, I, 231. See also Vincent of Beauvais, *Speculum doctrinale*, XII.II, c.1080, on 'De vomitu', which similarly describes the links between digestion, the head and the senses.

24 Colledge and Walsh (eds.), *Showings*, II, 306–7.

25 College and Walsh suggest OE *sufol*, 'cooked, digested food'. Nicholas Watson, 'Conceptions of the Word: The Mother Tongue and the Incarnation of God', *NML* 1 (1997): 85–124, corrects their etymology to OF *saoulee*, 'satiated with meat and drink' (86). More recently, Arabella Milbank, 'Medieval Corporeality and the Eucharistic Body in Julian of Norwich's *Revelation of Love*', *Journal of Medieval and Early Modern Studies* 46.3 (2016): 629–51, has suggested instead: 'sustenance as a whole' (635).

26 Hanna (ed.), *Liber Uricrisiarum*, p. 198.

27 Milbank's reading, 'Medieval Corporeality', stresses in particular Julian's exploration of the concept of enclosure in this analogy, and notes the possible meaning of 'harte' as stomach in Middle English, which would further extend the visceral focus of the passage (642).

28 On Julian's attitude to the natural and body, see further Alexandra Barratt, ' "In the Lowest Part of Our Need": Julian and Medieval Gynecological Writing', *Julian of Norwich: A Book of Essays*, ed. Sandra J. McEntire, Garland Medieval Casebooks 21 (New York: Garland, 1998), pp. 239–56. Milbank, 'Medieval Corporeality', argues against a defecatory reading of this image, preferring instead to emphasise its function as receptacle/container (see, e.g., 642).

29 See further my discussion of divine involvement in human defecation in 'The Child before the Mother: Mary and the Excremental in *The Prickynge of Love*', *Words and Matter: The Virgin Mary in Late Medieval and Early Modern Parish Life*, ed. Jonas Carlquist and Virginia Langum (Stockholm: Runica et Mediaevalia, 2015), pp. 151–65.

30 Furnivall and Locock (eds.), *Pilgrimage* (17,168–73).

31 Ibid. (17,492–4).

32 Ibid. (18,050; 18,055).

33 Ibid. (18,049). Cf. Gluttony in Furnivall and Locock (eds.), *Pilgrimage*. The 'sak' (12,793), which is also referred to as a 'paunche' (12,822), a 'mawe' (12,844), a 'bely' (12,860) and a 'sachel' (12,897), is synonymous with the stomach. The *Pilgrimage* continues to give a physiological description of swallowing and vomiting and a quasi-anatomical description of the gullet, see lines 12,839–48, and 12,893–900. Cf. Bakhtin, who asserts that grotesque images display 'not only the outward but inward features of the body: blood, bowels, heart and other organs. The outward and inner features are often merged into one', *Rabelais and His World*, p. 318.

34 Kitchell and Resnick (eds.), *On Animals*, i, 260. Elsewhere Albertus explains how '[with a straight intestine] the animal would constantly desire to eat, for the nourishment would always leave it and it would always be defecating. In this way it would be hindered in the performance of the many operations it has which are designed to help life', ii, 1027.

35 Fleischhacker (ed.), *Science of Cirurgie*, pp. 168–9. *MED*, s.v. 'segge' (n.(2)), 'A privy, latrine; a chamber pot, stool'; 'evacuation of the bowels or bladder'.

36 Staley (ed.), *Book*, p. 173.

37 Roger Ellis (ed.), *The Liber Celestis of St Bridget of Sweden*, Volume 1: *Text*, EETS os 291 (Oxford University Press, 1987), p. 351. The bowels, 'which clenses þe mete', is like contrition, which cleanses the soul (p. 351).

38 Oxford, Bodleian Library, Bodley MS 4, f. 60r, cited and translated in Craun, 'Aristotle's Biology', 299 and n.60.

39 Craun, 'Aristotle's Biology', 299.

40 Cf. Lindsay (ed.), *Etymologiae*, xi.i.5; trans. Barney and others, *The Etymologies*, p. 231: 'The Greeks called the human being ἄνθρωπος because he has been raised upright from the soil and looks upward in contemplation of his Creator … The poet Ovid describes this when he says (*Met.* 1.84): While the rest of the stooping animals look at the ground, he gave the human an uplifted countenance, and ordered him to see the sky, and to raise his upturned face to the stars. And the human stands erect and looks toward heaven so as to seek God, rather than look at the earth, as do the beasts that nature has made bent over and attentive to their bellies.'

41 This resonates with the four reasons Thomas Aquinas gives in the *Summa theologiae* for man's upright body: (1) so that the senses do not only hunt out food but get to know things, (2) so that the 'inner powers' can function unhindered, (3) so that he does not use his hands as forefeet, and (4) so that he does not have to gather food with his mouth, which would interfere with the faculty of speech. Aquinas's account therefore emphasises the way in which an upright posture specifically brings about the ennoblement of the mouth. Gilby (ed.), *Summa theologiae*, 1a.91.3 (pp. 28–9).

42 A literal translation might read along these lines: 'And while the other animals contemplate the earth leaning forwards, [God] gives a high mouth to men and

orders [them] to look up to the heavens and lift [their] faces towards the stars.' [Modern English translation my own.] Lewis and Short's *Latin Dictionary* records the use of 'os' to refer both to the mouth and more generally to the face, countenance or head. William D. Sharpe, 'Isidore of Seville: The Medical Writings', *Transactions of the American Philosophical Society* 54.2 (1964): 1–75 translates 'os' as 'countenance' (38); Innes, trans. *Metamorphoses*, less literally, as 'man stands erect' (p. 31).

43 Ernst Sieper (ed.), *Lydgate's Reson and Sensuallyte*, EETS es 84, 89, 2 vols. (London: K. Paul, Trench, Trübner & Co., 1901–3), 1, 393–7. It continues: 'He passeth bestys of reson, / Hys eye vp-cast ryght as lyne, / Where as bestes don enclyne / Her hedes to the erthe lowe' (398–401). On the question of the attribution of this work to Lydgate, see Jane Griffiths, *Diverting Authorities: Experimental Glossing Practices in Manuscript and Print* (Oxford University Press, 2014), p. 63 n. 26. See also K. Robertson, *Nature Speaks*, especially her discussion of Lydgate's use of the term 'demonstracion' in the poem (p. 301).

44 Notably, the Ovidian quotation appears a second time in Book xviii of *On the Properties of Things*, this time in the context of St Basil's warning of the ability of an unregulated appetite to overthrow the upright bearing and rationality of man. Seymour and others (eds.), *On the Properties of Things*, ii, 1095: 'Whanne an vnresonable beste is parfitliche ymade and yschape þe face þerof boweþ toward þe erþe þat is þe original and material matiere wherof it com. And oonliche to man kynde ordeigneþ and eseþ vpright stature; in þat mankynde is wonderliche ymade noble and passynge alle oþre bestes, as þe poete seiþ þat "kynde haþ 3iue to man an high mouþ and vertu to loken on heuene". Þerfore Basilius seiþ þat if man is defouled wiþ lust and likynge of fleissh and obedient to leccherie of þe wombe, þanne man is ymade pore and vnwise perliche to vnresonable bestes.'

45 Vincent of Beauvais, *Speculum naturale*, xxviii.3, c.1995: 'Non enim vt animalia rationis expertia, prona esse videmus in terram, ita creatus est homo, sed erecta in cælum corporis ammonet forma, eum quae sursum sunt sapere.'

46 Oxford, Oriel College MS 20, f. 140v, cited and translated in Craun, 'Aristotle's Biology', 300–1.

47 Craun, 'Aristotle's Biology', 301.

48 See Aristotle, *De partibus animalium*, in Barnes (ed.), *The Complete Works*, 1, 1071: 'in his [man's] infancy ... the upper parts are large, while the lower part is small, so that the infant can only crawl, and is unable to walk; and, at first cannot even crawl, but remains without motion.' Cf. *The Pricke of Conscience*'s observation that at birth man has 'nouther strenthe ne myght / Nouther to go ne yhit [yet] to stand', but can only 'ligge [lie] and sprawel', Richard Morris (ed.), *The Pricke of Conscience (Stimulus conscientiae): A Northumbrian Poem* (Berlin: A. Asher & Co., 1863), p. 13.

49 Albertus Magnus writes, children 'no more employ intellect during their infancy with respect to the powers of the soul than do the brute animals', Kitchell and Resnick (eds.), *On Animals*, 1, 587.

50 Thomas Hoccleve, 'La Male Regle de T. Hoccleve', in Roger Ellis (ed.), *'My Compleinte' and Other Poems* (University of Exeter Press, 2001), 105–16. Ellis glosses 'The custume of my replete abstinence' as 'the habit of only abstaining when stuffed'. See further Nicholas Perkins, 'Thomas Hoccleve, *La Male Reglé*', A *Companion to Medieval English Literature and Culture c.1350–c.1500*, ed. Peter Brown (Oxford: Blackwell, 2007), pp. 585–603 and his reading of 'excess' in this passage at p. 599.

51 Ellis (ed.), 'La Male Regle', ll. 110; 120.

52 Aristotle writes, 'human embryos lie bent, with nose between the knees and eyes upon the knees, and the ears free at the sides', *Historia animalium*, Barnes (ed.), *The Complete Works*, 1, 919. Isidore of Seville develops this Aristotelian observation and connects weeping and kneeling with the prepartum experience of being in the dark in the womb. See Lindsay (ed.), *Etymologiae*, XI.i.108–9. Trans. Barney and others, *The Etymologies*, p. 238.

53 On the symbolism of kneeling in medieval culture, see John Burrow, *Gestures and Looks in Medieval Narrative* (Cambridge University Press, 2002).

54 Charlotte D'Evelyn and Anna J. Mill (eds.), *The South English Legendary*, EETS os 236, 3 vols. (London: Oxford University Press, 1956–9), II, 425–6. See Jacqueline A. Tasioulas, 'Heaven and Earth in Little Space', *Medium Aevum* 76.1 (2007): 24–48, and her discussion of the accounts of embryology in *On the Properties of Things* and *The South English Legendary* (32–3). Tasioulas interprets these images as suggesting 'foetal life as a humiliation' (33). See also Pouchelle's reading of Isidore's etymology of knees and eyes, in Pouchelle, *The Body and Surgery*, p. 186; and Carruthers, *The Experience of Beauty*, where she discusses the connections between physiology, cognition and kneeling, e.g. pp. 145–6.

55 Barnum (ed.), *Dives and Pauper*, citing 'Ricardus de Media Villa, super iii Sententiis, d. ix, q.vlt', I/i, 104–5.

56 Aristotle, *De partibus animalium*, in Barnes (ed.), *The Complete Works*, I, 1070.

57 See also Furnivall and Locock (eds.), *Pilgrimage*, in which Sickness explains how in old age she 'make hir [i.e. humans] forto bowe hir chyne' (24,203).

58 Munich, Bayerische Staatsbibliothek, Clm. 19414, f. 180r. Elizabeth Sears, *The Ages of Man: Medieval Interpretations of the Life Cycle* (Princeton University Press, 1986), describes the illustration and gives a translation of the Latin text, here drawing on Aristotle, accompanying the image (notably the descriptions accompanying the other roundels draw instead on *De proprietatibus rerum*), p. 130 and fig. 65.

59 Cf. Leon R. Kass, *The Hungry Soul: Eating and the Perfecting of Our Nature* (New York: Maxwell Macmillan International, 1994), who writes, 'standing thus becomes a model of the unpremeditated natural human relation to nature: It requires effort, expended against [gravity]' (p. 65).

60 For the significance of kneeling in *Piers Plowman*, see James F. G. Weldon, 'Gesture of Perception: The Pattern of Kneeling in *Piers Plowman* B.18–19', *YLS* 3 (1989): 49–66. Notably, Weldon argues kneeling 'is closely connected with the unveiling of spiritual truth' (49). See also Mary C. Davlin, 'Devotional Postures in *Piers Plowman* B, with an Appendix on Divine Postures', *Chaucer Review* 42.2 (2007): 161–79.

61 Francis (ed.), *Book of Vices and Virtues*, p. 27; Diekstra (ed.), *Book for a Simple and Devout Woman*, p. 144.

62 Falling too might be connected with cognitive processes, since medieval prayer might be undertaken by prostrating oneself in order to induce tears, which, in turn, was thought to facilitate rational argument. See Mary J. Carruthers, 'On Affliction and Reading, Weeping and Argument: Chaucer's Lachrymose Troilus in Context', *Representations* 93 (2006): 1–21 (10).

63 Diekstra (ed.), *Book for a Simple and Devout Woman*, p. 144; see also p. 108 on St Paul and falling and the need for divine grace in rising.

64 Francis (ed.), *Book of Vices and Virtues*, however, describes a man so mired in sin that even bodily need does not seem to rouse him: 'for schrewednesse [he] ne wole not ones lift vp his tail to clepe to God ne repente hym' (p. 27).

65 Ibid., p. 126.

66 Scarry, *The Body in Pain*, pp. 32–3.

67 On *felix culpa*, see Hugh White, 'Langland, Milton and the *Felix Culpa*', *Review of English Studies* ns 45 (1994): 336–56.

68 Colledge and Walsh (eds.), *Showings*, 11, 496.

69 Ibid., 11, 602.

70 Ibid., 11, 603.

71 Ibid., 11, 514–15.

72 Ibid., 11, 515–16.

73 See further Larry Scanlon, 'Personification and Penance', *YLS* 21 (2007): 1–29, for a reading of Gloton in *Piers Plowman*, and (at 19–20) for the tradition of tavern sins and sins of the tongue that Langland draws on here. The sins of the tongue, likely 'the innovation of Peter Cantor', are taken up and expanded by William Peraldus, the compiler of the *Summa de vitiis*, 'the principal inspiration of the *Somme le roi* ... with its cognate, *Le miroir du monde*'. Scanlon is more sceptical of Nick Gray's suggestion in 'The Clemency of Cobblers: A Reading of "Glutton's Confession" in *Piers Plowman*', *Leeds Studies in English* 17 (1986): 61–75, that this scene is a parody of the act of confession (28). On the sin of gluttony and this episode in *Piers Plowman*, see also Langum, *Medicine and the Seven Deadly Sins* (e.g. p. 159).

74 Francis (ed.), *Book of Vices and Virtues*, p. 54. Cf. Diekstra (ed.), *Book for a Simple and Devout Woman*, pp. 261–2; Hanna (ed.) *Speculum Vitae*, 11, 447; Sullens (ed.), *Handlyng Synne*, pp. 162, 166.

75 See M. J. Toswell, 'Of Dogs, *Cawdels*, and Contrition: A Penitential Motif in *Piers Plowman*', *YLS* 7 (1993): 115–21, for an analysis of the tavern episode and the image of the unrepentant sinner returning to his sins like a dog. For a similar image, see also Edward H. Weatherly (ed.), *Speculum Sacerdotale*, EETS os 200 (London: Oxford University Press, 1936), p. 60.

76 L. O. Aranye Fradenburg, *Sacrifice Your Love: Psychoanalysis, Historicism, Chaucer*, Medieval Cultures 31 (Minneapolis: University of Minnesota Press, 2002), p. 81.

77 On smell and taste, see further p. 128 below.

78 Lesley Smith, 'William of Auvergne and Confession', *Handling Sin: Confession in the Middle Ages*, ed. Peter Biller and A. J. Minnis (Woodbridge: Boydell

& Brewer, 1998), pp. 95–107 (p. 106). Smith observes that William's treatises 'suggest an educated, interested, devout reading public which, though not ideologically trained, nevertheless wishes to know more of the Why, and not simply the How or What' (p. 107).

79 Cited in Smith, 'William of Auvergne', p. 95.

80 Seymour and others (eds.), *On the Properties of Things*, I, 201. Thus, if it is not performed properly ('imaade as he schulde'), the effect can also be deleterious. Cf. I, 396. See further Ogden (ed.), *Cyrurgie*, p. 564; Vincent of Beauvais, *Speculum doctrinale*, XII.II, c.1080. On the health benefits of purgation, see further Morrison, *Excrement*, e.g. p. 22.

81 On 'exemplarism' in *Piers Plowman*, see further Davis, ' "Save man allone" '.

82 Zeeman, 'Condition of *Kynde*', p. 16.

83 A version of this passage does not occur in either the A- or C-texts.

84 *MED*, s.v. 'helen' (v.(2)), 'To cover (sth.)', '*fig.* blot out (sin)'; 'To conceal (sth.), hide'.

85 See Margaret R. Miles, *Carnal Knowing: Female Nakedness and Religious Meaning in the Christian West* (Boston: Beacon Press, 1989), p. 92; see also James A. Brundage, 'Sex and Canon Law', *Handbook of Medieval Sexuality*, ed. Vern L. Bullough and James A. Brundage, Garland Reference Library of the Humanities 1696 (New York: Garland, 1996), pp. 33–50, in which he records that 'Human sexuality as we know it, according to one strand of Augustinian theory, departs in many important ways from the original intentions of the divine Creator. In paradise, before Adam and Eve, the progenitors of the entire human race, had committed the first sin, sexual feelings and sexual relations were radically different from anything that we now experience' (p. 34). This is primarily because the sexual organs were subordinate to reason and will; uncontrollable sexual appetite was therefore a consequence of sin.

86 See Chapter 1 for discussion of the sources of language in the body.

87 Schmidt (ed.), *Piers Plowman*, gives the translation as 'not to be wise more than it behoveth to be wise (Rom 12:3)' (p. 47).

88 *MED*, s.v. 'ars' (n), also arce, ers, eres, hars, hers, 'The anus, the rectum; excretory organ'; s.v. 'ere' (n(1)), pl. eren, ern, eres, 'The ear as a part of the body'.

89 Deguileville's figure of Grace Dieu argues that the Pilgrim's eyes need to be placed in his ears, 'Wherfor I shal (yiff that I may) / Bothe thyn Eyen take away, / And hem out off her placë fette [take with force]; / And in thyn Erys [ears] I shal hem sette', Furnivall and Locock (eds.), *Pilgrimage* (6253–6). The Pilgrim, fearing the physical monstrosity – the unnatural body – this will result in, is at first reluctant to consent to making himself 'so odius', to being thus 'transforme[d]' or 'dysfygure[d]' (6270–2).

90 Such an image may well take its visual cue from illustrations of the anal fistula like those accompanying a fifteenth-century Middle English translation of John of Arderne's medical treatise. The opening author portrait shows the surgeon Arderne treating a patient, who is figured only as a lower body, bending to expose his anal fistula to Arderne, whose finger is pointing to and

entering the anal sphincter. See Orlemanski, 'Jargon', 413–15 for a discussion of these illustrations.

3 Tasting, Eating and Knowing

1 Vincent of Beauvais, *Speculum naturale*, XXVIII.3, c.1995.
2 Zeeman, *Discourse of Desire*, p. 90.
3 On *lectio divina*, see Laura Sterponi, 'Reading and Meditation in the Middle Ages: *Lectio divina* and Books of Hours', *Text & Talk* 28.5 (2008): 667–89 (671).
4 On *sapientia* and sweetness, see Carruthers, *The Experience of Beauty*, especially ch. 4.
5 For Carruthers's outline of this tradition, see the discussion below, p. 96.
6 On the connections of eating and reading in vernacular literature, see the extracts in Part 3, Jocelyn Wogan-Browne and others (eds.), *The Idea of the Vernacular: An Anthology of Middle English Literary Theory, 1280–1520* (University Park: Penn State University Press, 1999), e.g. pp. 235–8, 281–5, 288–91.
7 Fowler and others (eds.), *The Governance of Kings and Princes*, p. 236.
8 Barnum (ed.), *Dives and Pauper*, 1/i, 129. It continues: 'and so oftentyme þey etyn and drynkyn and reseyuyn inward mechil vnthryfty thyng and venymyn hemself and hurtyn hemself in many wyse'. Cf. 1/124–7 on 'inclynacioun'.
9 Kitchell and Resnick (eds.), *On Animals*, II, 919. Vincent of Beauvais, citing Hippocrates, similarly records the fluid state of the spermatic substance of the brain in *Speculum doctrinale*, XIII.29, c.1188: 'a great amount of the substance of sperm is in the brain and runs down from two veins which are behind both ears' [Hippocrates ait, quod plurimum materia spermatis est in cerebro, & descendit ex duabus venis quæ sunt post ambas aures]. Cf. *Speculum doctrinale*, XIII.14–15, cc.1177–8; and Brian Lawn (ed.), *The Prose Salernitan Questions* (Oxford University Press, 1979), which records that the substance of the brain is fragile 'in the first origin', 'because it is assembled from the place of the foetus's conception, which is the uterus' [Huius itaque substantia in prima origine est tenerrima quod contrahit tum ex loco conceptionis fetus, scilicet matrice que velut sentina totius corporis existit], P 123, p. 252. [All Modern English translations from this text are my own.]
10 Fowler and other (eds.), *The Governance of Kings and Princes*, p. 220. Cf. p. 236, where Giles relates how: 'in þat age in þe whiche þe body is most nesche and most able to fonge diuerse schappes and diuerse inclinacioun, man is most nesche and most able to fonge diuerse schappes and inclinacioun by appetite'.
11 Fowler and other (eds.), *The Governance of Kings and Princes*, p. 219. Describing why we need to teach children 'goode maneres' in childhood, Giles, citing Aristotle's *Nichomachean Ethics*, notes: 'it is so kyndelich to vs to haue likyng þat in childhod we begynnen to haue likyng. Þerfore children hauen likyng anon whan þei bygennen to souke tetes and breestes.'

12 Aristotle, *De partibus animalium*, in Barnes (ed.), *The Complete Works*, I, 1028.

13 Diekstra (ed.), *Book for a Simple and Devout Woman*, p. 265.

14 Chaucer, 'The Manciple's Tale', *Riverside Chaucer*, ed. Benson, IX.322–4. Cf. the 'gat tothed' Wife of Bath in the General Prologue, I.468.

15 Edwin D. Craun, *Lies, Slander, and Obscenity in Medieval English Literature: Pastoral Rhetoric and the Deviant Speaker* (Cambridge University Press, 1997), p. 201, see also p. 206. Craun details in particular the tale's debt to teaching on the sins of the tongue derived from Peraldus.

16 Chaucer, 'The Manciple's Tale', *Riverside Chaucer*, ed. Benson, IX.316; 334.

17 Ibid., IX.332.

18 Vincent of Beauvais, *Speculum doctrinale*, XII.27, c.1090, similarly repeats the instruction to 'touch the palate with honey' [vt palatum cum melle tangatur].

19 Alexandra Barratt (ed.), *The Knowing of Woman's Kind in Childing: A Middle English Version of Material Derived from the Trotula and Other Sources*, Medieval Women's Texts & Contexts 4 (Turnhout: Brepols, 2001), Douce, lines 464–70, p. 72.

20 Jacqueline A. Tasioulas, 'The Mother's Lament: *Wulf and Eadwacer* Reconsidered', *Medium Aevum* 65 (1996): 1–18 (12). David Herlihy, *Medieval Households* (Cambridge, MA: Harvard University Press, 1985), records the details of the eighth-century Frisian tale of Liafburga in *Acta Sanctorum*: a grandmother, enraged because her daughter-in-law had not given birth to a son, sent *lictores* to take the baby 'before she took milk. For this was the custom of the pagans: if they wished to kill a son or daughter, they did so before they took material food. Liafburga was rescued and fed some honey' (pp. 53–4).

21 The dreamer in *Piers Plowman* is, for example, assaulted by Elde, who 'buffetted me aboute the mouth and bette out my wangteeth [molars]' (B.xx.191): losing his teeth, the dreamer also becomes impotent (B.xx.195–8), iterating a connection between teeth and sexual desire. Elsewhere, the association between toothlessness and a loss of reason is emphasised; see, for example, Graesse (ed.), *Legenda aurea*, p. 813 (trans. Ryan, *The Golden Legend*, II, 35).

22 Kitchell and Resnick (eds.), *On Animals*, II, 918–19.

23 Cf. Vincent of Beauvais, *Speculum doctrinale*, XIII.14, c.1177, where he likewise gives these four stages, citing Avicenna.

24 For example, Lawn (ed.), *Prose Salernitan Questions*: 'Dentium materia est ex cerebri substantia, et ex genarum medulla' [The material of teeth comes from the substance from the brain and from the marrow of the cheeks], P 123, p. 251; 'Ad dentium formationem tria concurrunt; fleuma ut materia, calor gingivas dilatans, frigiditas aeris consolidans' [Three things are needed in order to form teeth: phlegm so that there might be material, heat (for the purpose of) expanding the gums, and cold air (for the purpose of) solidifying (them)], P 242, p. 120.

25 Ibid., 'In iuvenibus remittitur fleuma et obtunditur, in senibus calor, unde in eis dentium non potest fieri reparatio', B 242, p. 120. Notably, the *Questions* also explains that, in old age, the substance of the brain 'becomes soft again,

just as at the place of the generation of the teeth matter is able to flow'. ['In ultimo vero senio, licet ipsum sit naturaliter siccum, ex humiditate tamen accidentali, actualitate cerebrum remollescit ut ad locum generationis dentium materia fluere possit'], P 123, p. 252.

26 Shulamith Shahar, *Childhood in the Middle Ages*, trans. Chaya Galai (London: Routledge, 1990), p. 92.

27 'A human being of the first age is called an infant (*infans*); it is called an infant, because it does not yet know how to speak, that is, it cannot talk. Not yet having its full complement of teeth, it has less ability to articulate words.' Trans. Barney and others, *The Etymologies*, p. 241. Lindsay (ed.), *Etymologiae*, XI.ii.9: 'Infans dicitur homo primae aetatis; dictus autem infans quia adhuc fari nescit, id est loqui non potest. Nondum enim bene ordinatis dentibus minus sermonis expressio.'

28 Shahar, *Childhood*, records the perception of childish speech as imitation of adult speech, p. 93.

29 See ibid., for example, pp. 24–55, 170–9; education begins in the second stage of childhood, which is normally at seven years old.

30 Vincent of Beauvais, *Speculum doctrinale*, XII.27, c.1090: 'Cum vero natiuitas dentium appropinquauerit, gingiuæ cum butyro & adipe gallinę sæpe fricandæ sunt, & aqua hordei liniendæ'; XII.30, c.1092: 'Tandem vero cum loqui cœperit fricandi sunt eius dentes, pręcipueque eorum radices.'

31 Monica H. Green (ed.), *The Trotula: An English Translation of the Medieval Compendium of Women's Medicine* (Philadelphia: University of Pennsylvania Press, 2001, 2002), p. 83.

32 Ogden (ed.), *Cyrurgie*, p. 483. These instructions are also found in Vincent of Beauvais, *Speculum doctrinale*; see, for example, XII.27, c.1090: 'Et postquam loquendi tempus approprinquauerit, nutrix frequenter eius linguam fricet, ante ipsum quoque frequenter loquendum est, & verba facilia leuiaque docendus est.' [And after the time of speaking has approached, the nurse should rub his tongue frequently, [and] before that one should speak frequently, and he should be taught with easy and light (e.g. not burdensome to the mouth) words.]

33 See Green (ed.), *Trotula*, p. 83. Shahar, *Childhood*, also records a medieval treatise that recommends the use of a mirror placed in front of a child, behind which a nurse speaks to encourage speech if a child does not develop it naturally, p. 93.

34 On weaning, see Barratt (ed.), *The Knowing of Woman's Kind*, Douce, pp. 74–6. This transition from breastfeeding to solids, according to *The Knowing of Woman's Kind in Childing*, is dependent on both the process of 'forgetting' and making the child's former attachment to the breast 'loth' to him. See also Green (ed.), *Trotula*, p. 84.

35 Josiah Forshall and Frederic Madden (eds.), *The Holy Bible, containing the Old and New Testaments … in the Earliest English Versions made from the Latin Vulgate by John Wycliffe and His Followers*, 4 vols. (Oxford University Press, 1850), IV.

36 St Jerome, *Letters and Select Works*, trans. W. H. Fremantle in *A Select Library of Nicene and Post-Nicene Fathers*, Second Series, ed. Philip Schaff and Henry Wace, 14 vols. (Oxford: Parker, 1893), VI, 259. For the Latin, see Letter 128, PL 22, col. 1098: 'Cum autem virgunculam rudem et edentulam, septimus ætatis annus exceperit, et ceperit erubescere, scire quid taceat, dubitare quid dicat.'

37 Those who were deaf or dumb were considered to lack reason. See Thomas Collett Sandars (ed.), *The Institutes of Justinian* (London: Parker, 1853), p. 445. Moreover, the *Institutes* forge a connection between *infans* and madmen, p. 446.

38 See Sandars (ed.), *Institutes*, p. 446. For the influence of Roman law in the medieval period, see Peter G. Stein, 'The Medieval Rediscovery of the Roman Civil Law', *The Civilian Tradition and Scots Law: Aberdeen Quincentenary Essays*, ed. David L. Carey Miller and Reinhard Zimmermann (Berlin: Duncker und Humblot, 1997), pp. 75–86; and Stephen Kuttner, 'The Revival of Jurisprudence', *Renaissance and Renewal in the Twelfth Century*, ed. R. L. Benson and Giles Constable (Oxford: Clarendon, 1982), pp. 299–323.

39 See also Aristotle, *Historia animalium*, in Barnes (ed.), *The Complete Works*, I, 797; Lindsay (ed.), *Etymologiae*, XI.i.53, trans. Barney and others, *The Etymologies*: 'From the teeth one can tell apart the sexes, for in men there are more, in women fewer' (p. 234).

40 Kitchell and Resnick (eds.), *On Animals*, II, 918.

41 Chaucer, 'The Reeve's Prologue', *Riverside Chaucer*, ed. Benson, 1.3888.

42 Chaucer, 'The Wife of Bath's Prologue', *Riverside Chaucer*, ed. Benson, III.449.

43 'Sir Gowther', *The Middle English Breton Lays*, ed. Anne Laskaya and Eve Salisbury (Kalamazoo: Medieval Institute Publications, 1995), pp. 263–96 (p. 277). Cf. Robert the Devil who has similarly destructive teeth, in Henry Morley (ed.), *Early Prose Romances* (London: Routledge, 1889), pp. 167–206 (p. 173). Shakespeare's Richard III is also born with teeth: *Henry VI*, pt. III, Act v, Scene 6.

44 On body *hexis*, see further Bourdieu, *Outline of a Theory of Practice*, who notes it is not merely bodily – a posture, a body movement, 'a durable manner of standing, speaking' – but also a manner of '*feeling* and *thinking*' (p. 93); and Carruthers, *Book of Memory*, who observes: body *hexis* 'is physiological, as the memory is trained to respond with certain movements, just as a dancer's muscles are, but it is also reasoned, for it is a "facilitated" rather than "automatic" response' (p. 69).

45 Hanna (ed.), *Speculum Vitae*, I, 8, describes the relation of the seven *Pater noster* petitions to the seven gifts of the Holy Ghost, the seven deadly sins, the seven remedial virtues and the seven beatitudes. See Hanna's overview, p. lxxi.

46 Ibid., I, 81 (2372).

47 Ibid., I, 91 (2676).

48 Ibid., I, 81–2 (2389–94).

49 Ibid., I, 82 (2395–8). Cf. Lydgate's poem, *Reson and Sensuallyte*, ed. Siepers, where taste also knows more truly than sight ('who taste aryght, / Contrarye

even to the syght') in discerning fruit, which is 'faire withoute' but 'corumpbable / They be wythin' (3924–9). See K. Robertson, *Nature Speaks*, p. 301 for a discussion of this episode.

50 Hanna (ed.), *Speculum Vitae*, i, 82–3 (2421–4).

51 Ibid., i, 115. The gift of understanding draws out the sin of lechery and sets in chastity, and its reward is to see the face of God.

52 Hanna (ed.), *Speculum Vitae*, ii, 485 (14,641–58).

53 Ibid., ii, 485–6 (14,659–67).

54 See, for example, Hanna (ed.), *Speculum Vitae*, i, 115. Moderation is thus a key concept of medical theory, understood to be crucial to maintaining health, but is also coloured by Classical and Christian discussions of vice and virtue and of temperance. For a wide-ranging discussion of the importance of measure in medieval thought, see Joel Kaye, *A History of Balance 1250–1375: The Emergence of a New Model of Equilibrium* (Cambridge University Press, 2014), which traces theories of balance across economic and political theory, as well as, in chs. 3 and 4, medical theory. On 'moderation' as an attribute of Nature, see also White, *Nature, Sex, and Goodness*, e.g. pp. 91–2.

55 See, for example, Hanna (ed.), *Speculum Vitae*, ii, 429, 483, 492–6, 497, 502–34.

56 See ibid., ii, 492 (14,853–4).

57 Jean Leclercq, O.S.B., *The Love of Learning and the Desire for God: A Study of Monastic Culture*, trans. Catharine Misrahi (New York: Fordham University Press, 1961, repr. 2003), p. 73.

58 Cited by Catherine Brown, 'In the Middle', *Journal of Medieval and Early Modern Studies*, 30.3 (2000): 547–74 (561).

59 Ynez Violé O'Neill, 'Diagrams of the Medieval Brain: A Study in Cerebral Localisation', *Iconography at the Crossroads*, ed. Brendan Cassidy (Princeton University Press, 1993), pp. 91–101 (p. 91). See also O'Neill's outline of William Conches's brain–stomach analogy, p. 96.

60 It is found, for example, in 'secular' contexts too, such as Geoffrey of Vinsauf, *Poetria nova*, rev. edn, trans. Margaret F. Nims, intro. to rev. edn, Martin Camargo, Medieval Sources in Translation 49 (Toronto: Pontifical Institute of Mediaeval Studies, 2010, first pub. 1967), pp. 76–7.

61 Carruthers, *Book of Memory*, p. 164.

62 Hanna (ed.), *Speculum Vitae*, i, 8–9 (128–30); 135–8; cf. Francis (ed.), *Book of Vices and Virtues*, p. 97.

63 Hanna (ed.), *Speculum Vitae*, i, 9–10 (143–52, 181–90).

64 Ibid., i, 78 (2277–80).

65 Ibid., i, 78 (2283–8).

66 Ibid., i, 78 (2289–91).

67 Ibid., i, 78 (2293–8). The exposition of these four words or units is extensive, running from p. 13 to p. 79. A useful, though extremely condensed, summary is offered, i, 78–9.

68 Hodgson (ed.), *The Cloud of Unknowing*, pp. 28–9. Elsewhere the *Cloud*-author writes that one word which bursts forth into audible sound is better

than 'any longe sauter [psalm] vnmyndfuly mumlyd [mumbled] in þe teeþ' (p. 75).

69 The exposition of the fourth petition, *Panem nostrum cotidianum da nobis hodie*, runs for several hundred lines, Hanna (ed.), *Speculum Vitae*, I, 90–8 (2641–879).

70 Ibid., I, 12 (227–8).

71 Ibid., I, 91 (2671–3).

72 Ibid., I, 98 (2883–92) summarises the three kinds of bread this petition obtains.

73 See ibid., I, 96–7 (2841–64) on the Eucharist as peculiarly 'substantial' food. Notably, by this period, the Host was typically only consumed once a year, at Easter after a period of fasting; the sacrament of the altar was thus more typically experienced as a visual and aural spectacle.

74 Hanna (ed.), *Speculum Vitae*, I, 93 (2721–6).

75 Diekstra (ed.), *Book for a Simple and Devout Woman*, p. 256.

76 Powell (ed.), *John Mirk's Festial*, I, 79.

77 Fowler and others (eds.), *The Governance of Kings and Princes*, pp. 230–1.

78 John Mirk, *Instructions for Parish Priests*, ed. Edward Peacock, EETS os 31 (London: Kegan Paul, Trench, Trübner, 1868; repr. 1902), p. 8.

79 Fiona Somerset, 'Here, There, and Everywhere? Wycliffite Conceptions of the Eucharist and Chaucer's "Other" Lollard Joke', *Lollards and Their Influence in Late Medieval England*, ed. Fiona Somerset, Jill C. Havens and Derrick G. Pitard (Woodbridge: Boydell, 2003), pp. 127–38 (p. 127).

80 On eucharistic theories, see Stephen E. Lahey, 'Late Medieval Eucharistic Theology', *A Companion to the Eucharist in the Middle Ages*, ed. Ian Christopher Levy and others (Leiden: Brill, 2012), pp. 499–539.

81 John A. F. Thomson, *The Transformation of Medieval England 1370–1529* (London: Routledge, 2014, first pub. 1983), p. 356.

82 Cited and discussed in Fiona Somerset, *Feeling Like Saints: Lollard Writings after Wyclif* (Ithaca: Cornell University Press, 2014), p. 263.

83 Francis (ed.), *Book of Vices and Virtues*, p. 109.

84 Furnivall and Locock (eds.), *Pilgrimage* (5383–508).

85 K. Robertson, *Nature Speaks*, p. 315 (see also p. 313). See further, in ch. 4, Robertson's discussion of Deguileville, the Eucharist and Aristotle, and these themes in Lydgate's translation in ch. 6.

86 Furnivall and Locock (eds.), *Pilgrimage* (5497–508, 5509–20).

87 Ibid. (5546–613).

88 Ibid. (5310–13).

89 Furnivall and Locock (eds.), *Pilgrimage* (5917–93). Cf. Aquinas's discussion in the *Summa theologiae*, 3a.76, 3 and K. Robertson, *Nature Speaks*, e.g. pp. 192, 314 on the mirror analogy.

90 Hanna (ed.), *Speculum Vitae*, I, 93 (2739–48).

91 Francis (ed.), *Book of Vices and Virtues*, p. 109.

92 Cf. Hanna (ed.), *Speculum Vitae*, I, 97 (2867–70), which elaborates: the words of this petition are as if to say ' "Þou it vs gif / Als lange als we sal here lif / Þat we mot here gode iourne make / And gladly habyde our hire to take" '.

93 See also 1 Peter 2:2–3.

94 Nicholas Love, *The Mirror of the Blessed Life of Jesus Christ: A Reading Text*, ed. Michael G. Sargent (University of Exeter Press, 2004), 10.15–16.

95 Cf. Bernard of Clairvaux, *On the Song of Songs: Sermones in Cantica Canticorum*, trans. a Religious of C.S.M.V. (London: Mowbray, 1952): 'seculars are babes requiring milk, as the apostle says; but you, the spiritual, need more solid food. Get your jaws ready, then, for bread, not milk – for most surpassingly delicious bread out of this book of Solomon's' (p. 21). On the circumscription of knowledge for laity in vernacular theology, see Michelle Karnes, *Imagination, Meditation, and Cognition in the Middle Ages* (University of Chicago Press, 2011). See also my 'Books and Bodies' on the ways in which 'boistous' becomes a powerful mode of knowledge for the laity.

96 Hanna (ed.), *Speculum Vitae*, 1, 34 (925–32). Cf. the encounter of the Pilgrim with Misericorde in the *Pilgrimage*, where the analogy of mother's milk to the milk of pity is tested. See further K. Robertson, *Nature Speaks*, pp. 209–11.

97 Colledge and Walsh (eds.), *Showings*, 11, 598.

98 For the sins of the tongue, see Sandy Bardsley, *Venomous Tongues: Speech and Gender in Late Medieval England* (Philadelphia: University of Pennsylvania Press, 2006), which builds on the earlier work of Craun, *Lies, Slander, and Obscenity*.

99 Hanna (ed.), *Speculum Vitae*, 11, 434–46, quotations at 437 (13,198), 437 (13,208), 443 (13,387), 445–6 (13,456–70).

100 Ibid., 11, 443 (13,399–404).

101 Ibid., 11, 444 (13,409–19).

102 Cf. Francis (ed.), *Book of Vices and Virtues*, p. 52. See Douglas Gray, *Later Medieval English Literature* (Oxford University Press, 2008), p. 60, for a summary of the regime for the household of the Duchess of York.

103 Staley (ed.), *Book*, p. 74.

104 Diekstra (ed.), *Book for a Simple and Devout Woman*, pp. 256–7.

105 In *De regimine principum*, reading while eating is likewise advocated as good everyday practice in the lay (noble) household. Giles recommends, not devotional material, but books on good governance among others, see Fowler and others (eds.), *The Governance of Kings and Princes*, p. 286.

106 J. Allan Mitchell's *Becoming Human: The Matter of the Medieval Child* (Minneapolis: University of Minnesota Press, 2014) devotes a chapter to the table ('The Mess'). See also Clare Sponsler's earlier study, 'Eating Lessons: Lydgate's "Dietary" and Consumer Conduct', *Medieval Conduct*, ed. Kathleen M. Ashley and Robert L. A. Clark (Minneapolis: University of Minnesota Press, 2001), pp. 1–22, on the cultivation of table manners in conduct books.

107 Zeeman, 'The Condition of *Kynde*', p. 8.

108 Jill Mann, 'Eating and Drinking in *Piers Plowman*', *Essays and Studies* 32 (1979): 26–43 (26–7); James Simpson, *'Piers Plowman': An Introduction to the B-Text* (London: Longman, 1990), p. 160. Mann's reading of eating and drinking in *Piers Plowman* sets a precedent of taking seriously material

images of eating and drinking ('the material world is not merely a vehicle for expressing the immaterial, but on the contrary contains the heart of its meaning and its mystery', 41).

109 Mann, 'Eating and Drinking', 34. Mann also looks at the example of Dame Studie in Passus x (34); Conscience's dinner party in Passus xiii (38); and Anima's discourse on the indigestibility of honey as the 'excessive desire for knowledge' (40). Cf. Schmidt, 'Elementary', 303, and his claims for the structural importance of food and drink images in *Piers Plowman*.

110 '[The] texts which are thus "digested" are themselves passages which use the images of eating and drinking'; the texts exploring the relationship between bread and the word act like ' "a hidden structure" in the poem', Mann, 'Eating and Drinking', 37–8.

111 Schmidt (ed.), *Piers Plowman*, see Passus ix, for example, pp. 131–3.

112 See further on Dame Studie's speech, Vincent Gillespie, 'The Senses in Literature: The Textures of Perception,' *A Cultural History of the Senses*, ed. Newhauser, pp. 153–73 (pp. 168–9). Emily Steiner, *Reading Piers Plowman* (Cambridge University Press, 2013), notes that Dame Studie 'puts the question of secular learning, as it were, "on the table" ' (p. 115).

113 On the economy of the hall, see Steiner's discussion of service in *Reading Piers Plowman*, pp. 113–24.

114 On Toby, see Steiner, *Reading Piers Plowman*, p. 116.

115 Cf. Steiner, *Reading Piers Plowman*, p. 115: 'intellectual consumption has become the currency of the hall ... To speak inappropriately is to overeat, and such improper speech is like a ritual out-of-place, as if one were to gobble down the sacramental body of Christ.'

116 Schmidt (ed.), *Piers Plowman*, B.x. 66–7.

117 See, for example, Psalm 33:9; 118:103; and see Rachel Fulton, ' "Taste and See that the Lord is Sweet" (Ps.33.9): The Flavor of God in the Monastic West', *Journal of Religion* 86.2 (2006): 169–204.

118 Diekstra (ed.), *Book for a Simple and Devout Woman*, p. 253.

119 Notably, in this passus, Scripture preaches on the theme of Matthew 22:14 – the feast to which many are invited but few are chosen – provoking a further testing of the relationship of knowledge to salvation, focused around the example of the righteous pagan, Trajan. Schmidt (ed.), *Piers Plowman*, B.xiii.

120 Gillespie, 'The Senses in Literature', p. 169, observes that the dreamer, at this point, 'has been on the verge of valorizing intellect and academic speculation above common sense'.

121 Later in the poem, original sin is further glossed as desire for knowledge beyond need – 'coveitise to konne and to knowe science' – which 'pulte out of Paradis Adam and Eve', Schmidt (ed.), *Piers Plowman*, B.xv.61–2.

122 Richard Morris (ed.), *Cursor Mundi, or The Cursur o the World*, EETS os 57, 6 vols. (London: Kegan Paul, Trench, Trübner, 1874–93), ii, 54.795–6. Cf. *St Erkenwald*: 'Adam oure alder, þat ete of þat appull / Þat mony a plyȝtles [innocent] pepul has poysned for euer. / ȝe were entouchid [poisoned] with his

tethe and taken in þe glotte [sin], / Bot mendyd with a medecyn 3e are made for to lyue,' *A Book of Middle English*, ed. J. A. Burrow and Thorlac Turville-Petre, 2nd edn (Oxford: Blackwell, 1992, 1996), pp. 201–14 (p. 212 (295–8)).

123 Mann, 'Eating and Drinking', 40.

124 Cf. Isidore of Seville: 'Death (*mors*) is so called, because it is bitter (*amarus*) … or else, death is derived from the bite (*morsus*) of the first human, because when he bit the fruit of the forbidden tree, he incurred death,' xi.ii.31; trans. Barney and others, *The Etymologies*, p. 243.

125 See, for example, Augustine, *Confessions*, trans. R. S. Pine-Coffin (London: Penguin, 1961), p. 256. Cf. Colledge and Walsh (eds.), *Showings*, ii, 346; ii, 645.

126 Graesse (ed.), *Legenda aurea*, p. 329: 'os nostrum est Christus dominus, quia est os nostrum et caro nostra'. Trans. Ryan, *The Golden Legend*, i, 301. Cf. St Jerome, *Moralium*, PL 76, col. 418–19.

127 Schmidt (ed.), *Piers Plowman*, p. 414.

128 Cf. Mann, 'Eating and Drinking', 27.

129 See Watson's analysis of this passage, in 'Conceptions of the Word', where he suggests that Christ is motivated by 'the wish to know their human condition from the inside' (114–16).

130 Sarah Elliott Novacich, *Shaping the Archive in Late Medieval England: History, Poetry and Performance* (Cambridge University Press, 2017), p. 138; and further, 'It is as if they [Adam and Eve] are passing through the mouth in order to begin a familiar story all over again' (p. 142).

131 This is an idea, traceable to Augustine's *Confessions* (p. 147), that emerges in the popular material of the *Legenda aurea*: ' "I [Christ] am the food of the full-grown! Grow and you will eat me, and you will not change me into yourself like the food of your body, but you will be changed into me" ' (trans. Ryan, *The Golden Legend*, ii, 119; for the Latin, see Graesse (ed.), *Legenda aurea*, p. 551).

4 The Epistemology of Kissing

1 On tactile engagement with devotional objects, see Bynum, *Christian Materiality*; on kissing books, see Kathryn M. Rudy, 'Kissing Images, Unfurling Rolls, Measuring Wounds, Sewing Badges and Carrying Talismans: Considering Some Harley Manuscripts through the Physical Rituals They Reveal', *Electronic British Library Journal* (2011): Article 5, 1–56.

2 Michael Camille, 'Gothic Signs and the Surplus: The Kiss on the Cathedral', *Yale French Studies* 80 (1991): 151–70, catalogues the instances of medieval kisses (the lecherous, spiritual, legal, courtly, treacherous, mystical, as well as the kiss of peace). Camille is predominantly interested in the kiss as a multivalent sign (152). Burrow, *Gestures and Looks*, explores the meanings of kisses in ceremonies of homage and fealty and as part of church ritual. In this context kissing signifies reconciliation, unity, love, peace, affection – though it is, of course, not without its dangers, for it might also mean sex (see pp. 50–6). Michael

Philip Penn, *Kissing Christians: Ritual and Community in the Late Ancient Church* (Philadelphia: University of Pennsylvania Press, 2005), provides a useful overview of the development of the kiss within Christian practice. Penn's emphasis is on the ways in which the kiss organises Christian community.

3 Bynum, *Christian Materiality*, p. 98 notes the example of the indulgences entailed on kissing an image of the wound of Christ. On kissing relics, see further Ronald C. Finucane, *Miracles and Pilgrims: Popular Beliefs in Medieval England* (London: Dent, 1977), e.g. p. 59, and see also Robyn Malo, *Relics and Writing in Late Medieval England* (Toronto University Press, 2013), who notes the ways in which touching relics at certain shrines may have been occluded, pp. 37 and 205 n. 46. See also Woolgar, *The Senses in Late Medieval England*, pp. 40–1, on the varieties of liturgical kisses and kissing relics.

4 Woolgar, *The Senses in Late Medieval England*, observes: 'There was a very strong interplay of theoretical analyses of perception, the product of a learned culture and derived from theology, natural philosophy and medicine, on the one hand, with popular beliefs and practices on the other' (p. 4).

5 Nicolas James Perella, *The Kiss Sacred and Profane: An Interpretative History of Kiss Symbolism and Related Religio-Erotic Themes* (Berkeley: University of California Press, 1969), traces the history of thinking around breath as soul and the kiss as a form of infusion or spiritual exchange, e.g. pp. 5, 18–21.

6 Cited in Perella, *The Kiss*, p. 27. Chrysostom writes in Homily 30 on 2 Corinthians that the kiss is given to 'be fuel unto love': 'And therefore when we return after an absence we kiss each other, our souls hastening unto mutual intercourse. For this is that member which most declares to us the workings of the soul.'

7 Perella, *The Kiss*, p. 29. See also Ambrose, *Hexameron, Paradise, and Cain and Abel*, trans. Savage: 'It is worthy of note too, that it is given to men alone to express with their lips what they feel with their hearts. Hence we make evident our tacit mental reflections with the speech that flows from our heart. What is the mouth of man but an avenue for discourse, a fount of disputation, a reception hall for words, a repository of the will?' (pp. 277–8).

8 Perella, *The Kiss*, p. 24. On the citation of Augustine on the need for accord between the mouth or lips and the heart in Middle English works, see, for example, Francis (ed.), *Book of Vices and Virtues*, p. 233; Hanna (ed.), *Speculum Vitae*, 1, 339; Barnum (ed.), *Dives and Pauper*, 1/i, 201.

9 Perella, *The Kiss*, p. 28. Cf. Ambrose, who understands Judas's kiss in similar terms (see Perella, *The Kiss*, p. 28). In Letter 41, Ambrose writes that the Jews do not have the kiss of communion: 'The Pharisee, then, had no kiss except perchance that of the traitor Judas. But neither had Judas the kiss; and so when he wished to show to the Jews that kiss which he had promised as the sign of betrayal, the Lord said to him: "Judas, betrayest thou the Son of Man with a kiss?" that is, you, who have not the love marked by the kiss, offer a kiss. You offer a kiss who know not the mystery of the kiss. It is not the kiss of the lips which is sought for, but that of the heart and soul.'

10 See Richard A. Norris (trans. and ed.), *The Song of Songs: Interpreted by Early Christian and Medieval Commentators* (Grand Rapids: Eerdmans, 2003), pp. 20–2.

11 Ibid., p. 23.

12 Ibid., p. 22.

13 See Bernard, *On the Song of Songs*, trans. a Religious of C.S.M.V., pp. 24–30.

14 Arjo Vanderjagt, 'Bernard of Clairvaux (1090–1153) and Aelred of Rievaulx (1110–1167) on Kissing', *Media Latinitas: A Collection of Essays to Mark the Occasion of the Retirement of L. J. Engels*, ed. R. I. A. Nip and others, Instrumenta Patristica et Mediaevalia 28 (Turnhout: Brepols, 1996), pp. 339–43 (p. 340).

15 Perella, *The Kiss*, p. 51.

16 Aelred of Rievaulx, *Aelred of Rievaulx's Spiritual Friendship*, trans. Mark F. Williams (London: Associated University Presses, 1994), p. 47. Aelred therefore talks of the 'kiss of the flesh' (pressing of lips), 'the kiss of the spirit' (coming together of souls) and 'the kiss of discernment' (outpouring of the Spirit of God), p. 47. See further Vanderjagt, 'Bernard of Clairvaux', who stresses the corporeal basis for twelfth-century theological considerations of the kiss, pp. 339, 342.

17 Williams (trans.), *Spiritual Friendship*, p. 47.

18 See also Perella, *The Kiss*, pp. 4, 7–9. In particular, the bestowal of the Holy Spirit by a kiss is commonplace in patristic writing and underlies Christian ritual and sacramental kissing; see ibid., pp. 18–19. Similarly, St Ambrose, *Select Works and Letters*, trans. H. De Romestin in *Nicene and Post-Nicene Fathers*, ed. Schaff and Wace, x, 448, writes: 'he kisses Christ who receives the Spirit, where the holy prophet says: "I opened my mouth and drew in the Spirit."'

19 Aelred warns that 'the base and perverse strive ... to season their own disgraceful acts even with the kiss of the flesh ... So greatly do they befoul the kiss with their baseness, that to be kissed by one of these people is nothing less than to be corrupted,' Williams (trans.), *Spiritual Friendship*, p. 47.

20 Williams (trans.), *Spiritual Friendship*, pp. 47–8. On Aelred, see further Burrow, *Gestures and Looks*, p. 41.

21 Perella, *The Kiss*, p. 39. Cf. Gregory of Nyssa, who writes, for example, that 'kissing ... is effected by the sense of touch. But there is also a higher order or spiritual sense of touch – hence, a spiritual kiss also – by which one comes into contact with the Word,' summarised by Perella, *The Kiss*, p. 38.

22 Staley (ed.), *Book*, p. 95.

23 Ibid., p. 170. See further on this episode, Jonathan Hsy, '"Be more strange and bold": Kissing Lepers and Female Same-Sex Desire in *The Book of Margery Kempe*', *Early Modern Women* 5 (2010): 189–99.

24 Seymour and others (eds.), *On the Properties of Things*, 1, 369.

25 Woolgar, *The Senses in Late Medieval England*, p. 39.

26 Ibid., p. 2. Cf. p. 13, where Woolgar, in a discussion of *The Doctrine of the Heart*, notes: 'The senses ... operated as receptors of information ... capable of changing the character of the perceiver and the perceived.'

27 Kitchell and Resnick (eds.), *On Animals*, II, 958.

28 Gilby (ed.), *Summa theologiae*, 1a.78, 3 (pp. 131, 135). The nature of change wrought by sense perception has been differently interpreted by modern readers. See, for example, M. F. Burnyeat, 'Aquinas on "Spiritual Change" in Perception', *Ancient and Medieval Theories of Intentionality*, ed. Dominik Perler (Leiden: Brill, 2001), pp. 129–53.

29 Woolgar, *The Senses in Late Medieval England*, p. 29.

30 *MED*, s.v. 'impressioun' (n.), 'The act or process of indenting a surface'; s.v. 'prenting(e' (ger.), 'An impression or imprint'. The terms also belong to a medical register, as symptoms of illness or a mode of diagnosis; thus Guy states that the signs of 'vdymya' (a swelling or abscess) are 'louse swellynge and softe, so þat it ȝeueth stede to þe fyngres and the inpressioun (i. pryntynge yn) is kepte after þe remevynge of þe fyngres', Ogden (ed.), *Cyrurgie*, p. 108.

31 *MED*, s.v. 'impressioun' (n.), 'the exertion of influence on the mind or emotions'; 'an image, a sensation, or an emotion produced in the mind, heart, soul, or sense'; s.v. 'prenting(e' (ger.), 'an image or impression produced in the mind or the senses'. On the involvement of the heart in sense perception, see further Heather Webb, *The Medieval Heart* (New Haven: Yale University Press, 2010), e.g. p. 54.

32 E. D. Blodgett (ed. and trans.), *The Romance of Flamenca*, Garland Library of Medieval Literature 101A (New York: Garland, 1995), p. 341 ('mais la boca no.s pot tener, / quan baisa, que del bon saber / a sos obs quesacom nom prenga avan que ren al cor ne venga', p. 340). See Perella's analysis of *Flamenca*, *The Kiss*, pp. 124–8.

33 For the Latin, see Guilelmus Peraldus [William Peraldus], *Summa de virtutibus et vitiis* (Venice: Paganino de Paganini, 1497), VI Treatise on Temperance, ch. 8, 86b. The Modern English translation is from Richard G. Newhauser, 'Introduction: The Sensual Middle Ages', *A Cultural History of the Senses*, ed. Newhauser, pp. 1–22 (p. 10).

34 See Camille, 'The Gothic Sign', e.g. 151.

35 Arnould (ed.), *Livre*, p. 177. Henry goes on to list three types of kisses: the lecherous kiss, the kiss of friendship and the kiss of peace, pp. 178–80; cf. with Woolgar, *The Senses in Late Medieval England*, in which he gives brief consideration to Henry's categorisation of kisses, pp. 39–41.

36 Klaus Bitterling (ed.), *Of Shrifte and Penance: The Middle English Prose Translation of 'Le manuel des péchés'*, Middle English Texts 29 (Heidelberg: Universitätsverlag C. Winter, 1998), p. 97. The exchange of winnings game in *Sir Gawain and the Green Knight*, in which Gawain exchanges with Bertilak the kisses he has won from Bertilak's wife, raises questions, however, about the safety of kisses between men, otherwise assumed (or at least left unnamed) in *Of Shrifte and Penance*. See further Carolyn Dinshaw, 'A Kiss Is Just a Kiss: Heterosexuality and Its Consolations in *Sir Gawain and the Green Knight*', *Diacritics* 24.2/3 (1994): 205–26.

37 Bartholomaeus is following Constantine here.

38 Thomas H. Bestul, *Texts of the Passion: Latin Devotional Literature and Medieval Society* (Philadelphia: University of Pennsylvania Press, 1996), notes 'there are many instances in medieval saints' lives in which holy persons are asked not only to kiss – but to spit into – the mouth of devotees', p. 89. Cf. Bynum, *Fragmentation and Redemption*, p. 184.

39 Kitchell and Resnick (eds.), *On Animals*, II, 1447. Cf. Seymour and others (eds.), *On the Properties of Things*, I, 209–10.

40 The *Polychronicon* is cited in *MED*, s.v. 'spotel' (n.).

41 Powell (ed.), *John Mirk's Festial*, I, 78.

42 Diekstra (ed.), *Book for a Simple and Devout Woman*, p. 263.

43 Trans. Barney and others, *The Etymologies*, p. 231. Lindsay (ed.), *Etymologiae*, XI.i.7. Cf. Gilby (ed.), *Summa theologiae*, 1a.90, I, 'Though even when a man breathes in the physical sense, he does not give out some of his own substance, but something of an extraneous nature' (p. 5).

44 See Vincent of Beauvais, *Speculum naturale*, XXV.3.

45 Aristotle, *De anima*, ed. Barnes, I, 574.

46 Chaucer, 'The Manciple's Prologue', *Riverside Chaucer*, ed. Benson, IX.32–3; 39. On infection and the Cook's breath in *The Canterbury Tales*, see further Shoaf, *Chaucer's Body* (e.g. p. 103).

47 Green, *Trotula*, pp. 45, 122.

48 Indeed, Green, *Trotula*, records a treatment for fissured lips caused by 'the excessive embraces of their lovers and their kisses with their lips rubbing between them' (p. 102).

49 Chaucer, 'The Miller's Tale', *Riverside Chaucer*, ed. Benson, I.3690. For Absolon's use of medicine to further his prospects in love, see Susanna Greer Fein, 'Why Did Absolon Put a "Trewelove" under His Tongue? Herb Paris as a Healing "Grace" in Middle English Literature', *Chaucer Review* 25 (1990): 302–17 (esp. 302, 304).

50 Chaucer, 'The Romaunt of the Rose', *Riverside Chaucer*, ed. Benson, p. 726, lines 3743–5.

51 Chaucer, 'The Franklin's Tale', *Riverside Chaucer*, ed. Benson, V.1455.

52 Siegfried Wenzel (ed.), *Fasciculus morum: A Fourteenth-Century Preacher's Handbook* (University Park: The Pennsylvania State University Press, 1989), p. 713. [' "Hoc, inquit, fecissem nisi credidissem omnium hominum ora sic olere." Ex quo verisimile fuit quod ipsa os alterius viri numquam tetigisset' (p. 712).]

53 Gilby (ed.), *Summa theologiæ*, XI, 1a.76,7, p. 83: 'Ad secundum dicendum quod, subtracto spiritu, deficit unio animæ ad corpus' (p. 82).

54 Powell (ed.), *John Mirk's Festial*, I, 177.

55 Bitterling (ed.), *Of Shrifte and Penance*, p. 67.

56 Here my thinking is indebted to, while it differs from, Camille's provocative characterisation of the kiss as 'sorplus' in 'Gothic Signs'.

57 Mary J. Carruthers, *The Search for St Truth: A Study of Meaning in 'Piers Plowman'* (Evanston: Northwestern University Press, 1973), remarks that 'Haukyn is the fullest mirror image that Will encounters in the poem' (p. 115),

and that 'Haukyn is perhaps the most completely mundane creature in the poem' (p. 118). John A. Alford, 'The Design of the Poem', *A Companion to 'Piers Plowman'*, ed. John A. Alford (Berkeley: University of California Press, 1988), pp. 29–65, remarks that Haukyn 'seems to be the perfect embodiment of the ideal sought but not obtained on Piers' half-acre' (p. 50). Robert Worth Frank, *'Piers Plowman' and the Scheme of Salvation: An Interpretation of Dowel, Dobet, and Dobest*, Yale Studies in English 136 (New Haven: Yale University Press, 1957), observes that '[Haukyn] remains a convincing, realistic character, largely because he is so consistently vigorous and earthbound' (p. 71).

58 Carruthers, *The Search for St Truth*, p. 115.

59 For Langland's spiritual economy, see James Simpson, 'Spirituality and Economics in Passus 1–7 of the B Text', *YLS* 1 (1987): 83–103.

60 Alford, 'The Design of the Poem', p. 147.

61 Scarry, *The Body in Pain*, p. 284.

62 Schmidt glosses this as 'a religious order composed of only one member, without any rule'.

63 '[Giving the impression] of desiring to live honestly', Schmidt (ed.), *Piers Plowman*, p. 219.

64 *MED*, s.v. 'studie' (n.), 'Zealous and diligent effort, zeal; labor, industry'; 'an endeavor, occupation, a pursuit'; 'devotion, affection'; 'Zealous and diligent pursuit of knowledge, study, intensive reading and contemplation'; 'Mental effort directed toward an end or a purpose'. For medieval formulations of 'studie' more generally and in *Piers Plowman* in particular, see Nicolette Zeeman, ' "Studying" in the Middle Ages – and in *Piers Plowman*', *NML* 3 (1999): 185–212 (esp. 193–5).

65 Schmidt (ed.), *Piers Plowman*, glosses lines 289–90 as 'with his faculties of intelligence and sense given over to imagining and brooding over how best to acquire a reputation for sexual prowess' (p. 219).

66 Reginald Pecock, *The Repressor of Over Much Blaming of the Clergy*, ed. Churchill Babington, 2 vols. (London: Longman, Green, Longman, and Roberts, 1860), II, 555.

67 Hanna (ed.), *Speculum Vitae*, II, 304 (9123–8).

68 Diekstra (ed.), *Book for a Simple and Devout Woman*, p. 210. Cf. Hanna (ed.), *Speculum Vitae*, I, 192 (5753–8): 'To trespass in vnderstandynge, / In sight, in heryng, or in felynge, / In smellynge, in tastynge with mouthe, / In kyssynge – þat es a taken couthe –, / In halsynge or in vndertakyng, / In beckenyng and in signes makyng'.

69 Cf. Perella, *The Kiss*, p. 1, who notes: 'Anthropologists, physiologists, and psychologists ... have put forth the theory that the kiss may very well be a vestigial remainder or a carry-over of a primitive habit of eating and thereby assimilating into the self any object felt to be "good" or desirable.'

70 Camille, 'Gothic Signs', 156.

71 Chaucer, 'The Miller's Tale', *Riverside Chaucer*, ed. Benson, 1.3682–4. See also Thomas J. Hatton, 'Absolon, Taste, and Odor in *The Miller's Tale*', *Papers in Language and Literature* 71 (1971): 72–5: referring to Chaucer's description of

Absolon, 'Sensynge the wyves of the parrishe faste' (3342), Hatton asserts that 'Absolon obviously "senses" the women in more than one way' (73).

72 Barnum (ed.), *Dives and Pauper*, I/ii, 95.

73 Powell (ed.), *John Mirk's Festial*, I, 61.

74 See Zeeman, *Discourse of Desire*, where she outlines devotional use of the figure of 'taste' and offers a reading of the Tree of Charity, the dreamer's desire to taste but also the loss to which that desire leads, p. 2.

75 On groping in *Piers Plowman*, see further Schmidt, 'Elementary'.

76 Drawing on Isidore's *Etymologiae*, Seymour and others (eds.), *On the Properties of Things*, I, 233, describes the 'groping' of the mother's breast by the newly born child; groping is part of an instinctive, natural impulse (motivated both by appetite and by bodily need) to learn and experience the world.

77 Powell (ed.), *John Mirk's Festial*, I, 75. Cf. Graesse (ed.), *Legenda aurea*, p. 185.

78 Cf. Sullen (ed.), *Handlyng Synne*, on the punishment of the body part that has sinned, p. 92.

79 Richard Hamer (ed.), *Gilte Legende*, EETS os 339, 3 vols. (Oxford University Press, 2012), I, 192. This is a Middle English translation of Jean de Vignay's French rendering of the *Legenda aurea*.

80 Jacques Le Goff, *Time, Work and Culture in the Middle Ages*, trans. Arthur Goldhammer (Chicago University Press, 1980), suggests that the kiss's potency derives from the perception that breath and/or saliva is exchanged, p. 252.

81 Bestul, *Texts of the Passion*, discusses the significance of Jews' spittle when they spit on Christ's face during the buffeting of Christ, pp. 85–9.

82 Staley (ed.), *Book*, p. 181.

83 For examples of the power of the Eucharist on the body of the communicant, see Powell (ed.), *John Mirk's Festial*, I, 155–6.

84 Barnum (ed.), *Dives and Pauper*, I/ii, 259.

85 Ibid., I/ii, 259.

86 Perella, *The Kiss*, p. 24.

87 Bitterling (ed.), *Of Shrifte and Penance*, p. 74.

88 Sullen (ed.), *Handlyng Synne*, p. 106.

89 Powell (ed.), *John Mirk's Festial*, I, 111. On pax-kissing, see Michael Penn's study (concerned specifically with the shift from an exchange of a mouth-to-mouth kiss in church ritual to kissing a board instead), which notes the function of the kiss as an act which excludes or which includes and creates (orthodox) Christian community, 'Ritual Kissing, Heresy and the Emergence of Early Christian Orthodoxy', *Journal of Ecclesiastical History* 54 (2003): 625–40.

90 Powell (ed.), *John Mirk's Festial*, II, 256.

91 Bitterling (ed.), *Of Shrifte and Penance*, p. 94.

92 Powell (ed.), *John Mirk's Festial*, notes: 'herte-coll: Not attested in *MED* (but *MED* herte n. Id, -cove, "a chamber of the heart?")'. Theodor Erbe's edition, *Mirk's Festial: A Collection of Homilies by Johannes Mirkus (John Mirk), edited from Bodleian Ms. Gough Eccl. Top. 4*, EETS es 96 (London: Kegan Paul, Trench, Trübner, 1905; repr. 1997) gives 'herte-cow', which Powell corrects, but Erbe similarly glosses the compound noun as 'cove, cell of the heart'.

93 Odo of Cheriton, *Summa de poenitentia*, Cambridge Trinity College, MS 356, f. 4rb, cited in Jacqueline Murray, 'Gendered Souls in Sexed Bodies: The Male Construction of Female Sexuality in Some Medieval Confessors' Manuals', *Handling Sin*, ed. Biller and Minnis, pp. 79–93 (p. 87 n. 49): 'Si quis pomum pulcherrimum morderet et uermem intus inuenerit, statim expueret. Pomum sapidum est pulcra mulier. Hoc pomum gustat qui hanc amplectitur. Set consideret uermem, id est, diabolum, siue peccatum, in tali pomo latitare, et statim per confessionem expuere festinet.' [Modern English translation my own.]

94 So St Jerome writes of Eve, 'as soon as she broke the command by eating the fruit, she experienced corruption', or rather loses her virginity (cited in Wenzel (ed.), *Fasciculus morum*, p. 631). Kissing as biting is not always viewed negatively in religious discourse, however. St John Chrysostom, *Homilies on First and Second Corinthians*, trans. Talbot W. Chambers in *A Select Library of Nicene and Post-Nicene Fathers*, First Series, ed. Philip Schaff, 14 vols. (New York: Christian Literature Co., 1889), XII, 143: 'This Body hath He given to us both to hold and to eat; a thing appropriate to intense love. For those whom we kiss vehemently, we oft-times even bite with our teeth.'

95 Wenzel (ed.), *Fasciculus morum*, p. 660 [' "Qui, inquit, meretricem deosculatur, pulsat inferni ianuam." Set certe delectantibus in signo cum facto patefacta est ianua. Et ideo oscula meretricis comparantur osculo Iude, quo Christum vendidit et ipsum Iudeis tradidit. Sic meretrix mediantibus osculis animam hominis demonibus vendit, et eciam tradit' (p. 661)].

96 Chaucer, 'The Parson's Tale', *Riverside Chaucer*, ed. Benson, x.855–6.

97 On the hellmouth, see further Pamela Sheingorn, ' "Who Can Open the Doors of His Face?" The Iconography of Hellmouth', *The Iconography of Hell*, ed. Clifford Davidson and Thomas H. Seiler (Kalamazoo: Medieval Institute Publications, 1991), pp. 1–19; Robert Lima, *Stages of Evil: Occultism in Western Theater and Drama* (Lexington: University Press of Kentucky, 2005); and Novacich, *Shaping the Archive*.

98 Staley (ed.), *Book*, p. 22.

99 Chaucer, 'The Manciple's Prologue', *Riverside Chaucer*, ed. Benson, ix.35–8. Directions in the Harrowing and Judgement plays themselves (such as those associated with Coventry and Towneley) often refer to hell as a gate; the Coventry Harrowing of Hell directs 'The sowle goth to helle gatys and seyn: "Attolite portas, principes vestras [etc.]" ', quoting Psalm 23; 'Play 33, Harrowing of Hell (I)', *The N-Town Plays*, ed. Douglas Sugano (Kalamazoo: Medieval Institute Publications, 2007). Later records clarify the entranceway to hell was commonly understood as a mouth: payments are recorded in 1561 for 'kepyng of the wynde and of hell mowthe xvj d', and in 1568 'for makynge of hellmothe new, xxj d', with regard to the Cappers' and Drapers' plays at Coventry respectively. See Philip Butterworth, *Staging Conventions in Medieval English Theatre* (Cambridge University Press, 2014), p. 149.

5 Surgical Habits

1 On the laicisation of the tools of spiritual discipline, see Nicole R. Rice, *Lay Piety and Religious Discipline in Middle English Literature* (Cambridge University Press, 2008).

2 See, for example, Rudolph Arbesmann, 'The Concept of "Christus Medicus" in St Augustine', *Traditio* 10 (1954): 1–28; and George Christian Anderson, 'Medieval Medicine for Sin', *Journal of Religion and Health* 2:2 (1963): 156–65, which documents the long penitential tradition viewing the confessor as physician and sin as sickness. See further Langum, *Medicine and the Seven Deadly Sins*; and Yoshikawa (ed.), *Medicine, Religion and Gender*.

3 Cited in Marjorie Curry Woods and Rita Copeland, 'Classroom and Confession', *Medieval English Literature*, ed. Wallace, pp. 376–406 (p. 392).

4 Francis (ed.), *Book of Vices and Virtues*, pp. 175, 128; see also, for example, pp. 127, 176. Cf. Hanna (ed.), *Speculum Vitae*, I, 184 (5487–90).

5 Of late medieval York, Philip Stell, 'Medical Practice in Medieval York', *Borthwick Papers* 90 (1996): 1–35, concludes that medical care 'was provided by the barbers from the first half of the fourteenth century, and it appears that they had largely replaced the *medici* by the second half of the fifteenth century' – a trend that seems to be reflective of practice in England as a whole (7). Cf. Michael R. McVaugh, *Medicine before the Plague: Practitioners and their Patients in the Crown of Aragon, 1285–1345* (Cambridge University Press, 1993), who suggests that 'by the 1340s barbers had become much more fully a part of medical life', and notes that 'evidence of many kinds seems to suggest that this process had begun in the 1330s, as barbers began to assume the role of surgeons' (p. 123). On healthcare more generally, see Carole Rawcliffe, *Urban Bodies: Communal Health in Late Medieval English Towns and Cities* (Woodbridge: Boydell, 2013).

6 Carole Rawcliffe, *Medicine and Society in Later Medieval England* (Kalamazoo: Medieval Institute Publications, 1995), p. 133.

7 Sidney Young, *The Annals of the Barber-Surgeons of London* (London: Blades, East & Blades, 1890), p. 51. See also John Flint South, *Memorials of the Craft of Surgery in England*, ed. D'Arcy Power (London: Cassell, 1886). On the education of barber-surgeons, see further Katherine Park, 'Medicine and Society in Medieval Europe, 500–1500', *Medicine in Society: Historical Essays*, ed. Andrew Wear (Cambridge University Press, 1992), pp. 59–90, who notes of this period that 'the culture of academic medicine, long the monopoly of the university educated, gradually found its way out into broader society; the medical faculties, even in northern Europe, began to offer occasional courses of lectures for surgeons and barbers' (p. 81).

8 I mostly use the postmedieval term 'barber-surgeon' (rather than 'barber' or 'surgeon') in this chapter, since this usefully brings in the full range of crafts, from shaving to tooth-drawing and, potentially, surgical proceedures, except where the examples give or require more specificity.

9 The 1381 Lay Poll Tax figures are recorded by Margaret C. Barnet, 'The Barber-Surgeons of York', *Medical History* 12 (1968): 19–30 (20–1). Cf. Stell, 'Medical Practice', who records that in York in the period 1350–99 there were fifteen *medici* and seventy-two barbers (6).

10 Citrome, *The Surgeon*, p. 1.

11 See, for example, Citrome, *The Surgeon*, pp. 7, 17, etc.

12 For a detailed overview of the role of digestion in ensuring the continuity of the body in medieval medical thinking, see further Karine van't Land, 'The Solution of Continuous Things: Wounds in Late Medieval Medicine and Surgery', *Wounds in the Middle Ages*, ed. Anne Kirkham and Cordelia Warr (Farnham: Ashgate, 2014), pp. 89–108.

13 Seymour and others (eds.), *On the Properties of Things*, 1, 204–5.

14 See ibid., 1, 148; see further, on 'apostemes', 1, 415–20. On the role of the pores of the skin and other orifices in purging the body in the stages of digestion, see further Hanna (ed.), *Liber Uricrisiarum*, e.g. p. 204.

15 Ogden (ed.), *Cyrurgie*, p. 4. Cf. Fleischhacker (ed.), *Science of Cirurgie*, p. 18, names the three kinds of work the surgeon does in equivalent terms: (1) 'vndoynge of þat, þat is hool', (2) 'to hele þat, þat is broke' and (3) 'remeuynge of þat, þat is to myche'.

16 Canon 18 of the Fourth Lateran Council placed prohibitions on the practice of medicine by the clergy: 'No subdeacon, deacon, or priest shall practice that part of surgery involving burning or cutting' (cited by Darrel W. Amundsen, 'Medieval Canon Law on Medical and Surgical Practice by the Clergy', *Bulletin of the History of Medicine* 52 (1978): 22–44 (40)). However, as historians of medicine, and in particular Amundsen, have been keen to point out, the scope of this injunction has been overestimated since it did not extend to the whole of the clergy, only to subdeacons, deacons and priests ('Medieval Canon Law', 26). See further Stell, 'Medical Practice', 8–9, 10; Citrome, *The Surgeon*, p. 3. Citrome also notes the surgeons' concern with the spiritual health of their patients – treatises sometimes instruct surgeons to recommend their patients to confess prior to treatment, p. 11.

17 Stell, 'Medical Practice', 9. Rawcliffe too has noted that 'the confessor and the physician were often the same person', *Medicine and Society*, p. 112.

18 Christiana Whitehead and others (eds.), *The Doctrine of the Hert: A Critical Edition with Introduction and Commentary* (Exeter University Press, 2010), p. ix. The Latin is extant in 208 manuscripts (p. xi). There are four extant manuscripts of the Middle English (p. xvii).

19 Whitehead and others (eds.), *The Doctrine of the Hert*, p. 79. The editors note, p. 167 n. 16, the Latin '*De doctrina* continues for an additional four pages … The barber figure is developed further: superiors are urged not to be like barbers who shave without the water of gentleness ("lenitas") or who use a nicked razor representing stinging correction.'

20 As the editors note, the translation includes a new prologue that 'very clearly indicates that this vernacular rendering has a non-*litteratus* audience of nuns in mind' (Whitehead and others (eds.), *The Doctrine of the Hert*, p. xxvi).

They further comment that while the audience of the original *De doctrina* is uncertain, 'the vernacular version at times omits material which would be better suited for a male audience. For example, the figure of the barber … is greatly reduced in the Middle English' (p. xxx).

21 Cf. Citrome's discussion of the punitive connections of surgeons and confessors, *The Surgeon*, e.g. pp. 9–12, *et passim*.

22 Whitehead and others (eds.), *The Doctrine of the Hert*, p. 79.

23 Powell (ed.), *John Mirk's Festial*, 1, 110.

24 Ibid., 1, 111. Powell notes: '*Schere Þursday*: From *MED* sker(e) adj. "clean", with reference to the cleansing of the soul in preparation for Easter Day', 11, 345.

25 *Summa de ecclesiasticis officiis* is printed as *Rationale Divinorum Officiorum*, PL 202, cols. 119–20: 'Abrasio enim capillorum et barbae, quae ex superfluis stomachi nascuntur humoribus, ut ungues ex superfluis humoribus cordis, significat quod debeamus vitia et peccata, quae nobis sunt superflua, resecare' [Indeed, shaving of the hair and beard, which are born from the superfluities of the stomach, as [shaving of] the nails, which are [born] from the superfluous humours of the heart, signifies that we ought to trim back the faults and sins which are superfluous in us.] [Modern English translation my own.]

26 *MED*, s.v. 'shaven' (v.), 'To scrape (sth.) with a knife of tool'; 'of a medicine: chafe or abrade'; 'to remove (sth.) by scraping or paring'; 'smooth or plane (sth.), polish'; '*med.* to scrape with a surgical instrument'; 'scrape away hair'; 'shave the face or head'. S.v. 'sheren' (v.), 'To cut or penetrate'; 'make an incision'; 'to cut (sth.) off'; 'to clip or trim with shears'; 'shave'.

27 From the twelfth century, barbers were involved with haircutting, shaving and bloodletting in both monastic and secular contexts. In the course of the late medieval period, they also began to perform a diverse range of medical procedures and organise themselves into guilds. While practised by barbers and surgeons alike, dentistry is one of the few areas of specialisation in the medieval period. Following Albucasis, for example, Guy de Chauliac consigns surgical craft in relation to teeth explicitly to barbers. See Ogden (ed.), *Cyrurgie*, p. 485. See further Rawcliffe, *Medicine and Society*, p. 133; Piers D. Mitchell, *Medicine in the Crusades: Warfare, Wounds and the Medieval Surgeon* (Cambridge University Press, 2004), p. 161.

28 Cited in G. Henslow, *Medical Works of the Fourteenth Century* (London: Chapman and Hall, 1899). See for tooth-worm, pp. 8, 95, 112; '3elw and stynkyng teþe', pp. 35, 70; 'touþ-ache', pp. 45, 95, 111; bad breath, p. 72; 'cancre', p. 80; speech impediments, p. 110; blisters, p. 111; and 'waggyng of teth', p. 112.

29 Book 30 draws on the seventh-century Greek encyclopaedia of Paulus Ægineta. See Francis Adams (ed.), *The Seven Books of Paulus Ægineta*, 3 vols. (London: Sydenham Society, 1844–7). The Latin translation is extant in at least twenty-eight manuscripts. See David Trotter, *Albucasis: Traitier de Cyrurgie: Édition de la traduction en ancien français de la Chirurgie d'Abū 'l Qāsim*

Halaf Ibn 'Abbās al-Zahrāwī du manuscrit BNF, français 1318 (Tübingen: Max Niemeyer Verlag, 2005), p. 1.

30 For the influence on medieval Italian and French surgeons, see D. A. Trotter, 'Arabic Surgery in Eastern France and the Midi: The Old French and Occitan Versions of *The Chirurgie d'Albucasis*', *Forum for Modern Language Studies* 35 (1999): 358–71. Trotter edits the single extant French translation, dated to the thirteenth century, as *Albucasis: Traitier de Cyrurgie*. The Paneth Codex (Yale Medical Library Manuscript 28), c.1300, preserves one such Italian manuscript copy of Cremona's translation.

31 For illustrations of Guy's surgical instruments, see Björn Wallner, 'Drawings of Surgical Instruments in MS. Bibl. Nat. Agnl. 25', *English Studies* 46 (1965): 182–6.

32 Ogden (ed.), *Cyrurgie*, p. 481. Cf. Trotter (ed.), *Traitier de Cyrurgie*, p. 117, 'de coper lou liien de la lengue'.

33 Ogden (ed.), *Cyrurgie*, p. 489.

34 The procedure of tooth extraction is described in ibid., pp. 488–90.

35 Ibid., p. 490.

36 Albucasis, *On Surgery and Instruments*, ed. M. S. Spink and G. L. Lewis (London: The Wellcome Institute of the History of Medicine, 1973), p. 272. For convenience I cite from the Modern English translation of Albucasis, but provide cross-references to the medieval French version of Cremona's Latin translation for comparison. The main section on oral treatments in the medieval French translation occurs in Trotter (ed.), *Traitier de Cyrurgie*, pp. 113–17, and covers, as the table of rubrics lists: 'De l'incision de la char que vient en gencives', 'De la rasure des dens au fer', 'De l'estraction des dens', 'De la sarrure des dens', 'De l'adrecement des dens', 'De l'incision don lien que vient desoz la lengue et tot la parole' and 'De l'estraction de la char engenree desoz la lengue' (p. 93).

37 Noted by Stell, 'Medical Practice', 22.

38 British Library MS Sloane 563, f. 13v. Cf. Vincent of Beauvais, *Speculum doctrinale*, XIV.78, c.1331: 'Corrosio dentibus & molaribus ex putredine fit, quæ ex humidtate mala efficitur, & ad ipsos defluit, putrescitque in eis, & ipsos comedit. Limositas est corpus croceum dentes vestiens, ex vaporibus à stomacho ascendentibus. Congelatio vero dentibus accidit, aut ab exterioribus, cum scilicet acerbum homo masticat; aut ab interioribus, vt ex acerbis qui in stomacho sunt humoribus.' [Corrosion of the teeth and molars happens because of rottenness, which is caused by evil moisture, and which flows to them and rots in them and consumes them. Sliminess/filthiness is a yellow substance clothing the teeth out of the vapours ascending from the stomach. Congelation of the teeth occurs either from the outside, as when a man chews bitter (things); or from the inside, because of the bitter liquids which are in the stomach.]

39 Spink and Lewis (eds.), *On Surgery and Instruments*, p. 288; cf. Trotter (ed.), *Traitier de Cyrurgie*, pp. 114–15.

40 Cf. Trotter (ed.), *Traitier de Cyrurgie*, p. 116.

41 Ogden (ed.), *Cyrurgie*, p. 490.

42 Spink and Lewis (eds.), *On Surgery and Instruments*, p. 290. Cf. Trotter (ed.), *Traitier de Cyrurgie*, p. 116: 'puis la plaine en la fin a tout aucun raseur, et se li dens est trop trenchans et il blece la lengue, si covient limer l'aspreteit tant qu'il soit iglaz, si qu'il ne blece la laengue ne ne corromple la parole'.

43 Vincent of Beauvais, *Speculum doctrinale*, XII.141, c.1164: '*Præterea* nonnumquam homini dens superfluus innascitur, & tunc intuendum est, vt si in alterius dentis radice cum organo quod rostro simile est auferatur, & si quid superfuerit lima explanetur. Si vero non in alterius radice, sed fundo nititur, cum forcipibus extrahatur.' [Moreover, sometimes a superfluous tooth is formed in man, and then it should be observed that if it is in the root of another tooth it should be removed with an instrument that is similar to a beak (rostrum), and if something is left over, it should be made plain with a file. But if it is not in the root of another (tooth), but leans on the lowest part, it should be extracted with a pair of forceps.]

44 Vincent of Beauvais, *Speculum doctrinale*, XII.141, c.1164: 'Porro si dentium quispiam iusto maior fuerit, quod manifeste turpe erit, oportet eum cum lima corrigi, & quod abundant tolli, quo cæteris æqualis fiat proportione competenti.'

45 Cf. Trotter (ed.), *Traitier de Cyrurgie*, p. 113, 'de la char des gencives'.

46 Fleischhacker (ed.), *Science of Cirurgie*, p. 265.

47 Ogden (ed.), *Cyrurgie*, p. 487.

48 Ibid., p. 482.

49 Ibid., p. 480.

50 Faye Marie Getz (ed.), *Healing and Society in Medieval England: A Middle English Translation of the Pharmaceutical Writings of Gilbertus Anglicus* (Madison: University of Wisconsin Press, 1991), p. 89.

51 Chaucer, 'The Miller's Tale', *Riverside Chaucer*, ed. Benson, 1.3747–8. For further occurrences of the term 'froten', see my note, 'The Middle English Term "Froten": Absolon and Barber Surgery', *N&Q* 53 (2006): 303–5.

52 Ogden (ed.), *Cyrurgie*, p. 489.

53 London, British Library MS Sloane 563, f. 15v.

54 Lawn (ed.), *The Prose Salernitan Questions*, 'Dentium materia est ex cerebri substantia, et ex genarum medulla. Unde philosophus quidam apud Delfos obiit quia dente abstracto cerebri substantiam amisit', P 123, pp. 251–2.

55 Ogden (ed.), *Cyrurgie*, p. 490.

56 Augustine, *Confessions*, p. 189; cf. Ogden (ed.), *Cyrurgie*, p. 484, where Guy names toothache the 'most grevous'.

57 This is explored further by Pouchelle, *The Body and Surgery*, pp. 31–6.

58 Monika Otter (trans.), 'Baudri of Bourgueil, "To Countess Adela"', *Journal of Medieval Latin* 11 (2001): 60–141 (95, lines 1201–10). Léopold Delisle (ed.), 'Poème adressé a Adèle, Fille de Guillaume le Conquérant par Baudri, Abbé de Bourgueil', *Mémoires de la Société des Antiquaires de Normandie* 28 (1869): 187–224 (220): 'Grammaticæ vero juxta renitebat imago, / Et

lateralis erat rethoricæ in trivio. / Limam dentatam gerit hæc in partibus octo, / Qua dentes scabros ipsa medens poliat. / Forpicibus medicis viciosa putando labella / Complet et hiulca, cito quod superest resecans. / Et refovens vulnus linit ilico pulvere quodam, / Sepia quem vel quem tetra favilla facit. / Namque sui juris infantum est ora docere, / Et male stridentes æquiparare sonos.'

59 Guy, drawing on Albucasis, lists (among other barber-surgeons' tools) files, 'scheres' and 'rasoures', Ogden (ed.), *Cyrurgie*, p. 5.

60 *Martianus Capella and the Seven Liberal Arts*, Volume II: *The Marriage of Philology and Mercury*, trans. William Harris Stahl and Richard Johnson, 2 vols. (New York: Columbia University Press, 1977), II, 66. On art historical depictions of Grammar, see Laura Cleaver, 'Grammar and Her Children: Learning to Read in the Art of the Twelfth Century', *Marginalia* 9 (2009): [n.p.].

61 John of Salisbury, *The Metalogicon of John of Salisbury*, trans. Daniel D. McGarry (Berkeley: University of California Press, 1962), p. 61; see also p. 37.

62 Rita Copeland and Ineke Sluiter (eds.), *Medieval Grammar and Rhetoric: Language Arts and Literary Theory* (Oxford University Press, 2009), p. 521. Cf. Hugutio of Pisa, *Magnae Derivatione*, in ibid., p. 359.

63 Cf. Richard de Bury, writing in Latin in 1345, who gives voice to the complaint of books about the clergy in the *Philobiblon*. Accused of having abandoned the books that nurtured them, the clergy are recalled as once having been helpless children who cried and 'begged to be made partakers of our milk'. Moved by the clergy's tears, books gave them instead 'the breast of grammar to suck, which ye plied continually with your teeth and tongue, until ye lost your native barbarousness and learned to speak with our tongues the mighty things of God'. *The Love of Books: The Philobiblon of Richard de Bury*, trans. E. C. Thomas (City of Birmingham School of Printing, 1946), p. 25.

64 Katharine Breen, *Imagining an English Reading Public, 1150–1400* (Cambridge University Press, 2010), p. 5.

65 Rita Copeland, 'Introduction: Dissenting Critical Practices', *Criticism and Dissent in the Middle Ages*, ed. Rita Copeland (Cambridge University Press, 1996), pp. 1–23 (p. 6).

66 Robert Francis Seybolt, trans., *The Manuale Scholarium: An Original Account of Life in the Mediaeval University* (Cambridge, MA: Harvard University Press, 1921). For university rituals more generally and that recorded in *The Manuale Scholarium*, see Hastings Rashdall, *The Universities of Europe in the Middle Ages*, ed. F. M. Powicke and A. B. Emden, 3 vols. (Oxford: Clarendon, 1936), III, 376–81.

67 Pouchelle, *The Body and Surgery*, p. 176; Le Goff, *Intellectuals*, p. 79.

68 Ruth Mazo Karras, *From Boys to Men: Formations of Masculinity in Late Medieval Europe* (Philadelphia: University of Pennsylvania Press, 2003), p. 193 n. 177 (citing the *Statutes of the Colleges of Oxford*, vol. 1, New College, p. 47). See further pp. 67–108 (esp. pp. 100–8) where Karras discusses the relation of the *Manuale* to actual practice.

69 Seybolt (trans.), *Manuale Scholarium*, pp. 24–33.

70 On this metaphor, see Virginia Langum, 'Discerning Skin: Complexion, Surgery, and Language in Medieval Confession', *Reading Skin in Medieval Literature and Culture*, ed. Katie L. Walter (New York: Palgrave, 2013), pp. 141–60 (p. 152); and Paul Sheneman, 'The Tongue as a Sword: Psalms 56 and 63 and the Pardoner', *Chaucer Review* 27.4 (1993): 396–400.

71 Hanna (ed.), *Speculum Vitae*, 11, 472 (14,261–2).

72 Chaucer, 'The Manciple's Tale', *Riverside Chaucer*, ed. Benson, ix.340–1. See further Craun, *Lies, Slander, and Obscenity*, pp. 192–3.

73 Francis (ed.), *Book of Vices and Virtues*, pp. 149–50. The four 'seruices' of the other side, in the will, are love, dread, joy and sorrow. When these are distempered then vices come, just as when the humours are, sickness does.

74 Francis (ed.), *Book of Vices and Virtues*, p. 151. Cf. Hanna (ed.), *Speculum Vitae*, I, 160 (4737–40).

75 Cf. Richard Morris and Pamela Gradon (eds.), *Dan Michel's Ayenbite of Inwyt, or Remorse of Conscience*, EETS 23, 278, 2 vols. (London: Trübner, 1866; Oxford University Press, 1979), I, 152, which translates the *Somme le roi* thus: 'Efterward he makeþ þane scele be mesure speke / and bleþeliche by stille. and speke onneþe. zuo þet þe speche come raþre to þe uile: þanne to þe tonge. Þet hi by y-weʒe ase guode moneye and y-proued. ase zayþ. salomon.'

76 Bernard Diensburg and Arne Zettersten (eds.), *The English Text of The Ancrene Riwle: The 'Vernon' Text*, EETS os 310 (Oxford University Press, 2000), p. 122. Cf. Barnum (ed.), *Dives and Pauper*, I/ii, 212, which warns those who keep silence and refuse to 'sekyn helpe of soule be schrifte or of body be oþir helpe & be good conceyl but *gnawyth & fretyth* hymself inward' (my emphasis).

77 Powell (ed.), *John Mirk's Festial*, I, 81.

78 Adrian James McCarthy (ed.), *Book to a Mother: An Edition with Commentary* (Salzburg: Institut für Anglistik und Amerikanistik, 1981), 38.21.

79 Rice, *Lay Piety*, p. 2.

80 On Mirk, see Breen, *Imagining an English Reading Public*, e.g. p. 34 ('Mirk seems to have conceived of *Instructions for Parish Priests* as a site of spiritual triage'); on *Piers Plowman*, see e.g. p. 174 ('If Langland wanted to imagine a potentially virtuous audience for his text, then, he had no choice but to engage with the negative dimension of habit as sin'). See also Aers, *Beyond Reformation?* on the poem's response to the crisis of virtue in late fourteenth-century England.

81 Lisa H. Cooper, *Artisans and Narrative Craft in Late Medieval England* (Cambridge University Press, 2014), p. 115.

82 The Dame Penance episode covers lines 4006–637. The allegory of the 'good chamberlyn' is found commonly in pastoral literature. See Francis (ed.), *Book of Vices and Virtues*, pp. 172–3, for example, which describes the three-stage process of penance through heart, mouth and deed, and observes that: 'After repentaunce schal come schrifte, þat is þe goode chamberleyn, þat swopeþ þe hous and casteþ out al þe dust and al þe filþe wiþ þe noise of þe tonge, wher-of Dauid spekeþ in þe Sauter.'

83 Notably, Lydgate's poem 'Tretise for Lauandres' offers a detailed exposition of what the task of laundering clothes entailed. See Maura Nolan, 'Lydgate's Worst Poem', *Lydgate Matters: Poetry and Material Culture in the Fifteenth Century*, ed. Lisa H. Cooper and Andrea Denny-Brown (New York: Palgrave, 2008), pp. 71–87, and her discussion of literary and devotional contexts for laundry; pp. 73–4 detail parallels between Dame Penance in *Pilgrimage* and the 'Tretise for Lauandres'.

84 As lines 4368–76 suggest, the 'mouth of man' or the sixth gate is drawn from the Old Testament ordure gate recorded in Nehemiah 3:14, which led to the rubbish dump outside the city. Cf. Wenzel (ed.), *Fasciculus morum*, which records a similar image of the mouth as an ordure gate, pp. 458–60.

85 The 'domestic' allegory of confession is widespread in medieval texts. See, for example, Morris and Gradon (eds.), *Ayenbite of Inwyt*: 'Efter þe uorþenchinge ssel come þe ssrifte þet is þe guode chomberier þet clenzeþ þet hous and kest out al þe uelþe mid þe besme of þe tonge', I, 171–2.

86 Arnould (ed.), *Livre*, p. 181: 'Tresdouz Sires, eietz mercy de moy et me donetz grace qe jeo peusse ou ma lang garrir l'ord plaie de ma bouche, et nettoier de l'ordure qe y est ou ma lange, c'est a dire pas regeier les ordes pecchés da ma bouche ou touz les autres par verraie confessione ou tristece de coer; et si jeo puisse ensi le male de ma bouche par ma bouche garrir, durement grande grace, douz Sires, me ferrietz de si tost et si legierment garrir.'

87 Pastoral texts such as Francis (ed.), *Book of Vices and Virtues*, p. 107, furnish similar images that invoke mining with pick and shovel.

88 Thomas N. Tentler, *Sin and Confession on the Eve of the Reformation* (Princeton University Press, 1977), p. 236.

89 Ogden (ed.), *Cyrurgie*, p. 489.

90 Ibid., p. 489.

91 Breen, *Imagining an English Reading Public*, p. 199.

92 Ibid., p. 204.

93 *MED*, s.v. 'palsy'. See Ogden (ed.), *Cyrurgie*, for a description of 'pallesie' caused either externally from blows or wounds, or internally from humoural imbalance (the tokens of which are quaking and fever, and the effects of which are a privation of feeling and movement), pp. 202–5; for 'pallesie' of the tongue (which hampers speech), see pp. 481–3.

94 Francis (ed.), *Book of Vices and Virtues*, p. 22.

95 Ibid., p. 25.

96 Pearsall (ed.), *Piers Plowman*, c.VI.74–5. The C-text relocates much of Haukyn's confession concerning 'backbiting' to Envy. Cf. Haukyn's similar phrase in the B-text: Envy 'with myght of mouth or thorugh mannes strengthe / Avenged me fele tymes, other frete myselve withinne / As a shepsteres shere, ysherewed men and cursed hem' (B.XIII.329–31).

97 Cf. *MED*, s.v. 'shapster' (n.), 'a female haircutter or barber'.

98 Pearsall (ed.), *Piers Plowman*, p. 112.

99 *MED*, s.v. 'defien' (v.(1)), 'To renounce (sth.), reject, repudiate; disavow'; (v.(2)) 'To digest (food, drink)'; 'assimilate'; 'To void (excrement)'.

100 Cf. Francis (ed.), *Book of Vices and Virtues*, pp. 146–7, which outlines the penitential process using a clinical model for treating pathological conditions: 'First schal a man legge þerto oynementes and plastres of faire amonestynges; and after, ȝif þat ne helpeþ not, þe fretynge poudres and scharpe of harde vndertakynges; after, þe yren of discipline; and ȝif he enpaireþ alwey, þan he bihoueþ to take þe swerd to smyte it of and part it from þe oþer membres, or by cursyng', etc.

101 *MED*, s.v. 'dia-' (pref.), '*Med.* ~penidion, ~pendion, a sweet drug in the form of a twisted thread, used to relieve coughing'.

102 On scrupulosity, see Tentler, *Sin and Confession*, e.g. p. 156, where he describes: 'the implacable search into the mental life of the penitent and the relentless demand that he make up his mind about the gravity of an act and the degree of his consent. Know thyself becomes an exhausting activity.'

103 William Langland, *Piers Plowman: The A Version*, ed. George Kane, rev. edn (London: Athlone Press, 1960; 1988), A.v.100–2. The C-text version reads thus: 'May no sugre ne swete thyng aswage my swellynge / Ne derworth drynke dryue hit fro myn herte / Ne noþer shame ne shryfte, but ho-so shrapede my mawe?' c.vi.88–90.

104 Scraping the stomach does also have culinary connotations. The *MED*, for example, gives s.v. 'scrapen': 'a 1450 Hrl.Cook.Bk.(1) 18: Take þe Mawes of Turbut, Haddock, or Codelyng, & pyke hem clene & scrape hem & Wasshem clene'. Cf. J. R. R. Tolkien and E. V. Gordon (eds.), *Sir Gawain and the Green Knight*, 2nd edn, rev. Norman Davis (Oxford: Clarendon Press, 1967), p. 37, lines 1330–1. Tolkien and Gordon observe in their notes on this hunting scene that 'the gullet was evidently scraped (*schaued* 1331) free of the flesh adhering to it, and tied to prevent the escape of the contents of the stomach' (p. 111).

105 Chaucer, 'Epilogue of the Man of Law's Tale', *Riverside Chaucer*, ed. Benson, II.1185–90.

106 Christine F. Cooper, ' "But Algates Therby Was She Understonde": Translating Custance in Chaucer's Man of Law's Tale', *Yearbook of English Studies* 36.1 (2006): 27–38 (28).

107 See further Derrick G. Pitard, 'Sowing Difficulty: The Parson's Tale, Vernacular Commentary, and the Nature of Chaucerian Dissent', *Studies in the Age of Chaucer* 26 (2004): 299–330. Pitard observes the Parson's 'clash with the Shipman ... demonstrates not just the nature of the friction between discursive classes but also ... between developing *vernacular* classes' (317, emphasis original).

Bibliography

MANUSCRIPTS

Cambridge
Trinity College

MS 356

Lincoln
Lincoln Cathedral, Dean and Chapter Library

MS 91

London
British Library

MS Sloane 6
MS Sloane 563

Munich
Bayerische Staatsbibliothek

Clm. 19414

New Haven
Yale Medical Library

MS 28

Oxford
Bodleian Library

Bodley MS 4

Oriel College

MS 20

PRINTED WORKS

Adams, Francis, ed. *The Seven Books of Paulus Ægineta*, 3 vols. (London: Sydenham Society, 1844–7)

Aers, David, *Beyond Reformation? An Essay on William Langland's Piers Plowman and the End of Constantinian Christianity* (University of Notre Dame Press, 2015)

Aers, David, and Lynn Staley, *The Powers of the Holy: Religion, Politics, and Gender in Late Medieval English Culture* (University Park: Pennsylvania State University Press, 1996)

Albert the Great [Albertus Magnus], *On Animals: A Medieval 'Summa Zoologica'*, trans. Kenneth F. Kitchell and Irven Michael Resnick, 2 vols. (Baltimore: The Johns Hopkins University Press, 1999)

Albucasis, *On Surgery and Instruments*, ed. M. S. Spink and G. L. Lewis (London: The Wellcome Institute of the History of Medicine, 1973)

Alford, John A., 'The Design of the Poem', *A Companion to Piers Plowman*, ed. John A. Alford (Berkeley: University of California Press, 1988), pp. 29–65

Allen, Judson Boyce, *The Ethical Poetic of the Later Middle Ages: A Decorum of Convenient Distinction* (University of Toronto Press, 1982)

Ambrose, Saint, *Hexameron, Paradise, and Cain and Abel*, trans. John J. Savage, Fathers of the Church 42 (New York: Fathers of the Church, 1961)

Amundsen, Darrel W., 'Medieval Canon Law on Medical and Surgical Practice by the Clergy', *Bulletin of the History of Medicine* 52 (1978): 22–44

Anderson, George Christian, 'Medieval Medicine for Sin', *Journal of Religion and Health* 2.2 (1963): 156–65

Arbesmann, Rudolph, 'The Concept of "Christus Medicus" in St Augustine', *Traditio* 10 (1954): 1–28

Aristotle, *The Complete Works of Aristotle: The Revised Oxford Translation*, ed. Jonathan Barnes, Bollingen Series 71, 2 vols. (Princeton University Press, 1984)

Augustine, *Confessions*, trans. R. S. Pine-Coffin (London: Penguin, 1961)

Bakhtin, Mikhail, *Rabelais and His World*, trans. Hélène Iswolsky (Bloomington: Indiana University Press, 1984)

Banks, Mary Macleod, ed. *An Alphabet of Tales: An English Fifteenth Century Translation of the Alphabetum Narrationum*, EETS os 126–7, 2 vols. (London: Kegan Paul, Trench, Trübner, 1904–5)

Bardsley, Sandy, *Venomous Tongues: Speech and Gender in Late Medieval England* (Philadelphia: University of Pennsylvania Press, 2006)

Barnet, Margaret C., 'The Barber-Surgeons of York', *Medical History* 12 (1968): 19–30

Barney, Stephen A., W. J. Lewis, J. A. Beach and Oliver Berghof, trans. *The Etymologies of Isidore of Seville* (Cambridge University Press, 2006)

Barnum, Priscilla Heath, ed. *Dives and Pauper*, EETS 275, 3 vols. (Oxford University Press, 1976)

Barratt, Alexandra, ed. *The Knowing of Woman's Kind in Childing: A Middle English Version of Material Derived from the Trotula and Other Sources*, Medieval Women's Texts & Contexts 4 (Turnhout: Brepols, 2001)

' "In the Lowest Part of Our Need": Julian and Medieval Gynecological Writing',
Julian of Norwich: A Book of Essays, ed. Sandra J. McEntire, Garland Medieval
Casebooks 21 (New York: Garland, 1998), pp. 239–56

Bartholomaeus Angelicus [Anglicus], *De rerum Proprietatibus* (Frankfurt: Minerva,
1601; repr. 1964)

Bayless, Martha, *Sin and Filth in Medieval Culture: The Devil in the Latrine*
(New York: Routledge, 2012)

Beadle, Richard, 'Middle English Texts and their Transmission, 1300–1500: Some
Geographical Criteria', *Speaking in Our Tongues: Medieval Dialectology
and Related Disciplines*, ed. Margaret Laing and Keith Williamson
(Cambridge: Brewer, 1994, pp. 69–92)

Beckwith, Sarah, *Christ's Body: Identity, Culture, and Society in Late Medieval
Writings* (London: Routledge, 1993)

Bennett, J. A. W., '*Nosce te ipsum*: Some Medieval Interpretations', *J. R. R. Tolkien,
Scholar and Storyteller: Essays in Memoriam*, ed. Mary Salu and Robert T.
Farrell (Ithaca: Cornell University Press, 1979), pp. 138–58

Bernard of Clairvaux, *On the Song of Songs: Sermones in cantica Canticorum*, trans.
a Religious of C.S.M.V. (London: Mowbray, 1952)

Bestul, Thomas H., *Texts of the Passion: Latin Devotional Literature and Medieval
Society* (Philadelphia: University of Pennsylvania Press, 1996)

Biernoff, Suzannah, *Sight and Embodiment in the Middle Ages*
(Basingstoke: Palgrave, 2002)

Bishop, Louise M., *Words, Stones, and Herbs: The Healing Word in Medieval and
Early Modern England* (New York: Syracuse University Press, 2007)

Bitterling, Klaus, ed. *Of Shrifte and Penance: The Middle English Prose Translation of
'Le manuel des péchés'*, Middle English Texts 29 (Heidelberg: Universitätsverlag
C. Winter, 1998)

Blodgett, E. D., ed. and trans. *The Romance of Flamenca*, Garland Library of
Medieval Literature 101A (New York: Garland, 1995)

Bloomfield, Morton, *'Piers Plowman' as a Fourteenth-Century Apocalypse* (New
Brunswick, NJ: Rutgers University Press, 1962)

Bourdieu, Pierre, *Outline of a Theory of Practice*, trans. Richard Nice (Cambridge
University Press, 1977; repr. 2007)

Breen, Katharine, *Imagining an English Reading Public, 1150–1400* (Cambridge
University Press, 2010)

'Langland's Literary Syntax, or Anima as an Alternative to Latin Grammar',
Answerable Style: The Idea of the Literary in Medieval England, ed. Frank
Grady and Andrew Galloway (Columbus: Ohio State University Press, 2013),
pp. 95–120

Brown, Catherine, 'In the Middle', *Journal of Medieval and Early Modern Studies*
30.3 (2000): 543–74

Brown, Elizabeth A. R., 'Death and the Human Body in the Later Middle
Ages: The Legislation of Boniface VIII on the Division of the Corpse', *Viator*
12 (1981): 221–70

Brundage, James, 'Sex and Canon Law', *Handbook of Medieval Sexuality*, ed. Vern L. Bullough and James A. Brundage, Garland Reference Library of the Humanities 1696 (New York: Garland, 1996), pp. 33–50

Bryan, Jennifer, *Looking Inward: Devotional Reading and the Private Self in Late Medieval England* (Philadelphia: University of Pennsylvania Press, 2007)

Burnett, Charles, 'The Superiority of Taste', *Journal of the Warburg and Courtauld Institute* 54 (1991): 230–8

Burnyeat, M. F., 'Aquinas on "Spiritual Change" in Perception', *Ancient and Medieval Theories of Intentionality*, ed. Dominik Perler (Leiden: Brill, 2001), pp. 129–53

Burrow, J. A., *Gestures and Looks in Medieval Narrative* (Cambridge University Press, 2002)

Langland's Fictions (Oxford: Clarendon, 1993)

Burrow, J. A., and Thorlac Turville-Petre, *A Book of Middle English*, 2nd edn (Oxford: Blackwell, 1992, 1996)

Butterworth, Philip, *Staging Conventions in Medieval English Theatre* (Cambridge University Press, 2014)

Bynum, Caroline Walker, *Christian Materiality: An Essay on Religion in Late Medieval Europe* (New York: Zone Books, 2015)

'The Female Body and Religious Practice in the Later Middle Ages', *Fragmentation and Redemption: Essays on Gender and the Human Body in Medieval Religion* (New York: Zone Books, 1991), pp. 181–238

Holy Feast and Holy Fast: The Religious Significance of Food to Medieval Women (Berkeley: University of California Press, 1987)

Jesus as Mother: Studies in the Spirituality of the High Middle Ages (Berkeley: University of California Press, 1982)

Metamorphosis and Identity (New York: Zone Books, 2001)

The Resurrection of the Body in Western Christianity, 200–1336 (New York: Columbia University Press, 1995)

'Why All the Fuss about the Body? A Medievalist's Perspective', *Critical Inquiry* 22 (1995): 1–33

Camille, Michael, 'Gothic Signs and the Surplus: The Kiss on the Cathedral', *Yale French Studies* 80 (1991): 151–70

Campbell, Neil, 'Aquinas' Reasons for the Aesthetic Irrelevance of Tastes and Smells', *British Journal of Aesthetics* 36.2 (1996): 166–76

Capella, Martianus, *Martianus Capella and the Seven Liberal Arts*, Volume II: *The Marriage of Philology and Mercury*, trans. William Morris Stahl and Richard Johnson (New York: Columbia University Press, 1977)

Carruthers, Mary J., 'On Affliction and Reading, Weeping and Argument: Chaucer's Lachrymose Troilus in Context', *Representations* 93 (2006): 1–21

The Book of Memory: A Study of Memory in Medieval Culture (Cambridge University Press, 1990)

The Experience of Beauty in the Middle Ages (Oxford University Press, 2013)

The Search for St Truth: A Study of Meaning in 'Piers Plowman' (Evanston: Northwestern University Press, 1973)

'Sweet Jesus', *Mindful Spirit in Late Medieval Literature: Essays in Honor of Elizabeth D. Kirk*, ed. Bonnie Wheeler (New York: Palgrave, 2006), pp. 9–19

Certeau, Michel de, *The Practice of Everyday Life*, trans. Steven Rendall (Berkeley: University of California Press, 1984)

Chaucer, Geoffrey, *The Riverside Chaucer*, gen. ed. Larry D. Benson, 3rd edn (Oxford University Press, 1987)

Chenu, M.-D., O.P., *Nature, Man, and Society in the Twelfth Century: Essays on New Theological Perspectives in the Latin West*, trans. and ed. Jerome Taylor and Lester K. Little (University of Toronto Press, 1997)

Citrome, Jeremy J., *The Surgeon in Medieval English Literature* (New York: Palgrave, 2006)

Classen, Constance, *The Deepest Sense: A Cultural History of the Sense of Touch* (Urbana: University of Illinois Press, 2012)

Cleaver, Laura, 'Grammar and Her Children: Learning to Read in the Art of the Twelfth Century', *Marginalia* 9 (2009): [n.p.]

Cohen, Jeffrey Jerome, *Medieval Identity Machines* (Minneapolis: University of Minnesota Press, 2003)

Colish, Marcia L., '*Habitus* Revisited: A Reply to Cary Nederman', *Traditio* 48 (1993): 77–92

Colledge, Edmund, and James Walsh, eds. *A Book of Showings to the Anchoress Julian of Norwich*, Studies and Texts 35, 2 vols. (Toronto: Pontifical Institute of Mediaeval Studies, 1978)

Collette, Carolyn P., *Species, Phantasms, and Images: Vision and Medieval Psychology in 'The Canterbury Tales'* (Ann Arbor: University of Michigan Press, 2001)

Cooper, Christine F., ' "But Algates Therby Was She Understonde": Translating Custance in Chaucer's Man of Law's Tale', *Yearbook of English Studies* 36.1 (2006): 27–38

Cooper, Lisa H., *Artisans and Narrative Craft in Late Medieval England* (Cambridge University Press, 2014)

Copeland, Rita, 'Introduction: Dissenting Critical Practices', *Criticism and Dissent in the Middle Ages*, ed. Rita Copeland (Cambridge University Press, 1996), pp. 1–23

Copeland, Rita, and Ineke Sluiter, eds. *Medieval Grammar and Rhetoric: Language Arts and Literary Theory* (Oxford University Press, 2009)

Copeland, Rita, and Marjorie Curry Woods, 'Classroom and Confession', *The Cambridge History of Medieval English Literature*, ed. David Wallace (Cambridge University Press, 1999), pp. 376–406

Courcelle, Pierre, *Connais-toi toi-même. De Socrate à Saint Bernard*, 3 vols. (Paris: Études Augustiniennes, 1974–5)

Crane, Susan, *Animal Encounters: Contacts and Concepts in Medieval Britain* (Philadelphia: University of Pennsylvania Press, 2012)

Craun, Edwin D., 'Aristotle's Biology and Pastoral Ethics: John of Wales's *De Lingua* and British Pastoral Writing on the Tongue', *Traditio* 67 (2012): 277–303

Lies, Slander, and Obscenity in Medieval English Literature: Pastoral Rhetoric and the Deviant Speaker (Cambridge University Press, 1997)

Davis, Rebecca A., ' "Save man allone": Human Exceptionality in *Piers Plowman* and the Exemplarist Tradition', *Medieval Latin and Middle English Literature: Essays in Honour of Jill Mann*, ed. Christopher Cannon and Maura Nolan (Cambridge: Brewer, 2011), pp. 41–64

Davlin, Mary Clement, 'Devotional Postures in *Piers Plowman B*, with an Appendix on Divine Postures', *Chaucer Review* 42.2 (2007): 161–79

'*Kynde Knowyng* as a Major Theme in *Piers Plowman* B', *Review of English Studies* ns 22 (1971): 1–19

Delisle, Léopold, ed. 'Poème adressé à Adèle, Fille de Guillaume le Conquérant par Baudri, Abbé de Bourgueil', *Mémoires de la Société des Antiquaires de Normandie* 28 (1869): 187–224

Denery II, Dallas G., *Seeing and Being Seen in the Later Medieval World: Optics, Theology and Religious Life* (Cambridge University Press, 2005)

D'Evelyn, Charlotte, and Anna J. Mill, eds. *The South English Legendary*, EETS os 236, 3 vols. (London: Oxford University Press, 1956–9)

Diekstra, F. N. M., ed. *Book for a Simple and Devout Woman: A Late Middle English Adaptation of Peraldus's "Summa de Vitiis et Virtutibus" and Friar Laurent's "Somme le Roi"* (Groningen: Egbert Forsten, 1998)

Diensburg, Bernard, and Arne Zettersten, eds. *The English Text of The Ancrene Riwle: The 'Vernon' Text*, EETS os 310 (Oxford University Press, 2000)

Dinshaw, Carolyn, 'A Kiss Is Just a Kiss: Heterosexuality and Its Consolations in *Sir Gawain and the Green Knight*', *Diacritics* 24.2/3 (1994): 205–26

Edwards, A. S. G., 'Bartholomaeus Anglicus' *De Proprietatibus Rerum* and Medieval English Literature', *Archiv für das Studium der neueren Sprachen und Literaturen* 222 (1985): 121–8

Egmond, Florike, and Robert Zwijnenberg, eds. *Bodily Extremities: Preoccupations with the Human Body in Early Modern European Culture* (Aldershot: Ashgate, 2003)

Ellis, Roger, ed. *The Liber Celestis of St Bridget of Sweden*, Volume 1: *Text*, EETS os 291 (Oxford University Press, 1987)

Epstein, Steven A., *The Medieval Discovery of Nature* (Cambridge University Press, 2012)

Erbe, Theodor, ed. *Mirk's Festial: A Collection of Homilies by Johannes Mirkus (John Mirk), edited from Bodleian Ms. Gough Eccl. Top. 4*, EETS es 96 (London: Kegan Paul, Trench, Trübner, 1905; repr. 1997)

Eyler, Joshua R., ed. *Disability in the Middle Ages: Reconsiderations and Reverberations* (Farnham: Ashgate, 2010)

Fein, Susanna Greer, 'Why Did Absolon Put a "Trewelove" under His Tongue? Herb Paris as a Healing "Grace" in Middle English Literature', *Chaucer Review* 25.4 (1991): 302–17

Finucane, Ronald C., *Miracles and Pilgrims: Popular Beliefs in Medieval England* (London: Dent, 1977)

Fleischhacker, Robert von, ed. *Lanfrank's 'Science of Cirurgie'*, EETS os 102 (London: Kegan Paul, Trench, Trübner, 1894)

Ford, Judy Ann, 'The Autonomy of Conscience: Images of Confession in Mirk's *Festial*', *Renaissance and Reformation* 35.3 (ns 23.3) (1999): 5–27

 John Mirk's 'Festial': Orthodoxy, Lollardy, and the Common People in Fourteenth-Century England (Cambridge: Brewer, 2006)

Forshall, Josiah, and Frederic Madden, eds. *The Holy Bible, containing the Old and New Testaments […] in the Earliest English Versions made from the Latin Vulgate by John Wycliffe and His Followers*, 4 vols. (Oxford University Press, 1850)

Foucault, Michel, *The History of Sexuality*, trans. Robert Hurley, 3 vols. (London: Penguin, 1990)

Fowler, David C., Charles F. Briggs and Paul G. Remley, eds. *The Governance of Kings and Princes: John Trevisa's Middle English Translation of the 'De Regimine Principum' of Aegidius Romanus*, Garland Medieval Texts 19 (New York: Garland, 1997)

Fradenburg, L. O. Aranye, *Sacrifice Your Love: Psychoanalysis, Historicism, Chaucer*, Medieval Cultures 31 (Minneapolis: University of Minnesota Press, 2002)

Francis, W. Nelson, ed. *The Book of Vices and Virtues: A Fourteenth Century English Translation of the Somme le roi of Lorens d'Orléans*, EETS os 217 (London: Oxford University Press, 1942)

Frank, Robert Worth, '*Piers Plowman' and the Scheme of Salvation: An Interpretation of Dowel, Dobet, and Dobest*, Yale Studies in English 136 (New Haven: Yale University Press, 1957)

Fulton, Rachel, ' "Taste and See that the Lord is Sweet" (Ps.33.9): The Flavor of God in the Monastic West', *Journal of Religion* 86.2 (2006): 169–204

Gasse, Roseanne, 'The Practice of Medicine in *Piers Plowman*', *Chaucer Review* 39.2 (2004): 177–97

Gavrilyuk, Paul L., and Sarah Coakley, eds. *The Spiritual Senses: Perceiving God in Western Christianity* (Cambridge University Press, 2012)

Geoffrey of Vinsauf, *Poetria nova*, rev. edn trans. Margaret F. Nims, intro. to rev. edn Martin Camargo, Medieval Sources in Translation 49 (Toronto: Pontifical Institute of Mediaeval Studies, 2010, first pub. 1967)

Getz, Faye Marie, 'Charity, Translation, and the Language of Medical Learning in Medieval England', *Bulletin of the History of Medicine* 64 (1990): 1–17

Getz, Faye Marie, ed. *Healing and Society in Medieval England: A Middle English Translation of the Pharmaceutical Writings of Gilbertus Anglicus* (Madison: University of Wisconsin Press, 1991)

Giles of Rome [D. Aegidii Romani], *De regimine principum Libri III* (Rome: Bladum, 1556)

Gillespie, Vincent, 'The Senses in Literature: The Textures of Perception', *A Cultural History of the Senses in the Middle Ages*, ed. Richard G. Newhauser (London: Bloomsbury, 2014), pp. 153–73

 'Vernacular Theology', *Oxford Twenty-First Century Approaches to Literature: Middle English*, ed. Paul Strohm (Oxford University Press, 2007), pp. 401–20

Grant, Edward, *The Nature of Natural Philosophy in the Late Middle Ages* (Washington, DC: Catholic University of America Press, 2010)

Gray, Douglas, *Later Medieval English Literature* (Oxford University Press, 2008)

Gray, Nick, 'The Clemency of Cobblers: A Reading of "Glutton's Confession" in *Piers Plowman*', *Leeds Studies in English* 17 (1986): 61–75

Green, Monica H., ed. *The Trotula: An English Translation of the Medieval Compendium of Women's Medicine* (Philadelphia: University of Pennsylvania Press, 2001, 2002)

Griffiths, Jane, *Diverting Authorities: Experimental Glossing Practices in Manuscript and Print* (Oxford University Press, 2014)

Grigsby, Bryon, 'The Social Position of the Surgeon in London 1350–1450', *Essays in Medieval Studies* 13 (1996): 71–80

Grmek, Mirko Dražen, and Pierre Huard, *Mille ans de chirurgie en occident: Ve–XVe siècles* (Paris: Dacosta, 1966)

Hagen, Susan, *Allegorical Remembrance: A Study on 'The Pilgrimage of the Life of Man' as a Medieval Treatise on Seeing and Remembering* (Athens: University of Georgia Press, 1990)

Hamer, Richard, ed. *Gilte Legende*, EETs os 339, 3 vols. (Oxford University Press, 2012)

Hamling, Tara, and Catherine Richardson, eds. *Everyday Objects: Medieval and Early Modern Material Culture and Its Meanings* (Farnham: Ashgate, 2010)

Hanna, Ralph, ed. 'Henry Daniel's *Liber Uricrisiarum (Excerpt)*', *Popular and Practical Science of Medieval England*, ed. Lister M. Matheson (East Lansing: Colleagues, 1994), pp. 185–218

  'Sir Thomas Berkeley and His Patronage', *Speculum*, 64.4 (1989): 878

  ed. *Speculum Vitae: A Reading Edition*, EETS os 331–2, 2 vols. (Oxford University Press, 2008)

Harvey, E. Ruth, 'The Swallow's Nest and the Spider's Web', *Studies in English Language and Literature: 'Doubt Wisely': Papers in Honour of E. G. Stanley*, ed. M. J. Toswell and E. M. Tyler (London: Routledge, 1996), pp. 327–41

Hasse, Dag Nikolaus, 'The Soul's Faculties', *The Cambridge History of Medieval Philosophy*, Volume 1, ed. Robert Pasnau (Cambridge University Press, 2010), pp. 305–19

Hatton, Thomas J., 'Absolon, Taste, and Odor in *The Miller's Tale*', *Papers in Language and Literature* 71 (1971): 72–5

Heller-Roazen, Daniel, *The Inner Touch: The Archaeology of a Sensation* (New York: Zone Books, 2007)

Henry of Lancaster, *Le Livre de seyntz medicines, the Unpublished Devotional Treatise of Henry of Lancaster*, ed. E. J. Arnould, Anglo-Norman Text Society 11 (Oxford : Blackwell, 1940)

Henry, Avril, ed. *The Pilgrimage of the Lyfe of the Manhode*, EETS os 288, 292, 2 vols. (London: Oxford University Press, 1985–8)

'*Þe Pilgrimage of Þe Lyfe of Þe Manhode*: The Large Design, with Special Reference to Books 2–4', *Neuphilologische Mitteilungen* 87 (1986): 229–36

Henslow, G., *Medical Works of the Fourteenth Century* (London: Chapman and Hall, 1899)

Herlihy, David, *Medieval Households* (Cambridge, MA: Harvard University Press, 1985)

Hill, Boyd H., Jr., 'The Grain and the Spirit in Mediaeval Anatomy', *Speculum* 40 (1965): 63–73

Hoccleve, Thomas, '*My Compleinte' and Other Poems*, ed. Roger Ellis (University of Exeter Press, 2001)

Hodgson, Phyllis, ed. *The Cloud of Unknowing and The Book of Privy Counselling*, EETS os 218 (London: Oxford University Press, 1944; repr. 1973)

Holbrook, Sue Ellen, 'A Medieval Scientific Encyclopaedia "Renewed by Goodly Printing": Wynkyn de Worde's English *De Proprietatibus Rerum*', *Early Science and Medicine* 3 (1998): 119–56

Hsy, Jonathan, ' "Be more strange and bold": Kissing Lepers and Female Same-Sex Desire in *The Book of Margery Kempe*', *Early Modern Women* 5 (2010): 189–99

Huby, Pamela M., 'Soul, Life, Sense, Intellect: Some Thirteenth-Century Problems', *The Human Embryo: Aristotle and the Arabic and European Traditions*, ed. G. R. Dunstan (University of Exeter Press, 1990), pp. 113–22

Inagaki, Bernard Ryosuke, '*Habitus* and *Natura* in Aquinas', *Studies in Medieval Philosophy*, ed. John F. Wippel (Washington, DC: The Catholic University of America Press, 1987), pp. 159–76

Innes, Mary M., trans. *The Metamorphoses of Ovid* (Harmondsworth: Penguin, 1955)

Jacobi a Voragine [Jacobus de Voragine], *Legenda aurea: vulgo historia Lombardica dicta*, ed. Theodore Graesse, 3rd edn (Bratislav: Guilelmum Keobner, 1890)

Jacobus de Voragine, *The Golden Legend: Readings on the Saints*, trans. William Granger Ryan, 2 vols. (Princeton University Press, 1993)

Jacquart, Danielle, and Claude Thomasset, *Sexuality and Medicine in the Middle Ages*, trans. Matthew Adamson (Cambridge: Polity, 1988)

Jay, Martin, *Downcast Eyes: The Denigration of Vision in Twentieth-Century French Thought* (Berkeley: University of California Press, 1993)

Jones, Peter Murray, *Medieval Medical Miniatures* (London: The British Library, 1984)

Karnes, Michelle, *Imagination, Meditation, and Cognition in the Middle Ages* (University of Chicago Press, 2011)

Karras, Ruth Mazo, *From Boys to Men: Formations of Masculinity in Late Medieval Europe* (Philadelphia: University of Pennsylvania Press, 2003)

Kass, Leon R., *The Hungry Soul: Eating and the Perfecting of Our Nature* (New York: Maxwell Macmillan International, 1994)

Kaye, Joel, *A History of Balance 1250–1375: The Emergence of a New Model of Equilibrium* (Cambridge University Press, 2014)

Keenan, Joseph M., 'The Cistercian Pilgrimage to Jerusalem in Guillaume de Deguilville's *Pèlerinage de la Vie Humaine*', *Studies in Medieval Cistercian History II*, ed. John R. Sommerfeldt, Cistercian Studies Series 24 (Kalamazoo: Cistercian Publications, 1976), pp. 166–85

Keiser, G. R, 'XXV. Works of Science and Information', *A Manual of the Writings in Middle English, 1050–1500*, ed. Albert E. Hartung and others, 11 vols. (New Haven: Connecticut Academy of Arts and Science, 1998)

Keller, Angelina, 'Grotesquely Articulate Bodies: Medicine, Hermeneutics and Writing in *The Canterbury Tales*', *Fleshy Things and Spiritual Matters: Studies on the Medieval Body in Honour of Margaret Bridges*, ed. Nicole Nyffenegger and Katrin Rupp (Cambridge Scholars Publishing, 2011), pp. 79–124

Kerby-Fulton, Kathryn, '*Piers Plowman*', *The Cambridge History of Medieval English Literature*, ed. David Wallace (Cambridge University Press, 1999), pp. 513–38

Krug, Rebecca, '*Piers Plowman* and the Secrets of Health', *Chaucer Review* 46.1/2 (2011): 166–81

Kuttner, Stephan, 'The Revival of Jurisprudence', *Renaissance and Renewal in the Twelfth Century*, ed. R. L. Benson and Giles Constable (Oxford: Clarendon, 1982), pp. 299–323

Lahey, Stephen E., 'Late Medieval Eucharistic Theology', *A Companion to the Eucharist in the Middle Ages*, ed. Ian Christopher Levy, Gary Macy and Kristen Van Ausdall (Leiden: Brill, 2012), pp. 499–539

Lambek, Michael, and Andrew Strathern, eds. *Bodies and Persons: Comparative Perspectives from Africa and Melanesia* (Cambridge University Press, 1998)

Land, Karine van't, 'The Solution of Continuous Things: Wounds in Late Medieval Medicine and Surgery', *Wounds in the Middle Ages*, ed. Anne Kirkham and Cordelia Warr (Farnham: Ashgate, 2014), pp. 89–108

Langland, William, *Piers Plowman: The A Version*, ed. George Kane, rev. edn (London: Athlone Press, 1960; 1988)

Piers Plowman: An Edition of the C-Text, ed. Derek Pearsall (London: Edward Arnold, 1978)

The Vision of Piers Plowman: A Critical Edition of the B-Text based on Trinity College Cambridge MS B.15.17, ed. A. V. C. Schmidt, 2nd edn (London: Dent, 1978)

Langum, Virginia, 'Discerning Skin: Complexion, Surgery, and Language in Medieval Confession', *Reading Skin in Medieval Literature and Culture*, ed. Katie L. Walter (New York: Palgrave, 2013), pp. 141–60

Medicine and the Seven Deadly Sins in Late Medieval Literature and Culture (New York: Palgrave, 2016)

Laskaya, Anne, and Eve Salisbury, eds. *The Middle English Breton Lays* (Kalamazoo: Medieval Institute Publications, 1995)

Lavezzo, Kathy, 'The Minster and the Privy: Rereading "The Prioress's Tale"', *PMLA* 126.2 (2011): 363–82

Lawn, Brian, ed. *The Prose Salernitan Questions* (Oxford University Press, 1979)

Leclercq, Jean, O.S.B., *The Love of Learning and the Desire for God: A Study of Monastic Culture*, trans. Catharine Misrahi (New York: Fordham University Press, 1961; repr. 2003)

Lefebvre, Henri, *Everyday Life in the Modern World*, trans. Sacha Rabinovitch (London: Allen Lane, 1971)

Le Goff, Jacques, *The Birth of Europe*, trans. Janet Lloyd (Oxford: Blackwell, 2005)
  Intellectuals in the Middle Ages, trans. Teresa Lavender Fagan (Cambridge, MA: Blackwell, 1993)
  Time, Work and Culture in the Middle Ages, trans. Arthur Goldhammer (Chicago University Press, 1980)
  'What Did the Twelfth-Century Renaissance *Mean?*', *The Medieval World*, ed. Peter Linehan and Janet L. Nelson (London: Routledge, 2001), pp. 635–47
Lewis, C. S., *The Allegory of Love: A Study in Medieval Tradition* (London: Oxford University Press, 1936)
Lewis, Charleton T., and Charles Short, *A Latin Dictionary* (Oxford: Clarendon, 1879)
Lima, Robert, *Stages of Evil: Occultism in Western Theater and Drama* (Lexington: University Press of Kentucky, 2005)
Lindsay, W. M., ed. *Isidori Hispalensis Episcopi Etymologiarum sive Originvm libri XX*, 2 vols. (Oxford: Clarendon, 1911)
Love, Nicholas, *The Mirror of the Blessed Life of Jesus Christ: A Reading Text*, ed. Michael G. Sargent (University of Exeter Press, 2004)
Lydgate, John, *The Pilgrimage of the Life of Man*, ed. F. J. Furnivall and Katharine B. Locock, EETS es 77, 83, 92 (London: Kegan Paul, Trench, Trübner, 1899–1904)
McAvoy, Liz Herbert, and Teresa Walters, eds. *Consuming Narratives: Gender and Monstrous Appetite in the Middle Ages and the Renaissance* (Cardiff: University of Wales Press, 2002)
McCarthy, Adrian James, ed. *Book to a Mother: An Edition with Commentary* (Salzburg: Institut für Anglistik und Amerikanistik, 1981)
McGarry, Daniel D., trans. *The Metalogicon of John of Salisbury* (Berkeley: University of California Press, 1962)
McNamer, Sarah, *Affective Meditation and the Invention of Medieval Compassion* (Philadelphia: University of Pennsylvania Press, 2010)
McVaugh, Michael R., *Medicine before the Plague: Practitioners and their Patients in the Crown of Aragon, 1285–1345* (Cambridge University Press, 1993)
Malo, Robyn, *Relics and Writing in Late Medieval England* (Toronto University Press, 2013)
Mann, Jill, 'Eating and Drinking in *Piers Plowman*', *Essays and Studies* 32 (1979): 26–43
  'Speaking Images in Chaucer's *Miller's Tale*', *Speaking Images: Essays in Honor of V. A. Kolve*, ed. Charlotte C. Morse and Robert F. Yeager (Asheville, NC: Pegasus Press, 2001), pp. 237–53
Mannyng, Robert, of Brunne, *Handlyng Synne*, ed. Idelle Sullens, Medieval & Renaissance Texts & Studies 14 (Binghamton: Medieval & Renaissance Texts & Studies, 1983)
Metzler, Irina, *Disability in Medieval Europe: Thinking about Impairment in the High Middle Ages, c.1100–c.1400* (London: Routledge, 2006)
Middleton, Anne, 'The Audience and Public of *Piers Plowman*', *Middle English Alliterative Poetry and Its Literary Background: Seven Essays*, ed. David Lawton (Cambridge: Brewer, 1982), pp. 101–23

'Narration and the Invention of Experience: Episodic Form in *Piers Plowman*', *The Wisdom of Poetry: Essays in Early English Literature in Honor of Morton W. Bloomfield*, ed. Larry D. Benson and Siegfried Wenzel (Kalamazoo: Medieval Institute Publications, 1982), pp. 91–122

Migne, J.-P., gen. ed. *Patrologiae cursus completus: Series latina*, 221 vols. (Paris: Migne, 1844–64)

Milbank, Arabella, 'Medieval Corporeality and the Eucharistic Body in Julian of Norwich's *A Revelation of Love*', *Journal of Medieval and Early Modern Studies* 46.3 (2016): 629–51

Miles, Margaret R., *Carnal Knowing: Female Nakedness and Religious Meaning in the Christian West* (Boston: Beacon Press, 1989)

Mills, Robert, *Suspended Animation: Pain, Pleasure and Punishment in Medieval Culture* (London: Reaktion Books, 2005)

Milner, Matthew, *The Senses and the English Reformation* (Farnham: Ashgate, 2011)

Minnis, Alastair, 'Medieval Imagination and Memory', *The Cambridge History of Medieval Literary Criticism*, Volume II: *The Middle Ages*, ed. Alastair Minnis and Ian Johnson (Cambridge University Press, 2005), pp. 239–74

Medieval Theory of Authorship: Scholastic Literary Attitudes in the Later Middle Ages, 2nd edn (Aldershot: Scolar Press, 1984, 1988)

Mirk, John, *Instructions for Parish Priests*, ed. Edward Peacock, EETS os 31 (London: Kegan Paul, Trench, Trübner, 1868; repr. 1902)

Mitchell, J. Allen, *Becoming Human: The Matter of the Medieval Child* (Minneapolis: University of Minnesota Press, 2014)

Mitchell, Piers D., *Medicine in the Crusades: Warfare, Wounds and the Medieval Surgeon* (Cambridge University Press, 2004)

Morley, Henry, ed. *Early Prose Romances* (London: Routledge, 1889)

Morris, Richard, ed. *Cursor Mundi, or The Cursur o the World*, EETS os 57, 99, 101, 3 vols. (London: Kegan Paul, Trench, Trübner, 1874–93)

The Pricke of Conscience (Stimulus conscientiae): A Northumbrian Poem (Berlin: A. Asher & Co., 1863)

Morris, Richard, and Pamela Gradon, eds. *Dan Michel's Ayenbite of Inwyt, or Remorse of Conscience*, EETS 23, 278, 2 vols. (London: Trübner, 1866; Oxford University Press, 1979)

Morrison, Susan Signe, *Excrement in the Late Middle Ages: Sacred Filth and Chaucer's Fecopoetics* (New York: Palgrave, 2008)

Murdoch, John E., *Album of Science: Antiquity and the Middle Ages* (New York: Scribner, 1984)

Murray, Jacqueline, 'Gendered Souls in Sexed Bodies: The Male Construction of Female Sexuality in Some Medieval Confessors' Manuals', *Handling Sin: Confession in the Middle Ages*, ed. Peter Biller and A. J. Minnis (Woodbridge: Boydell Press, 1998), pp. 79–93

Nederman, Cary J., 'Nature, Ethics, and the Doctrine of "Habitus": Aristotelian Moral Psychology in the Twelfth Century', *Traditio* 45 (1989/90): 87–110

Newhauser, Richard G., ed. *A Cultural History of the Senses in the Middle Ages* (London: Bloomsbury, 2016)

'Introduction: The Sensual Middle Ages', *A Cultural History of the Senses in the Middle Ages*, ed. Richard G. Newhauser, London: Bloomsbury, 2016, pp. 1–22

'John Gower's Sweet Tooth', *Review of English Studies* 64 (2013): 752–69

'Peter of Limoges, Optics, and the Science of the Senses', *Senses & Society* 5.1 (2010): 28–44

'The Senses, the Medieval Sensorium, and Sensing (in) the Middle Ages', *Medieval Culture: Fundamental Aspects and Conditions of the European Middle Ages*, ed. Albrecht Classen, 3 vols. (Berlin: De Gruyter, 2015) vol. III, pp. 1559–79

Newhauser, Richard G., and Arthur J. Russell, 'Mapping Virtual Pilgrimage in an Early Fifteenth-Century *Arma Christi* Roll', *The Arma Christi in Medieval and Early Modern Material Culture, with a Critical Edition of 'O Vernicle'*, ed. Lisa H. Cooper and Andrea Denny-Brown (Farnham: Ashgate, 2014), pp. 83–112

Nichols, Stephen G., Andreas Kablitz and Alison Calhoun, eds. *Rethinking the Medieval Senses: Heritage, Fascinations, Frames* (Baltimore: The Johns Hopkins University Press, 2008)

Nolan, Maura, *John Lydgate and the Making of Public Culture* (Cambridge University Press, 2005)

'Lydgate's Worst Poem', *Lydgate Matters: Poetry and Material Culture in the Fifteenth Century*, ed. Lisa H. Cooper and Andrea Denny-Brown (New York: Palgrave, 2008), pp. 71–87

Norris, Richard A., ed. and trans. *The Song of Songs: Interpreted by Early Christian and Medieval Commentators* (Grand Rapids, MI: Eerdmans, 2003)

Novacich, Sarah Elliott, *Shaping the Archive in Late Medieval England: History, Poetry and Performance* (Cambridge University Press, 2017)

O'Boyle, Cornelius, 'Surgical Texts and Social Contexts: Physicians and Surgeons in Paris, c.1270 to 1430', *Practical Medicine from Salerno to the Black Death*, ed. Luis García-Ballester, Roger French, Jon Arrizabalaga and Andrew Cunningham (Cambridge University Press, 1994), pp. 156–85

Ogden, Margaret S., ed. *The Cyrurgie of Guy de Chauliac*, EETS 265 (London: Oxford University Press, 1971)

Olson, Glending, *Literature as Recreation in the Later Middle Ages* (Ithaca: Cornell University Press, 1982)

O'Neill, Ynez Violé, 'Diagrams of the Medieval Brain: A Study in Cerebral Localisation', *Iconography at the Crossroads*, ed. Brendan Cassidy (Princeton University Press, 1993), pp. 91–101

Speech and Speech Disorders in Western Thought before 1600, Contributions in Medical History 3 (London: Greenwood Press, 1980)

Orlemanski, Julie, 'Jargon and the Matter of Medicine in Middle English', *Journal of Medieval and Early Modern Studies* 42.2 (2012): 395–420

Otter, Monika, trans., 'Baudri of Bourgueil, "To Countess Adela"', *Journal of Medieval Latin* 11 (2001): 60–141

Pahta, Päivi, *Medieval Embryology in the Vernacular: The Case of 'De Spermate'*, Mémoires de la Société Néophilologique de Helsinki 53 (Helsinki: Société Néophilologique, 1998)

Pahta, Päivi, and Irma Taavitsainen, eds. *Medical and Scientific Writing in Late Medieval English* (Cambridge University Press, 2004)

'Vernacularisation of Medical Writing in English: A Corpus-Based Study of Scholasticism', *Early Science and Medicine* 3 (1998): 157–85

'Vernacularisation of Scientific and Medical Writing in its Sociohistorical Context', *Medical and Scientific Writing in Late Medieval English*, ed. Päivi Pahta and Irma Taavitsainen (Cambridge University Press, 2004), pp. 1–22

Park, Katharine, 'The Life of the Corpse: Division and Dissection in Late Medieval Europe', *Journal of the History of Medicine* 50 (1995): 111–32

'Medicine and Society in Medieval Europe, 500–1500', *Medicine in Society: Historical Essays*, ed. Andrew Wear (Cambridge University Press, 1992), pp. 59–90

Paulmier-Foucart, Monique, with Marie-Christine Duchenne, *Vincent de Beauvais et le Grand miroir du monde* (Turnhout: Brepols, 2004)

Pearsall, Derek, *John Lydgate* (London: Routledge & Kegan Paul, 1970)

Pecock, Reginald, *The Repressor of Over Much Blaming of the Clergy*, ed. Churchill Babington, 2 vols. (London: Longman, Green, Longman, and Roberts, 1860)

Penn, Michael, *Kissing Christians: Ritual and Community in the Late Ancient Church* (Philadelphia: University of Pennsylvania Press, 2005)

'Ritual Kissing, Heresy and the Emergence of Early Christian Orthodoxy', *Journal of Ecclesiastical History* 54 (2003): 625–40

Peraldus, Guilelmus [William Peraldus], *Summa de vitiis et virtutibus* (Venice: Paganino de Paganini, 1497)

Perella, Nicolas James, *The Kiss Sacred and Profane: An Interpretative History of Kiss Symbolism and Related Religio-Erotic Themes* (Berkeley: University of California Press, 1969)

Perkins, Nicholas, 'Thomas Hoccleve, *La Male Regle*', *A Companion to Medieval English Literature and Culture c.1350–c.1500*, ed. Peter Brown (Oxford: Blackwell, 2007), pp. 585–603

Petkov, Kiril, 'The Cultural Career of a "Minor" Vice: Arrogance in the Medieval Treatise on Sin', *Sin in Medieval and Early Modern Culture: The Tradition of the Seven Deadly Sins*, ed. Richard G. Newhauser and Susan J. Ridyard, York Medieval Press (Woodbridge: Boydell and Brewer, 2012), pp. 43–65

Pitard, Derrick G., 'Sowing Difficulty: The Parson's Tale, Vernacular Commentary, and the Nature of Chaucerian Dissent', *Studies in the Age of Chaucer* 26 (2004): 299–330

Pouchelle, Marie-Christine, *The Body and Surgery in the Middle Ages*, trans. Rosemary Morris (New Brunswick: Rutgers University Press, 1990)

Pouzet, Jean-Pascal, '"Space this Werke to Wirke": Quelques figures de la complémentarité dans les manuscrits de Robert Thornton', *La Complémentarité: Mélanges offerts à Josseline Bidard et Arlette Sancery à l'occasion de leur départ en retraite*, ed. Marie-Françoise Alamichel (Paris: AMAES, 2005), pp. 27–43

Powell, Susan, 'A Critical Edition of the *Temporale* Sermons of MSS Harley 2247 and Royal 18 B XXV', 2 vols., unpublished doctoral thesis, University of London, King's College (1980)

'John Mirk's *Festial* and the Pastoral Programme', *Leeds Studies in English* ns 22 (1991): 85–102

ed., *John Mirk's Festial edited from British Library MS Cotton Claudius A.II*, EETS 334–5, 2 vols. (Oxford University Press, 2009–11)

Rashdall, Hastings, *The Universities of Europe in the Middle Ages*, ed. F. M. Powicke and A. B. Emden, 3 vols. (Oxford: Clarendon, 1936)

Rawcliffe, Carole, *Medicine and Society in Later Medieval England* (Stroud: Sutton Publishing, 1995)

Sources for the History of Medicine in Late Medieval England (Kalamazoo: Medieval Institute Publications, 1995)

Urban Bodies: Communal Health in Late Medieval English Towns and Cities (Woodbridge: Boydell, 2013)

Reynolds, Philip Lyndon, *Food and the Body: Some Peculiar Questions in High Medieval Theology* (Leiden: Brill, 1999)

Rice, Nicole R., *Lay Piety and Religious Discipline in Middle English Literature* (Cambridge University Press, 2008)

Riddy, Felicity, 'Looking Closely: Authority and Intimacy in the Late Medieval Urban Home', *Gendering the Master Narrative: Women and Power in the Middle Ages*, ed. Mary Carpenter Erler and Maryanne Kowaleski (Ithaca: Cornell University Press, 2003), pp. 212–28

'Temporary Virginity and the Everyday Body: *Le Bone Florence of Rome* and Bourgeois Self-Making', *Pulp Fictions of Medieval England: Essays in Popular Romance*, ed. Nicola McDonald (Manchester University Press, 2004), pp. 197–216

Robertson, Elizabeth, '*Noli me tangere*: The Enigma of Touch in Middle English Religious Literature and Art for and about Women', *Reading Skin in Medieval Literature and Culture*, ed. Katie L. Walter (New York: Palgrave, 2013), pp. 29–55

Robertson, Kellie, *Nature Speaks: Medieval Literature and Aristotelian Philosophy* (Philadelphia: University of Pennsylvania Press, 2017)

Rubin, Miri, *Corpus Christi: The Eucharist in Late Medieval Culture* (Cambridge University Press, 1991)

Rudy, Gordon, *Mystical Language of Sensation in the Later Middle Ages* (London: Routledge, 2002)

Rudy, Kathryn M., 'Kissing Images, Unfurling Rolls, Measuring Wounds, Sewing Badges and Carrying Talismans: Considering Some Harley Manuscripts through the Physical Rituals They Reveal', *Electronic British Library Journal* (2011): Article 5, 1–56

Salmón, Fernando, 'A Medieval Territory for Touch', *Studies in Medieval and Renaissance History* 3rd Series 2 (2005): 59–81

Sandars, Thomas Collett, ed. *The Institutes of Justinian* (London: Parker, 1853)

Scanlon, Larry, 'Personification and Penance', *YLS* 21 (2007): 1–29

Scarry, Elaine, *The Body in Pain: The Making and Unmaking of the World* (Oxford University Press, 1985)

Schaff, Philip, ed. *A Select Library of Nicene and Post-Nicene Fathers*, First Series, 14 vols. (New York: Christian Literature Co., 1889)

Schaff, Philip, and Henry Wace, eds. *A Select Library of Nicene and Post-Nicene Fathers*, Second Series, 14 vols. (Oxford: Parker, 1893)

Schmidt, A. V. C., ' "Elementary" Images in the Samaritan Episode of *Piers Plowman*', *Essays in Criticism* 56 (2006): 303–23

Schoenfeldt, Michael C., *Bodies and Selves in Early Modern England: Physiology and Inwardness in Spenser, Shakespeare, Herbert and Milton* (Cambridge University Press, 1999)

Scully, Jackie Leach, 'Disability and Vulnerability: On Bodies, Dependence, and Power', *Vulnerability: New Essays in Ethics and Feminist Philosophy*, ed. Catriona Mackenzie, Wendy Rogers and Susan Dodds (New York: Oxford University Press, 2014), pp. 204–21

Sears, Elizabeth, *The Ages of Man: Medieval Interpretations of the Life Cycle* (Princeton University Press, 1986)

Seybolt, Robert Francis, ed. *The Manuale Scholarium: An Original Account of Life in the Mediaeval University* (Cambridge, MA: Harvard University Press, 1921)

Seymour, M. C., and others, eds. *On the Properties of Things: John Trevisa's Translation of Bartholomaeus Anglicus 'De Proprietatibus Rerum'*, 3 vols. (Oxford: Clarendon, 1975)

Shahar, Shulamith, *Childhood in the Middle Ages*, trans. Chaya Galai (London: Routledge, 1990)

Sharpe, William D., 'Isidore of Seville: The Medical Writings', *Transactions of the American Philosophical Society* 54.2 (1964): 1–75

Sheingorn, Pamela, ' "Who Can Open the Doors of His Face?" The Iconography of Hellmouth', *The Iconography of Hell*, ed. Clifford Davidson and Thomas H. Seiler (Kalamazoo: Medieval Institute Publications, 1991), pp. 1–19

Shoaf, R. Allen, *Chaucer's Body: The Anxiety of Circulation in the 'Canterbury Tales'* (Gainesville: University of Florida Press, 2001)

Sieper, Ernst, ed. *Lydgate's Reson and Sensuallyte*, EETS es 84, 89, 2 vols. (London: K. Paul, Trench, Trübner & Co., 1901–3)

Simpson, James, *'Piers Plowman': An Introduction to the B-Text* (London: Longman, 1990)

'The Role of *Scientia* in *Piers Plowman*', *Medieval English Religious and Ethical Literature: Essays in Honour of G. H. Russell*, ed. Gregory Kratzmann and James Simpson (Cambridge: Brewer, 1986), pp. 49–65

Sciences and the Self in Medieval Poetry: Alan of Lille's 'Anticlaudianus' and John Gower's 'Confessio Amantis' (Cambridge University Press, 1995)

'Spirituality and Economics in Passus 1–7 of the B Text', *YLS* 1 (1987): 83–103

Siraisi, Nancy G., *Medieval and Early Renaissance Medicine: An Introduction to Knowledge and Practice* (London: University of Chicago Press, 1990)

Smith, Lesley, 'William of Auvergne and Confession', *Handling Sin: Confession in the Middle Ages*, ed. Peter Biller and A. J. Minnis (Woodbridge: Boydell & Brewer, 1998), pp. 95–107

Smith, Mark M., *Sensing the Past: Seeing, Hearing, Smelling, Tasting and Touching in History* (Berkeley: University of California Press, 2007)

Somerset, Fiona, *Clerical Discourse and Lay Audience in Late Medieval England* (Cambridge University Press, 1998)

　Feeling Like Saints: Lollard Writings after Wyclif (Ithaca: Cornell University Press, 2014)

　　'Here, There, and Everywhere? Wycliffite Conceptions of the Eucharist and Chaucer's "Other" Lollard Joke', *Lollards and Their Influence in Late Medieval England*, ed. Fiona Somerset, Jill C. Havens and Derrick G. Pitard (Woodbridge: Boydell, 2003), pp. 127–38

South, John Flint, *Memorials of the Craft of Surgery in England*, ed. D'Arcy Power (London: Cassell, 1886)

Spearing, A. C., *The Medieval Poet as Voyeur: Looking and Listening in Medieval Love-Narratives* (Cambridge University Press, 1993)

Sponsler, Clare, 'Eating Lessons: Lydgate's "Dietary" and Consumer Conduct', *Medieval Conduct*, ed. Kathleen M. Ashley and Robert L. A. Clark (Minneapolis: University of Minnesota Press, 2001), pp. 1–22

Staley, Lynn, ed. *The Book of Margery Kempe* (Kalamazoo: Medieval Institute Publications, 1996)

Steel, Karl, *How to Make a Human: Animals and Violence in the Middle Ages* (Columbus: Ohio State University Press, 2011)

Stein, Peter G., 'The Medieval Rediscovery of the Roman Civil Law', *The Civilian Tradition and Scots Law: Aberdeen Quincentenary Essays*, ed. David L. Carey Miller and Reinhard Zimmermann (Berlin: Duncker und Humblot, 1997), pp. 75–86

Steiner, Emily, *Reading Piers Plowman* (Cambridge University Press, 2013)

Stell, Philip, 'Medical Practice in Medieval York', *Borthwick Papers* 90 (1996): 1–35

Sterponi, Laura, 'Reading and Meditation in the Middle Ages: *Lectio divina* and Books of Hours', *Text & Talk* 28.5 (2008): 667–89

Stewart, Dana E., *The Arrow of Love: Optics, Gender, and Subjectivity in Medieval Love Poetry* (London: Associated University Presses, 2003)

Sturzinger, J. J., ed. *Le Pèlerinage de Vie Humaine de Guillaume de Deguileville*, Roxburghe Club 124 (London: Nichols, 1893)

Sugano, Douglas, ed. *The N-Town Plays* (Kalamazoo: Medieval Institute Publications, 2007)

Tasioulas, Jacqueline A., 'Heaven and Earth in Little Space', *Medium Ævum* 76.1 (2007): 24–48

　'The Mother's Lament: *Wulf and Eadwacer* Reconsidered', *Medium Ævum* 65.1 (1996): 1–18

Tentler, Thomas N., *Sin and Confession on the Eve of the Reformation* (Princeton University Press, 1977)

Thomas Aquinas, *Summa theologiae*, ed. Thomas Gilby, 61 vols. (London: Blackfriars, 1964–81)

Thomas, E. C., trans., *The Love of Books: The Philobiblon of Richard de Bury* (City of Birmingham School of Printing, 1946)

Thomson, John A. F., *The Transformation of Medieval England 1370–1529* (London: Routledge, 2014, first pub. 1983)

Tolkien, J. R. R., and E. V. Gordon, eds. *Sir Gawain and the Green Knight*, 2nd edn, rev. Norman Davis (Oxford: Clarendon, 1967)

Toswell, M. J., 'Of Dogs, *Cawdels*, and Contrition: A Penitential Motif in *Piers Plowman*', *YLS* 7 (1993): 115–21

Trotter, David, *Albucasis: Traitier de Cyrurgie: Édition de la traduction en ancien français de la Chirurgie d'Abū'l Qāsim Halaf Ibn 'Abbās al-Zahrāwī du manuscrit BNF, français 1318* (Tübingen: Max Niemeyer Verlag, 2005)

'Arabic Surgery in Eastern France and the Midi: The Old French and Occitan Versions of the *Chirurgie d'Albucasis*', *Forum for Modern Language Studies* 35 (1999): 358–71

Twomey, Michael W., 'Towards a Reception History of Western Medieval Encyclopaedias in England before 1500', *Pre-Modern Encyclopaedic Texts: Proceedings of the Second COMERS Congress, Groningen, 1–4 July 1996*, ed. Peter Binkley (Leiden: Brill, 1997), pp. 329–62

Vanderjagt, Arjo, 'Bernard of Clairvaux (1090–1153) and Aelred of Rievaulx (1110–1167) on Kissing', *Media Latinitas: A Collection of Essays to Mark the Occasion of the Retirement of L. J. Engels*, ed. R. I. A. Nip, H. van Dijk, E. M. C. van Houts, C. H. J. M. Kneepkens and G. A. A. Kortekaas, Instrumenta Patristica et Mediaevalia 28 (Turnhout: Brepols, 1996), pp. 339–43

Vincentius Bellovacensis [Vincent of Beauvais], *Speculum Quadruplex sive Speculum Maius*, Volume I: *Speculum Naturale* (Douai: Bibliotheca Mundi, 1624; repr. Graz, Austria: Akademische Druck -u. Verlagsanstalt, 1964)

Speculum Quadruplex sive Speculum Maius, Volume II: *Speculum Doctrinale* (Douai: Bibliotheca Mundi, 1624; repr. Graz, Austria: Akademische Druck - u. Verlagsanstalt, 1964)

Voigts, Linda Ehrsam, and Patricia D. Kurtz, compilers, *Scientific and Medical Writings in Old and Middle English: An Electronic Resource*, CD-ROM (Ann Arbor: University of Michigan Press, 2001)

Wallner, Björn, 'Drawings of Surgical Instruments in MS Bibl. Nat. Angl. 25', *English Studies* 46 (1965): 182–6

ed. *The Middle English Translation of Guy de Chauliac's Anatomy* (Lund: CWK Gleerup, 1964)

Walter, Katie L., 'Books and Bodies: Ethics, Exemplarity and the "Boistous" in Medieval English Writings', *NML* 14 (2012): 95–125

'The Child before the Mother: Mary and the Excremental in *The Prickynge of Love*', *Words and Matter: The Virgin Mary in Late Medieval and Early Modern Parish Life*, ed. Jonas Carlquist and Virginia Langum (Stockholm: Runica et Mediaevalia, 2015), pp. 151–65

'Discourses of the Human: Mouths in Late Medieval Religious Literature', unpublished doctoral thesis, University of Cambridge (2007)

'The Middle English Term "Froten": Absolon and Barber-Surgery', *N&Q* 53 (2006): 303–5

Watson, Nicholas, 'Censorship and Cultural Change in Late-Medieval England: Vernacular Theology, the Oxford Translation Debate, and Arundel's Constitutions of 1409', *Speculum* 70 (1995): 822–64

'Conceptions of the Word: The Mother Tongue and the Incarnation of God', *NML* 1 (1997): 85–124

Weatherly, Edward H., ed. *Speculum Sacerdotale*, EETS os 200 (London: Oxford University Press, 1936)

Webb, Heather, 'Cardiosensory Impulses in Late Medieval Spirituality', *Rethinking the Medieval Senses: Heritage, Fascinations, Frames*, ed. Stephen G. Nichols, Andreas Kablitz and Alison Calhoun (Baltimore: The Johns Hopkins University Press, 2008), pp. 265–85

The Medieval Heart (New Haven: Yale University Press, 2010)

Weldon, James F. G., 'Gesture of Perception: The Pattern of Kneeling in *Piers Plowman* B.18–19', *YLS* 3 (1989): 49–66

Wenzel, Siegfried, ed. *Fasciculus morum: A Fourteenth-Century Preacher's Handbook* (University Park: The Pennsylvania State University Press, 1989)

'The Pilgrimage of Life as a Late Medieval Genre', *Mediaeval Studies* 35 (1973): 370–88

Wetherbee, Winthrop, trans. *The Cosmographia of Bernardus Silvestris* (New York: Columbia University Press, 1973; 1990)

White, Hugh, 'Langland, Milton and the *Felix Culpa*', *Review of English Studies* ns 45 (1994): 336–56

Nature, Sex, and Goodness in a Medieval Literary Tradition (Oxford University Press, 2000)

Whitehead, Christiana, Denis Renevey and Anne Mouron, eds. *The Doctrine of the Hert: A Critical Edition with Introduction and Commentary* (Exeter University Press, 2010)

Williams, David, *Deformed Discourse: The Function of the Monster in Mediaeval Thought and Literature* (University of Exeter Press, 1996)

Williams, Deanne, *The French Fetish from Chaucer to Shakespeare* (Cambridge University Press, 2004)

Williams, Mark F., trans. *Aelred of Rievaulx's Spiritual Friendship* (London: Associated University Presses, 1994)

Wittig, Joseph S., '*Piers Plowman* B, Passus IX–XII: Elements in the Design of the Inward Journey', *Traditio* 28 (1972): 211–80

Wogan-Browne, Jocelyn, Nicholas Watson, Andrew Taylor and Ruth Evans, eds. *The Idea of the Vernacular: An Anthology of Middle English Literary Theory, 1280–1520* (University Park: The Pennsylvania State University Press, 1999)

Wogan-Browne, Jocelyn, and others, eds. *Language and Culture in Medieval Britain: The French of England, c.1100–c.1500* (Woodbridge: York Medieval Press in association with Boydell Press, 2009)

Woolgar, C. M., *The Senses in Late Medieval England* (New Haven: Yale University Press, 2006)

Yamamoto, Dorothy, *The Boundaries of the Human in Medieval English Literature* (Oxford University Press, 2000)

Yoshikawa, Naoë Kukita, ed. *Medicine, Religion and Gender in Medieval Culture* (Cambridge: Brewer, 2015)

Young, Sidney, *The Annals of the Barber-Surgeons of London* (London: Blades, East & Blades, 1890)

Zeeman, Nicolette, 'The Condition of *Kynde*', *Medieval Literature and Historical Inquiry: Essays in Honor of Derek Pearsall*, ed. David Aers (Cambridge: Brewer, 2000), pp. 1–30

'*Piers Plowman*' *and the Medieval Discourse of Desire* (Cambridge University Press, 2006)

' "Studying" in the Middle Ages – and in *Piers Plowman*', *NML* 3 (1999): 185–212

Ziegler, Joseph, *Medicine and Religion c.1300: The Case of Arnau de Vilanova* (Oxford: Clarendon, 1998)

Index

CAMBRIDGE STUDIES IN MEDIEVAL LITERATURE

General Editor
ALASTAIR MINNIS, *Yale University*